Transformation of the Classical Heritage

Peter Brown, General Editor

GREGORY THE GREAT

p. 41
184
188
192
n.3, 194
201
203
207
Catry = 209
Stoics = 213 f.
Aubin - 216
(int./ext.)
Szarmach (horse/
ground) 217
Penitence, etc. 218
→ (of remedy)
222
Contemplation 226
reverberatio 228
Stability in contemplation 233
Attraction of secular pursuits 232
N.B. n.5.
237
on Stoics 240
Why God allows Job's trials 241
Virtue / Vice 244
Remedies 247
act./Contemp. 258
Imperf. /
Perf. 256

Gregory the Great, from a twelfth-century mosaic in Cefalù cathedral. Courtesy of Alinari.

CAROLE STRAW

GREGORY THE GREAT

PERFECTION
IN IMPERFECTION

UNIVERSITY OF CALIFORNIA PRESS
Berkeley • Los Angeles • London

University of California Press
Berkeley and Los Angeles, California

University of California Press, Ltd.
London, England

© 1988 by
The Regents of the University of California

Library of Congress Cataloging-in-Publication Data

Straw, Carole Ellen.
  Gregory the Great.

  (Transformation of the classical heritage; 14)
  Bibliography: p.
  Includes index.
  1. Gregory I, Pope, ca. 540-604.   I. Title.
II. Series
BX1076.S67   1988   270.2′092′4[B]   87-1667
ISBN 0-520-05767-8 (alk. paper)

Printed in the United States of America

1   2   3   4   5   6   7   8   9

FOR FREDERICK

. . . φίλτρον πολύ, καὶ οἷον ἐν ἑκατέρῳ
ὑπὲρ τὸν ἄλλον ὑπονοεῖσθαι, ἡ γλυκεῖα
ἐκείνη φιλονεικία τὸ ἑαυτὸν βούλεσθαι
νικᾶν ἐν τῇ ἀγάπῃ ἑκάτερον.
—Gregory of Nyssa, *virg.* 3.2.

CONTENTS

LIST OF FIGURES

NOTE ON SOURCES
AND ABBREVIATIONS

Ancient and patristic writers are cited from standard authoritative texts. Abbreviations for classical Greek authors and their works are from Liddell and Scott, *Greek-English Lexicon*, supplemented with G.W.H. Lampe, *Patristic Greek Lexicon*. Classical and patristic Latin sources are from the *Thesaurus Linguae Latinae*. Abbreviations to periodicals are from *L'Année philologique*, supplemented with Johannes Quasten's *Patrology*. Translations of Gregory's scriptural citations are my own.

ACKNOWLEDGMENTS

This book began as a doctoral dissertation at the University of California, Berkeley, completed under the direction of Gerard Caspary and Peter Brown. While my greatest debts are to these two scholars, I would like to thank all my professors at Berkeley for the many happy hours spent in their classes, especially Robert Brentano, whose imaginative classes drew me to graduate school to pursue the studies he made so delightful. I also had the honor of studying and beginning my dissertation with the late Paul Alexander as my second director. The elegant clarity of his work has remained a model I have striven to emulate.

Whatever skill I possess as a historian I owe principally to Gerry Caspary. His formidable intellect and challenges have shaped how I analyze and write about texts, and my work is built on the foundation of his careful teaching. In a much more profound way, his guidance and friendship have illuminated and sustained my career as a scholar. Peter Brown has been kind enough to read several versions of this manuscript as it has evolved. His comments and suggestions have been invaluable, and I appreciate deeply the time he has taken to sift the "silver" from the "gold" that I might improve my manuscript.

Two eminent scholars of Gregory the Great have been especially helpful in the preparation of this manuscript. Paul Meyvaert and Robert Markus read early drafts and offered valuable critiques from their own vast knowledge of Gregory. I have been touched by their generosity—the books lent, the articles that I could not obtain through our library system, and, most of all, their unfailing kindness and encouragement of my work.

I would like to thank many other scholars who have shared their work on Gregory with me and so encouraged my own: Rodrigue Bélanger, Marc Doucet, Joan Petersen, and Grover Zinn. I must thank James O'Donnell especially for his editorial suggestions, which proved to be a healthful discipline. Charles McClendon, Michael Davis, and Wendy Watson offered information on art history. A Faculty Summer Grant from Mount Holyoke College aided my library research, and the support of my fellow historians at Mount Holyoke has been much appreciated. My editors, Doris Kretchmer, Mary Lamprech, and Amy Einsohn made working with the University of California Press a pleasure. Mark Campbell of Xyquest, Inc., supplied technical computer assistance with admirable professionalism. Vivienne Webb of Smith College has my gratitude for her general assistance and the many favors which have rendered her a true friend.

This book is dedicated to my husband, Frederick McGinness, a fellow historian and my greatest friend. He has sacrificed time better devoted to his own research in order to help me in innumerable ways, yet his greatest gift is simply the grace of his presence: his wry wisdom, his calm and reassuring disposition.

INTRODUCTION

On meeting St. Anthony, the old hermit Paul recalls the world, and for all his years of isolation in the desert he cannot quite forsake the fortunes of cities and empires: "Because true love embraces all things, please tell me how the human race is getting along: whether new roofs rise in the ancient cities, whose empire now rules the world, and whether any still exist, snared in the error of demons."[1]

The life of perfection includes charity for others; indeed, it is nothing without such charity. Though a thousand reasons bid the monk to leave the world, polluted as it is with enticements of demons, those who escape are never wholly comfortable about the fate of those left behind, imperiled and perhaps lost. Even in its most ascetic expression, late antique Christianity is never a flat rejection of the world. The gnawing recollection of Christ's lament cannot be dispelled, "O, Jerusalem, Jerusalem, the city that murders the prophets and stones the messengers sent to her! How often have I longed to gather your children, as a hen gathers her brood under her wings; but you would not let me. Look, look, there is your temple forsaken by God" (Mt 23:37–38).

To see this temple forsaken and destroyed is to witness God's justice, but one testifies to God's terrible vengeance with grief for those lost, for the suffering of people and the decline of cities once great. Apocalypticism is woven of bereavement as well as anticipation.[2] Is there more one

1. Hier. *vita Pauli* 10 (PL 23, 25).
2. Cf. *Ep.* 3.29 (CCL 140, 175); *Ep.* 3.61 (CCL 140, 209–11); *Ep.* 11.37 (CCL 140A, 931–32). For Gregory's apocalypticism see Claude Dagens, "La Fin des temps et l'église selon saint Grégoire le Grand," *RecSR* 58 (1970): 273–88, and *Saint Grégoire le Grand* (Paris, 1977), 345–430; René Wasselynck, "L'Orientation eschatologique de la vie chrétienne d'après saint Grégoire le Grand," in *Assemblées du Seigneur* 2 (1962): 66–80. See two articles by Raoul Manselli, "Escatologismo di Gregorio Magno," in *Atti del Primo Congresso Internazionale di Studi*

could do? "*Age quod agis!*"[3] Get on with business, do what you must do. Never cease to work, do all you can. Such is the advice in the late sixth century of Gregory I, gazing from the see of Peter at so many adumbrations of the end. Gregory responds with remarkable energy and imagination to work in his dying world, feeling a duty to serve others despite the perils to his own soul.[4] Gregory is often credited with founding the medieval papacy; and for many, his literary works mark the beginning of a truly medieval spirituality. Gregory achieved much, then, despite the disorders of the sixth century.

Gregory's times were the stuff of apocalyptic dreams and visions to impressionable minds such as his. The last western Roman emperor was deposed in 476, an event not particularly noticed, but by this time almost the whole of the Western empire was ruled by German kings. Italy's first *rex*, Odoacer, lasted less than twenty years and was replaced by the Ostrogoth Theodoric in 493. Theodoric ruled conscientiously for thirty-three years, although he could not remedy the structural weaknesses of the Italian economy. A shortage of manpower, high taxes, and low productivity continued to thwart capital formation, and the countryside drifted further toward a natural economy.[5] Theodoric died unable to secure his kingdom for the future, and Italy fell prey to Justinian's ambitions. Determined to restore the empire to its former glory, Justinian sent out forces to reconquer the West in 535. Italy was beset with wars of varying intensity for almost two decades and suffered unparalleled destruction; Rome was besieged at least four times. Starvation and the plague accompanied the wars, and the population dwindled.[6] The last half of the sixth century was marked by a serious economic recession.[7]

Longobardi, 383–87; and "L'escatologia di S. Gregorio Magno," in *RStR* 1 (1954): 72–83; and Paulo Siniscalco, "Le età del mondo in Gregorio Magno," Jacques Fontaine, Robert Gillet, and Stan Pellestrandi, eds., *Grégoire le Grand*, Colloques Internationaux du Centre National de la Recherche Scientifique, Chantilly 15–19 September 1982 (Paris, 1982), 377–387. See also Brian Daley, *Eschatologie in der Schrift und Patristik*, in *Handbuch der Dogmengeschichte* vol. 4, fasc. 7a, ed. Michael Schmaus et al. (Freiburg, Basel, Vienna, 1986): 245–47. A modern trend is to downplay the severity of the crisis that Gregory considers catastrophic; cf. Michel Rouche, "Grégoire le grand face à la situation économique de son temps," in Fontaine et al., eds., *Grégoire le Grand*, 41–57.

3. *HEv.* 2.37.9 (PL 76, 1279); *Dial.* 4.58.1 (SC 265, 194).

4. See esp. Patrick Catry, "Amour du monde et amour de Dieu chez saint Grégoire le Grand," *StudMon* 15 (1973): 253–75. The duty to serve others despite inconvenience to self is found also in Cic. *off.* 1.21; cf. Ambr. *off.* 1.9.28–29.

5. T. S. Brown, *Gentlemen and Officers* (Rome, 1984), 5.

6. Brown notes we have no means of gauging the population as a whole and eschews estimates, see *Gentlemen*, 63; also 6, 7, 144, 97. Michel Rouche estimates a decline in Rome from the fourth century to Gregory's time, passing from 700,000 to 200,000; the peninsula

The peace Justinian secured in 554 lasted only until 568, when a new and fierce tribe, the Lombards, crossed the Alps. The fortunes of the Lombards ebbed and flowed throughout the rest of the century, but their depredations were particularly difficult for the Church. Dozens of episcopal sees were disrupted, and Gregory did much to consolidate the remaining bishoprics.[8] Politics in Italy became a three-cornered affair among the Lombards, the Papacy, and the East as represented by the "exarch" of Ravenna.[9] Often at odds with both Byzantine and Lombard policies, the Papacy became increasingly autonomous. Yet Gregory never relinquished the ideal of a Christian empire somehow uniting disparate peoples.

Slowly, memories faded of Rome's splendid past as the imperial capital. The Senate ceased to function effectively soon after the Reconquest, and early in the seventh century the *curia senatus* was actually turned into the Church of S. Adriano. Rome became increasingly the holy city of saints and martyrs cherished by pilgrims,[10] an evolution reflected pointedly in building patterns. Secular structures were allowed to decay, despite the sunny provisions of Justinian's Pragmatic Sanction of 554. Only the Ponte Salaria was rebuilt in 565. Eventually the Papacy assumed responsibility for the vital aqueducts, even as it undertook many other civic traditions, such as maintaining the grain supply and feeding the poor. Nor was aristocratic patronage lavish in the late sixth century, focusing rather around small foundations associated with churches and charitable institutions. Only the large intramural churches and the cemetery-churches devoted to martyrs received much attention.[11]

Such rapid political and economic changes accounted for the vertiginous fluidity of Gregory's society. T. S. Brown has described admirably

---

as a whole declined from 5 million to 3.5 million, figures that are rather high; see Rouche, "Grégoire le Grand face à la situation économique de son temps," in Fontaine et al., eds., *Grégoire le Grand*, 42ff., also A. H. M. Jones, *The Later Roman Empire* (Norman, Okla., 1964), 2: 1040–45.

7. The evidence of pottery, inscriptions, and excavations indicate a decline in the number of settlements and of material culture; see the discussion by Brown, *Gentlemen*, 6–7.

8. Jeffrey Richards, *Consul of God* (London, 1980), 100–104, says at least forty-two sees disappeared during the Lombard period. See also L. Duchesne, "Les Evêchés d'Italie et l'invasion lombarde," *MEFR* 23 (1903): 83–116; 25 (1905): 356–99, noting that twenty-seven sees were disrupted in the late sixth century. Cf. Brown, *Gentlemen*, 40.

9. On the difficulties of utilizing this title, which first appeared in 584, see Brown, *Gentlemen*, 48–53. In Gregory's time, the exarch was in charge of all army units in Italy, even in matters of pay and promotion. Still, Gregory's letters testify to the exarch's ineffectiveness around Rome.

10. See esp. Peter Llewellyn, *Rome in the Dark Ages* (London, 1970), 173–98.

11. Bryan Ward-Perkins, *From Classical Antiquity to the Middle Ages* (Oxford, 1970), 45ff. and 56ff.

the social revolution of the late sixth century: the rapid formation of a new military aristocracy that came to dominate society at the expense of the civilian senatorial aristocracy, the conflation of civilian and military authority and administration that eventually enhanced the military elite.[12] Gregory's letters and exegetical works provide an important perspective on these developments, revealing a world of mercurial mobility, of brazen usurpation of the property, rights, authority, and even the regalia of others. Gregory was continuously wary of those who sought to find a career and worldly success in the Church. These carnal-minded Christians might better have chosen civilian pursuits instead. They seemed all too familiar with the arrogance and power of military vocations. Gregory cautioned against using such unseasoned wood "unless dried of their humors," for such "newness" could destabilize the Church. In a revealing simile, Gregory argued that bishops must be trained thoroughly, just as generals are trained before commanding troops.[13] Surely his audience could appreciate this obvious truth.

Gregory came to view the world as clearly divided into realms of purity and impurity: the righteous of the world were forced to live among the reprobate, like Job becoming the "brother of dragons and the friend of ostriches" (cf. Jb 30:29).[14] Though mingling with the unclean, the righteous must retain a sense of separateness. Gregory's society was turbulent and confused; yet, like a whirling flock of birds that suddenly divides in the heavens, its members disperse on divergent trajectories: either toward a holy life purified of secular temptations or toward a life of sin and pollution devoted to worldly gains. Increasingly polarized, Gregory's society gradually lost a neutral and civilian middle ground. Too often the Church stood face-to-face with the sword. Only a rigorous hierarchical order could be trusted to contain the violent potential of the secular members of society. Yet if each knew his place, obeying the rank assigned by *merit* rather than *power*, a majestic social concord could be orchestrated from such inherently discordant elements.

Gregory's earliest years coincided with Italy's shambling and laborious instability, but Gregory was more fortunate than most. While he is no longer believed to be of the *gens* Anicia or Decia, his family was of noble lineage and handsomely rich. In addition to the family estate on

12. Brown, *Gentlemen*, esp. 8–20. Brown notes the lack of division between civil and military power after the Gothic War and in the sixth century: "In practice civil and military spheres overlapped continually, but most of the pressures worked against the autonomy of the state power" (p. 9).

13. *Ep.* 5.58 (CCL 140, 356); *Ep.* 9.219 (CCL 140A, 787–88); *Ep.* 5.60 (CCL 140, 361).

14. *Ep.* 11.27 (CCL 140A, 904).

the Caelian hill, the family possessed properties in the neighborhood of Rome and farms in Sicily. Befitting their position, his family was prominent in the Church. Gregory's great-great-grandfather had ruled the see of Peter as Felix III (483–492), and Pope Agapitus (535–536) was a kinsman. Gregory's father, Gordianus, was a minor officer in the Church, and his three paternal aunts lived under vows in a family residence, albeit with varying success. Gregory's education was probably the best available in sixth-century Rome. Early lives boasted that he was second to none in grammar, rhetoric, and dialectic, and he probably had legal training as well.[15] Gregory began his career in public service, holding the office of urban prefect by 573. His brother Palatinus succeeded him and was the last to hold this office for over a century.[16] In 574, Gregory resigned to form a monastic community in his paternal home on the Caelian hill. As a simple monk, he spent his happiest years at this monastery dedicated to St. Andrew. But his tranquillity was short-lived, for in 579 he was called to serve the Church in the world as apocrisiarius (a papal legate) in Constantinople for Pope Pelagius II. He returned to Rome in the middle of the next decade and served as a deacon, and probably drafted some of Pelagius's letters. In 590, he was elected pope to succeed Pelagius, and he held office until his death in 604.

As pope, Gregory attempted to accommodate the Church to the world and yet to purify the Church from secular corruption. Even as the Papacy assumed greater responsibilities in the secular realm—maintaining the supplies of food and water, paying soldiers, negotiating treaties, administering estates, and systematizing charitable operations—Gregory still sought to preserve the Church from the pollution of secular values. He campaigned tirelessly against simony and demanded that the Church return properties gained in questionable circumstances. He excluded lay attendants from the Lateran palace and continually preferred clerics over laymen, and monks over clerics, in his appointments: only they who despised power could be trusted to exercise it wisely, even as they regulated their carnal natures with relentless discipline. Gregory's genius as an administrator was rooted in the same temperance and self-control that governed his spiritual life.

15. For early lives of Gregory, see: *The Earliest Life of Gregory the Great, by an Anonymous Monk of Whitby*, ed. Bertram Colgrave (Lawrence, Kans., 1968); Paulus Diaconus, *Vita beatissimi Gregorii papae urbis Romae*, ed. H. Grisar, *ZKTh* 11 (1887): 158–73, appearing also in an edition by W. Stuhlfath, *Gregor I der Grosse* (Heidelberg, 1913); Io. Diac., *vita Greg.* (PL 75, 59–242). See also *Liber Pontificalis*, ed. L. Duchesne, 2d ed. (Paris, 1955), 1: 312–14; and Bede, *hist. eccl.* 2.1.

16. Brown, *Gentlemen*, 11. After 599, no record of this office appears, and the office is effectively supplanted by the praetorian prefecture. The office reappears in 772.

Gregory's varied writings reveal a breadth of personality and vocation that has intrigued and, on occasion, baffled historians. His exegetical works on Job, Ezechiel, the Song of Songs, and 1 Kings possess an intellectual power and spiritual insight that justify his title as a Doctor of the Church. These works, and probably his lost works on Proverbs, the Heptateuch, and the Prophets, were directed largely to monastic audiences. While they enjoyed varying degrees of success, each is a serious and sophisticated effort to marshal the learning of the past and open new frontiers of spiritual knowledge.[17] In contrast (or so it seems) to these works of elevated ambition, the *Dialogues* and *Homilies on the Gospel* stand as works of a more popular spirit.[18] Filled with clear directives and comforting miracles, they teach his audience more effectively than mere instruction[19] and seem to express the side of Gregory known for learned ignorance (*indocta scientia, docta ignorantia*).[20] Gregory appears as the consummate professional in his terse, formulaic manual for the clergy, *Pastoral Rule*, an astute handbook useful not only to ecclesiastical rectors but to anyone bearing power.[21] Finally, a register of over eight hundred and fifty letters testifies to Gregory's administrative talents. But apart from scattered letters, the register is peculiarly silent about the spiritual world so vividly recounted in other works.[22] Gregory can seem to embrace very different personalities. Along with the sheer and perplexing variety of his works, autobiographical data are scanty, and moments of deliberate, self-

17. On Gregory's works and his audience, see Judith McClure, "Gregory the Great: Exegesis and Audience" (D. Phil. diss., Oxford, 1978); Michel Banniard, "*Iuxta uniuscuiusque qualitatem*: L'Ecriture médiatrice chez Grégoire le Grand," in Fontaine et al., eds., *Grégoire le Grand*, 477–87.

18. Frances Clark's argument that the *Dialogues* are spurious reflects the apparent incongruity of this work with Gregory's exegesis; see his "The Authorship of the Gregorian *Dialogues*: A Challenge to the Traditional View," *Studia Patristica* (to appear).

19. *Dial.* praef. 9–10 (SC 260, 16–18).

20. See Dagens, *Saint Grégoire*, 45–50.

21. See Robert A. Markus, "Le *Rector* de Grégoire le Grand et sa genèse," in Fontaine et al., eds., *Grégoire le Grand*, 137–146.

22. On Gregory's letters, see the works of Dag Norberg, *In Registrum Gregorii Magni studia critica* (Uppsala, 1937 and 1939), 2 vols; *Critical and Exegetical Notes on the Letters of St. Gregory the Great* (Stockholm, 1982); and "Qui a composé les lettres de saint Grégoire le Grand?" *StudMed* 21 (1980): 1–17. Norberg distinguishes two genres of letters: (1) Letters written to personal friends, to the imperial family, to kings, to patriarchs, and to others not under his jurisdiction. These letters contain such personal material that they were doubtless dictated by the pope himself. (2) Letters addressed to subordinates, generally treating administrative problems. In this category are formularies antedating Gregory, probably written by notaries such as Paterius, who was *secundicerius notariorum*, and administrative letters whose form dates from Gregory's time. Some of the letters were dictated by Gregory, others redacted by notaries recording Gregory's decisions. Gregory's own letters can be identified by his disregard for regular clausular endings.

conscious reflection are few. Certainly Gregory changes with time. He revises his position on the destruction of idols in England;[23] he varies his notion of the stages of sin.[24] He grows more pessimistic with age, more sensitive to the difficulties of the mixed life.[25] And yet no chronological evolution can be adduced to explain his diversity, his persistent ambivalence, and the recurrence of common themes. Gregory is elusive. Artless and honest, he is nevertheless a mysteriously subtle personality not easily confined to conventional categories.

This elusiveness is caught by Pierre Boglioni, writing of the contrast between the practical pope of the letters and the credulous monk of *The Dialogues*, noting as well the difference between the refined spiritual sophistication of the commentaries and the schematic simplicity of *Pastoral Rule*.[26] Boglioni's work illustrates the uneasiness of the modern reader in Gregory's world, thereby calling attention to modern difficulties in understanding Gregory. The historical imagination is surely taxed in reconciling the shrewd administrator and the ingenuous monk who speaks of devils weighing down rocks and dragons guarding the gates of monasteries. In the nineteenth century, such talk elicited the scathing ridicule of Adolph Harnack.[27] While modern writers are more sensitive to differences of history and culture, most still tend to treat Gregory's miraculous

23. *Ep.* 11.37 (CCL 140A, 929) orders Adilbert, king of the Angles, to destroy idols; *Ep.* 11.56 (CCL 143B, 961–62) orders Abbot Mellitus to have pagan altars purified and reconsecrated.

24. See chapter 5, n. 56.

25. In *HEz.* the tension between active and contemplative lives is more acute than in *Mor.*; still the ideal of uniting the two lives remains. While *In lib. I Reg.* exalts monastic life, the mixed life is still present. McClure's argument of chronological evolution utilizes dating now disputed, "Exegesis and Audience," 39 and passim. See Paul Meyvaert's "The Date of Gregory the Great's Commentaries on the Canticle of Canticles and on I Kings," *SEJG* 23 (1978–79): 191–216; and A. de Vogüé, "Les vues de Grégoire le Grand sur la vie religieuse dans son commentaire des Rois," *StudMon* 20 (1978): 19ff., independently supporting Meyvaert's late dating of *In lib. I Reg.* Meyvaert argues that the *Mor.* was preached during Gregory's stay in Constantinople (c. 579–585/6), and completed by 591; *Reg. Past.* completed by 591; *HEz.* by 591–592 (assuming the uncertainty of the date of Agilulf's march on Rome, which Gregory mentions at the beginning of book 2, the text is usually thought to date from 593, which would in any case be a signal of early composition for the first book); *HEv.*, completed by 593; *Dial.* late 593 to early 594; *Cant.*, 595–598, existing as the unrevised notes of Claudius of Ravenna; *In lib. I Reg.*, preached in 595–598 (de Vogüé, 597–598) and revised from Claudius's notes in 599–604 (de Vogüé, 598). R. Bélanger argues that Claudius actually edited notes of *Cant.*; see the introduction to his edition of Grégoire le Grand, *Commentaire sur le Cantique des Cantiques*, SC 314 (Paris, 1984), 22–28.

26. Pierre Boglioni, "Miracle et nature chez Grégoire le Grand," in *Cahiers d'études médiévales*, I: *Epopées, légendes et miracles* (Montreal and Paris, 1974), 11–102.

27. According to Adolf Harnack, Gregory appealed to a declining civilization sunk in superstition and magic, and he created a crude work-religion (*ergismus*); cf. *History of Dogma* (New York, 1961), 5: 262.

side as something requiring explanation, if not apology.[28] Yet this mirac- ulous side needs to be understood as an integral part of his thought, for it is emblematic of a larger vision of the world, one that violates modern perceptions and classifications. The unity, coherence, and internal logic of Gregory's mind and world view often escape his critics because Greg- ory's world can be so alien and inaccessible to modern minds.

Gregory's world is different from the modern world with its clinical objectivity, where any trace of the extraordinary is scoured impatiently from contemporary life. Gregory's world is still the late antique uni- verse populated by Principalities, Thrones, and Powers; a reality whose boundaries witness an energetic traffic of visitors to and from the other world. Yet Gregory's world differs subtly from the late antique world of Augustine, or that of the Desert Fathers, for theirs are worlds where one is still cautious of crossing these boundaries, still conscious of how this dull life differs from the shimmering brilliance of the other side. The late antique "upperworldliness" Peter Brown describes is a world of such dis- tinctions.[29] The other world is most often above, invisible, and difficult of access. It is something the soul strives to reach; it is not at one's elbow, tugging at one's very sleeve. Moments when boundaries are crossed are cherished as rare and numinous. Plotinus strives a lifetime for perfection, yet he reaches the All-in-All only four times during the years he spends with Porphyry. And Porphyry, sitting long at the feet of his master, enters into union only once, in his sixty-eighth year.[30] Lesser students may have had even less success. For their part, neo-Pythagoreans find the other world remote and far different from known experience. Only the most extravagant asceticism can be expected to refine and lighten the soul suf- ficiently for the ascent.[31] Late antique people may embrace the holy man and the martyr as true mediators of the other world, but they also spend considerable time verifying their credentials.[32] Living on familiar, if un- friendly, terms with demons, even the Desert Fathers can be frankly sus- picious of crossing over to the other world. "If you see a young man ascend to heaven by his own will, catch him by the foot and throw him to the ground, for it does him no good," runs the advice in the *Vitae patrum*.[33] It is no accident that in late antiquity so much of the contact

28. Cf. Sofia Boesch Gajano, "Demoni et miracoli nei *Dialogi* di Gregorio Magno," in *Hagiographie, cultures et sociétés iv–xii siècles* (Paris, 1981), 263.

29. Peter Brown, *The Making of Late Antiquity* (Cambridge, 1978), 68 and passim.

30. Porphyry, *On the Life of Plotinus and the Arrangement of His Work*, 23.13–18.

31. Cf. Herbert Musurillo, "The Problem of Ascetical Fasting in the Greek Patristic Writers," *Traditio* 12 (1956): 1–64.

32. Brown, *Making of Late Antiquity*, 1–26.

33. *Vitae patr*. 5.10.111 (PL 73, 932).

with the spiritual world is confined to dreams, those moot courts of inspiration.[34]

For most of his life, Augustine shares this caution and reticence. Augustine stresses the distance and the tenuous paradoxical relationship between the transcendent world of the spirit and the visible world of daily experience, for this distinction is ultimately a function of God's omnipotence. The two different orders of reality are linked only paradoxically, in a way that ensures mystery. Visible signs both partly conceal and partly reveal invisible reality, making impossible a certain correlation between external sign and invisible reality.[35] Of necessity signs are ambiguous because God's mysterious majesty remains inscrutable to mere human beings. Knowing this, Augustine repeatedly warns his listeners not to presume to discern God's will in earthly affairs; nor should they read visible signs around an individual as indications of his secret election.[36] Only in the elderly Augustine is Gregory foreshadowed. Late in life Augustine speaks warmly of miraculous events, writing especially of medical cures gained by the faithful around him. He has now come to appreciate the need of frail humanity for proofs of "an unbelievable, distant transformation."[37] In this aged Augustine—and in a writer such as Paulinus of Milan, who recorded lovingly the miracles of Ambrose's death and life—one finds a glimpse of Gregory's vision.[38]

To understand Gregory one must begin by recognizing that he has modified the paradoxes of the mature Augustine and that the fluid boundaries of late antiquity have all but vanished. The supernatural is mingled with the world of ordinary experience, and in surprising ways. Visible and invisible, natural and supernatural, human and divine, carnal and spiritual are often directly and causally connected. Where Augustine stresses the mystery and ambiguity of signs, hiding yet hinting at supernal realities, Gregory is far more interested in carnal signs as mediating links between this world and the spiritual reality beyond. While

---

34. On the place and importance of dreams in late antiquity, see esp. Artemidorus, *The Interpretation of Dreams: Oneirocritica by Artemidorus*, trans. Robert White (Park Ridge, N.J., 1975), esp. 1–10.

35. See Maurice Pontet, *L'Exégèse de s. Augustin, prédicateur* (Paris, 1945), 257–303; Robert A. Markus, "St. Augustine on Signs," in *Augustine: A Collection of Critical Essays*, ed. Robert A. Markus (New York, 1972), 61–91.

36. In *civ.* this is the general criticism of pagans who blame Christians for the fall of Rome; it is also an argument Augustine uses against Donatists in his exegesis of the parable of the wheat and the tares; see my "Augustine as Pastoral Theologian: The Exegesis of the Parable of the Field and Threshing Floor," *AugStud* 14 (1983): 129–51.

37. Peter Brown, *Augustine of Hippo* (Berkeley and Los Angeles, 1969), 417. See esp. *civ.* 22.8f.

38. Emilien Lamirande, *Paulin de Milan et la "Vita Ambrosii"* (Montreal, 1982).

Augustine stresses the inscrutability of God's order, Gregory is apt to spell out just what God's possibilities are: good fortune and prosperity can mean either election or abandonment; but then so can misfortune and adversity. In any individual case, the outcome of God's actions may be unknown, but the general principles of God's dispensation are known, and proper human action can be prescribed. In so labeling the possible meanings of God's dispensation, Gregory systematizes the unknown and draws a clear map to guide the pilgrim's return to his homeland.[39]

In Gregory's world, invisible reality exists alongside the visible reality it sustains and determines. The other world is at one's very elbows, though often hidden to those of carnal minds. Yet those whose vision is restored, like the holy man and the good Christian, see invisible causes all the more clearly since they are, in fact, the more "real." Consequently, the familiar distinctions that once governed reality now become blurred. Natural causation is eclipsed by supernatural intervention.[40] Natural disasters such as earthquakes, fires, or storms are expressions of God's wrath, or his trial of man; a nun's indigestion is not caused by the cabbage, but by the devil lurking in its leaves.[41]

Gregory tends to link causally flesh and spirit, present and future worlds, displaying a certainty and predictability in their interconnection. To abase the power of the flesh is to exalt the aims of the spirit,[42] and the more painful the afflictions and scourges suffered in this life, the greater the joys in the world beyond.[43] Reaching the other world is much simpler now because it is so immediately present. Union with God is eminently attainable: one can even cling to the light inwardly at the same time one is busied outwardly in secular affairs.[44] As the spiritual and carnal boundaries are broken for body and soul, this world and the next, so too the boundaries between the self and others weaken, and social unity is intensified. Each individual exists only as a member of the larger, transcendent body of Christ, which is political and social as well as religious; a delicate hierarchy preserves the right order and harmony of the universe.

39. For other examples of such systematization, see: *Mor*. 26.27.50 (CCL 143B, 1304–5); *HEz*. 1.1.1ff. (CCL 142, 5ff.); *HEz*. 1.12.16 (CCL 142, 191–92).

40. Cf. Boglioni, "Miracle et nature," 28–35.

41. *Dial*. 1.4.7 (SC 260, 42–43).

42. Typical formulas are found in *Mor*. 7.15.19 (CCL 143, 346): "Nam quo uirtutem carnis humiliat, intentionem spiritus exaltat"; and *Ep*. 11.18 (CCL 140A, 887): "Quoniam qui ex carnis blandimento multa peccauimus, ex carnis afflictione purgamur."

43. *HEv*. 1.14.5 (PL 76, 1130): "tanto illic laetior, quanto hic durius afflictus."

44. *Ep*. 7.23 (CCL 140, 475); *HEz*. 1.9.22 (CCL 142, 135–36); *HEz*. 1.3.13 (CCL 142, 40).

To pursue a separate course is to subvert both self and society, to imitate the devil's delusion of self-sufficiency.

In Gregory's world, the shape of history and of individual lives is sketched only from a celestial perspective.[45] Augustine's sense of secular history independent of God's intention is lost.[46] Nor is there the canny sense of secular politics one finds reflected in Eusebius.[47] God's providence orders every event, and his will is communicated each minute in the rewards and punishments he sends. History becomes the record of God's communication with the elect, while individual lives become mosaics of black and white tracing the path of God's hand in the adversity and prosperity he sends. Nothing remains neutral or indifferent; ordinary reality—the natural, the secular, the human, the carnal—is subsumed and directed to transcendent ends. Earthly life is very much Job's trial, an arena where "our athlete" goes forth to fight the devil in the great *agon*, where everything that happens and all that exists is somehow a part of God's pedagogic game.[48] While the angels sit as silent spectators in the great theater of the heavens, the moral theologian becomes a commentator who explains the possible meaning of every turn of fortune that the athlete suffers in battle. All worlds and realities intersect in that great drama of the athlete in the arena.

Gregory sees direct links and dependencies between the two orders of reality, carnal and spiritual, this world and the next. He rejects the very distinctions that defend the transcendence and omnipotence of God in Augustine's theology. But Gregory's concerns are not Augustine's. To Gregory, God is not less majestic and mysterious because man knows he sends the whirlwind of adversity and the sweet smile of prosperity, but more so. The very fact that God controls everything, either by active ordination or passive permission, is sufficient proof of his terrible power and of his abiding mercy as well. While this realization might unsettle modern minds, it would come only as a relief to Gregory and his contemporaries, who were so familiar with the cavalier and ruthless enterprises of the devil. Reassured of God's ultimate control, they can envision limits

45. Cf. Boglioni, "Miracle et nature," 28–35.

46. See Robert A. Markus, *Saeculum: History and Society in the Theology of St. Augustine* (Cambridge, 1970), 157ff.

47. See Harold Allen Drake, *In Praise of Constantine: A Historical Study and New Translation of Eusebius' Tricennial Orations* (Berkeley, 1976). Eusebius's orations are carefully written to appeal to pagan Neoplatonists as much as to Christians.

48. *Mor.* 1.3.4 (CCL 143, 27); *Mor.* 10.1.1 (CCL 143, 534). God's pedagogy is a recurrent theme in Dagens, *Saint Grégoire*; see also Marc Doucet, "Pédagogie et théologie dans la *Vie de saint Benoît* par saint Grégoire le Grand," *CollCist* 38 (1976): 158–73.

to the devil's power and trust that the chaos around them is really part of a greater providential order. So while Augustine stresses the mysterious chasm between an omnipotent God and his contingent creatures, Gregory knows man's helplessness well enough to stress God's connection with man. Gregory prefers to speak of God's use of physical, visible, and temporal changes of fortune to soothe man, or shake him to the core. Gregory's God chastens with punishments and comforts with blessings, but he always remains the Father calling his prodigal son to return home.

To stress the unity and continuity of all reality is ultimately to emphasize the hand of God in the carnal side of life; that is, in the physical world, in the body, in pain, and in that darker presence known as evil. Here Gregory anticipates the physicality so characteristic of the later Middle Ages in figures as diverse as Anselm and St. Francis.[49] He is also reminiscent of the anti-Pelagian Augustine studiously arguing the "Catholic view" as "a view that can show a just God in so many pains and in such agonies of tiny babies."[50] The devil is God's *exactor*—his executioner, his "enforcer." The devil strikes man with evils, having the full permission of God to vent such wrath. The flesh and particularly its torments become an important means of attaining spiritual ends. Now suffering and evil are transformed into partial goods, for they are known to be the discipline of the Father chastening the sons He loves; they are integral and essential parts of God's plan.

Without hesitation or dread, Gregory recognizes that God is ultimately responsible for suffering, be it the illness visited upon the body, the instability that shakes political order, or the trials burdening a fragile soul. While others might rush to repel this deduction with academic niceties, Gregory embraces it as a confession, even a tribute to God's omnipotence. Yet such a confession is not easy, and it exacts a high price from repose. Gregory's feelings weave back and forth between loving the good Creator and fearing the evil he permits in judgment. But submission to God's dispensation is inescapable: man might resist, but God's will is always done.[51] Traces of this conflict and rebellion persist in the ambivalence found on many levels of Gregory's thought. Gregory always works toward a balance and resolution of these positive and negative feelings, be they described as hope and despair, humility and pride, or love and fear.

49. See chapter 2, n. 54.
50. Augustine, *c. Iul. op. imp.* 1.22, quoted by Brown, *Augustine of Hippo*, 397.
51. *Mor.* 6.18.28 (CCL 143, 304–5); *Mor.* 9.16.23 (CCL 143, 473); *Dial.* 3.21.4 (SC 260, 354).

In many ways, Gregory only articulates what is latent in earlier Christianity. Though Gregory owes much of his intellectual vocabulary to Cassian, Augustine, and Ambrose, it is remarkable to compare his writings with theirs. Gregory pulls to the very surface the dialectics and paradoxes that structure Christian thought. What is often the invisible architecture in earlier writers becomes in Gregory the visible Church, with the beams and buttresses clearly articulated. Gregory's spirituality is often little more than variations of tradition; yet slight changes can be of great consequence, creating new, distinctive styles. Gregory shows that the shift from late antique to medieval spirituality is gradual, a change by quantitative degrees that eventually becomes qualitative and dramatic.

Old ideas are recombined, new emphases appear, and subtle but stubborn differences distinguish Gregory from the earlier writers who inspired him. This is particularly true of Gregory's relation to Augustine. Although Augustine's work may have served as a reference library where Gregory found authoritative definitions and images, Gregory is often nearer the Greek tradition in his sensibilities and reads Augustine in that spirit. While it is doubtful Gregory knew Greek himself, he seems to have known in translation works of Origen, Gregory Nazianzen, and Gregory of Nyssa. Conversations with friends may have given him further access to Greek thinkers, such as Theodoret of Cyrus.[52] Gregory knows Cassian

52. On Gregory's Greek, see Joan Petersen, "Did Gregory Know Greek?" in *The Orthodox Churches and the West*, ed. Derek Baker (Oxford, 1976), 121–34; "Did Gregory the Great Know Greek?: A Reconsideration" (unpublished manuscript); and *The "Dialogues" of Gregory the Great in Their Late Antique Cultural Background* (Toronto, 1984), esp. 1–14, 151–91. See also A. de Vogüé's introduction to the *Dial.* (Paris, 1978) SC 251, 110–40, and the footnotes of all three volumes; and Paul Meyvaert, "A New Edition of Gregory the Great's Commentaries on the Canticle and I Kings," *JThS* n.s. 19 (1968): 215–25, noting Gregory's use of Origen. Gregory has familiarity with untranslated Greek sources: the writings of Lucian of Samosata, Theodoret of Cyrus's *Historia Religiosa*, and a story found only in the Greek version of the *Life of Symeon Stylites*. Gregory may have had oral knowledge of Theodoret's and of Gregory of Nyssa's commentaries on the Song of Songs, if he wrote the letter on the Three Chapters for Pelagius II (cf. MGH *Ep.* 2 *App.* 3 (3), 449–67). Translations known to be available to Gregory were those of Jerome, the most important of which were: Didymus, *spir.*; Eusebius, *chron. a. Abr.*; Epiphanius of Salamis, *c. Orig.*; several homilies of Origen: *in Is.*, *in Luc.*, *in Ier.*, *in cant.*, *in Ezech*; Theophilus of Alexandria: *epp.* 87, 92, 96, 98, 100; *reg. Pachom.*; and the Bible. Rufinus's most important translations were: Pamphilius, *apol. Orig.*; Eusebius, *hist.*; several works of Origen: *princ.*, *in psalm. 36–8.*, *in gen.*, *in exod.*, *in Lev.*, *in Ios.*, *in iud.*, *in num.*, *in Rom.*, *in cant.*; Ps-Clement: *recog.* and *epist. ad Iac.*; Basil: *reg. br.* and *reg. fus.* (edited as one rule) and nine homilies; Gregory Nazianzen: *orat.* 2, 6, 16, 17, 26, 27, 38, 39, 40; Evagrius Ponticus: *sent. mon.* and *sent. virg.*, also Sextus, *sent.*; and the *hist. mon.* In addition, Dionysius Exiguus translated Gregory of Nyssa, *hom. op.*, and the *vita Pachom.* Hilary of Poitiers translated a homily on Job by Origen, fragments of which survive. A translation of the *vita Anton.* also existed in sections of the *Vitae patr.* On the problem of Diony-

very well, and he has thoroughly absorbed the Neoplatonism of Ambrose. He doubtless knew sections of the *Vitae patrum*—particularly those translated by the deacon who became Pope Pelagius I (556–561) and the subdeacon later named Pope John III (561–574)—also those of Paschasius and Martin of Dumio,[53] and Rufinus's *Historia Monachorum.*[54] Several lives of saints were also at hand.[55] This spirit of asceticism from the desert is always a silent partner in his work, leading Gregory in new directions away from Augustine and the Western Fathers. He will often exhibit striking similarities with others of his era also steeped in Eastern monastic culture, such as Dorotheos of Gaza or John Climacus. This monastic sensibility, the restless vision of the athlete's battle with the devil, left a deep impression on Gregory. Yet Gregory sees less the display of ascetic valor in the desert and more the suffering and sacrifice the monks endure in that warfare.

To this grounding in Eastern monasticism must be added Gregory's own apocalypticism, fanned equally by the depredations of the barbarians and the imperial forces, who were as little trusted as their Germanic foes. Gregory's sense that the end is close at hand is no mere rhetorical device. The imminence of the end inspires an intolerant anxiety, and Gregory reacts by being doubly conscientious. With chilling severity, he scrutinizes every step along the way, for one false move might mean the loss of a soul. The battle Gregory fights in the arena is the beginning of that final great struggle with Satan and the Antichrist. Wars, famine, disease, invading soldiers—all are tribulations and adversities inflicted by the devil in this intensified conflict presaging the end.[56] The familiarity

---

sius the Areopagite, see chapter 1, n. 23. For Jerome's and Rufinus's translations and other information about Gregory's sources, see Martin Schanz, *Geschichte der römischen Literatur bis zum Gesetzgebungswerk des Kaisers Justinian*, pt. 4:1 (Munich, 1920), 374–81 and 415–23; and pt. 4:2, 605–22.

53. Existing as the *Verba seniorum* in the *Vitae patr.* (PL 73): book 3 is a translation by Pseudo-Rufinus, books 5–6 by Pelagius and John; book 7 by Paschasius of Dumio. In PL 74, the *sent. patr.* 109 is by Martin of Dumio (= Martin of Braga) and the *Heraclidis Paradisus*, a part of the *Historia Lausiaca* of Palladius is translated anonymously. See esp. José Geraldes Freire, *A Versão Latina por Pascásio de Dume dos Apophthegmata Patrum*, 2 vols. (Coimbra, 1971), from which I will cite Paschasius. See also W. Bousset, *Apophthegmata* (Tübingen, 1923), 1–208; and A. Wilmart, "Le recueil latin des Apophthegmes," *RBen* 34 (1922): 185–98.

54. PL 21, 393–462.

55. See A. de Vogüé's introduction to his edition of Grégoire le Grand, *Dialogues* (SC 251), 113ff.

56. *Mor.* 34.1.1 (CCL 143B, 1733). See also *Ep.* 5.36 (CCL 140, 307); *Ep.* 5.39 (CCL 140, 316); *HEz.* 2.6.22–24 (CCL 142, 310–13).

Gregory displays with the other world comes from his own experience in this battle: the nearer the end, the more one sees of the next world.[57] Sight of the next world is expected and welcome. Considering Gregory's intimate involvement in this battle, the equanimity he possesses is its own kind of courage.

Gregory's classical education reinforces the desert tradition he loves, often simply because the science, medicine, and natural history of his era are a legacy little changed from classical times. Gregory's readings of Cicero and Seneca, and his familiarity with other Christian writers such as Ambrose and Augustine, kept him in touch with Stoic ideas.[58] Like other educated men of his time, he understands the world and the human body through a science brewed from several strains of classical thought: Stoicism, Neoplatonism, Pythagoreanism, Hippocratism. Of course, Stoic and Platonic ideas, in particular, were already part of the Christian intellectual tradition, having been absorbed by many earlier Christian writers of East and West.[59] This classical influence is especially evident in the ideas of self-discipline and discernment (*discretio*) found in Cassian and in the Desert Fathers,[60] and in the general sense of world order found

57. *HEz.* 2.4.12 (CCL 142, 268).

58. Cf. M. Doucet, "Le Récit par saint Grégoire le Grand (*Dial.* 2.35) de la vision de saint Benoît, et les *Tusculanes* (1.14–21) de Cicéron," paper presented at the Ninth International Conference on Patristic Studies (Oxford, 5–10 September 1983); J. Stelzenberger, *Die Beziehungen der frühchristlichen Sittenlehre zur Ethik der Stoa, eine moralgeschichtliche Studie* (Munich, 1933), 374–75; Leonhard Weber, *Hauptfragen der Moraltheologie Gregors des Grossen* (Freiburg in der Schweiz, 1947), 53f. Also useful are P. Ewald, *Die stoisch-ciceronianischen Moral auf die Darstellung der Ethik bei Ambrosius* (Leipzig, 1881); and F. Homes Dudden, *The Life and Times of Ambrose*, 2 vols. (Oxford, 1935), 2: 502ff. In speaking of Gregory's Stoicism, it is best to consider his contact with writers themselves influenced by Stoic ideas. A rigorous application of Stoicism is inappropriate.

59. For Stoicism essential sources are: Michel Spanneut, *Le Stoïcisme des Pères de l'Eglise de Clément de Rome à Clément d'Alexandrie*, Patristica Sorbonensia, 1 (Paris, 1969); idem, *Permanence du stoïcisme de Zenon à Malraux* (Gembloux, Belgium, 1973); and now Marcia L. Colish, *The Stoic Tradition from Antiquity to the Middle Ages*, Studies in the History of Christian Thought, edited by Heiko A. Oberman, vols. 34–35 (Leiden, 1985); for Neoplatonism, see especially *Neoplatonism and Early Christian Thought. Essays in Honour of A. H. Armstrong*, ed. H. J. Blumenthal and Robert A. Markus (London, 1981); and A. A. Long, *Hellenistic Philosophy: Stoics, Epicureans, Sceptics* (New York, 1974), *The Cambridge History of Later Greek and Early Medieval Philosophy*, ed. A. H. Armstrong (Cambridge, 1970), which also treats minor philosophical trends. Medicine and geography also have many ideas in common with Stoicism.

60. On *discretio* see esp. Eloi Dekkers, "'Discretio' chez Benoît et saint Grégoire," *CollCist* 46 (1984): 79–88; Dagens, *Saint Grégoire*, 117–24; A. Cabassut, "Discrétion," *DS* 9:1311–30; Fr. Dingjan, *Discretio: les origines patristique et monastique de la doctrine sur la prudence chez saint Thomas d'Aquin* (Assen, Holland, 1967), 86–102; A. de Vogüé, "'Discretione praecipuam': A quoi Grégoire pensait-il?," *Benedictina* 22 (1975): 325–27; Robert Gillet, in-

in Augustine and Ambrose. Ideas of balance, equilibrium, and moderation would have been keynotes in Gregory's classical education and in
his Christian sources. Yet because Gregory is so concerned with God's
paradoxical ordering of the universe, and because he sees justice, righteousness, and virtue as reciprocity and equilibrium—that is, a mean between extremes—his writings are often reminiscent of Aristotle, Cicero,
Plotinus, and any number of ancient writers who shared so many ideas
about the harmony of the cosmos. Gregory also has a striking fondness
for the binary oppositions that intrigued the Pythagoreans and other philosophers and are so pervasive in Western thought in general. This is not
to say he read ancient philosophers in depth. More likely, his own desire
to map out the mysteries of God's order and to define possibilities led him
to draw on the residue of Greek philosophy latent in Christianity.

Gregory's temperament and historical situation led him to a selective
use of sources. No single inspiration or tradition captures his essence as
a thinker. He takes much from many sources, and his borrowing is eclectic and free-spirited, never slavish. In addition to the major writers already mentioned, traces of writers such as Hilary of Poitiers, Julianus
Pomerius, and even Juvenal can be found in Gregory's works. Yet Gregory always digests and transforms the ideas of others, shaping them to
his own requirements. His thought is the proverbial paradox: the whole
that is more than the sum of its parts.

The uniqueness and originality of Gregory's thought and his contribution to the later tradition of medieval spirituality have yet to be appreciated, perhaps because of the methods so often used to examine his
works. Gregory's writings are an encyclopedia of spiritual experience,
wide ranging, sagacious, eminently practical. Yet these writings need to
be read with the same diligence given poetry. Form and content, struc-

---

troduction to Grégoire le Grand, *Morales sur Job* I–II, trans. André Gaudemaris, SC 32 (Paris,
1952). On Cassian, who influenced Gregory's idea of *discretio*, see Owen Chadwick, *John
Cassian*, 2d ed. (Cambridge, 1968), esp. 82–136 and 148–62. Cassian and the Desert Fathers
are the important sources influencing Gregory; see *conl.* 1.20; 1.22–23; 2 (entire); 4.9; 4.19;
7.5; 16.22; 16.27; 17.23; *inst.* 5.4.2; 5.20.1; 5.36.1; 7.1.1; 11.4.1; 11.8.1; 12.17.3; also *Vitae patr.*
5.10 (entire). Discretion is also found in Ambrose, Augustine, Gregory Nazianzen, and the
Benedictine Rule, and it is especially associated with Aris. *Nich. Eth.* Discretion is both the
power to discern the ideal and distinguish differences from that ideal (διάκρισις: *discernere,
discutere, distinguere, examinare, considerare, pensare, perpendere*, etc.). It is also the power to
moderate one's conduct so that one might obtain the ideal (μέτρον: *moderare, moderamen
discretionis, temperare*). It is often symbolized by scales: *trutina, Mor.* 33.35.60 (CCL 143B,
1724–26); *Mor.* 8.4.5 (CCL 143, 384); *libra, Mor.* 3.13.24 (CCL 143, 130); the eyes, *Mor.* 6.37.57
(CCL 143, 327); *Mor.* 7.28.37 (CCL 143, 361–62); or the nose, *Reg. Past.* 1.11 (PL 77, 24), *Mor.*
31.44.85 (CCL 143B, 1608–9), *Mor.* 28.10.23 (CCL 143B, 1413–14).

ture and idea are inseparable in Gregory's writings, more so than for many early Christian theologians. To understand Gregory's message, one must focus on the mental processes and the various configurations of ideas that structure his thought, for these patterns determine the very definitions and prescriptions he gives for the spiritual life. Because this internal grammar, or structure of thought, is so important in Gregory's spirituality, and so striking even to the casual reader, it has rightly concerned every scholar of Gregory, to a greater or lesser degree.[61]

To define this structure, to present Gregory's complex *mentalité*, requires the skills of the literary critic, the anthropologist, and the historian. A close study of Gregory's writings must focus not only on the explicit argument but also on incidental and implicit information. By discovering the hidden logic of comparisons and associations and tracing the various interconnections of ideas, one can determine the criteria defining various mental categories and discern the function of specific ideas in the whole network of thought. From a knowledge of the underlying principles governing the operation and grammar of Gregory's thought, we can understand more fully the intuitions, prejudices, and assumptions that shape his values and judgments, and perhaps appreciate more fully the subtleties that distinguish his vision of reality from those of other writers.

Numerous scholars have studied structural features of Gregory's thought or have concerned themselves especially with the form and methodology of his thinking. Ferruccio Gastaldelli and Leonhard Weber have discussed rhetorical devices and the influence of rhetoric in general.[62] Jean Leclercq and Robert Gillet have noted patterns of alternation, while Jean LaPorte has argued that Gregory is systematic in his teaching, even though he is not to be considered a systematic theologian.[63] Pierre Aubin's investigation of interiority and exteriority was a milestone,[64] and the later works of Claude Dagens, Rodrigue Bélanger, Marc Doucet, and others have built upon Aubin's basic insight.[65] Dagens in particular has

61. See, e.g., Boglioni, "Miracle et nature," 67.

62. F. Gastaldelli, "Teologia e retorica in s. Gregorio Magno," *Salesianum* 28 (1967): 267–99; Weber, *Hauptfragen*, 53–74.

63. Jean Leclercq, *The Spirituality of the Middle Ages* (New York, 1961), 2:3–30; Gillet, introduction to *Morales sur Job I–II*, 29ff.; Jean LaPorte, "Une Théologie systematique chez Grégoire," in Fontaine et al., eds., *Grégoire le Grand*, 235–42; Weber, *Hauptfragen*, 53–74.

64. Pierre Aubin, "Intériorité et extériorité dans les *Moralia in Job* de saint Grégoire le Grand," *RSR* 62 (1974): 117–66.

65. Dagens, *Saint Grégoire*; Rodrigue Bélanger, "Anthropologie et Parole de Dieu dans le commentaire de Grégoire le Grand sur le Cantique des cantiques," in Fontaine et al., eds., *Grégoire le Grand*, 245–54; Marc Doucet, "'Vera philosophia.' L'Existence selon saint Grégoire le Grand," *CollCist* 41 (1979): 227–53.

elaborated the interiority/exteriority contrast, and it becomes for him the fundamental structure governing Gregory's definitions of spiritual experience. These studies, along with many others, are to be lauded for avoiding the neoscholastic approach that has characterized Gregorian studies of earlier generations. Yet these studies, as excellent as they are, still leave work to be done.

A greater overall pattern can be discerned that embraces those structures of alternation, interiority/exteriority, and others already noted by scholars. This grammar of reconciliation and complementarity underlies the vision of unity and the sacramental reality that is distinctively and characteristically Gregorian.[66] Gregory sees carnal and spiritual realms as interrelated, connected as endpoints of a continuum. Like faces of a coin, ends of a stick, or poles of a magnet, they are extremities of a single whole. Two relationships are evident: one of opposition, which is metaphoric and paratactic; one of connection or unity, which is metonymic and syntagmatic.[67] Though opposite, carnal and spiritual realms are very much united through various degrees of complementarity and reconciliation. At any one moment, only a single aspect of the relationship might appear, such as the conflict between spirit and flesh, or the sympathy of body and soul. But when opposition is overt, unity is latent, and vice versa. Gregory's line of discretion (*linea discretionis*) illustrates this structure of unity and opposition. Like the old Stoic sage, one should pursue moderation and follow the line carefully, diverging neither too far to the right in the spiritual excess of severity, nor too far to the left in the carnal excess of laxity. Qualities or states that are extreme opposites are, by their very opposition, interrelated as margins of the same line. Similarly, the

66. For this notion of "sacramental reality" in the Middle Ages, see Gerd Tellenbach, *Church, State and Christian Society at the Time of the Investiture Contest*, trans. R. F. Bennett (New York, 1970), 47ff.

67. See Edmund Leach, *Culture and Communication* (Cambridge, 1976), 14ff. For a summary of these anthropological terms, see Roman Jakobson and Morris Halle, *Fundamentals of Language*, Janua Linguarum: Series Minor 1 (The Hague, 1956), and Claude Lévi-Strauss, *The Savage Mind* (Chicago, 1966) and his other works. In metaphoric and paratactic associations, a separation and distance exist between two elements because their association is wholly arbitrary, though conventional. In metonymic and syntagmatic chains, there is an intrinsic connection through the participation and organic interrelation of elements. Gregory often moves between these two ways of thinking, and the distinction should be appreciated. For instance, the vices are a metaphoric disease of the soul, and yet a metonymic relationship is present as well, because the humors of the body can affect the soul. Man is both a metaphoric world in miniature, and he shares in the four elements of the world metonymically. These relations affect causation and the relations between this world and the next. Augustine's signs are paradoxical and metaphoric, for they both reveal and yet conceal hidden truths. Gregory's signs are sacramental and metonymic: carnal signs reveal hidden spiritual truths, at least to those with discretion.

scales of the soul are to be balanced. One should be neither too high in the spiritual pride of contemplation, nor too low in the carnal numbness of worldly activity. Movement on one side of the scale affects the other: the lower, left, and outward carnal side balances the higher, right, and inward spiritual side. In equilibrium the soul experiences a mixed life of activity and contemplation, humility and hope.

Gregory wishes especially to stress the reciprocity and complementarity of spiritual and carnal. In this concept he has begun to modify the traditional polarities and the dialectical movement between spiritual and carnal, as found in Saint Paul and earlier Fathers from Tertullian to Augustine and beyond.[68] Gerard Caspary adeptly summarizes these complex patterns: "[t]he Covenant of Grace is the Covenant of the Law, enhanced and renewed. . . . it is the duality of spirit and letter that explains both the perfect continuity and the utter opposition between Law and Gospel."[69] The Old Dispensation is ethically opposed to the New. Law and grace are at odds. Yet the Old Dispensation is related to the New as means is to end; so the Old is subordinated hierarchically to the New. The Old Dispensation of the flesh precedes the New Dispensation of the spirit in time; law comes before grace, the old man before the new, Adam before Christ. Perceptually, the Old Dispensation is a visible, external, and less valuable "shell" concealing yet revealing an invisible, inner, and more valuable core. The letter hides and yet points to the inner spiritual meaning. Four dimensions are distinguished: ethical opposition, hierarchical subordination, temporal precedence, and a perceptual contrast of inner and outer. Caspary's schema captures this Pauline dialectic: one must first move through the lesser, external, carnal Dispensation to attain the more valuable, inner, and invisible Dispensation of spirit, paradoxically accepting the carnal to obtain the spiritual.

Gregory's most striking modification of Pauline thought can be seen in the complementarities governing his moral theology, the line of discretion and the scale of the soul. Gregory is able to create a complementarity out of the dialectical opposition of spirit and flesh because each pole has become ambivalent. The original division between the ethical good of the spirit and the evil of the flesh now becomes replicated at each pole. Having partly "switched charges," neither pole is now wholly positive

68. On the Pauline patterns and exegetical tradition, see esp. Aloys Grillmeier, *Christ in Christian Tradition*, trans. John Bowden, 2d ed. (Atlanta, 1975), 15–26. On Gregory's use of Augustine, see, e.g., Gillet, introduction to *Morales sur Job*, 7–109; Henri DeLubac, *Exégèse médiévale: les quatre sens de l'Ecriture*, 2 vols., 4 parts (Paris, 1959–1964); Pontet, *L'Exégèse de s. Augustin*, 257–303.

69. Gerard Caspary, *Politics and Exegesis: Origen and the Two Swords* (Berkeley, Los Angeles, London, 1979), 17; see also 11–39.

nor wholly negative, and while still opposites, the poles are also complements. There is reconciliation, for each pole supplies the qualities that
remedy the deficits of its mate; and evil now lies in the extremes of each
pole, arising when either pole is viewed apart from the complement that
checks its negative potential. Gregory's formulation of the balance between activity and contemplation and even sin and virtue ensures the
humility often wanting from ascetic virtue and the contemplative life.
Complete devotion to the contemplative life is dangerous, as is the pure
pursuit of the active life. Good stands in balance and equilibrium, which
is achieved when both poles are embraced properly for the good qualities
each possesses.

This kind of complementarity typifies the general pattern of reconciliation in Gregory's thought. But the complementarity of carnal and
spiritual creates a double paradox, and so modifies the original dialectic
of Paul. Now, one moves not only through the flesh to reach the spirit;
one must return back again to the carnal to become truly spiritual. This
cyclical movement returns to its origins; it is a pattern of unity analogous
to the line whose extremes are endpoints of a single unity. As Gregory
sees it, Jacob begins with Leah, attains Rachel, and returns to Leah—activity precedes contemplation, but contemplation must be expressed in
service to one's neighbor. More surprising, the merciful grace of Christ
becomes a New Law recapitulating, indeed strengthening, the Old Law
that it supplants; and it is even possible to find the grace of God fulfilled
in the wrath of the devil. Gregory forges a new unity through this return
to the carnal, which in turn supports his sacramental vision of reality.
Visible carnal signs point toward the invisible spirit, and now these signs
return to reveal the spiritual world in the present. Consequently, the citizens of heavenly Jerusalem can be discerned by their earthly acts, and
even glimpses of hell are perceptible in the flaming craters of volcanoes.
At the center of this pattern of sacramental unity—indeed, the very reason it exists—lies the incarnation and sacrifice of Christ. In Christ is the
perfect unity of spirit and flesh; he is the type of all succeeding unities of
flesh and spirit. Sacrifice becomes the center of Gregory's theology, be it
the sacrifice of Christ, the Mass, or the individual Christian, for sacrifice
is the means whereby the two sides of reality are joined and reconciled.
Through sacrifice, the carnal becomes spiritual.

There is a whole continuum of reconciliations between spiritual and
carnal, offering a wide range of intensities. The reconciliation between
God and the devil (representing the spiritual and the carnal poles of the
supernatural) is very weak; indeed, it is surprising to find any at all.
Nevertheless, the devil is God's *exactor* and his servant. This reconcilia-

tion is different from the mixed life of activity and contemplation, where each acts in a reciprocal way to remedy the weakness of the other. In Christ, reconciliation becomes identity, for he is both sides of reality simultaneously: God and man, spirit and flesh, reconciled and reconciler. The universe encompasses the carnal and the spiritual woven together in various intensities, yet all combining to form a design of harmony and extraordinary order.

These patterns of reconciliation affect the stylistic devices Gregory chooses, and they give his thought a distinctive texture. Because complementarity, continuity, opposition, and paradox play so important a role in Gregory's thought, certain rhetorical figures are particularly apt. There are simple paradoxes of contradiction or opposition: God is both *with* and yet *not with* the Israelites in the desert. Dialectical paradoxes abound, for they express complementarity: one is lifted to joy through tears, or healed by being wounded. Daring reversals are few but memorable: sin becomes virtue, and virtue becomes sin. Oxymora are numerous, where reconciliation takes the form of the union of opposites: joyful sadness, merciful severity, immutable mutability. So, too, chiasmus is employed frequently to express the balance that can be constructed with paradoxes: in holding, God repels; in repelling, he holds. Imagery of balance is particularly significant: weights and measures, scales, lines and roads, and other formulations of a mean between extremes.

Oppositional contrasts are of three basic types. The original Pauline polarity of carnality and spirituality always remains at least latent in Gregory's thought, expressing the primary values one achieves paradoxically. In this category are such contrasts as upright and fallen, sight and blindness, fixity and wandering. The majority are complementary dialectical pairs: ascent and descent, sweetness and bitterness, softness and hardness. The pairs work together and ideally strike a balance. Also, there are contrasts of the negative extremes generated when each pole is not checked by its complement, such as zeal and laxness, or pride and despair. These are extremes of the proper complements, authority and humility, and humility and hope. Finally, to secure the complementarity of halves that are in some sense dependent upon one another, Gregory frequently uses correlatives such as *tanto . . . quanto, eo . . . quo,* or *sic . . . ut tamen.* The density of such rhetorical figures gives Gregory's writings a tight, aphoristic, and at times almost mathematical quality that sets him apart from other patristic writers.

Gregory's distinctive style of thought, both in its art and its content, accounts largely for his enormous influence and popularity in the Middle Ages. His formulaic paradoxes can be extremely pleasing mnemonic devices, and once the reader has taken hold of Gregory's thought there can be a delightful predictability to his manner of expression. If Gregory mentions God's sweetness in one breath, the next breath is certain to mention God's trials; and the third will doubtless convey his "sweet tortures" and "delectable pains."[70] Gregory is eminently readable, but more than that, he is easily preached and discussed with others. His work is simple, in the archaic sense of the word. It possesses clarity, integrity, unity of thought, and purity of style. Gregory confronts problems directly and, most important, gives answers. His answers are indeed paradoxical, but they are neither so abstruse nor so speculative that only a highly educated elite could appreciate them. Such unpretentious forthrightness commanded wide appeal in the Middle Ages, if the proliferation and distribution of Gregory's manuscripts are valid indicators.

Ironically, while waiting anxiously for the world to end, Gregory provided an intellectual framework to integrate all aspects of life with Christianity. While decrying power, he showed how the Church and the Christian could use and benefit from power and earthly achievements. While wishing for withdrawal and purity, he presented a model of returning to life amid sinful and unsettling circumstances. Gregory is at once progressive, because his thought is flexible and comes to terms with the world, yet conservative in his ideals. His thought is dynamic, always offering the means of converting defeat to victory, yet somehow static, for success turns all too easily to failure.

Gregory deals profoundly and sensitively with the ambivalences that plague human life: why tears of love and grief are so closely allied, why sin nips the very heels of virtue, why the loving God must also have the devil as his *exactor*. His works express a quiet regret, a sadness that any resistance lingers in his soul, however unwilled. Like Job, with whom he identifies,[71] Gregory humbly confronts the universe, but he struggles as Job never did to make his will truly love what God wills. He offers his soul freely in conscious obedience. Yet this sacrifice is most poignant in his bitter contention against those hidden stirrings of the unconscious mind that most men only dimly perceive. Gregory wants fervently to know and control each step of the heart: every footprint must be scrutinized, every feeling sifted through the febrile hand of discretion.

---

70. *HEz.* 2.4.3 (CCL 142, 260): "Vnde et donis suis flagella permiscet, ut nobis omne quod nos in saeculo delectabat amarescat, et illud incendium surgat in animo quod nos semper ad caeleste desiderium inquietet, excitet, atque, ut ita dicam, delectabiliter mordeat, suauiter cruciet, hilariter contristet."

71. Cf. *Ad Leand.* 5 (CCL 143, 6).

What conversions must a man feel to thank God for the strokes, rather than resist him? These conversions Gregory knew very well: one should no longer fight against God as an enemy, nor fear his avenging wrath. One should grow to love him and long passionately for the Kingdom. The fight must be waged against that part of oneself differing from the Father one loves. One must agree with God and support his chastening punishment against one's rebellious self.

If Gregory knew the conversions, he also knew the reversals, the exasperating mutiny of the carnal man that must be uprooted and destroyed. Like a candle searching the inmost parts of the belly (Prv 20:27), self-examination scrutinizes the hidden recesses of the mind for secret sins, and then immolates those sins in the fires of penitence, burning with deepest compunction.[72] Examination of self pierces the soul and destroys its carnality, like teeth tearing the flesh and mincing it to nothingness. Man's former rebellion in carnality burns on the altar of penitence as a sacrifice of obedience to God. This sacrifice arises from love and longing for the Kingdom, but beneath these tears of joy are clearly discernible the earlier fear of wrathful judgment and the tears of grieving for one's possible torment in hell. In a word, ambivalence is again apparent. We see a man who sacrifices himself for love *and* fear of God; one who must fight against the self he unfortunately possesses and inadvertently gratifies.

Gregory was ambivalent and divided, though he earnestly wished not to be. His inventive moral theology stems from an unconventional life. Drawing on personal experience, Gregory studied the paradoxical relation between active and contemplative lives, between sin and virtue, adversity and prosperity. He will succeed in reconciling such divisions in

---

72. Compunction is especially important in Gregory's spiritual doctrine. For the tradition of this term, whose Greek equivalent is *penthos*, see esp. Irénée Hausherr, *Penthos*, trans. Anselm Hufstader, Cistercian Studies 53 (Kalamazoo, Mich., 1982). Hausherr (7f.) notes that πένθος is used in Mt 5:4; a later synonym is κατάνυξις. Cassian is Gregory's main influence (e.g., *conl.* 1.17; 1.19; 2.11; 4.5; 4.19; 9.28–29; *inst.* 4.43.1; 12.15.1; 12.18.1; 12.27.5). The influence of Origen is also important, indirectly and directly, as are the Desert Fathers; see *Vitae patr.* 5.3 (entire). For Augustine's influence, see Jean Doignon, "'Blessure d'affliction' et 'blessure d'amour' (*Moralia* 6.25.42): une jonction de thèmes de la spiritualité patristique de Cyprien à Augustin," in Fontaine et al., eds., *Grégoire le Grand*, 297–303. See also Pie Raymond Régamey, "La Compunction du coeur," *VS*, suppl. 44 (1935): 65–84; Joseph Pegon, "Compunction," *DS* 4: 1312–21. See also P. Catry, "Désir et amour de Dieu chez saint Grégoire le Grand," *RecAug* 10 (1975): 269–303. *Compunctio* and *compungere* are difficult to translate. To feel compunction means one is pierced by a sharp feeling, be it fear of judgment and grief of sins, or love and longing for God. Gregory distinguishes a compunction of fear and one of love.

a Christian who is perfect in imperfection. Gregory's conversion to monastic life came slowly, as Dagens has noted.[73] *Diu longeque* . . . "For a long time I drove away the grace of conversion," he wrote to Leander of Seville. It is not known exactly how long nor for what reasons he continued in public service. A sensitive conscience pursued him relentlessly, if slowly, a Monica more subdued, though equally dogged. As noted earlier, Gregory resigned his civil office (574) and retired to the monastery only to be thrust out into the world again as apocrisiarius to Constantinople (579). He returned to serve as deacon to Pelagius II (585/6) and was elected to succeed him as pope (590). His early letters as pope reflect his inner turmoil and resistance, as he grieved over the loss of his tranquillity and the burdens he had to bear.

His high birth and office bespeak a man accustomed to considerable wealth and power. Perhaps the donation of his family property to create monasteries and his distribution of wealth to the poor reveal most dramatically his desire to reverse his past. He bore a deep suspicion of those in power, whether they were secular rulers or clergy. Yet always a leader, Gregory was tied to his past and consciously aware of all the temptations and gratifications he could find there. More important, he knew part of him responded to these offerings. The simplest and purest life is the monastic "grave," where both world and monk are dead to one another. All too treacherous is the life of the prelate, whom the world denies repose but instead devours as the sea swallows the living and expels the dead. Gregory was of the living, and he was forced to face a worldly life that could offer fulfillment of just those impulses he struggled to abnegate. The converted man suffers the peculiar horror of being punished by his former pleasures, of suffering with grief what he had once pursued with delight. He begins by taking on worldly conversation as a condescension and a burden, but he ends by clinging to it with pleasure: such observations account for Gregory's obsessive anxiety about secret sins. Yet this suffering and these unwitting sins can be offered as a sacrifice to God if carefully washed with cleansing tears of compunction.

The plaint closing the *Moralia*[74] is a deeply moving revelation of this anxiety: would that none of his words were spoken from the desire for human praise, but only in praise of God. But as Gregory examines his inward intention, he finds that in "some unknown secret way" the desire for human praise has blended with his higher intentions. By his exposi-

---

73. Dagens, "La 'Conversion' de saint Grégoire le Grand," *REAug* 15 (1969): 149–62.
74. *Mor.* 35.20.49 (CCL 143B, 1810–11); and cf. *Reg. Past.* 4.1 (PL 77, 125).

tion he has revealed his gifts and will not withdraw the healing remedy of his words from his audience. But by his confession he has exposed his wounds and neither will he conceal them from us. Will his readers confer on him the solace of their prayers before the strict Judge? Will their tears wash away the filth of every sin they discover in him? Gregory's personal agonies translate the penitence and compunction of the Desert Fathers to the medieval world, as man's fundamental posture of sacrifice before God.

Although resolved to retire to a life of contemplation, Gregory was forced back unwillingly into a world that part of him still loved despite all his determination. Because of this, Gregory will emphasize self-control, self-examination, and penitence as a means of dealing with this basic conflict and ambivalence. Rational action and discipline can perform the penitence necessary for inadvertent, secret sins. Having been tossed back into the world unwillingly, Gregory will add a new meaning to the self-control found in the monastic tradition. The monastery is the citadel of security; yet controls are external, localized in the monastic cell. Now the *arx mentis*, the citadel of the mind, must be the primary bastion of stability. It must both regulate the impulses of man's carnal nature and weather the vicissitudes of the world outside. A stable, unshaken fortress, the mind must overcome all mutability of the world, whether personal or social.

If the true citadel of virtue is the mind and heart, and not simply the cell, then a kind of ascesis can become accessible to all levels of Christians in varying degrees of achievement. By making perfection paradoxical, so integrating worldly involvement and the inevitability of sin, Gregory can give all Christians a chance to develop *discretio, compunctio, stabilitas,* and *tranquillitas*—virtues formerly associated with monastic life. Gregorian Christianity is inclusive and open-ended.[75] In the *Dialogues* 1.12.4, Gregory cheers his disciple Peter, assuring him that even today there are holy men of great stature, as there were of yore. Though their saintliness now appears more often as inward virtue than as outward miracles, they are no less holy. This adjustment of doctrine to historical circumstance is calibrated to meet the world as it is and to christen it. No part of life remains untouched by the sacred, no part of life need necessarily be excluded from the Christian. Not that Gregory joyously affirms the world, as Teilhard de Chardin did: Gregory always remains wedded somberly to his

---

75. Weber's point is well taken: Gregory is not hostile to the world as such, but speaks of leaving it for the sake of heaven; see *Hauptfragen*, 125–28, esp. 128, n. 2.

apocalypticism and to his desire for the true repose of the monastery. He knew very well how demons polluted every corner of carnal life. But through sacrifice and repentance, carnal life could be offered to God, cleansed and purified by tears of contrition. Through sacrifice, the things of the flesh could be reunited with those of the spirit.

If Gregory's notion of stability ultimately sustains a conquest of the world and life in the flesh for the Christian, it is important to recognize that his stability is not only internal and personal but also social and political. Stability is also a desire for order in a sea of violence churning between the twin evils of tyranny and lawlessness. Gregory will find the counterpart of personal stability in political and social hierarchies that can unify disparate minds and bridle arrogance and cruelty. If there is a certain self-containment in the citadel of the soul on a personal level, this is balanced by the rejection of isolation and selfishness on a political and social level. The unity of spiritual and carnal characteristic of Gregory's vision implies also a corporate definition of personality. Any modern sense of the individual as autonomous and self-determining will be rejected, for single egos cannot be separated from a greater general mind without grave social and personal disharmony. A parallel pattern exists for self and society: if the focus of personal stability is in the citadel of the mind exerting discipline over irrational members, the focus of social and political stability is an authority exercising control over a similar "body" of which it is "head." In both cases, a unity embraces carnal and spiritual extremes of the entity, be it man or the social body of Christ, and unity is possible because of the inner connection of those two extremes.

Of Gregory's contributions to later spirituality, this broader integration of the carnal side of life in a unified vision of reality is little recognized. Gregory is remembered more narrowly for his confrontation with evil and suffering and for the message bequeathed to individual Christians in similar struggles. This personal message has proved very compelling; Gregory's suffering may well be one of the great events in Western spirituality. His triumph lies in his minute exposition of self-control, in his ability to transform suffering and trial into spiritual progress. He shows how the Christian should struggle to govern responses to the painful and delectable ambivalences of human experience, and through discretion retain equanimity of soul. Gregory has faith enough to see the hidden prosperity in every adversity, yet is wary enough to fear the secret adversity that prosperity can bring. Whether the hand of God caresses or strikes a blow, man should be able to redress the balance in the scale of his soul, for he expects uncertainty and accepts God's will. Ideally, positive and negative feelings are reconciled: for Gregory, the strokes do not vitiate the love. Does not the Lord chasten every son he receives? The passage Gregory cites of Paul expresses this acceptance of life's ambivalence, and the love enabling him to endure it: "I know both how to be brought low, and I know how to enjoy abundance: everywhere and in all things I am instructed both to be full and to be hungry; both to abound and to suffer need. I can do all things through Christ Who strengthens me" [Phil 4:12–13].[76]

76. *HEz.* 2.7.15 (CCL 142, 329).

· I ·

MICROCOSM AND MEDIATOR

"[I]f we look carefully at exterior things, they call us back to interior things, for the marvelous works of visible creation are surely the footsteps of our Creator."[1] The universe is filled with traces of God, hint by hint disclosing deeper truths. Ever the preacher and teacher, Gregory wishes his audience to learn the wisdom the universe teaches, particularly the lessons of humility and fear of God.[2] But more than this, from the vast, busy world outside man learns about himself.[3] By studying the workings of the visible cosmos, the Christian, like the Stoic sage, begins slowly to discern the invisible laws regulating the human condition.[4] When man begins to understand the underlying principles of God's dis-

1. *Mor.* 26.12.17 (CCL 143B, 1277–78); see also *HEz.* 2.5.10 (CCL 142, 283). Gregory's understanding of the physical universe is more or less the conventional wisdom of late antiquity. See esp. Samuel Sambursky, *The Physical World of Late Antiquity* (London, 1962). For a treatment of distinctly Stoic cosmology, see Marcia L. Colish, *The Stoic Tradition from Antiquity to the Early Middle Ages*, I: *Stoicism in Classical Latin Literature*, Studies in the History of Christian Thought, ed. Heiko A. Oberman (Leiden, 1985), 34: 116–19. Colish's definition of Stoic cosmology is extremely rigorous and precise and seems inappropriate for Gregory's more eclectic intellectual era. See below, note 6.

2. *Mor.* 26.12.18 (CCL 143B, 1279).

3. As Claude Dagens and others have noted, there has been no work to provide us with a synthetic account of Gregory's views of man: see Dagens, *Saint Grégoire le Grand* (Paris, 1977), 167, n. 2. Dagens treats the human condition in dealing with the structures of interiority and exteriority; cf. 165–245. Three older works are useful: F. Homes Dudden, *Gregory the Great* (London, 1905), 2.374–92; Franz Lieblang, *Grundfragen der mystischen Theologie nach Gregors des Grossen Moralia und Ezechielhomilien* (Freiburg im Breisgau, 1934), 29–43; and Leonhard Weber, *Hauptfragen der Moraltheologie Gregors des Grossen* (Freiburg in der Schweiz, 1947), 106–16, 128–64, 224–33. See also R. Bélanger, "Anthropologie et Parole de Dieu . . . ," in Jacques Fontaine et al., eds., *Grégoire le Grand* (Paris, 1986), 499; and Gregorio Penco, "S. Gregorio e la teologia dell'immagine," *Benedictina* 18 (1971): 32–45.

4. H. Savon, "Maniérisme et allégorie dans l'oeuvre d'Ambroise de Milan," *REL* 55 (1977): 219, noting Seneca and Ambrose on this idea. See also Pierre Hadot, *Exercices spirituels et philosophie antique* (Paris, 1981), 71–83.

pensation, how it is fitting and right (*rectum, justum*), and how so often it is woven in a pattern of paradox, then he has traveled some distance toward understanding himself and remedying his unfortunate predicament. If the Christian understands God's order, he knows God has planned it to be flexible and reversible: "Where we have fallen, there we lie that we may rise again. . . . If we have fallen from the invisible because of the visible, it is fitting that we strive to rise again through the visible to the invisible."[5]

Gregory's views of man and the universe are founded upon very old traditions of world harmony and hierarchical order, long a part of Christian tradition.[6] Nevertheless, his vision reflects his historical situation and personal predilections.[7] Gregory believes that man mirrors the cosmos, that the social differences of human society are reflections of the greater divisions of the cosmos. But this is an endless set of reflecting mirrors, because Gregory's vision of universal order is shaped by his own

5. *Mor.* 26.12.18 (CCL 143B, 1278).

6. For Stoic cosmology in the Fathers, see Michel Spanneut, *Le stoïcisme des Pères de L'Eglise de Clément de Rome à Clément d'Alexandrie* (Paris, 1969), 90–95, 350–421; and *Permanence du stoïcisme de Zenon à Malraux* (Gembloux, 1973), 130–78; Pierre Boyancé, *Etudes sur le songe de Scipion* (Bordeaux and Paris, 1936); A.-J. Festugière, *Le Dieu cosmique* (Paris, 1949); S. K. Heninger, Jr., *Touches of Sweet Harmony: Pythagorean Cosmology and Renaissance Poetics* (San Marino, Calif., 1974); Hermann Krings, *Ordo. Philosophisch-Historische Grundlegung einer abendländischen Idee* (Halle, E. Germany, 1941); Leo Spitzer, *Classical and Christian Ideas of World Harmony: Prolegomena to an Interpretation of the Word "Stimmung"* (Baltimore, 1963); and M. Colish, *The Stoic Tradition, II: Stoicism in Christian Latin Thought through the Sixth Century*, Studies in the History of Christian Thought, 35: 70–116. For emanation and participation in the Neoplatonic tradition, see esp. A. H. Armstrong, "Plotinus," in *The Cambridge History of Later Greek and Early Medieval Philosophy* (Cambridge, 1970), 195–268; idem, *Plotinian and Christian Studies* (London, 1979), esp. nos. 2 and 22; A. C. Lloyd, "The Later Neoplatonists," in *Cambridge History of Later Greek and Early Medieval Philosophy*, 271–325. Augustine also appreciated the orderly rank assigned to creatures, which created a harmonious order; see *civ.* 12.5; also Robert A. Markus, "Marius Victorinus and Augustine," in *Cambridge History of Later Greek and Early Medieval Philosophy*, 329–419; Etienne Gilson, *The Christian Philosophy of Saint Augustine*, trans. L. E. M. Lynch (New York, 1960), esp. 210–24. For Origen, see David L. Balas, "The Idea of Participation in the Structure of Origen's Thought. Christian Transposition of a Theme of the Platonic Tradition," *Origeniana, Quaderni di Vetera Christianorum* 12 (1975): 257–75.

7. Gregory's concern for hierarchical order is shared by other writers of his era, e.g., Dionysius the Areopagite, Maximus the Confessor, John Climacus, and Isidore of Seville; and the very large role this order plays in Gregory's thought separates him from Augustine. See René Rocques, *L'Universe dionysien: structure hiérarchique du monde selon le Pseudo-Denys* (Paris, 1954); idem, "Dionysius Aréopagita" in *RACH*, 3:1075–1121; Ronald F. Hathaway, *Hierarchy and the Definition of Order in the Letters of Pseudo-Dionysius* (The Hague, 1969); Jean Vanneste, *Le Mystère de Dieu: essai sur la structure rationnelle de la doctrine mystique du Pseudo-Denys l'Aréopagite* (Bruges, Belgium, 1959); Jacques Fontaine, *Isidore de Seville et la culture classique dans l'Espagne wisigothique* (Paris, 1983), 2:647–76; Lars Thunberg, *Microcosm and Mediator: The Theological Anthropology of Maximus the Confessor* (Lund, Sweden, 1965), 52–99.

values. Man mirrors a cosmic order shaped by Gregory's own preoccupation with the bittersweet harmony of spirit and flesh that accompanies all human experience. Consciously and unconsciously, Gregory ponders the organization of human society and of man himself in considering how God has ordered the universe: how body and soul can be friends and yet enemies, how a society divided into classes of greater and lesser worth can nevertheless find a concord in such diversity. Since the Fall, man is out of tune with himself, with others, and especially with his God.

Gregory has an intense desire to demonstrate the fundamental unity of God's order, despite its patent divisions and differences. Though the Fall has brought separation and discord, the pattern of original unity persists, despite profound dislocation. The essential connection of all life can still be traced in the now paradoxical relations of Creator and creatures, spirit and flesh, this world and the next, God and the devil. Gregory sees the universe as an ontological continuum, flowing from pure spirituality to pure carnality. Spiritual and carnal are antithetical as are beauty and deformity, permanence and change; but an underlying continuity unites them in the same order of comparison as complementary opposites. A mysterious unity of paradox and complementarity replaces the simpler unity of happier times in paradise. If man can perceive the true unity and continuity of the universe, he has proof of God's providential care, and he can be assured that God's Providence underlies the conflict and discord wracking earthly life. Learning how the bitter oppositions of life are part of God's plan, he can cherish the hope that one day perfect unity and peace will be regained in paradise.

As preacher and teacher, Gregory helps the Christian recognize the ultimate unity of God's universe beneath the discord and divisions so obvious and troublesome in daily life. Comprehending God's order, the Christian learns who he is and why he is poised so precariously between heaven and hell. A convicted sinner, he justly suffers God's wrath in the unnerving disorders of daily life. Yet this deepened understanding of himself and the human predicament gives him hope by showing him how to reverse his fall from grace. An emphasis on human activity and a justification of ascetic practices are implicit in Gregory's study of the unity and harmony of the universe. Certainly Gregory confesses man's need for humility, warning that human curiosity can never unravel the mysteries of the divine dispensation; faith should prevail over reason.[8] Nevertheless, God has arranged the universe in a harmonious order that is accessible to human reason, at least in part. God's omnipotent power

---

8. *Mor.* 6.15.19 (CCL 143, 296–97).

is also a sublimely rational power. The marvelous works of God are arranged with a "mightiness of power" that fittingly spans the heavens above the earth and balances the earth above the abyss, wonderfully creating the whole universe of things visible and invisible.[9] Because God abides within all things, upholding, ruling, and sustaining them,[10] his power and personality make things the way they are: rightly ordered by divine justice. Nothing happens by caprice or accident, for God cares about all human affairs.[11] The very aesthetic perfection of divine order assures man of God's care and foresight, even if he cannot always penetrate the mysteries of God's justice. Man trusts that God would not "deliberately destroy" what he so "mercifully created."[12]

God has so arranged the world that it speaks to man, if he is a careful listener. The orderly ranks of angels, the topography of the world, and the playful tricks of animals have meaning for the Christian, showing how the entire universe is bound in unity and sympathy with man. Creation is a sensitive web borne on the breath of God. The Author of all existence,[13] God is the "cause of causes, the life of the living and the reason of rational creatures."[14] He breathes life and movement into invisible rational beings, who in turn impart sensation and movement to visible bodies.[15] All things animate and inanimate are put into being by God: the sea, the heavens, the angels who comfort men.[16] Even the physical mechanics of the world are orchestrated by God and carried out by spiritual forces; the visible world is sustained by the invisible.[17] All creatures are interconnected and bound in a certain sympathy because their very existence links them with God.

Although all creation is joined harmoniously, all creatures are not equal. Some creatures are nearer the immutable God, others the dead weight of matter, though, alas, all creatures by definition are subject to

---

9. *Mor.* 6.15.18 (CCL 143, 296).

10. *Mor.* 2.12.20 (CCL 143, 72); *Mor.* 27.18.35 (CCL 143B, 1357–58).

11. Cf. *Mor.* 27.17.34 (CCL 143B, 1356).

12. *Mor.* 26.20.35 (CCL 143B, 1292–93); *Mor.* 9.15.22 (CCL 143, 472).

13. The best treatment of Gregory's ideas of God is still Michael Frickel, *Deus totus ubique simul. Untersuchungen zur allgemeinen Gottgegenwart im Rahmen der Gotteslehre Gregors des Grossen*, Freiburger Theologische Studien 96 (Freiburg im Breisgau, 1956). See also Lieblang, *Grundfragen*, 44f., which especially treats God as Illuminator, and Dudden, *Gregory*, 2:310–24, noting: "Gregory's doctrine of God is derived almost entirely from Augustine, though the more strictly philosophical parts of Augustine's theory are barely touched."

14. *Mor.* 30.4.17 (CCL 143B, 1503): "Deus enim sicut est causa causarum, sicut uita uiuentium, ita etiam ratio rationabilium creaturarum."

15. *Dial.* 4.5.8 (SC 265, 38).

16. *Mor.* 16.37.45 (CCL 143A, 825).

17. *Dial.* 4.5.4ff. (SC 265, 34–38).

change and ultimately nonbeing. Creation ranges along a hierarchical scale graded in degrees of being and value: the immutability or mutability that determines one's level of existence carries a moral significance. The more reason and resistance to mutability one possesses, the more spiritual one becomes. Concomitantly, one is closer to God, true being, and perfect goodness, the more reason rules one's life. The stronger one's ties to matter and the physical world, the more one is cursed with mutability. One approaches nothingness and evil in proportion to one's involvement with the flesh and its irrational senses and impulses.

Matter and physical existence are relative evils because they represent change and, of necessity, a cruel degeneration. In contrast, reason is a rejection of change, a stability that enables one to exist more truly and authentically. In such attitudes, Gregory differs very little from ancient tradition. Change is deeply disturbing, for it represents a lack of control over the chaotic forces that can shatter man's integrity and destroy his freedom. However rational and disciplined he may be, man is still hostage to forces that can diminish him by subverting his good intentions. Things transient and changeable must be shunned because "they can be lost against one's will."[18] Through change one ceases to be what one was and becomes something one was not. Indeed, every change is a form of death,[19] beckoning man's return to the nothingness whence God summoned all creation.[20] Most distressing, change disrupts man's struggle for perfection, for change admits the loss of virtues one enjoys. This is why only God, being immutable, is true existence: God *is* his goodness, wisdom, power, and so forth.[21] God can never lose his qualities, never become less than he is. Displaying a classical optimism about reason, Gregory links immutability with reason and self-control, assuming that reason always chooses the good. A rational person would choose to be stable; Gregory assumes this is self-evident. Change is rooted in the body and emotions because the body decays and emotions are notoriously unstable and unpredictable.

Gregory departs from Augustine in emphasizing the innate goodness of reason and in associating evil and change so closely with matter and physical existence. Gregory's universe has striking polarities. True, a continuum connects Creator and creation, but it does so by placing matter and physical existence in mirror opposition to God; both have exact

---

18. *Mor.* 31.28.55 (CCL 143B, 1590–91).

19. *Mor.* 25.6.9 (CCL 143B, 1235).

20. *Mor.* 25.6.10 (CCL 143B, 1235–36).

21. *Mor.* 16.43.54 (CCL 143A, 830); *Mor.* 17.30.46 (CCL 143A, 877); *Mor.* 18.50.81 (CCL 143A, 944–45); *HEz.* 1.8.3 (CCL 142, 102–103); of Christ, *HEv.* 2.22.4 (PL 76, 1176).

and analogous differences. Ultimately, this opposition between spirit and flesh is more important than the distinction between God and creation, and in this Gregory differs again from Augustine. To ensure man's humility, Augustine strongly affirmed that God and creation were two entirely different orders of reality. Creation was wholly contingent upon God; and man, totally dependent upon God's grace. Gregory focuses on the polar opposition of spirit and flesh not to deny the role of grace, but rather to underscore human activity and progress. Sharing the ascetic mentality of the Desert Fathers, Gregory believes spiritual perfection lies especially in the subjection of the flesh. Matter and physical existence are set directly opposite God and the spiritual world, as enemies to be conquered. Even though they are also God's creations, they are external forms of life apart from God.

Since this opposition of spiritual and carnal is clearly acknowledged, Christians can use the things of this world to teach themselves of the next by contrast and comparison. "Experiencing in themselves that the invisible is better than the visible," they can rise toward God through contemplation of the visible world.[22] The universe is composed of progressive degrees of being, ranging from the perfect spirituality of God to the dull carnality of lifeless matter.[23] Angels, men, beasts, and even plants and rocks have their place along this scale, and visible creation forms a "ladder of contemplation" (scala considerationis).[24] Each level increases in rationality and spirituality as it leaves behind matter and emotion, as man climbs to gain knowledge of his Creator. God "leads us marvelously through exterior forms to interior things; with immense wonder he makes known what he is, by outwardly showing the marvels which he is not."[25] Even man's physical senses should lead him toward spiritual perception.[26] Knowing something of God, man learns what he should be.

22. *Mor.* 15.46.52 (CCL 143A, 781).

23. Gregory's hierarchical continuum echoes that of Pseudo-Dionysius, for whom proportional ranks and participation are important ideas. See Hathaway, *Hierarchy*, 47–51. For a summary of this controversy about Gregory's knowledge of Dionysius, see Dagens, *Saint Grégoire*, 151, n. 40; and Joan Petersen, "Did Gregory Know Greek?" in *The Orthodox Churches and the West*, ed. Derek Baker (Oxford, 1976), 121–34.

24. *Mor.* 15.46.52 (CCL 143A, 781): "Quia ergo rebus uisibilibus inuisibilia praestantiora sunt, carnales quique ex semetipsis pensare debuerunt, atque per hanc ut ita dixerim, scalam considerationis tendere in Deum; quia eo est quo inuisibilis permanet, et eo summus permanet quo comprehendi nequaquam potest." See also *Mor.* 26.12.17–18 (CCL 143B, 1277–79). See also Dagens, *Saint Grégoire*, 177f. This tradition will evolve to become "the great chain of being" in the Renaissance; see Arthur O. Lovejoy, *The Great Chain of Being: A Study of the History of an Idea* (Cambridge, Mass., 1971).

25. *Mor.* 26.12.17–19 (CCL 143B, 1277–78).

26. *Mor.* 11.6.8 (CCL 143A, 590).

"The beauty of the creature [is a] lesson to our mind," for created and corporal things show us how distant we are from the greatness and highness (*sublimitas*) of the Creator. Everything we see warns us to be humble.[27]

Creation forms a ladder of contemplation, step by step revealing the unity and continuity of God's creation and disclosing glimpses of God from his visible works. As the universe unfolds, man's own identity becomes more distinct and comprehensible. Angels are equidistant from God and man, illustrating the serene delight of a more spiritual life. The blessed angels excel man in reason, knowledge, and purity, but surely fall far short of God's perfection: though "huge to man, they are little to God."[28] Their very mutability mediates between God and man. Insofar as angels are creatures, they do possess a *vicissitudo mutabilitatis*, pulling them away from the immutable God, toward change and a return to nothingness. But happily angels have overcome this potential instability by clinging to God in contemplation.[29] This stability comes easily to angels because they are purely rational creatures lacking actual flesh. Compared to man, angels have no bodies; but compared to God, their spirits are indeed bodies.[30] Lacking material bodies, angels suffer no rebellion of the flesh (*corporea oppositio*). Their perception is wholly spiritual, as Adam's was before the Fall. Angels "hear" God through contemplation and understand invisible secrets without words being spoken.[31] Since the body poses no obstruction, comprehension is instantaneous, intimate, and tremblingly alive.

Man can gain some knowledge of perfection (and of his own imperfection) by pondering the angels' reverent and exemplary behavior, for of all creatures, angels are closest to man and tell the most about him. Man is created tenth in the number of the elect, of whom angels constitute the first nine orders.[32] It is said man was made with the angels, for both are rational creatures made in God's image.[33] Possessing reason, these two are set off from the rest of creation, which is incapable of knowledge or learning. Being rational, both men and angels can partici-

27. *Mor.* 26.12.18 (CCL 143B, 1279).
28. *Mor.* 2.2.3 (CCL 143, 61): "Eorum itaque scientia comparatione nostrae ualde dilata est, sed tamen comparatione diuinae scientiae angusta. . . ." Cf. *Mor.* 18.44.71 (CCL 143A, 936–37).
29. *Mor.* 5.28.68 (CCL 143, 267).
30. *Mor.* 2.3.3 (CCL 143, 61); cf. *Mor.* 4.3.8 (CCL 143, 168–69), and *Mor.* 32.12.17 (CCL 143B, 1640–42).
31. *Mor.* 2.7.9 (CCL 143, 65).
32. *HEv.* 2.34.6 (PL 76, 1249).
33. *Mor.* 32.12.17 (CCL 143B, 1642). On man's image and likeness to God, see Penco, "La Teologia dell'immagine," 37f. The exegesis arises from Job 40:10: "Ecce Behemoth, quem feci tecum."

pate in God; yet while man failed to remain fixed in God, the angels succeeded. But possessing reason, man's task is to discover why this is so.
Fortunately, God offers many aids.

Even the sky and the heavens serve as metaphors for the angels'
beauty,[34] offering man a visible reminder of their brilliance and guidance
in everyday life. Moreover, the Scriptures teach that angels span the distance between God and man in nine orderly ranks,[35] a hierarchical order
that has numerous implications for a human society so in need of stability
and equilibrium. The ranks of angelic society are defined along a continuum from the higher and more spiritual grades to the lower and more
carnal. The inequality found in the angelic host is a clear lesson for man:
equality should not be expected in universal order. To be sure, inequality
between *men* is the remedial punishment resulting from sin.[36] Nevertheless a greater inequality, or rather a measured distinction of status, of *dignitas*, is simply part of universal order, for concord can only be achieved
from the smooth integration of members performing different and complementary roles. Each has his own status and proper function.[37] Gregory's characteristic oppositions of inner and outer, invisible and visible,
contemplation and activity are aspects of the essential polarity of spirituality and carnality governing universal order. For angels as well as man
the quality of such oppositions determines hierarchical order. Mention-
ing Dionysius the Areopagite in his *Homilies on the Gospel* 2.34, Gregory
begins by elaborating the orderly ranks of angels. The supreme rank, the
Seraphim, is the most inward and invisible, for they seldom if ever leave
the intersanctum, where they stand in the presence of God and in continual contemplation and burning love. The Cherubim have a plenitude
of knowledge, and also contemplate God continuously. Gregory is uncertain whether they themselves are messengers or whether they order
lesser angels to minister to men. In any case, the lower angels perform
outward services. They rule the world on God's behalf and execute his
vengeance, often becoming visible when bringing messages to man.[38]
Still these lesser angels never depart from inward contemplation.[39]

At least in part, a chain of command makes each rank responsible for

34. *Mor.* 32.12.17 (CCL 143B, 1642).

35. *HEv.* 2.34.7f. (PL 76, 1249f.); also *Mor.* 32.23.48 (CCL 143B, 1666).

36. *Reg. Past.* 2.6 (PL 77, 34): "omnes homines natura aequales genuit, sed variante
meritorum ordine alios aliis culpa postponit. Ipsa autem diversitas quae accessit ex vitio,
divino judicio dispensatur; ut quia omnis homo aeque stare non valet, alter regatur ab altero." Also, *Mor.* 21.15.22 (CCL 143A, 1082). Cf. Aug. *civ.* 19.15; Ambr. *epist.* 37.8.

37. This notion of justice goes back to Pl. *Rep.*, esp. 4.427C–445D.

38. *Mor.* 4.29.55 (CCL 143, 199); *Mor.* 9.16.26 (CCL 143, 476); *HEv.* 2.38.5 (PL 76,
1285).

39. *HEv.* 2.34.10–14 (PL 76, 1251–55).

the rank or ranks beneath it. This obtains for the Dominations, who control the Principalities and lower ranks. Principalities control good angels, and Powers hold Virtues in check.[40] While these hierarchical ranks set forward the differentiation and inequality of the angels, a second principle of participation establishes an equity through a sharing of virtues.[41] Each angel possesses the properties of all others through the love of the spirit, even though the various ranks of angels discharge different offices. A shared spirit checks any possible jealousy due to differences of status and ensures an identity of interests between superiors and subordinates. Though diverse in duties and talents, the angels are united in love and benevolent cooperation, a model of harmony and concord the Church should replicate on earth.

Since men will share heavenly citizenship with the angels, it is fitting that they bear similar distinctions.[42] The various occupations of men resemble the different orders of angels, and men will be classed according to the ranks of these celestial beings. Those who understand little but nevertheless teach what they know will be grouped with the Angels. Those who expound mysteries through divine grace will be with the Archangels. Miracle workers will join the Virtues, while exorcists will be with the Powers. Those who are better than good and excel among the elect, who rule their brothers in justice, will find their place among the Principalities. Men such as Moses, who control themselves so impeccably that they seem to be "god[s]" to men like Pharaoh (cf. Ex 7:1) are surely numbered with the Dominations. Rulers who cling to God in contemplation while judging others and governing his Church will be among the Thrones. The Cherubim will be joined by the elect who love neighbor and God with a special fullness. Finally, the contemplatives, cleansed of all earthly desire, are honored with the highest rank. Burning with heavenly love, they inspire and teach others most effectively. Igniting their brothers with love of God and enlightening their dim vision, these fiery contemplatives kindle others to repent of their sins. Such contemplatives who teach will join the Seraphim.

These hierarchical ranks of man reflect the angelic orders, and, like theirs, the highest orders are the most inward and contemplative, the lower the more active and outward. Yet each life is a "mixed life," a com-

40. *HEv.* 2.34.7f. (PL 76, 1249f.); and *Mor.* 4.29.55 (CCL 143, 199).
41. *Mor.* 34.21.40 (CCL 143B, 1762).
42. *HEv.* 2.34.11–12 (PL 76, 1252–53). This hierarchy may be inspired by Dionysius the Areopagite, *de ecclesiastica hierarchia.* Although Dionysius uses different orders (bishops, priests, ministers, monks, holy people, and purified orders) there is some similarity of function of the orders because both human hierarchies reflect the angelic hierarchy.

bination of heavenly understanding and service to others. The rungs of the hierarchy are determined by the sophistication and purity of one's understanding of heavenly truths, and those whose comprehension is most perfect serve their neighbors in the most exalted way by leading them to salvation. Even the contemplative must be a preacher, so to speak.[43] This contemplative preacher is the pattern of Gregory's own life, or at least the ideal he hoped to achieve. The contemplative's own knowledge of God must be generative and creative in promoting the salvation of others.

The angels offer a pure yet practical order prescriptive for human society. The heavenly ranks of the angels validate human social distinctions and set forward the vision of fraternal responsibility and cooperation that Gregory believes is necessary for a peaceful and happy society. Being purely rational and spiritual, angels lead lives of open-hearted obedience and cheerful service to God. Though their individual contributions may differ, they are never competitive nor hostile toward one another. Gregory emphasizes man's kinship with the angels both to demonstrate how valid and applicable their concord is to human affairs and also to intimate just how possible and how close such concord is to man. If man could stretch a little to reach the rationality of his more spiritual brothers, if he could just put aside the selfishness imposed by his refractory carnal nature, perhaps he could find the harmony that the angels enjoy. Yet, as a consequence of his very constitution, man has certain problems to conquer that the angels never face.

Man is midway in the continuum of creation, a position that emphasizes his potential for activity and change, even while it points out the difficulties man faces in recovering the lost virtues of his original innocence. Man stands at the great divide separating what can be redeemed and what must always remain outside God's embrace. Being spiritual and carnal, man exists between angels and animals and shares something of their respective natures. He is both immortal, possessing a spirit, and mortal, being endowed with a body.

> Now, since man was created midway between angels and beasts, to be lower than the angel and higher than the beast, so he has something in common both with the highest and with the lowest. His spirit shares

---

43. An interesting parallel to this active, preaching contemplative exists in *In lib. I Reg.* Helcana has two wives, symbolizing the active and contemplative lives: Phenenna, who is fertile, and Anna, who is sterile for a long while (1.64 [CCL 144, 89–90]). Helcana prefers Anna, who finally gives birth to Samuel. Gregory sees this child representing the *ordo praedicatorum*, who possess a special strength and grace in having knowledge of the divine and the ability to bring others to conversion (1.42–43 [CCL 144, 77–78]).

immortality with the angels, but with the animals, he is doomed to death of the flesh.[44]

Man mediates between the two opposites of creation by sharing in each. Since he embraces both kinds of existence, he can favor one side or the other, becoming more angelic or more bestial according to his choice of direction.

A second expression of man's mediation specifies the various levels of creation, each with its proportion of mortal flesh and immortal spirit. While the angels are immortal living spirits, animals are living but mortal, because they are burdened with mutable flesh. Man is living and yet immortal; for although man is clothed with labile and vulnerable flesh, he does not perish with the pitiful disintegration of his body.[45] One half of creation is spiritual and immortal, the other half carnal and mortal; again man stands in the center, sharing something of each. Man's mediation has a mathematical exactitude, for if the spiritual qualities of the angels are wholly positive and the carnal qualities of the animals wholly negative, man mediates their difference in being half negative and half positive, as it were.

44. *Dial.* 4.3.2 (SC 265, 24): "Homo itaque, sicut in medio creatus est, ut esset inferior angelo, superior iumento, ita aliquid habet commune cum summo, aliquid commune cum infimo, inmortalitatem scilicet spiritus cum angelo, mortalitatem uero carnis cum iumento." Cf. Dionys. Exig. *Gr. Nyss. hom. op.* 17, which stresses man as the mean between rational spirits and irrational beasts. In following this sharp dichotomy of body and soul, Gregory is also close to Ambr. *hex.* 9.7.42; also *hex.* 6.7.43; *inst. virg.* 20, *exc. Sat.* 2.130; *Noe* 86 and 99; *in psalm. 118* 10.13–15; *in psalm. 43.* See also Aug. *civ.* 12.21; Dionys. Exig. *Gr. Nyss. hom. op.* 17; Rufin. *Gr. Naz. orat.* 38.11, also Gr. Naz. *or.* 45.7, *or.* 32.9 (both untranslated, of which Gregory may have had oral knowledge). Gregory's view of man's mediation should be compared with that of Philo; see Marguerite Harl, "Adam et les deux arbres du paradis ou l'homme milieu entre deux termes chez Philon d'Alexandre," *RSR* 50 (1962): 321–88, esp. 326–27; on Ambrose, see A. Loiselle, *"Nature" de l'homme et histoire du salut: étude de l'anthropologie d'Ambroise de Milan* (Lyon, 1970); G. Madec, *Saint Ambroise et la philosophie* (Paris, 1974), esp. 67–91; and E. Dassmann, *Die Frömmigkeit des Kirchenvaters Ambrosius von Mailand* (Münster in Westfalen, 1965); on Augustine see: Robert O'Connell, *St. Augustine's Early Theory of Man, A.D. 386–391* (Cambridge, Mass., 1968), and [Tarsicius] Johannes van Bavel, "The Anthropology of Augustine," *Louvain Studies* 5 (1974): 34–47; and on Gregory of Nyssa, see Gerhart B. Ladner, "The Anthropology of Gregory of Nyssa," *DOP* 12 (1958): 61–94; M. Alexandre, "Protologie et eschatologie chez Grégoire de Nysse," *Arche e Telos. L'Antropologia di Origene e di Gregorio di Nissa*, ed. U. Bianchi, Studia Patristica Mediolanensia 12 (Milan, 1981), 122–59. M. Doucet has noted the parallels between Gregory's ideas of the soul in *Dial.* 2.35 and *Tusc.* 1.14–21; see his "Le Récit par saint Grégoire le Grand (*Dial.* 2.35) de la vision de saint Benoît, et les *Tusculanes* (1.14–21) de Cicéron," paper presented at the Ninth International Conference on Patristic Studies (Oxford, 5–10 September, 1983); see esp. Peter Brown, *The Body and Society* (to appear) for his extensive treatment of patristic anthropology, also Paul Veyne, ed., *A History of Private Life: From Pagan Rome to Byzantium*, trans. Arthur Goldhammer (Cambridge, Mass. and London, England, 1987), esp. 235–550.

45. *Dial.* 4.3.1 (SC 265, 22–24).

In his most exalted expression of man's mediation, Gregory places man at the center of creation, recapitulating all life. In an exegesis of Job 5:10 ("Who gives rain upon the face of the earth, and waters the universe with waters?"), Gregory writes, "Moreover, man is symbolized in the name of the universe, since a true likeness and a great communion with the universe is shown in him."[46] In this traditional view of man as microcosm, Gregory sees man as an image of the whole universe and as a mediator participating in its various levels of existence. Man shares a great *communio*, a mutual participation in the rest of the world. Like the stones, he exists; like the trees, he exists and is alive; like the beasts, he exists, is alive, and is sensate; and like the angels, he exists, is alive, is sensate, and has understanding. As the whole universe consists of visible and invisible things, in creating man, God "gathered together another world in miniature," making him an admixture of flesh and soul, dust and spirit.[47] Like the rest of the universe, he shares invisible causation, the spirit. And like most of creation, he shares visible effect, the body.

Elsewhere, we learn that man shares the physical properties of the universe, for his body is made of the four types of matter from which all physical life is composed: hot, cold, moist, and dry.[48] These four qualities correspond to the humors of the body, which affect man's temperament, binding body with the soul and in turn linking man with changes in the physical world.[49] Virtue and vice are inseparable from the physical con-

---

46. *Mor.* 6.16.20 (CCL 143, 298): "Uniuersitatis autem nomine homo signatur quia in ipso uera species et magna communio uniuersitatis ostenditur." Cf. Ambr. *hex.* 6.9.55. To Gregory of Nyssa, this is no compliment; being in God's image is: cf. Dionys. Exig. *Gr. Nyss. hom. op.* 17. See Spanneut, *Le Stoïcisme*, 410ff.

47. *Mor.* 6.15.18 (CCL 143, 296): "Quod ex rebus inuisibilibus omnis haec uniuersitas ac uisibilibus exsistit quod hominem fecit ut ita dixerim, in breui colligens mundum alterum sed rationalem; quod hunc ex anima et carne constituens, inuestigabili uirtutis dispositione permiscuit spiritum et lutum?" Cf. *HEz.* 1.8.16 (CCL 142, 109); and Ambr. *hex.* 6.55; Dionys. Exig. *Gr. Nyss. hom. op.* 8, where man contains all previous levels of creation. Ladner believes that this Stoic view in which the universe unfolds in progressive levels derives from Posidonius, probably through Galen; cf. "Anthropology," 71, n. 47. This idea echoes the progress of nature from inanimate to animate in Arist. *HA.* 8.1.588b; Spanneut, *Le Stoïcisme*, discusses this cosmic evolution in Clement and Athenagoras. The microcosm/macrocosm contrast is especially strong in Posidonius and is used by Philo, Origen, Gregory of Nyssa, and Augustine. See also George P. Conger, *Theories of Macrocosms and Microcosms in the History of Philosophy* (New York, 1922); Rudolph Allers, "Microcosm from Anaximander to Paracelsus," *Traditio* 2 (1944): 319–407; and Marie-Thérèse d'Alverny, "L'Homme comme symbole. Le microcosme," *Simbol e Simbologia* nell' alto medioevo. Settimane di Studio del Centro Italiano di Studi sull' alto medioevo (Spoleto, 1976) 23: 123–145.

48. *Mor.* 35.16.42 (CCL 143B, 1802): "Corporaliter uero quattuor qualitatibus continetur, quia uidelicet ex materia calida et frigida, humida et sicca componitur." Cf. Cic. *Tusc.* 1.17; but this is a general Stoic and medical doctrine.

49. Stoic philosophers had carefully elaborated correspondences between the uni-

dition of the body. For instance, gluttons are swollen with satiety, their bellies so distended with moist humors that lust is aroused.[50] Such excessive humors stimulate other vices as well, namely, loquacity and levity— a looseness of tongue and a windiness of spirit. In severe cases, excessive humors "harden" into the "swelling of pride."[51] In contrast, the chaste and abstemious have "worn down" their bodies and "dried up" their humors with discipline.[52]

Various combinations of humors determine temperament, and such combinations can be affected by season, weather, age, diet, and habits. In turn, one's temperament can predispose one to certain vices.[53] Bitter tempers (*asperi*) tend toward cruelty, wrath, and pride; mild tempers (*blandi*) toward lechery, lack of discipline, frivolity, and boasting.[54] A

---

verse and the human soul, stressing the organic unity and sympathy of each level of physical life with human life. Such ideas, held in common with the Hippocratic tradition, viewed emotional and even moral states as arising from the balance of humors, that is, of hot, cold, wet, or dry components in the body. According to Galen, the most influential exponent of this tradition, the elements of man are not the four primary bodies (fire, air, water, and earth) but their qualities: the warm, cold, dry, and humid. See Galen, *Introd. s. med.*, 9, quoted by Sambursky, *Physical World*, 119. Galen is following Athenaios, founder of the "Pneumatic School" in the first half of the first century. See also Wesley D. Smith, *The Hippocratic Tradition* (Ithaca and London, 1979), 108ff; and F. H. Sandbach, *The Stoics* (New York, 1975), 71–78. Isidore of Seville may be used as an index of medical thought during Gregory's era: medical concepts became fixed toward the end of the first century A.D. and scarcely changed until the fourteenth century, cf. Jackie Pigeaud, *La Maladie de l'âme: étude sur la relation de l'âme et du corps dans la tradition médico-philosophique antique* (Paris, 1981), 21. Isidore glosses over this distinction but does define four humors corresponding to the four elements, both sets of which preserve the body: blood (*sanguis*) corresponds with the air and is hot and moist; yellow bile (*cholera*) with fire, and is hot and dry. Black bile (*melancholia*) corresponds with the earth, and is cold and dry. Phlegm (*phlegma*) like water, is cold and wet. Isidore, *orig.* 4.5.5; *orig.* 9.1ff.; see Fontaine, *Isidore of Seville*, 2d ed., 2:665ff. for Isidore and the tradition before him. Isidore associates blood with pleasantness, phlegm with coldness, choler with agitation, and black bile with *melancholia*. Isidore also associates humors with organs of the body in *orig.* 11.1.125–28: the spleen with laughter, the gall bladder and its bile with anger, the heart with understanding, and love, pleasure, and sensual desires with the liver. Health lies in the proper balance of humors (*eucrasia*); disease results from their faulty mixture (*dyscrasia*). Healing consists in running a middle course between health and disease, because, Isidore explains, if healing were not congruent with the disease, it would not produce health, *orig.* 4.5.1–3. Gregory would have found mention of the four humors in Cic. *Tusc.* 1.24.56; 4.10.23.

50. *Reg. Past.* 3.19 (PL 77, 81); *Ep.* 11.56a (MGH, II, 342); see also *Reg. Past.* 1.11 (PL 77, 26).

51. Cf. *Mor.* 13.15.18 (CCL 143A, 678–79); *Mor.* 5.1.1 (CCL 143, 218–19).

52. *Mor.* 33.3.8–9 (CCL 143B, 1676–78); *Mor.* 20.41.78 (CCL 143A, 1061). Also *Mor.* 33.12.23 (CCL 143B, 1693–94), where humility dries the swelling of pride.

53. Cicero discusses tempers and their proneness to vice in *Tusc.* 4.12.27–4.13.21; and the four humors in *Tusc.* 1.24.56; 4.10.23.

54. *Mor.* 14.13.15 (CCL 143A, 706–7).

warmth of wit makes one talkative and curious.[55] The perspicacious ad-
monitions in Gregory's *Pastoral Rule* depend on such distinctions of temperament as well as of social circumstance. Joyful temperaments, which
are close to lechery, must be treated one way; the sad, who are near anger, must be treated another way. The joyful are administered fear or
punishment, the sad the joy of reward.[56] Meek and gentle souls (*mansueti*)
tend toward laxity, softness, and torpor, a word Gregory associates elsewhere with coldness.[57] Their opposites, the passionate (*iracundi*), tend to
be impetuous, severe, and on fire with zeal. Each type is to be given the
proper opposite remedy, be it warm encouragement or icy rebuke, to restore balance.

The connection of body and soul is altogether real in Gregory, although not as strong as that perceived by monastic writers such as Cassian or Dorotheos of Gaza. As a preacher, Gregory's method is rhetorical.
He will speak metaphorically of vices as diseases of the soul, and of the
balance that is true health.[58] He will emphasize the interdependence of
all virtues[59] and the relentless succession of all vices,[60] for perfection encompasses body and soul. Above all, he wishes to stress the mysterious
sympathy man possesses with all creation to show that creation can in
turn have an effect upon him. Being both flesh and spirit, man responds

55. Cf. *Mor.* 3.22.45 (CCL 143, 143).

56. *Reg. Past.* 3.3 (PL 77, 53–54).

57. *Reg. Past.* 3.16 (PL 77, 75–77); *Mor.* 9.58.88 (CCL 143, 519).

58. E.g., *Reg. Past.* 1.11 (PL 77, 23–26). Cf. *Mor.* 33.6.13 (CCL 143B, 1683); *Mor.*
7.28.34ff. (CCL 143, 357–58); cf. Gr. Naz. *or.* 32.27 (untranslated; of which Gregory may
have had oral knowledge). Virtue and vice work as contraries: *HEv.* 2.32.1 (PL 76, 1232–33):
"Sed coelestis medicus singulis quibusque vitiis obviantia adhibet medicamenta. Nam sicut
arte medicinae calida frigidis, frigida calidis curantur, ita Dominus noster contraria oppo-
suit praedicamenta peccatis, ut lubricis continentiam, tenacibus largitatem, iracundis man-
suetudinem, elatis praeciperet humilitatem." This medical imagery of contraries also carries
over to images of warfare: *HEz.* 1.12.25 (CCL 142, 198); *In lib. I Reg.* 5.9 (CCL 144, 421).
Virtues appear as the remedies of vice in Aug. *agone.* 11.12. On the relation between Cassian's and Gregory's list of vices see Robert Gillet, introduction to Grégoire le Grand, *Morales sur Job* I–II (SC 32), 89f. The proper virtue can be applied to cure a specific vice, imbalance is redressed, and the health of the soul returns. The ideas of sin as a disease and virtue
as the health of the soul go back as far as Democritus and Plato, and came to be stressed by
the Stoics; see Pigeaud, *La Maladie de l'âme*, 17f., 245–371.

59. *Mor.* 1.32.42f. (CCL 143, 84ff.); *Mor.* 22.1.2–3 (CCL 143A, 1042–43); *Mor.* 1.36.54
(CCL 143, 55–56); *Mor.* 1.27.38 (CCL 143, 82–83); *Mor.* 2.49.76f. (CCL 143, 105f.); *HEv.*
2.27.1 (PL 76, 1205); *HEz.*1.3.8 (CCL 142, 37); *HEz.* 2.7.7 (CCL 142, 320–22); *HEz.* 2.20.18
(CCL 142, 393–94); *HEz.* 2.8.4 (CCL 142, 338); *HEz.* 1.9.31 (CCL 142, 159–60). Cf. Ambr. *off.*
2.43; also 1.129; 2.48; *parad.* 22. See D. Lottin, "La Connexion des vertues avant saint
Thomas d'Aquin," *RechTh* 2 (1930): 21ff.; Edward V. Arnold, *Roman Stoicism* (1911; repr. ed.,
London, 1958), 294f.; Spanneut, *Le Stoïcisme*, 242f.

60. *Mor.* 31.45.87 (CCL 143B, 1610); *Mor.* 33.37.65 (CCL 143B, 1728–29). Cf. Cassian,
conl. 13.3. See also Siegfried Wenzel, *The Sin of Sloth: Acedia* (Chapel Hill, N.C., 1960).

to both the visible and invisible realities in the rest of the universe. These sensitive connections with reality enable him to change and reform as he responds to God's will as presented in the world's prosperity and adversity. Physical comfort can undermine self-control, even as harsh circumstances can strengthen the soul's discipline.

Man is at the very center of creation, in communion with the universe. But the universe he reflects and recapitulates is itself deeply divided, an indication of Gregory's solemn misgivings about the human condition. Flesh and spirit are opposites, each pulling in a different direction toward the realm of its origin. Gregory's explanation of the Pauline warfare of spirit and flesh in Romans 7:23 is straightforward and dualistic. The spirit raises (*levare*) man internally and draws him to the height (*trahere ad summa*) to experience an invisible world. The flesh weighs him down (*aggravare*) externally and drags him to the depths (*trahere ad ima*), so binding him to a visible world.[61] The presence of an "interior" and an "exterior" man also signifies this distinction. Each is vivified in a different way: "As we draw in breath that the body might live, so the Spirit is drawn in from the inward depths of wisdom that the soul might live."[62] Each side of man has its own sensation and perception,[63] its own understanding of punishment and delight: "For as the flesh is nourished by softness, the spirit is nourished by hardness. Mildness pampers the one, harshness exercises the other. One is fed by delights, the other flourishes on bitterness."[64] Man possesses both a voice of the flesh and a voice of the soul (*vox carnis, vox animae*).[65] Gregory often uses dualistic images to emphasize man's conflicting exterior and interior natures, such as the house and its inhabitant or the prison and its prisoner.[66]

The interior reason is the higher side of man that links him with the angels. Indeed, Gregory locates the *imago* and *similitudo* of God in reason,

---

61. *Mor.* 19.6.12 (CCL 143A, 964).

62. *Mor.* 18.51.83 (CCL 143A, 946).

63. See esp. Gregorio Penco, "La Dottrina dei sensi spirituali in S. Gregorio," *Benedictina* 17 (1970): 161–201.

64. *Mor.* 10.24.42 (CCL 143, 567).

65. *Mor.* 19.6.12 (CCL 143A, 964); also *HEz.* 1.8.13 (CCL 142, 108). On the place of the "interior" and the "exterior" man in Gregory, see *Mor.* 9.53.80 (CCL 143, 511–12): "Sicut lutum quippe homo noster interior exsistit, quia sancti Spiritus gratia terrenae menti infunditur, ut ad intellectum sui conditoris erigatur. Humana namque cogitatio quae peccati sui sterilitate aruit, per uim sancti Spiritus quasi irrigata terra uiridescit . . ."; *HEz.* 1.8.13 (CCL 142, 108). See Pierre Aubin, "Intériorité et extériorité dans les *Moralia in Job* de Saint Grégoire le Grand," *RSR* 62 (1974): 129f.; Dagens, *Saint Grégoire*, 133ff.; Gillet, Introduction to *Morales sur Job*, I–II, passim. The interior man and exterior man is found in Augustine; see Gareth Matthews, "The Inner Man," in Robert A. Markus, ed., *Augustine: A Collection of Critical Essays* (Garden City, N.Y., 1972), 176–90.

66. *HEz.* 2.5.9 (CCL 142, 282); *HEv.* 1.9.1 (PL 76, 1106); *Mor.* 15.46.52 (CCL 143A, 780–81); *Mor.* 8.23.40 (CCL 143, 411).

for reason joins man with God through knowledge and contemplation.[67] Reason offers man stability in clinging to God and is ultimately the source of his immortality.[68] The immutability and stability conferred by reason keep man from passing away to the nothingness of death.[69] It is not surprising, therefore, that Gregory has little positive to say about the body. Of course, Gregory acknowledges the goodness of the body at creation,[70] but he is anxious about the danger the body poses to man's spiritual well-being. The body—constituted of the four elements that make up the physical world—pulls man downward toward mutability and nothingness, making him all too vulnerable to change.

But Gregory's attitude goes beyond the relative neutrality of seeing the body as part of the physical world; his disgust can be ostentatious. Gregory associates the body with defilement, pollution, and the irrational desires of animals. A solid, intractable mass, the body is made of clay,

67. *Mor.* 32.12.17 (CCL 143B, 1641–42); and *Mor.* 5.34.63 (CCL 143, 262): "Rationalis uero creatura eo ipso quo ad imaginem auctoris est condita ne ad nihilum transeat . . ."; *Mor.* 29.10.21 (CLL 143B, 1448): "Ex luto quippe homo conditus, et mentis accepta ratione, similitudine, diuinae imaginis decoratus. . . ."; see also *Mor.* 9.49.75 (CCL 143, 509). Cf. Aug. *trin.* 11.5.8; *divers. quaest.* 51.2; *civ.* 12.23; Ambr. *hex.* 9.7.43. Gregory uses *imago* and *similitudo* interchangeably, often together as in Gn 1:26, and gives them a moral emphasis. The image is what one *is* (i.e., a spiritual being), not what one *has*. See *HEv.* 2.28.3 (PL 76, 1212); note, too, *Mor.* 30.17.56 (CCL 143B, 1529) where the soul "ad auctoris sui imaginem ac similitudinem sit condita meminit [Gn 1:26], et iuxta perceptae similitudinis ordinem incedit." The image and likeness account for contemplation; cf. *HEv.* 2.34.6 (PL 76, 1249). On the whole Gregory's emphasis on contemplation achieved through the image and likeness echoes Augustine; see T. A. Fay, "*Imago Dei*. Augustine's Metaphysics of Man," *Antonianum* 49 (1974): 173–97. In practical terms, "imago etenim et similitudo dei est inclyto odio malum odire et amore perfecto bonum diligere"; cf. *In lib. I Reg.* 2.106 (CCL 144, 176). Gregory follows Origen in seeing the lost drachma of Luke 15:9 as the image of God; cf. *HEv.* 2.34.6 (PL 76, 1249); and it is a coin (*nummum*) defiled by the filth of sin in *In lib. I Reg.* 2.106 (CCL 144, 175–76). On this passage, see Joan Petersen, "Greek Influences in Gregory the Great's Exegesis of Luke 15, 1–10 in *Evang.* II, 34 (PL 76, 1246ff.)," in Fontaine et al., eds., *Grégoire le Grand*, 521–29. The image is restored (*reparare*) by penitence and the avoidance of evil, cf. *In lib. I Reg.* 2.106 (CCL 144, 175 76): "In nummo quippe imago domini sculpitur, ut eius esse cognoscatur, a quo formari praecipitur. Nummus itaque dei similitudo eius accipitur. . . ."). See Penco, "Teologia dell'immagine," 33–42 and p. 42, n. 50, discussing the controversy of a different use of *imago* and *similitudo* in Gregory; also Dudden, *Gregory*, 376, and Weber, *Hauptfragen*, 106ff. For the theology of reform the classic work is Gerhart B. Ladner, *The Idea of Reform* (New York, 1959; repr. ed., 1967).

68. *Mor.* 14.15.17 (CCL 143A, 707–8): "Ex rationali quippe anima habet homo ut in perpetuum uiuat."

69. *Mor.* 5.34.63 (CCL 143, 262): "Omnis quippe creatura quia ex nihilo facta est, et per semetipsam ad nihilum tendit, non stare habet sed defluere. Rationalis uero creatura eo ipso quo ad imaginem auctoris est condita ne ad nihilum transeat, figitur. Irrationalis autem nequaquam figitur, sed donec uisionis suae ministerio uniuersitatis speciem impleat, transeundo tardatur. . . . Stare ergo, solius creatoris est per quem cuncta non transeuntem transeunt et in quo aliqua ne transeant, retinentur." See also *Mor.* 11.50.68 (CCL 143A, 624–25); *Mor.* 12.15.19 (CCL 143A, 640); *Mor.* 25.3.4 (CCL 143B, 1232).

70. See, e.g., *Mor.* 9.36.58 (CCL 143, 498–99).

the lowest matter.[71] Composed of the dust of the earth, the body pollutes man. Job sits on his dunghill to remind himself that he will return to stench.[72] And each of the body's products defiles man; from the *superflua* of the bowels and of the face (i.e., the hair) to the bloody humors oozing from Job's skin—all are pollutants. Excrement is the body's sin, hairs are carnal passions, and humors are corruption.[73] The body's very mutability (*fluxus*) is itself corruption, a tendency to degenerate and return to primal elements, dust and ashes. Because it was created *ex nihilo*, the body is prone to revert to this nothingness.[74] Ultimately, mutability means dissolution, a return to the gaping void of numbness and nonexistence.

The body renders man "dissimilar" to himself,[75] and causes him to lose his true identity in unrestricted change and finally in death. The ideal likeness to God found in man's reason is woefully deformed when muddled and infected with change. The body is a shell of alien, lifeless matter threatening the soul, its animating principle and man's authentic self.[76] In receiving the flesh, man is actually given "something through which he would be less than himself."[77] Even though Gregory occasionally identifies man with the body,[78] reason remains man's true identity. Only the flesh keeps man from perfection, or so it seems: "And still, though this same dignity of ours shines through the image, [man] is far removed from the perfection of beatitude through the flesh, since when the spirit is mixed with dust, in a certain way, it is joined to weakness."[79]

With reason as God's image and the true essence of man, the flesh is alien and unwelcome, for it threatens to undermine man by pulling him away from perfection and blessedness. Gregory sees man as a composite of fiercely dissimilar elements:

> And so every man, since he exists from soul and flesh, is composed, so to speak, of strength and weakness. For from that part by which he was created a rational spirit, he is not unfittingly called strong, but from that

71. *Mor.* 6.15.18 (CCL 143, 296); *Mor.* 29.10.21 (CCL 143B, 1448); *Mor.* 14.15.17 (CCL 143A, 707–8); *Mor.* 9.50.76 (CCL 143, 510).

72. *Mor.* 3.7.10 (CCL 143, 120).

73. *Mor.* 5.33.59 (CCL 143, 260): "Semper enim caro superflua generat quae semper spiritus ferro sollicitudinis recidat."

74. See, e.g., *Mor.* 5.34.63 (CCL 143, 262); cf. Dionys. Exig. *Gr. Nyss. hom. op.* 17. Of course angels and souls are also created *ex nihilo*, but their success achieving stability contravenes the pull back to nothingness.

75. *HEz.* 2.5.10 (CCL 142, 283). See also, *Mor.* 9.36.58 (CCL 143, 498–99). The word *dissimilar* recalls the Plotinian Augustine; cf. *conf.* 7.10.6.

76. *HEz.* 2.5.9 (CCL 142, 282); *Mor.* 9.50.76 (CCL 143, 510); *Dial.* 4.1.4–5 (SC 265, 20–22).

77. *Mor.* 9.50.76 (CCL 143, 510).

78. *HEz.* 2.1.9 (CCL 142, 215).

79. *Mor.* 9.49.75 (CCL 143, 509).

part by which he is flesh he is weak. The strength of man is his rational soul by which he is able to resist attacking vices through reason.[80]

Schooled in the physics of the human condition, man can better understand the conflicts he feels and perhaps defend himself in the warfare that the flesh imposes on the soul. But while it may seem an unhappy fate to be rent with such battles and internal tension, Gregory sees God's Providence at work in this stunning paradox, and this is his central point. God has wrought a miracle in making man. Even though soul and body stand strongly opposed, they are marvelously united in a relationship of interdependence and complementarity, so that the sufferings of one can affect the other:

> Certainly you were created from spirit and clay, one invisible, the other visible; one sensible, the other insensible. How therefore can spirit and clay be mixed in you, so that from diverse things arise something which is not diverse, so that spirit and clay are mixed in such great harmony that when the flesh is weakened, the spirit droops, and when the spirit is afflicted the flesh wastes away?[81]

Spirit and flesh are such mutually hostile elements it seems impossible that the two could be joined in one creation. But the power of God in making man is awesome, and the bitter opposition between man's spirit and his flesh testifies to the force of God's powers. The visible clay is mixed so harmoniously with the invisible spirit, flesh and spirit are so mysteriously linked, that their antipathy gives rise to their sympathy. At times their relation is positive and direct: as flesh suffers, soul suffers. The unity and interaction of soul and flesh are particularly obvious in this relation of deepest sympathy. More typical, however, is the inverse relationship where flesh and spirit are at odds because of their natural diversity, where one flourishes only at the expense of the other. Indeed, the cost must be exacted from one in order to benefit the other. The suffering of the flesh improves the welfare of the soul; wounds inflicted on the body cure wounds of the soul.[82]

The positive and negative interconnections of body and soul sustain two models of perfection in Gregory's thought. The ascetic model, the more conventional and more common, is best exemplified by the monk

---

80. *Mor.* 14.15.17 (CCL 143A, 707–8). This sense that man is comprised of fiercely opposed natures is strong in Dionys. Exig. *Gr. Nyss. hom. op.* 17.

81. *HEz.* 2.8.9 (CCL 142, 343): "Certe ex spiritu es creatus et limo, uno inuisibili, altero uisibili, uno sensibili, altero insensibili. Quomodo ergo permisci in te potuit spiritus et limus atque ex diuerso fieri res non diuersa, ita ut in tanta conuenientia misceretur spiritus et limus, ut cum caro atteritur spiritus marceat, et cum spiritus affligitur caro contabescat?" Cf. Dionys. Exig. *Gr. Nyss. hom. op.* 14.

82. *Mor.* 33.19.35 (CCL 143B, 1705–6). Cf. Tert. *anim.* 5, arguing that such sympathy of body and soul could not happen unless the soul were corporeal.

who mortifies the flesh for the sake of his spirit. A more dangerous and daring model is that of the contemplative preacher, the ascetic who returns to the world—the pattern Gregory created for himself. Unwillingly immersed in the good things of life that tempt him and pamper the flesh, the contemplative preacher can become perfect in imperfection, for he learns to use good fortune as even greater suffering and trial.[83] These two models, which will be examined later at length, suggest a central ambivalence. Man certainly is a unity to Gregory, a composite of body and soul, but in which does his true identity lie? Reason is the authentic side of man, but the body is crucial in his salvation. Gregory succeeds in mastering a difficult dilemma by having it both ways. If reason reaches perfection, this is to be praised, but if the body presents obstacles, one need not surrender to despair. The works of the body can be transformed and offered to God in sacrifice, precisely because the unity of flesh and spirit works along two pathways of integration, one of melodic cooperation, another of harmony in dissonance.

Standing in the middle of the universe, at the juncture of spiritual and carnal existence, man holds a privileged position as mediator and microcosm. Not only is man a noble creation, but in Christ God has even favored human weakness above the angels.[84] Just as the universe is a continuous ladder of spirit and flesh, so man replicates this continuum in himself in the sensitive unity and interconnection of his body and soul. If his volatile personality often sweeps him to change and decay, it can nevertheless lift him toward the exquisite mysteries of the eternal. Mediating and recapitulating all creation, he can become almost anything, angel or beast. Should he follow the spirit, the whole man might be dominated by its scintillating power, making him "spiritual in the flesh" (*carne spiritualis*).[85] But if he follows the sodden ways of the flesh, he will become even "carnal in the mind" (*mente carnalis*).[86] Man's position is dynamic and challenging: he can rise to become God's intimate friend or fall to become his despised and forlorn enemy.

83. *Mor.* 33.19.35–36 (CCL 143B, 1705–7).
84. *Mor.* 27.15.29–30 (CCL 143B, 1352–53).
85. *Mor.* 5.34.61 (CCL 143, 261): "Homo enim, qui si praeceptum seruare uoluisset, etiam carne spiritualis futurus erat, peccando factus est etiam mente carnalis . . ."
86. Ibid. For the terms *carne spiritualis* and *mente carnalis*, see Aug. *civ.* 14.15.

· II ·

A SACRAMENTAL VISION

Gregory's world is full of surprises, not all of them pleasant. A bear honors a saint,[1] and the sea bellows with God's anger.[2] Such engaging incidents illustrate how this world can embody the spiritual realities of the next. Yet a darker side exists. In the *Dialogues*, Gregory describes the dismal passing of a monk in his own community. As the physician Justus lies dying, he confesses to hoarding three gold pieces among his various medicines. With ferocious zeal, Gregory forces the monk to die friendless and alone, then throws his body and coins on a manure heap to rot with a curse, "Take your money with you to perdition" (cf. Acts 8:20). Punishment of sins can begin even on one's deathbed, and the bitter experience actually speeds Justus's release from hell.[3] Such incidents reflect what might be called a sacramental vision of reality. This visible world of flesh and blood and mere human experience reveals a variety of mysterious links with the transcendent, invisible world of the spirit. Such mediation is possible because existence is continuous: the ladder of being stretches from God to dust, from perfection and pure existence to nothingness and evil. Though the two ends of this scale are polar opposites, paradoxically they are also united in sharing the same order of comparison.

In Gregory's sacramental vision, carnal signs mediate between this world and the next. Carnal means attain spiritual ends, and the things of this world are often vehicles of spiritual experience. The soul can be bruised through the body: ascetic practices and the suffering of external

1. *Dial*. 3.11.1–3 (SC 260, 292–94).
2. *Dial*. 3.36.1–5 (SC 260, 408–10).
3. *Dial*. 4.57.9–11 (SC 265, 188–90). Jeffrey Richards notes this "comes rather badly from one who still owned several farms at least thirteen years after becoming a monk," *Consul of God* (London, 1980), 36.

adversities can help chasten and improve the soul.[4] Though they be dusted with the sin of the world, ordinary human activities can become sacrifices offered to God, linking man with the world beyond, just as the daily sacrifice of the Mass mediates between worlds,[5] and the sacrifice of Christ mediates continually with God.[6] In this sacramental vision of reality, the saint and holy man also mediate between two worlds. To lesser mortals blinded by the Fall, they reveal the invisible world which is always very much present. The saint and holy man participate in the life of God while still on earth, for each has managed to link his soul with God so completely that God dwells within him with a special fullness. Physical relics conduct a flow of power from the world beyond into the present world, and human action intersects both carnal and spiritual realms, this world and the next. This is a world where a cross made over bread baking in hot embers can be perceptible when the bread is removed from the ashes, for it is possible to draw a spiritual force into visibility through a physical act.[7] In one way or another, all these kinds of mediation depend on the inner continuity of spiritual and carnal reality, despite their obvious opposition.

This dialectic of flesh and spirit changes the reality one experiences. In Gregory's vision, the carnal side of reality is instrumental for the spiritual. Thus elevated or transformed, the carnal symbolizes spiritual truths and links man with the spiritual realm. Even as the carnal begins to take on spiritual significance, the spirit takes on many carnal aspects as well. The ordinary accidents of daily life can embody transcen-

---

4. Gregory relates that in order to cure the flames of lust, Benedict threw himself into thornbushes, and by the wounds of the body cured the wounds of the soul; cf. *Dial.* 2.2.2 (SC 260, 138). Despite this passage and his frequent references to the *flagella Dei* visited upon man, Gregory does not endorse self-inflicted punishment with scourges or other instruments of discipline; see Robert Gillet, "Spiritualité et place du moine dans l'Eglise selon saint Grégoire le Grand," *Théologie de la vie monastique* (Paris, 1961), 336, and Olegario M. Porcel, *La doctrina monástica de San Gregorio Magno y la "Regula Monachorum"* (Washington, D.C., 1951), 89–90. See also Robert Gillet, "Saint Grégoire le Grand," *DS*, 4:882; and Patrick Catry, "Epreuves du juste et mystère de Dieu: Le Commentaire litteral du Livre de Job par saint Grégoire le Grand," *REAug* 18 (1972), 124–44. Gregory's words for disciplinary (and supererogatory) suffering include: *cruciare, tormentum, mordere, maceratio corporis, castigare, afflictio.* An instance of corporal discipline of the clergy appears in *Ep.* 4.24 (CCL 140, 243), where concerning the cleric Paul, Gregory states: "corporali prius proueniente uindicta, praeuidimus in paenitentiam dari, quatenus et secundum apostolicam sententiam ex carnis afflictione spiritus saluus fiat, et terrenas peccatorum sordes, quas prauis contraxisse fertur operibus, lacrimarum possit assiduitate diluere." Still Gregory condemns the use of excessive force on the clergy, *Ep.* 12.8 (CCL 140A, 979–80); *Ep.* 3.52 (CCL 140, 197–99); on parishioners, cf. *Ep.* 3.45 (CCL 140, 190).

5. *Dial.* 4.60–61 (SC 265, 200–204).

6. Ibid.

7. *Dial.* 1.11.1 (SC 260, 110–12).

dent truths; the breaking of a lamp or a sudden fire can make one shudder at the presence of spiritual forces. The tribulations man suffers from natural or political disasters can disclose God's wrath, for "the invisible judge moves the breath of the gentlest breeze."[8] The most banal form of carnality, evil itself, can even have its spiritual side when one recognizes that the devil is only God's minion. The suffering inflicted by the devil is elevated and imbued with spiritual consequence once one realizes that suffering is a trial from God. In a complementary way, what is spiritual can be touched by the heavy hand of the flesh. Heaven takes on a very earthly appearance, and even God has something of a carnal side when his wrath and his control of evil are understood fully.

In Gregory's world, to meet someone might be to learn the inner secrets of his soul, if one possessed discernment (*discretio*). Election is not always a mysterious truth hidden from men. Gregory deeply believes the words of Matthew 7:20, "by their fruits you will know them." Inner spiritual dispositions are very often manifest in visible works.[9] Indeed, inner charity must be displayed in works to be considered true virtue: works must be joined to faith.[10] For this reason, the nature of the heavenly Jerusalem can be seen in its citizens on earth,[11] just as the damned reveal themselves by their unregenerate behavior. Like Augustine, Gregory acknowledges that external appearance can belie inner reality, but their emphases differ. Augustine was acutely aware of God's omnipotence and believed that God's dispensation was necessarily mysterious and inscrutable to mere human beings. The hidden justice of election inextricably mixed good and evil men like wheat and tares in the field, or grain and chaff on the threshing floor. Good could be discerned only by God, who alone knew the secrets of the human heart. Wickedness was visible, but God might snatch the sinner from the snares of the devil at the last moment and place him among the elect. Only on the threshing floor of the Last Judgment would Christ reveal the elect and the damned for all to see.

Gregory's shift of Augustine's position is slight, but significant. Augustine's God plays hide-and-seek with man, now concealing or revealing truths to keep man humble and mindful of his dependence. Gregory chooses rather to emphasize God's involvement with creation and the

8. *HEv*. 1.1.6 (PL 76, 1081).

9. *Mor*. 31.8.13 (CCL 143B, 1559); *HEz*. 2.4.19 (CCL 142, 308).

10. *HEv*. 2.30.2 (PL 76, 1221); *HEz*. 1.9.6 (CCL 142, 126); *HEz*. 2.10.17 (CCL 142, 392); *Reg. Past*. 3.24 (PL 77, 94); *Mor*. 33.6.12 (CCL 143B, 1682); and *HEz*. 2.9.2 (CCL 142, 357), citing Jas 2:20: "Fides sine operibus mortua est."

11. *Dial*. 3.35.6 (SC 260, 406): "Magna uitae aedificatio est uidere uiros mira facientes, atque in ciuibus suis Hierusalem caelestem in terra conspicere."

sacramental presence of spiritual truths in the things of this world. When Gregory sees a disparity between the external sign and the inner spiritual reality, he knows it is the malignant deceit and trickery of the devil, rather than a sublime mystery designed to keep man humble. One expects to see the heart revealed in works, but one is always prepared to detect hypocrisy, the deliberate perversion of right order, which is the work of that beast who "disguised himself as an angel of light."[12] While Augustine wished to emphasize man's powerlessness before God's omnipotence, Gregory hopes to stir man to take action against evil. Since Christ has conquered the devil, that first hypocrite, Christians now have tactics to ferret out deceit. To possess *discretio* is to see the invisible reality, and to discern spirits accurately enough to expose the hypocrite hiding behind a false exterior.[13]

While the hidden election of a soul can be revealed in the external works of a Christian, on a larger scale, all the world can manifest invisible spiritual messages.[14] The natural world is close to man and in sympathy with him, a sympathy that recalls Stoic teaching.[15] Since the whole universe is harmoniously composed of invisible and visible existence, with each level possessing various proportions of matter and spirit, there is a natural sympathy of participation among all these interacting parts of the universe. As man is made of the four elements composing the universe, his link with the world is material and metonymic as well as metaphoric and rhetorical. Even as man is a "little universe," so too the universe is like man. On occasion, Gregory displays a tendency toward anthropomorphism and animism. He sees a hierarchical animation of the world echoing that of human life. "The earth is made fruitful by the air; the air, by the heavens," Gregory writes, as if animation travels a downward path from heaven to earth.[16] God imbues the world with existence from the top downward; just as he breathes life into man's soul, and the soul in turn animates man's body, so the invisible forces of the heavens activate the earth. The parallel between man and the universe suggests their inner likeness. Like man, the universe ages with time and in old age becomes prey to sickness and disaster.[17] This sympathy is so great that in

12. Cf. *Mor.* 33.24.44 (CCL 143B, 1712).

13. *HEz.* 1.7.7 (CCL 142, 86–87).

14. *Mor.* 4.29.55 (CCL 143, 199–200). See esp. Roger Sorrel, "Dreams and Divination in Certain Writings of Gregory the Great" (B. Litt. Thesis, Oxford, 1978), 189ff.

15. For Stoics the world was alive and possessed a soul, ideas Gregory of course rejects; see Michel Spanneut, *Permanence du stoïcisme de Zenon à Malraux* (Gembloux, 1973), 157–59. The sensibility of the world for man happens only as a miracle of God's ordination.

16. *Mor.* 4.29.55 (CCL 143, 199).

17. *Mor.* 34.1.1 (CCL 143B, 1733). Gregory is unusual in drawing a parallel between

the daily cycles of sun and moon and the seasonal changes of the elements, nature herself predicts the resurrection of the flesh.[18] All the natural elements testified that Christ was the true Messiah:[19] the star at his birth, the earthquake at his death, the many miracles he wrought.

This sensitivity explains why natural disasters can both portend human difficulties and reflect human virtues. When Abbot Suranus dies, the earth trembles, "as if to declare openly that the fall of the saint was too much for it to bear."[20] Nature obeys the saint, for he shares the same power Christ possessed over animals and the elements. Consider Bishop Sabinus, who sends a written order to the River Po, ordering it to return to its banks. The river recedes and never again dares to leave its banks.[21] Animals also can have "almost a human heart," like the ferocious bear sent to devour Bishop Cerbonius. The bear recognizes the bishop's saintliness and is converted. Now gentle, the bear licks the bishop's hands and feet in humble submission.[22] In a corresponding way, animals can also be vehicles of demonic inspiration, as they were on occasion in the Gospel. Troublesome pigs and restless cattle are possessed by demons in the *Dialogues*.[23]

An even subtler sympathy exists between animals and man, for animals also perform an important duty in teaching man about himself.[24] The animals themselves are simply unreflective and pure in pursuing their natural instincts. But should man betray his rational side and follow his bestial nature, his despicable perversion mimics their own innocent irrationality. Ostriches suggest the deceit of hypocrites, whose wings of contemplation are puny, while their bodies are heavy with sensuality.[25] The slithery newt suggests the laxity of sinners, who are "numb" with "negligence" but nevertheless clever in getting what they want.[26] Bulls

---

the ages of the world and of man (Cf. *HEv.* 1.19.2ff.); see Paulo Siniscalco, "Le Età del mondo," in Jacques Fontaine et al., eds., *Grégoire le Grand* (Paris, 1986), 377–87.

18. *Mor.* 14.50.70 (CCL 143A, 741–42).

19. *HEv.* 1.10.2 (PL 76, 1111).

20. *Dial.* 4.23.2 (SC 265, 80); also *Dial.* 3.1ff. (SC 260–66). Cf. Mt 28:51.

21. *Dial.* 3.10.2–3 (SC 260, 290). See de Vogüé's edition for an exhaustive treatment of literary parallels to this and other incidents.

22. *Dial.* 3.11.1–3 (SC 260, 292).

23. *Dial.* 3.30.3 (SC 260, 380).

24. For a study of Gregory's use of animals to explicate the moral and spiritual senses of Scripture, see R. Hesbert, "Le Bestiaire de Saint Grégoire," in Fontaine et al., eds., *Grégoire le Grand*, 455–66; and B. O'Malley, *The Animals of St. Gregory* (London, 1981). Origen also uses animals in moral exegesis; see Patricia Cox, "Origen and the Bestial Soul: A Poetics of Nature," *VChr* 36 (1982): 115–40. See also Dionys. Exig. *Gr. Nyss. hom. op.* 19.

25. *Mor.* 7.28.36 (CCL 143, 359–60), also *Mor.* 31.8.11f. (CCL 143B, 1557).

26. *Mor.* 6.10.12 (CCL 143, 292).

symbolize the stiff neck of pride, while wild asses show how sinners are unbridled and run riot in the "grass" of carnal pleasure.[27] When sinners hide from rebuke of their wickedness, they are like hedgehogs curling up in self-defense.[28] And what could the bold horn of the rhinoceros represent except the swelling pride of the secular prince?[29] The elect are like the eagles, who live in high places of contemplation; they are also like hawks and herons having small bodies and huge, powerful wings (Jb 39:13).[30] Preachers can see themselves in the sturdy oxen harnessed to serve others, bent low in the defiling dust of the world. They are also locusts who soar in contemplation yet fall to earth in service of others.[31]

While animals serve as moral lessons, exemplifying man's strengths and weaknesses, the physical and natural world can express God's aims toward man with great immediacy, intervening directly in man's life with God's message. Natural catastrophes are adversities sent as expressions of God's wrath, while fertility of the earth, peace, good weather, and such are his blessings of prosperity. Sometimes both grace and wrath are expressed by the same event, like the alarming gale sent against Maximian on the Adriatic. While battering his ship with violent winds, God still kept the bark afloat, preserving Maximian's life and those of his monks.[32] Such lessons teach humility while preserving hope.

Not only does the natural world carry messages from God, its very structure helps man understand himself and the problems he faces in life. The world displays a certain pattern of binary oppositions of a piece with the spiritual and carnal polarities of man's life. Each part of the world reflects the other; man and his society mirror the natural order of the cosmos. The very nature of things, the immutable arrangement of God's dispensation, echoes the dissonance of soul and body, of men and women, of the more rational and thoughtful citizens and those more bestial and worldly. To find the world arranged in such clear and systematic oppositions is to acknowledge the divisions in human experience, yet also to awaken the hope and need to resolve such aching tensions and create a unified, harmonious whole, like life before the Fall.

The universe is riddled with polarities, some of which are themselves ambivalent. With its setting sun, the West suggests the decay of carnal

27. *Mor. praef.* 8.18 (CCL 143, 22); *Mor.* 7.12.14 (CCL 143, 343–44).

28. *Mor.* 33.29.53 (CCL 143B, 1719–20).

29. *Mor.* 31.2.2 (CCL 143B, 1549–50).

30. *Mor.* 31.8.12 (CCL 143B, 1558–59); *Mor.* 31.47.94f. (CCL 143B, 1614f.).

31. *Mor. praef.* 8.18 (CCL 143, 22). Animals too can symbolize vices: the caterpillar crawling in the earth is lust, the locust, vainglory, etc.; cf. *Mor.* 33.37.65 (CCL 143B, 1728–29); *Mor.* 31.25.49 (CCL 143B, 1584–85).

32. *Dial.* 3.36.1–5 (SC 260, 408–10).

corruption and the fall to sin. From the East dawns virtue and a reminder that our conversation is in heaven (cf. Phil 3:20).[33] The cold north wind is the raw numbness of the evil spirit, while the south wind warms and thaws the soul with the Holy Spirit.[34] Warmth generally represents internality and the love inspiring good works and conversion of the heart, while coldness suggests externality, sloth, insensibility, and sin.[35] Yet the south wind can also represent the warmth that relaxes the body and encourages a dissolute life.[36] One might also "burn" with carnal desires and be "cooled" by holy thoughts.[37] Heat can be associated with vices such as loquacity and curiosity, as well as the virtue of charity.[38] Presumably, the "heat" of vices arises from the humors associated with bodily digestion, itself a "hot" process.

Gregory links dryness with virtue and rational control, for the spirit should be "dried" of bodily humors. Moisture and heaviness suggest the damp clay of matter and the suspicious humors of man's "slippery mutability," especially those of lust.[39] Yet one can also be dessicated spiritually and in need of spiritual refreshment. For this, the moisture of Scripture or the preacher's words can return the soul to the greenness and fertility of good works.[40] Strength and firmness describe a soul collected and governed by reason and discretion. Weakness and softness suggest the relaxation of discipline leading to sin, especially of the body.[41] However, the

---

33. *Mor.* 1.31.43 (CCL 143, 48); *HEz.* 2.6.24 (CCL 142, 313). The imagery of day and night is of course associated with East and West. On this directional symbolism, see Sorrell, "Dreams and Divination," 137ff.; also D. F. Pocock, "North and South in the Book of Genesis" in *Studies in Social Anthropology: Essays Presented in Memory of E. E. Evans-Pritchard*, ed. J. H. M. Beattie and R. G. Lienhardt (Oxford, 1975), 273–84.

34. *HEz.* 1.2.8–9 (CCL 142, 21–22), where the north wind also has apocalyptic meaning. Also *HEz.* 2.7.6 (CCL 142, 320); *Mor.* 12.4.5 (CCL 143A, 631); *Mor.* 31.12.19 (CCL 143B, 1564); *Mor.* 3.22.45 (CCL 143, 143).

35. In addition to the preceding note, see *Mor.* 11.50.68 (CCL 143A, 625); *Mor.* 4.23.42 (CCL 143, 188–89); *Mor.* 12.53.60 (CCL 143A, 665); *Mor.* 9.58.88 (CCL 143, 519); *Mor.* 16.50.63 (CCL 143A, 835); *Mor.* 20.12.23 (CCL 143A, 1020–21); *Mor.* 31.10.15 (CCL 143B, 1560); *Mor.* 7.27.33 (CCL 143, 356); *Mor.* 27.38.64 (CCL 143B, 1381–82); *Mor.* 25.7.15 (CCL 143B, 1239–40); *Mor.* 29.30.58 (CCL 143B, 1475); *HEz.* 1.2.9–12 (CCL 142, 22–24). Such associations are strong in Cassian; e.g., *inst.* 2.10.1; 2.13.3; *conl.* 4.3; 4.19.

36. *Mor.* 7.30.39 (CCL 143, 364); *HEz.* 1.2.3. (CCL 142, 18–19).

37. *Mor.* 30.26.79 (CCL 143B, 1546).

38. *Mor.* 3.22.45 (CCL 143, 143); *HEz.* 1.2.3. (CCL 142, 19).

39. Cf. *HEz.* 1.2.3 (CCL 142, 18); *Mor.* 33.3.8–9 (CCL 143B, 1676–78); *Mor.* 20.41.78 (CCL 143A, 1061); *Mor.* 33.12.23 (CCL 143B, 1693).

40. *HEz.* 1.5.16 (CCL 142, 65–66); *Mor.* 14.20.24 (CCL 143A, 711–12); *Mor.* 9.53.80 (CCL 143, 511); *Mor.* 12.53.60 (CCL 143A, 665).

41. Variously, *fortitudo, robor, constantia* and *mollities, fluxus*; see *Mor.* 32.21.40 (CCL 143B, 1658–59); *Mor.* 28.11.28 (CCL 143B, 1416–17); *Mor.* 14.15.17 (CCL 143A, 707–8); *Mor.* 18.28.45 (CCL 143A, 914–15); *Mor.* 30.25.72 (CCL 143B, 1539); *Mor.* 30.10.39 (CCL 143B,

NOTHINGNESS   DEVIL

↑

SIN

FLESH

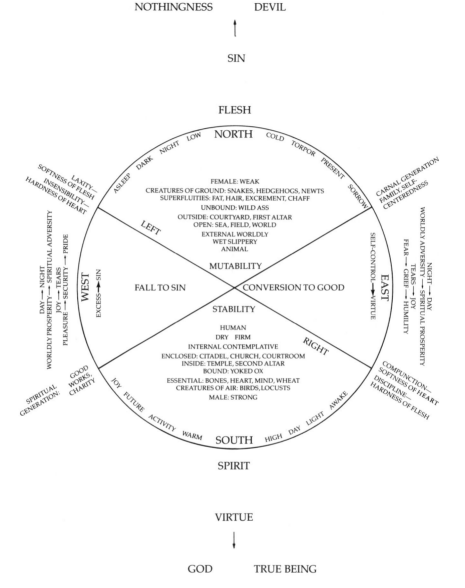

1. Synopsis of Oppositions in Gregory's World View

VIRTUE

↓

GOD   TRUE BEING

reprobate can also be strong and hard, refusing to be softened by the scourge of God's discipline. Correspondingly, the elect are weak and soft, so they are easily pierced with compunction.[42] Man represents the strong rational mind that rightly rules, and woman the weak animal body properly subjected to his dominion.[43] Light and dark are virtue and sin; day and night, morning and evening bear similar associations.[44] To go to the left is to enjoy sinning and think of the present, while to go to the right is to be virtuous and think of the future.[45] The contrasts between up and down and inward and outward are also morally weighted, representing spirituality and carnality in various forms.[46] Highness suggests the heavens, lowness the earth and the "heaviness" of sin. The external is linked with the visible cold world of the present flesh, the internal with the invisible warm life of the transcendent spirit.[47] Most of the oppositions found in Aristotle's table of Pythagorean opposites appear at one time or another in Gregory's writing.[48] These and other binary oppositions can be diagrammed (Figure 1).[49] The reader should imagine himself standing on high ground in the south, looking toward low ground in the north. To his right, the sun rises in the east, to his left, it sets in the west.

1518–19); *Mor.* 9.53.80–81 (CCL 143, 511–13); *Mor.* 7.21.24 (CCL 143, 349); *Mor.* 7.37.59 (CCL 143, 379); *Mor.* 7.30.43 (CCL 143, 367); *HEv.* 1.6.3 (PL 76, 1097); *HEv.* 1.15.3 (PL 76, 1133). See also *Mor.* 11.6.8 (CCL 143A, 589–90); *Mor.* 19.27.50 (CCL 143A, 996–97); *Mor.* 9.66.106 (CCL 143, 531–32).

42. Variously, *fortitudo, duritia, durus,* and *emolliri, mollire, mollescere*; see *Mor.* 7.21–22.24–46 (CCL 143, 349–51); *HEv.* 1.17.14 (PL 76, 1146); *Mor.* 11.9.13 (CCL 143A, 592); *Mor.* 30.26.78 (CCL 143B, 1545); *Mor.* 16.41.51 (CCL 143A, 828); *Mor.* 3.12.20 (CCL 143, 127); *Mor.* 29.30.58 (CCL 143B, 1475); *HEz.* 1.11.25 (CCL 142, 181); *Ep.* App. 9 (CCL 140A, 1102).

43. *Mor.* 30.16.54 (CCL 143B, 1528); *Mor.* 9.66.106 (CCL 143, 531–32); *Mor.* 30.25.72 (CCL 143B, 1540).

44. *Mor.* 2.9.15 (CCL 143, 69); *Mor.* 4.13.24–25 (CCL 143, 179–80); *Mor.* 24.23.50 (CCL 143B, 1224–25); *Mor.* 4.11.19 (CCL 143, 176–77).

45. *Mor.* 16.31.38 (CCL 143A, 821–22); *HEz.* 2.5.12 (CCL 142, 285). Also *HEz.* 1.4.3 (CCL 142, 49); *Mor.* 30.25.77 (CCL 143B, 1544).

46. See Pierre Aubin, "Intériorité et extériorité dans les *Moralia in Job* de saint Grégoire le Grand," *RSR* 62 (1974): 129–38.

47. Cf. *Mor.* 12.53.60 (CCL 143A, 665).

48. Arist. *Meta.* A5 986a 22ff. These binary oppositions are not only characteristic of Western culture, but are found in other cultures as well. As the meaning and origin of these binary oppositions are disputed, it is best to analyze how Gregory uses these contrasts rather than speculate on their genesis. See G. E. R. Lloyd, *Polarity and Analogy: Two Types of Argumentation in Greek Thought* (Cambridge, 1966); idem, "Right and Left in Greek Philosophy," in *Right and Left: Essays on Dual Symbolic Classification*, ed. Rodney Needham (Chicago, 1973), 167–86; and Paul Roubiczek, *Thinking in Opposites* (Boston, 1952).

49. I have been inspired by anthropologists such as Pierre Bourdieu, *Outline of a Theory of Practice* (Cambridge, 1977), 156–57; Claude Lévi-Strauss, *The Naked Man*, trans. Jonathan Cape (New York, 1981), esp. 128, 309, 351, 618.

The perilous conflict of spirit and flesh is echoed in the winds, the elements, the seasons—indeed, virtually all aspects of physical life reveal the underlying continuity of nature and human life. Just as levels of being are continuous in nature and man, so too the present and the future form a continuous reality. The Church is the very "entrance-court" of heaven, and one can speak allegorically of the Church already as the "kingdom of heaven."[50] Death is but the gateway to true life,[51] and the passage between life and death becomes the reverse of what might be expected: in death, life is not extinguished but intensified. Choirs of angels fill the air with song, beautiful visions are beheld, friendly saints or even Christ may welcome the soul.[52] If one is sufficiently virtuous, the physical body may continue to reflect the soul after death. The body need not decay, but smells sweet; wounds heal and deformities may be repaired.

This continued connection of soul and body after death explains the awesome power of relics. If the soul animates the body in earthly life, how much more does it continue to animate the body after death? The sick are healed, perjurers confounded, those possessed delivered from Satan. Such deeds show the "fullness of life the saints now enjoy in heaven, if their dead bodies on earth are alive with such miraculous power."[53] Life continues to flow through the body, but now it is the *true* power of invisible life, so potent it heals on contact. The force of life in a relic can be so real that the relic can even bleed. Gregory tells Constantina a story about how Pope Leo dealt with doubters questioning the authenticity of a cloth relic (*brandeum*). To confound them, Leo cut the cloth with scissors, and blood flowed from the cut.[54]

In fact, the power of relics is so potent it can be transmitted through

---

50. *HEv.* 2.38.10 (PL 76, 1288); *HEv.* 2.38.2 (PL 76, 1282–83).

51. *Dial.* praef. 1.3 (SC 260, 12); *Dial.* 4.5ff. (SC 265, 32–38); *Mor.* 7.15.18 (CCL 143, 345–46). See also Claude Dagens's discussion of death, *Saint Grégoire le Grand* (Paris, 1977), 405–10.

52. *Dial.* 4.12–18 (SC 265, 48–72).

53. *Dial.* 4.6.2 (SC 265, 38–41).

54. *Ep.* 4.30 (CCL 140, 249). On relics, see John M. McCulloh, "The Cult of Relics in the Letters and 'Dialogues' of Pope Gregory the Great: A Lexicographical Study," *Traditio* 32 (1976): 145–84. McCulloh notes the different words used for relics and possible differences of the relics: *reliquiae* refer to both physical remains and objects sanctified by contact with the body of a saint; *brandea* (cloths placed in boxes and inserted into the saint's tomb) are the most important because Romans shunned dismembering bodies to obtain parts of the body itself. *Sanctuaria* is synonymous with *reliquae*, and usually refers to objects sanctified by the body or tomb of a saint; *sanctuaria* also refers to the memorial housing these relics. *Beneficia* is occasionally synonymous with *reliquiae*, and *benedictio* for fragments of something that was in contact with a saint when he was alive and is given for personal wearing, such as keys with filings from Peter's chains. See also Robert A. Markus, "The Cult of Icons in Sixth-Century Gaul," in *From Augustine to Gregory the Great*, Variorum reprints, CS 169 (London, 1983), XII: 151–57.

physical objects and projected across distances. Because relics achieve their effectiveness by uniting the power of the saint and the faith of the petitioner, the quality of miracles varies. Some relics are so powerful that they do not even require the faith of the Christian. Gregory tells of a demented woman, not having the faintest idea where she is, wandering into Benedict's cave at Subiaco. She falls asleep in the cave and awakens the next morning completely cured.[55] Gregory explains that sometimes greater miracles are performed away from the burial place of the saint's body because the weakness of human faith may cause people to question the presence of the saint and his ability to answer prayers.[56] Of course, those with the greater "merit of faith" realize that the martyrs are always present to answer prayers, even if their bodies lie elsewhere.[57] Thus two reasons explain why great miracles can occur at a distance from the tomb of a saint: the superior merit of the believer and the greater condescension of God to human weakness.

In most instances, however, the faith of the petitioner and proximity to the body directly determine the power of the relic. The body of the saint is so potent that Romans do not dare to touch it. Instead they put a cloth (*brandeum*) in a box and place it next to the body of the saint. The cloth then absorbs the power of the saint through physical proximity.[58] These kinds of relics are exceptionally powerful, and often an altar is dedicated and a church is built around them. Even the dust from such an altar has extraordinary virtue when used by one of requisite sanctity. A holy man raises a man from the dead with dust from the altar of the church at Bussento.[59] Relics worn as personal talismans put one into direct contact with the saint, and from these one gains a multitude of blessings: the saint's intercession, release from sin, cure of sickness, and protection from evil.[60]

---

55. *Dial*. 2.38.1 (SC 260, 246).

56. Peter's question may arise from the prevalence of contact or secondary relics in parish churches, where altar and tomb are "joined" through the use of *brandea*. Roman reticence for dismembering bodies encouraged this growth of secondary relics; see McCulloh, "Cult of Relics," 178. On the joining of altar and tomb in late antiquity, see Peter Brown, *The Cult of the Saint in Late Antiquity* (Chicago, 1981), 9ff.; and on *brandea*, see 87–88.

57. *Dial*. 2.38.3 (SC 260, 246).

58. McCulloh, "Cult of Relics," 184 cites a Georgian text of John Moschos's *Pratum Spirituale*, possibly reflecting Roman customs ca. 614–619, when Moschos lived in Rome. The text records Christians depositing a cloth or object on a tomb and there waiting the night in prayer. In the morning they take up the object and weigh it. If it is heavier than it was the previous night, they know their prayers were answered. Such practices would accord with Gregory's very physical sense of relics.

59. *Dial*. 3.17.1–5 (SC 260, 336–40).

60. McCulloh, "Cult of Relics," 173, n. 110 cites examples of intercession in Gregory's letters: *Ep*. 1.19; 1.30; 6.6; 11.43; 12.2; release from sin: *Ep*. 7.25; 8.33; 9.228; protection: *Ep*. 6.6; 11.43; curing: *Ep*. 1.25; 1.29; 1.30.

Even as the saint's power bridges the grave and shows the continuity of all life, so the future world in general appears very much an extension of the present. What might be understood as a symbolic expression of a spiritual state is taken literally and physically. Heaven and hell are amazingly carnal places, and one's fate after death corresponds minutely to the details of one's earthly life. Hell is under the earth; volcanoes are peepholes to the fires of the inferno.[61] Heaven is above the earth in the sky.[62] Gregory's characteristic logic of what is fitting and complementary extends to man's fate in heaven or hell. There is an "order of punishments" for those who differ from the Creator's will in this life,[63] and punishments and rewards are based on the unity of spirit and flesh. If the incorporeal soul of man is held in a corporeal body, so it is fitting that it be held in corporeal fires after death.[64] Corresponding to the many mansions of heaven, hell also has its varied forms of torment.[65] Aptly, those whose lives were consumed and polluted by the stench of lust in this life will be seared with brimstone and nauseated by sulfur as punishment after death.[66] So, too, the rich man who scorned to give Lazarus the crumbs from his table will beg that same Lazarus for a drop of water to cool his tongue.[67] Hell is paradoxically "death without death, end without end, destruction without destruction."[68] The very order of the universe requires that hell exist; otherwise God would be deceitful.[69]

Heaven also combines spiritual and carnal dimensions, and it mirrors and continues earthly experience. Should grace make one heir to heaven, one would witness the reversals heaven brings to earthly life: prosperity turns to adversity, light into darkness, smiles into grief, sweetness into worms.[70] Heaven is an inverse reflection of earth, yet it is again the same image reflected in the mirror. Heaven has its *societas* of citizens.[71] Distinctions of status (*dignitas*) correspond to the merit one has earned through

61. *Dial.* 4.44.1–3 (SC 265, 156–58), and *Dial.* 4.36.12 (SC 265, 122).

62. Ibid.

63. Cf. *Mor.* 9.66.100 (CCL 143, 527–28). See Alfred Rush, "An Echo of Christian Antiquity in St. Gregory the Great: Death a Struggle with the Devil," *Traditio* 3 (1945): 369–81. Dagens, *Saint Grégoire*, 401–30, argues that Gregory has stronger eschatological beliefs than Augustine (409, n. 30); this is explained in detail by Giuseppe Cremascoli, *"Novissima Hominis" nei "Dialogi" di Gregorio Magno* (Bologna, 1979), 37ff.

64. *Dial.* 4.30.1 (SC 265, 100): "Si uiuentis hominis incorporeus spiritus tenetur in corpore, cur non post mortem, cum incorporeus sit spiritus, etiam corporeo igne teneatur?"

65. *Mor.* 9.65.98 (CCL 143, 526–27). Cremascoli, *"Novissima Hominis,"* 87–102, 121–29.

66. *Dial.* 4.39.1 (SC 265, 138); see also 4.38f. (SC 265, 138f.).

67. *Dial.* 4.30.3 (SC 265, 100–102).

68. *Mor.* 9.46.100 (CCL 143, 528).

69. *Dial.* 4.45–46.1–3 (SC 265, 158–162).

70. *In lib.I Reg.* 5.38 (CCL 144, 443); *In lib.I Reg.* 5.58 (CCL 144, 456); *Mor.* 15.55.62 (CCL 143A, 789).

71. *In lib.I Reg.* 2.29 (CCL 144, 137).

suffering and performing good deeds on earth; the many mansions of reward will accommodate the differing merits of those saved.[72] Those whom we benefit by almsgiving in this life will work for us in the next.[73] Indeed, to give alms is to lay up treasures in heaven (cf. Lk 18:22).[74] As hell has its surfeit of pain (death without dying, end without end) and as earth has its ambivalences (sweet tortures and delectable pains), so heaven is perfect happiness, with no admixture of pain. Following Augustine, Gregory sees heaven as "joy without defect," a "burning of love that does not torture," a love that "satiates without tedium."[75]

The next life is thus a continuation of the present and it is temporally nearby, not only because Gregory sees the end of the world as imminent, but also because judgment takes place both in the adversities of the present life and in an immediate judgment of the soul after death. In this context, Cyril Vogel notes a fundamental shift in Gregory's eschatology from that of the early Church. The dead no longer sojourn in *refrigerium* or *tormentum*, awaiting the Last Judgment. Gregory explains, rather, that the soul undergoes immediate judgment and flies to heaven, hell, or places of purgation.[76] To Gregory's anxiety about the closeness of the Last Judgment must be added his additional concern for God's immediate judgment of the soul after death.

If punishment comes hard on the heels of this life, the salvation of the soul continues after death: some sins can be forgiven in this world, and some in the world to come.[77] A purging fire will cleanse the soul of minor faults before judgment.[78] The prayers of others can free a soul from

72. *HEz.* 2.4.6 (CCL 142, 263): "in retributione ultima quamuis eadem dignitas omnibus non sit, una tamen erit omnibus uita beatitudinis. Vnde et per semetipsum Dominus dicit: 'In domo Patris mei mansiones multae sunt'" [Jn 14:2]; see also *Mor.* 9.65.98 (CCL 143, 526–27); *Dial.* 4.36.13 (SC 265, 122–24).

73. *Dial.* 4.37.16 (SC 265, 134).

74. *Dial.* 4.38.16 (SC 265, 134); *Dial.* 4.9.8 (SC 265, 42); cf. *Dial.* 2.28.1 (SC 260, 216); *Dial.* 4.9 (SC 265, 42–44).

75. *HEz.* 1.8.15 (CCL 142, 108–9): "quae sit in eis sine fine festiuitas uisionis Dei, quae laetitia sine defectu, qui amoris ardor non crucians, sed delectans, quantum in eis sit desiderium uisionis Dei cum satietate, et quanta satietas cum desiderio. In quibus nec desiderium poenam generat, nec satietas fastidium parit."

76. Cyril Vogel, "Deux conséquences de l'eschatologie grégorienne: la multiplication des messes privées et les moines-prêtres," Fontaine et al., eds., *Grégoire le Grand*, 267–76. Vogel says the change presupposes a change in religious sensibilities, the signs of which are the multiplication of masses, the growth of monk priests, and the beginning of numerous abuses. See also Jacques Le Goff, *The Birth of Purgatory*, trans. Arthur Goldhammer (Chicago, 1984). Le Goff argues that Gregory remains close to Augustine, but is incorrect in stating that earthly tribulation was *not* a part of purgation (91); it certainly was, cf. *Mor.* 7.19.22 (CCL 143, 348); see also Cremascoli, "*Novissima Hominis*," 105–18.

77. *Dial.* 4.41.3–4 (SC 265, 148).

78. *Dial.* 4.40–41 (SC 265, 138–50). On purgatory, see Cremascoli, "*Novissima Hominis*," 105–18; M. McC. Gatch, "The Fourth Dialogue of Gregory the Great: Some Problems

torment after death because the good works of one soul can be transferred to another, and the sacrifice of the Mass reaches from this world
to the next.[79] Acts in this life immediately carry over to the next world,
and in a way man and God are drawn nearer in the matter of salvation.
Man accepts a certain responsibility for his own salvation with penitence,
just as his will cooperates with the grace God gives him.

This world and the next are opposites, yet they share much, for they
are part of a continuum of man's life, body and soul. The afterlife resembles this life, even as the present life abounds in so many supernatural
qualities. Given this continuum of spiritual and carnal, two governing
assumptions become clear. First, man's debts can be paid either in this
world or in the next; if rewards and punishments are absent from one
realm, they certainly exist in the other. Second, because this world is related dialectically to the next, with man returning to eternal joys through
temporal losses and deprivations,[80] and receiving rewards in proportion
to his suffering,[81] suffering and sacrifice can either expunge sins already
committed, or, if one is innocent, like Job, increase one's reward. God's
justice dictates that man does not suffer in vain.[82]

Since temporal loss can point to eternal gain, and present suffering
to eternal joy, definitions of good and evil for body and soul are reversed:
the temporal evil of the body is the eternal good of the soul, and vice
versa. Suffering and all evil become ambiguous, painful yet profitable.
Afflictions are recognized as malevolent, yet confessed as beneficial; they
are actions of the devil and yet visitations of God's wrath to discipline
man and teach him a lesson. Evils are instrumental to good; afflictions
are somehow bound up with the nature of good.[83]

of Interpretation," *Studia Patristica* 10 (1970): 70–83. Gatch agrees there is a purging fire; the
problem is when: right after death (as the texts seem to read) or before the Second Coming
(which is unlikely). See A. Michel, "Purgatoire," *DTC* 13:1225–26, and Le Goff, *Birth of Purgatory*, passim, for whom the problem is not time but place.

79. *Dial.* 4.60.1 (SC 251, 200).

80. *Mor.* 26.16.26 (CCL 143B, 1283–84), where the anchor of the exegesis is Job 34:10:
"'Cui dedit carmina in nocte': Carmen in nocte est laetitia in tribulatione, quia etsi pressuris
temporalitatis affligimur, spe iam tamen de aeternitate gaudemus. . . . Ecce de nocte pres-
suram nominat, et tamen liberatorem suum inter angustias exsultationem uocat. Foris quidem nox erat in circumdatione pressurae, sed intus carmina resonabant de consolatione
laetitiae. Quia enim ad aeterna gaudia redire non possumus, nisi per temporalia detrimenta, tota scripturae sacrae intentio est ut spes manentis laetitiae nos inter haec transitoria
aduersa corroboret. . . . Carmen quoque et uae continent, quia sic de spe gaudium prae-
dicant, ut in praesenti tamen pressuras atque angustias incident. Carmen et uae continent,
quia etsi illic dulcia appetimus, prius necesse est ut hic amara toleremus."

81. Cf. *HEv.* 2.35.8 (PL 77, 1264); *Mor.* 10.19.36 (CCL 143, 563).

82. *Mor.* 32.4.5 (CCL 143B, 1630–31); *Mor.* 14.31.36 (CCL 143A, 719–20); *Mor.* 24.18.44
(CCL 143B, 1221–22).

83. *Mor.* 26.37.68 (CCL 143B, 1317–18).

Perhaps the most complex and troubling continuity of spiritual and carnal emerges in unraveling this problem of good and evil and human suffering.[84] Surely a clear polarity in the universe separates God and the devil, good and evil. The devil and his wicked works are a cosmic mirror of God's righteousness. As God has his kingdom, so too the devil presides over his own kingdom. He is the "proud king" who lords it over his servants, unlike God who provides freedom in servitude.[85] Exercising his "dominion of sin,"[86] the devil is assisted by apostate angels as associates who stand opposed to the choirs of angels attending God.[87] As God has his judgment, so the devil has his courtroom, where he makes his demons render account of the evil they have done.[88] As the saints are called Sion, the devil and his reprobates are called Babylon.[89] As Christ has a body in the good, so there is a corresponding body in the wicked: all are members of Satan, joined to him in wickedness; there is one body of the wicked, and Satan is head.[90] Gregory even uses the language of the Incarnation to speak of Satan's historical appearance as Antichrist.[91]

While God is Creator, the devil is destroyer, the enemy who makes war upon God and man. Brandishing weapons of temptation, he seeks to drag man into his kingdom of sin and make him a helpless captive.[92] Firing the first salvo against Adam, the devil has continued to wage war against man, becoming increasingly savage as the world nears its end. Mindful of Cassian and the Desert Fathers, Gregory depicts the struggle between the devil and God as fierce and deadly. In the *Moralia* this stark battle between good and evil in the desert is translated into Job's battle with the devil. Fear of the devil is so acute that it inspires man's humble subordination to God as his protector, and man's deliverance in turn in-

84. Cf. Cassian *conl*. 6.1 ff. treats the problem of evil; *conl*. 6.9–11 is probably the inspiration for Gregory's theme of Job's constancy in adversity and prosperity.

85. *Mor*. 4.23.42 (CCL 143, 188).

86. *Mor*. 4.36.71 (CCL 143, 215).

87. *Mor*. 12.43.48 (CCL 143A, 658); *Mor*. 29.7.15 (CCL 143B, 1443–44).

88. *Dial*. 3.7.4–5 (SC 260, 280–82).

89. *Mor*. 5.21.42 (CCL 143, 247).

90. *Mor*. 13.34.38 (CCL 143A, 689); *Mor*. 33.14.29 (CCL 143B, 1698–99).

91. *Mor*. 4.11.18 (CCL 143B, 175–76), and *Mor*. 14.21.25 (CCL 143A, 712–13). Cf. Pierre Boglioni, "Miracle et nature chez Grégoire le Grand," in *Cahiers d'études médiévales*, I: *Epopées, légendes et miracles* (Montreal and Paris, 1974), 42–43.

92. *Mor*. 8.32.52 (CCL 143, 423); *Mor*. 17.30.46 (CCL 143A, 877): "Ipse namque diabolus in illa nos parentis primi radice supplantans, sub captiuitate sua quasi iuste tenuit hominem qui libero arbitrio conditus, ei iniusta suadenti consensit." See also *Mor*. 8.8.13 (CCL 143, 391); *Mor*. 34.21.40 (CCL 143B, 1761–62); and *Mor*. 4.36.71 (CCL 143, 215–16). Enslavement to the flesh, sin, and the devil are traditional ideas going back as far as Irenaeus; cf. Norman P. Williams, *Ideas of the Fall and Original Sin* (London, 1938), 244; Hastings Rashdall, *The Idea of Atonement in Christian Theology* (London, 1919), 243, who cites Iren. *haer*. 5.1.1 and 3.22.2. The idea is carried through Tert. *fuga*. 2.1. Augustine emphasizes that dominion to the devil is a juridical sentence, *trin*. 13.15.

spires boundless gratitude as man recognizes the terrible power of the enemy.[93] The devil's power is so great that God must be thanked for bridling his fury.

Despite this almost Manichaean conflict between good and evil waged in the cosmos and on the battlefield of the heart, Gregory pointedly affirms the omnipotence of God and the unity of the divine dispensation. Unity and continuity are intrinsic to the divine dispensation, for only the Creator, the source of all existence, possesses the power to act and the power to control the workings of the universe.[94] As a mere creature, Satan has no power to accomplish evil by himself, just as he has no power to subsist by himself. He can do nothing without God's permission, not even attack the lowest pig, as Gregory is fond of telling us.[95] The devil's power to perpetrate evil derives from God, so his power is just. But the evil the devil accomplishes comes from a perverse will entirely his own. Ironically, he "fulfills" God's will by his very "resistance" to it.[96] Because of this curious situation, the devil and his demons are both "robbers" and yet "God's robbers,"[97] "evil spirits" and yet "spirits of the Lord."[98] God unleashes the devil in his wrath and severity, permitting him to rage in the "punishment of strict justice." Evils and suffering result from God's "indignation and not his will," from his "indignation" rather than his "tranquil majesty of divinity."[99]

The devil has a "contract" with God, [100] in which he becomes the "servant" or "slave of God" in exchange for the gratification of his own desires. The agreement is mutually advantageous, for the devil's desire for evil is satisfied, while the will of the "Just Dispensator" is fulfilled. Paradoxically, the anger and evil of the devil brings to completion the kindness and mercy of God: "in the secret order of the dispensation, when the devil is permitted to rage, then the kindness of God is brought about

93. *Mor.* 32.11.14 (CCL 143B, 1639–40); *HEz.* 2.10.24 (CCL 142, 397–98).

94. *Mor.* 2.10.16 (CCL 143, 70).

95. *Mor.* 32.24.50 (CCL 143B, 1668).

96. *Mor.* 16.38.47 (CCL 143A, 827): "Apostatae quippe angeli peruersa uoluntas est, sed tamen a Deo mirabiliter ordinatur ut ipsae quoque eius insidiae utilitati bonorum seruiant, quos purgant dum temptant."

97. *Mor.* 14.51–52.59–60 (CCL 143A, 733–34). This ambivalence about the devil's power is found before Gregory in Augustine and Leo, and is continued after Gregory. See Jean Rivière, *Le Dogme de la rédemption après saint Augustin* (Paris, 1930), 75.

98. *Mor.* 18.2.4 (CCL 143A, 887–88). Augustine also believes in the just injustice of the devil; cf. *c.Faust.* 14.6–7, cited by Rivière, *Le Dogme de la rédemption*, 12.

99. *In lib.I Reg.* 4.7–10 (CCL 144, 299–300).

100. *Mor.* 33.14.28 (CCL 143B, 1697–98): "In pacto namque discordantium partium uoluntas impletur, ut ad uotum suum quaeque perueniat et iurgia desiderato fine concludat. . . . Haec ipsa ergo temptationis licentia pactum uocatur, in qua et desiderium temptatoris agitur, et tamen per eam miro modo uoluntas iusti dispensatoris impletur."

in mercy."[101] Not only are God's wrath and justice executed through the devil, but his kindness as well.

This contract allows the devil to make war upon man, a war enabling God to prove his servant's virtue and loyalty.[102] The trial is ordained out of God's strict or merciful judgment, and the devil acts as God's minion and surrogate; he is the "hammer" God uses to smite man.[103] God is the "Judge," the devil his *exactor*.[104] The judge hands the guilty over to the *exactor*, who in turn throws him into prison and executes punishment.[105] God decides when to "permit and restrain, loose and bind our enemy,"[106] "when to let Satan's sword strike, and when to bend the sword back."[107] Sometimes the Lord will let the fighter be defeated in the contest against the devil; other times he controls the contest so his fighter wins.[108]

In so unleashing the devil against man, God afflicts man justly or mercifully.[109] God's just and righteous affliction visits strict judgment upon reprobates. Here the sinner is neither amended nor improved but rather abandoned to the devil as a foretaste of punishments to come.[110] Merciful affliction promotes the welfare of the good, for it chastens them, purifies their sins, or proves their strength.[111] Not all suffering is the result of sin, and here lies one of God's great mysteries. Gregory argues that the affliction of the just is another exercise of God's mercy. Weighing God's actions,[112] Gregory frankly admits the scourges of adversity Job suffered were not just recompense, for Job was innocent. But if God's *mercy* is considered, the scale shifts in the opposite direction, for God's scourges give Job the chance to increase his merit.[113]

Consequently, man's attitude toward suffering is transformed, or at least should be, when he recognizes that pain and affliction come from

101. Ibid.
102. Cf. Dagens, *Saint Grégoire*, 100, 107, 187f.; Robert Gillet, introduction to Grégoire le Grand, *Morales sur Job* I–II (SC 32 bis), 57.
103. *Mor.* 34.12.23 (CCL 143B, 1748)
104. *HEv.* 2.39.5 (PL 76, 1297); *Mor.* 4.35.69 (CCL 143, 214). For Augustine the devil is also the *exactor*; cf. Rivière, *Le Dogme de la rédemption*, 71.
105. *HEv.* 2.39.5 (PL 76, 1297); cf. *Mor.* 4.35.69 (CCL 143, 214).
106. *Mor.* 2.11.19 (CCL 143, 71): "Consideranda est in uerbis Domini dispensatio sanctae pietatis, quomodo hostem nostrum permittit et retinet, relaxat et refrenat."
107. *Mor.* 32.24.50 (CCL 143B, 1668).
108. *Mor.* 2.11.19 (CCL 143, 71–72).
109. *Mor.* 33.14.28 (CCL 143B, 1697); cf. *In lib.I Reg.* 4.10 (CCL 144, 300–301).
110. *Mor.* 34.12.23 (CCL 143B, 1748).
111. Ibid.; *Mor.* 2.11.19 (CCL 143, 71–72); cf. *Mor.* 16.38.47 (CCL 143A, 827).
112. *Mor.* 19.6.12 (CCL 143A, 964).
113. *Mor.* 2.10.18 (CCL 143, 71): "Cuius petitione callida nequaquam prouocata Veritas uincitur sed ad deceptionem suam hosti conceditur, quod fideli famulo ad augmentum muneris suffragetur."

God. One should be like Job, thanking God for the scourges and even seeking the trial that proves the soul.[114] Gregory neither minimizes nor denies the pain of this affliction. In so recognizing that it is God who visits man with scourges, that the devil is only his minion, the Christian recognizes God as he who should truly be feared: "that power alone must be feared which allows the enemy to rage and turns the unjust will of the devil to just judgment."[115] Only God, the power behind the devil, is truly worthy of fear. Correspondingly, the devil is less feared.

The devil may be the terrible enemy, but he is also the trickster of the *Dialogues*, the forerunner, as F. Homes Dudden observes, of the comical medieval devil who flung a stone at Dominic and got splattered by Luther's ink.[116] The devil's games can be humorous: he teases Benedict by calling him "Maledict."[117] Sometimes he is little more than a jealous competitor easily beaten by man's virtue. A strong man can challenge the devil and win, like Saint Martin placing his hand in the serpent's mouth and daring him to sting.[118] The devil taunts man and plays impish tricks on him, and sometimes man seems more than his match.

The devil and God have a deeply complementary relationship. The devil and his wickedness are not purely evil, but are salutary expressions of God's indignation and severe judgment. The devil serves God as his *exactor*, chastising and punishing man's errant ways, and the devil's sheer cruelty is useful pedagogy, teaching man how much more God should be loved as deliverer. But if the devil and his evil are partly transformed, God is also changed, at least from man's point of view. Where man once wholly feared the devil, he now learns to fear God all the more as God is acknowledged as the true source of man's affliction. While the devil is less feared, God is more so. The trickster and the wrathful Judge are inseparable partners within the drama of the divine dispensation.

God and the devil are opposite poles of the divine dispensation, yet this dispensation is a single unity because God is omnipotent and claims the devil as his *exactor*. The original polarity between God and the devil, good and evil, becomes displaced to either pole. God is both loved and

114. *HEz.* 2.10.24 (CCL 142, 397–98); cf. *Mor.* 33.19.35 (CCL 143B, 1706).

115. *Mor.* 2.10.17 (CCL 143, 70): "Formidari igitur non debet qui nihil nisi permissus ualet. Sola ergo uis illa timenda est, quae cum hostem saeuire permiserit ei ad usum iusti iudicii, et iniusta illius uoluntas seruit."

116. F. Homes Dudden sees in Gregory's work the typical devil of the Middle Ages; see *Gregory the Great* (London, 1905), 2:367–68.

117. *Dial.* 2.8.12 (SC 260, 170).

118. *Dial.* 3.16.3 (SC 260, 328). This account may be an "animalized" version of Sulp. Sev. *V. Mart.* 17, where a man is possessed and exorcised by Martin placing his hand in the victim's mouth. Gregory turns it into an incident illustrating the devil's jealousy.

feared for his severity. Man both fears the devil as the hateful enemy and yet has confidence facing the trickster employed by God. The very unity of the divine dispensation blurs the realms and creates an ambivalence between spiritual and carnal, God and the devil. They become complementary opposites, partaking of one another's qualities.

The whole universe is a unity and proportional mixture of spiritual and carnal elements, ranging from the heights of heaven to the depths of hell, from the pure spirit of God to the lifelessness of matter. Gregory's Christianity is never removed from the world—it is very much in it. For to perceive the world and natural life in sympathy with man is to possess a closeness to that world, a certain communion with the universe. Such a spirituality cannot ignore or reject either the natural world or the secular world of men. God's universe is an organic whole, embracing so many and such different forms of life. Accommodation and integration remain open possibilities.

· III ·

THE SAINT AND THE SOCIAL
MEANING OF STABILITY

The righteous are like stars "enlightening the darkness of the present life," Gregory writes in his preface to the *Moralia*. "Look, what shining stars we see in the sky that we may walk along the pilgrimage of our night without stumbling."[1] Rome had long been showered with such "stars" in the saints and martyrs buried in her shrines and cemeteries, and in the late sixth and early seventh centuries, Rome became a center for pilgrims zealous in pursuit of the holy. Relics proliferated. Gregory was fond of sending filings of St. Peter's chains to select correspondents, or golden keys to unlock the blessed sepulcher of the saint.[2] On occasion, he supplied or secured relics for the foundations of churches.[3] Gregory's devotion to the saints took other forms as well. He organized elaborate penitential processions to avert God's wrath.[4] Many of his prayers praised saints as models and pleaded for their intercession on behalf of man's iniquities.[5]

---

1. *Mor.* praef. 6.13 (CCL 143, 18–19).

2. Jeffrey Richards lists fourteen such gifts, *Consul of God* (London, 1980), 23, n. 73.

3. *Ep.* 6.50 (CCL 140, 423); *Ep.* 3.19 (CCL 140, 165). *Dial.* 1.10.2 (SC 260, 94), and 3.30.2 (SC 260, 380) concern miracles surrounding relics in churches. See John McCulloh, "The Cult of Relics in the Letters and 'Dialogues' of Pope Gregory the Great: A Lexicographical Study," *Traditio* 32 (1976): 173f.

4. A procession was held in 590 during the plague and was repeated at least once, probably in 603, cf. *Ep.* App. 9 (CCL 140A, 1102). Judith McClure speculates that it may have been repeated in 599, also a year of disease, McClure, "Gregory the Great: Exegesis and Audience" (D. Phil. diss., Oxford, 1978), 131–37. Cf. *Ep.* 9.232 (CCL 140A, 814–15).

5. Eighty-eight prayers became part of the Hadrianum Sacramentary, see H. Ashworth, "The Liturgical Prayers of Gregory the Great," *Traditio* 15 (1959): 106–61; idem, "Further Parallels to the 'Hadrianum' from St. Gregory the Great's Commentary on the First Book of Kings," *Traditio* 16 (1960): 364–73.

As the mystique of Rome grew, the character of the holy city slowly changed. Pilgrims needed accommodations, and the Papacy supported hostels, often founded in the great houses of the waning aristocracy. Later, national communities settled around many shrines, such as the borgo (borough) of Anglo-Saxons near St. Peter's, whose name survives to this day.[6] Traffic to shrines became ritualized, as pilgrims wound their way along the city's perimeter clockwise or counterclockwise, visiting every holy place in turn. Guidebooks were issued, the earliest of which may date from the time of Pelagius II, Gregory's immediate predecessor. These guides reflect Rome's changed fortunes: her antiquities and imperial artifacts are ignored, her cemeteries and shrines celebrated.[7] Even Roman architecture echoed this enthusiasm for the saints. Perhaps the most significant architectural development of the sixth century was the response to the cult of relics in which altar and church were united with the martyr's tomb.[8] If we can trust the *Liber Pontificalis*, Gregory himself was responsible for the insertion of crypts at St. Peter's and St. Paul's Outside the Walls, an Eastern practice Gregory may have seen on his travels to Constantinople.[9]

But above all, the *Dialogues* stand out as Gregory's response to the hunger of Christians for communion with the holy. At the behest of the monks and clerics of his entourage, Gregory began writing the *Dialogues* in the summer of 593 and finished by 594, but this work is the fruit of decades spent hearing and collecting the stories of holy men.[10] The work has long puzzled many scholars, among them J. M. Wallace-Hadrill, who mused: "The *Dialogues* are the joker in Gregory's pack. What are we to make of them in the grand company of the *Moralia*, the *Homilies*, the *Regula Pastoralis* and the *Register*?"[11] While recent scholarship has begun to clarify Gregory's purposes,[12] a certain inconsistency remains. In the *Mo-*

6. Peter Llewellyn, *Rome in the Dark Ages* (London, 1970), 178–79.

7. One of the earliest guides, *De Locis Sanctorum Martyrum quae sunt foris Civitate Roma* is probably revised from an earlier edition; cf. Llewellyn, *Rome*, 177.

8. Richard Krautheimer, *Corpus basilicarum Christianarum Romae. The Earliest Christian Basilicas of Rome (IV–IX cent.)*, 5 vols. (Vatican City, 1937–1977); idem, *Early Christian and Byzantine Architecture* (Baltimore, 1965); idem, *Rome: Profile of a City, 312–1308* (Princeton, 1980), 85f.; F. Deichmann, "Märtyrerbasilika, Martyrion, Memoria und Altargrab," *Römische Mitteilungen* 77 (1970): 144–69, reprinted in his collected essays, *Rom, Ravenna, Konstantinopel, Naher Osten. Gesammelte Studien zur spätantiken Architektur, Kunst und Geschichte* (Wiesbaden, 1982), 375–400. See also the forthcoming work of Charles McClendon, tentatively titled "The Architectural Contribution of the Early Middle Ages."

9. *Lib. pont.* 1.66, 312. Suggested by McClendon in correspondence with the author.

10. A. de Vogüé, introduction to Grégoire le Grand, *Dialogues* (SC 251), 27–29.

11. J. M. Wallace-Hadrill, quoted in "Memoirs of Fellows and Corresponding Fellows," in *Speculum* 61 (1986): 769.

12. Sofia Boesch Gajano, "Dislivelli culturali e mediazioni ecclesiastiche nei *Dialogi* di

ralia and other works, Gregory views miracles as historically necessary to nourish the faith of early Christians, or convert those hard of heart. Through miracles the Church has "conquered" the fearsome "waves" of the world,[13] but now such visible displays of divine power are no longer essential. Instead, the charity of good deeds should kindle hearts with heavenly love. Still, outward miracles can change the hearts of those numb to invisible truths, and they can encourage those whose faith is too feeble to penetrate deeper mysteries.[14]

While acknowledging the awesome power of miracles to nourish faith, Gregory's *Dialogues* aim to carry the audience beyond a fascination with external miracles. A preoccupation with miracles can lead to pessimism and despair. At the beginning of the *Dialogues*, Gregory's disciple Peter laments ruefully that the world is bereft of living saints. No one in Italy possesses such virtue that he displays signs and powers (*signa, virtutes*), Peter complains.[15] Gregory tries to cheer Peter. Even if great miracles are wanting, he contends, virtue abounds and this is the true measure of worth.[16] The *Dialogues* present continually a distinction between external and internal virtues, as Gregory strives to lead his audience inward. Chastity and abstinence are external signs just as those more wondrous feats, such as suspending a stone in mid-air or multiplying loaves of bread. Both kinds of deeds are external phenomena set in contrast to internal charity.[17] Though charity is what really matters, sometimes the full strength of this virtue remains hidden in this life simply because others lack the spiritual discernment to see it. The true virtue of a saint may appear only after death, when his relics proclaim his happiness in heaven. Euthicius passes through life undistinguished from his peers. But after death, the miracle wrought with his cloak proves his strength

---

Gregorio Magno," *Quaderni storici* 14 (1979): 398–415; idem, "Demoni e miracoli nei *Dialogi di Gregorio Magno,*" in *Hagiographie, cultures et sociétés iv–xii siècles,* Actes du Colloque organisé à Nanterre et à Paris (2–5 May 1979) (Paris, 1981), 263–64.

13. *Mor.* 28.16.36 (CCL 143B, 1422–23); *Mor.* 9.10.11 (CCL 143, 463–64).

14. *Mor.* 27.18.36–37 (CCL 143B, 1358–59); *Mor.* 30.25.75 (CCL 143B, 1543–44); *Mor.* 26.18.32 (CCL 143B, 1289–90); *Mor.* 34.3.7 (CCL 143B, 1737); *Mor.* 30.2.6 (CCL 143B, 1494–95); *Ep.* 11.36 (CCL 140A, 926); *HEv.* 2.29.4 (PL 76, 1215–16); *HEv.* 2.38.15 (PL 76, 1290). See also Claude Dagens, *Saint Grégoire le Grand* (Paris, 1977), 225–28.

15. *Dial.* 1. praef. 7 (SC 260, 14). This lament is a topos found in the Benedictine Rule, see de Vogüé's introduction to *La Règle de saint Benoît* (SC 181), 39–44.

16. *Dial.* 1.12.4 (SC 260, 116): "Neque enim si talia signa non faciunt, ideo tales non sunt. Vitae namque uera aestimatio in uirtute est operum, non in ostensione signorum. Nam sunt plerique, qui etsi signa non faciunt, signa tamen facientibus dispares non sunt." Cf. Cassian, *conl.* 15.2f.

17. *Mor.* 20.7.17 (CCL 143A, 1016).

was merely hidden to those around him.[18] Clearly, Gregory does not wish his audience to be seduced by the glory of external miracles so that they equate holiness only with spectacular feats of power.[19]

Yet, as a pastor sensitive to Peter's needs, Gregory reassures him that the holy men of modern Italy *do* indeed have their miracles.[20] Like saints of the past, modern holy men perform great miracles in imitation of the Lord;[21] and generally, the men of God shine with virtues in this life, so they can serve their neighbors as well as God.[22] Elsewhere, Gregory affirms the prediction of the Gospel that signs and wonders will increase as the world nears its end.[23] Miracles may even be expected in this final battle with the forces of evil. In sum, Gregory's affirmation of the miraculous is thorough but restrained. He remains the pastor whose primary concern is the spiritual reform of his audience.

Consequently, in pursuing Peter's quest for living saints, Gregory sets out an alternative to the martyrological literature of the sixth century, which had been implicitly directed against paganism.[24] The *Dialogues* offer Gregory's own sense of what is needed: not just records of impressive acts of power that humiliate pagan gods, but rather a cogent portrait of holiness presenting the quotidian virtues of Christian life: charity, obedience, and discipline of the flesh. In the apt description of Robert Markus, the work is "Gregory's answer to the need he perceived for a new

18. *Dial.* 3.15.18–19 (SC 260, 326).

19. Cf. Cassian, *conl.* 15.2.

20. *Dial.* 1.2.1f. (SC 260, 24ff.); 3.25.1f. (SC 260, 364ff.).

21. For instance, *Dial.* 3.37.8 (SC 260, 416): "Mira res, atque in exemplo dominici operis uehementer stupenda."

22. Peter Brown notes the tendency of living saints to appear in Eastern sources of the sixth century, in contrast to the West, as represented by Gregory of Tours, where "the only good holy man is a dead one." See Brown, "Eastern and Western Christendom in Late Antiquity: A Parting of the Ways," in *The Orthodox Churches and the West* (1976), 1–24, reprinted in *Society and the Holy in Late Antiquity* (Berkeley, 1982), 166–95. See modifications suggested by John Petersen, "Dead or Alive? The Holy Man as Healer in East and West in the Late Sixth Century," in *JMedHist* 9 (1983): 91–98. Gregory's emphasis of living saints reflects his connections with the East. Theodoret of Cyrus may have been a particularly important inspiration for the *Dialogues*. For Eastern influences on the *Dialogues* and monastic theory, see Lellia Cracco-Ruggini, "Grégoire le Grand et le monde byzantin," in Jacques Fontaine et al., eds., *Grégoire le Grand* (Paris, 1986), 83–94. See also de Vogüé's introduction to the *Dialogues* (SC 251); Michel von Parys, "L'accès à l'Orient monastique chez saint Benoît," *Irenikon* 47 (1974): 48–58; William Seston, "Remarques sur le rôle de la pensée d'Origène dans les origines du monachisme," *RHR* 108 (1933): 197–213; P. Resch, *La Doctrine ascétique des premiers maîtres égyptiens du quatrième siècle* (Paris, 1931), 91f.

23. *Dial.* 4.43.2 (SC 265, 154).

24. Sofia Boesch Gajano, "La proposta agiografica dei *Dialogi* di Gregorio Magno," *StudMed* 21 (1980): 623–64.

kind of integration of the elements of Christian living, notably an integration of the ideal of the *rectores*, the bearers of ecclesiastical authority, and the power of the *viri Dei*, the holy men of the Italian countryside."[25]

Gregory's pedagogical aims are quite clear. Written in a traditional genre of instruction, the *Dialogues* are self-consciously didactic. While the Scriptures tell how to attain virtue, the miracles of saints show how this acquired virtue reveals itself in those who persevere.[26] These examples of the saints are a two-fold aid to the souls of listeners, filling them with love and longing, yet humbling them before the greater deeds of others.[27] Like medicine nursing the balance of health, the stories inspire hope and love, while preserving humility and a salutary fear of judgment. In this didactic and pastoral function, the historicity of deeds is less important than their appropriateness as models of Christ.[28]

Yet it remains to be seen just how the ideal of the *rector* is integrated with that of the holy man, and just what this integration means in Gregory's thought. The familiar polarities are evident: carnal/spiritual, mutable/immutable, exterior/interior, this world/the next world, and so on. In the *Dialogues*, the social implications of such a vision of reality unfold. Gregory focuses especially on the tension between autonomy and participation in a hierarchical order, between selfishness and social harmony. These contrasts are richly evocative, depending ultimately on Gregory's cosmology and anthropology. Through his depiction of the holy man as *rector*, as a charismatic minister of God possessed of status in the church, Gregory can reconcile the apparent contradictions of humility and authority, personal charisma and institutional obedience, and, on a more intimate level, the aching strife between rational control and carnal impulses. The Eucharist assumes special importance as the visible symbol of these various reconciliations. The Eucharist manifests now the harmony and resolution of cosmic dissonance promised with the eschatological triumph of Christ. Expressing the holy man's unity with God now, the Eucharist embodies the fundamental attunement of the human spirit with

25. Robert Markus, "The Sacred and the Secular: From Augustine to Gregory the Great," *JThS* n.s. 36 (1985): 91.

26. *Dial.* 1. praef. 9 (SC 260, 16). The *Dialogues* should not be treated as historical biography but rather as miracle stories; see Giorgio Cracco, "Uomini di Dio e Uomini di Chiesa nell'Alto Medioevo (per una reinterpretazione dei *Dialogi* di Gregorio Magno)," *Ricerche di storia sociale e religiosa* n.s. 12 (1977): 163–202.

27. *Dial.* 1. praef. 9 (SC 260, 16).

28. See discussion by Frantisek Graus, *Volk, Herrscher und Heiliger im Reich der Merowinger. Studien zur Hagiographie der Merowingerzeit* (Prague, 1965), 62–139; and P. Brown, "The Saint as Exemplar in Late Antiquity," *Representations* 1 (1983): 1–25.

the divine. In turn, the holy man may reveal all the more easily the essential though often puzzling continuities between this world and the next.

The *Dialogues* present an idealized picture of the saint in society: he is an ambassador between worlds. As such, Gregory's saint follows the tradition of the holy man established in Athanasius's *Life of Anthony*. But Gregory has his own particular agenda of spiritual reform. He wishes to strengthen and purify the corporate life of the Church by emphasizing the importance of hierarchical order and obedience to authority. A spiritual guide and moral exemplar, Gregory's saint also intercedes with God for his weaker brothers and, as an intercessor, he is very much in the Church. In the largest sense, all saints "preach," whether they lived before or after Christ; they teach the Christian message by word and example.[29] The saint is avid for the salvation of others, a vocation he shares with the prelate, the *rector*, and the missionary. Gregory's saint focuses attention on the Church that embodies Christ's teachings, and he underscores the importance of obeying her ministers.

Gregory's saint has a variety of appellations and vocations.[30] He is *vir dei, homo dei, famulus Dei, servus Dei, vir sanctus, vir venerabilis*, and *sanctissimus vir*.[31] These are basically the same epithets Gregory accords Job and other biblical figures in the *Moralia* and members of the elect in his other works—be they prelates, monks, or Christians of a mixed life. No one technical term distinguishes a saint from others of the elect. Yet many saints come to hold ecclesiastical offices or leadership roles in monastic communities; for all their charm and simplicity, monks and hermits are overshadowed by their brothers with authority.[32] This trend is surprising, given Gregory's distrust of the clergy, his suspicions that they are easily prey to flattery, ambition, and careless discipline.[33]

The predominance of abbots over monks is another clue to Gregory's purposes. The picture painted of monastic and ecclesiastical order is far

29. Cf. *Mor.* 29.31.68ff. (CCL 143B, 1481ff.).

30. On the inclusive variety of social and cultural levels of persons in the *Dialogues*, see Boesch Gajano, "Dislivelli culturali," 398–415.

31. Giorgio Cracco, "Ascesa e ruolo dei *Viri Dei* nell' Italia di Gregorio Magno," *Hagiographie, cultures et sociétés iv–xii siècles* (Paris, 1981), 283, 292, n. 7; see also his "Uomini di Dio e uomini di Chiesa," 163–202.

32. See the exchange between Boesch Gajano and Cracco in Cracco, "Ascesa e ruolo del *Viri Dei*," 296; de Vogüé, "Benoît, modèle de vie spirituelle d'après le Deuxième Livre des *Dialogues* de saint Grégoire," *CollCist* 38 (1976): 147–57, remarks that despite all his other heroes, Benedict the monk is Gregory's favorite; see also idem, *Saint Benôit. Sa Vie et son oeuvre. Etudes choisies* (Bellefontaine, 1983).

33. See, for instance, *Dial.* 1.4.1f. (SC 260, 38f.). Dagens notes his preference for monks over clerics, *Saint Grégoire*, 17.

from harmonious, and Gregory recognizes that carnal members and notorious hypocrites dwell even in the more exalted ranks of the Church.[34] Saint Benedict's monks try to poison him,[35] and an ambitious archdeacon gives poison to Bishop Sabinus.[36] Certain abbots persecute their monks. Both Libertinus and Nonnosus suffer from the severity of their abbots. At least Libertinus conquers through humility, for his suffering softens his abbot's cruelty.[37]

Gregory sympathizes with the good who have suffered abuses from their carnal brothers.[38] In the traditional topos of the misunderstood holy man Gregory finds new meaning. He praises the holy men Equitius and Honoratus for their autonomy from "the establishment." In contrast to the secularism that endangers the Church,[39] such holy men exemplify the pristine virtues of the Gospel, which flourish best in monastic life. Abbot Equitius preaches throughout the countryside, antagonizing the Pope over this breach of ecclesiastical discipline. He is vindicated when the Pope's emissary is unable to arrest him.[40] Of servile background, Abbot Honoratus is unlettered and mocked for his conspicuous and irritating idealism. But Gregory tells Peter that Honoratus's lack of instruction is of no consequence, for the gift of the Holy Spirit is not restricted by any law.[41] In his explanation, Gregory distinguishes between two kinds of Christians: some are directly guided from within by the Spirit, but weaker souls must be subject to discipline and can never be allowed this freedom.[42] He continues:

34. The presence of this theme of monastic disorder suggests that Gregory's primary audience for the *Dialogues* was the monks themselves. Concern for the internal working of monastic life, especially for obedience to authority, is a major theme in *In lib. 1 Reg.*, as noted by de Vogüé, "Les vues de Grégoire le Grand sur la vie religieuse dans son commentaire des Rois," *StudMon* 20 (1978): 29ff. De Vogüé sees such parallels between the monastic organization reflected in the *Dialogues* and that of the *Regula Magistri* that he locates the provenance of the *RM* to Subiaco; see "La Règle du Maître et les Dialogues de s. Grégoire," *RHE* 61 (1966): 44–76.

35. *Dial*. 2.3.4 (SC 260, 142).

36. *Dial*. 3.5.3f. (SC 260, 274f.).

37. *Dial*. 1.2.1ff. (SC 260, 30ff.); 1.7.1ff. (SC 260, 64ff.).

38. A similar criticism of clergy appears in *In lib.I Reg.* 1.76 (CCL 144, 97), where bishops refuse to let clergy enter monasteries. Cited by de Vogüé, "Les Vues de Grégoire le Grand sur la vie religieuse," 28.

39. Cf. *Mor*. 29.6–7.12–17 (CCL 143B, 1440–45).

40. *Dial*. 1.4.11ff. (SC 260, 48ff.). De Vogüé identifies this pope as Agapitus I, "Le Pape qui persécuta saint Equitius: essai d'identification," *AB* 100 (1982): 319–25.

41. *Dial*. 1.1.6 (SC 260, 22): ". . . sed lege non stringitur sancti Spiritus donum. . . . Sed tamen sunt nonnumquam qui ita per magisterium Spiritus intrinsecus docentur, ut, etsi eis exterius humani magisterii disciplina desit, magistri intimi censura non desit."

42. See C. Dagens, "Grégoire et la culture: de la *sapientia huius mundi* à la *docta igno-*

It is right practice that he who has not learned to obey should not dare to lead, nor to order obedience of subjects which he has not learned to give prelates. However, there are some who are so taught inwardly by the instruction of the Spirit that even if the discipline of human teaching is lacking outwardly, they do not lack the judgment of the Inward Teacher. Nevertheless, their freedom of life is not to be taken as an example by the weak, lest when each one presumes he is similarly inspired by the Holy Spirit, he refuses to be the pupil of men, and becomes instead the teacher of errors.[43]

The Holy Spirit guides some so powerfully that their judgment, their *discretio*, is molded directly by the Inward Teacher. Such holy men may be freed safely from the authority of other men and institutions. But those blessed with such discretion are truly a fortunate few. Gregory surprises Peter with his remark that even bishops of Rome can make mistakes: after all, they are human.[44] Certainly, institutional office cannot compensate for a lack of personal sanctity nor for the absence of direct guidance of the Holy Spirit. Servants of God are rightly freed from the constraints of custom, having superior guidance of the Spirit. Their charismatic personal authority can at times be jarringly different from the authority of those holding office. But it need not be.

Gregory's achievement in the *Dialogues* lies in placing these servants of God with their real power of divine inspiration firmly within the Church's hierarchy.[45] Christ is present now in the body of his elect, very often recognized as leaders in the Church—bishops, priests, abbots— who possess institutional as well as personal authority.[46] These members perfect Christ's suffering in their own flesh and convey his power in their deeds. Living beside their more carnal brothers, they supplement their

---

rantia," REAug 14 (1968): 17–26. Dagens argues (22f.) that Gregory follows Augustine in seeing the Holy Spirit and the wisdom of Christ as the interior teacher; cf. *beat. vit.* 4.35; *soliloq.* 1.1.1; and *mag.* 11.38.

43. *Dial.* 1.1.6 (SC 260, 22). Cf. Cassian *inst.* 2.3.1f.

44. *Dial.* 1.4.19 (SC 260, 54–56): "Quid miraris, Petre, quia fallimur, qui homines sumus? . . . Cumque animus diuiditur ad multa, fit minor ad singula, tantoque ei in una qualibet re subripitur, quanto latius in multis occupatur."

45. Sulpicius Severus also believed spirituality and ecclesiastical office should correspond, see Philip Rousseau, "The Spiritual Authority of the Monk-Bishop," *JThS* n.s. 22 (1971): 407. Rousseau sees this as a general trend for the West by the fifth century.

46. The importance of authority and power as themes in Gregory's work and life has been noted by Paul Meyvaert, "Gregory the Great and the Theme of Authority," in *Benedict, Gregory, Bede, and Others*, Variorum Reprints, CS 61 (London, 1977). See also Robert Markus, "Le *Rector* de Grégoire le Grand et sa genèse," in Fontaine et al., eds., *Grégoire le Grand*, 137–46; E. Carton de Wiart, "Une Ame de chef: Grégoire le Grand," *VS* 21 suppl. (1929), 45–54.

brethren's weakness.[47] The presence of the saint enlivens the authority of office, vivifying it with a fresh infusion of the Holy Spirit. Even Honoratus and Equitius become abbots of flourishing monasteries, enforcing rules with the internal governance of the Spirit. The churlish pope accommodates Equitius, and Honoratus finds a safe haven in his monastery at Fondi. Benedict, of course, becomes a leader whose awesome *discretio* amazes and confounds others.

Gregory believes the Church is flexible enough to change and close enough to the Spirit to recognize and respond to it. Anticipating the Middle Ages, Gregory believes that the things of this world can continue to incorporate and manifest the spiritual. Incarnational spirituality can even transform the nature of office, unifying the external institutional role and the internal transcendent authority. The saint thus assures continued access to the divine through the mediation of the Church, as the Mass does on another plane. Indeed, the *Dialogues* include many miracles involving the Eucharist, for the saint can be said to be like the Eucharist, a sacrament offered through the Church. Such analogues contribute to Gregory's vision of a whole pattern of Christian society organized around the Church and particularly her leaders. The Church of the *Dialogues* is presented as an organic, corporate whole defined and animated by the authority of God speaking through his ministers, his *rectores*. The Eucharist symbolizes the harmony of this Church in uniting earthly and heavenly realms, for the sacrifice of the God-Man heals the troubling divisions of universal order. The ministers who offer this sacrifice are correspondingly the power uniting the Church and ensuring its harmony. As such they command particular attention.

Saintliness possesses its freedom to know divine laws directly, but holiness lies above all in an obedience to God that is deeply social: the Christian dwells within a hierarchical structure animated by the Holy Spirit; he must not separate himself from God nor from his fellow man. Even Gregory's recluses serve others, setting forth examples to teach their disciples and nourishing faith with miracles. In such a role, the holy man imitates Christ, who as Teacher educates men and brings them to salvation. Gregory does not suppose that all servants of God are necessarily leaders, though in fact many of them are, but rather that holiness lies in one's continuity with others, as well as in one's participation with God. This unity with God and others is the primary lesson of harmony the holy man exemplifies and teaches to others.

---

47. As Cracco notes, the holy man begins where the bishop leaves off; this is true, but the holy man often is or becomes a bishop. See Cracco, "Ascesa e ruolo dei *Viri Dei*," 296.

Thus, holiness is grounded in the right order of participation in God and corporate society: servants of God become one with God (*unus fit cum Domino spiritus*), cling to him with a devoted mind (*devota mente Deo adhaerere*), and know the mind of the Lord to the extent they are one with him.[48] The holy men possess to an eminent degree what every Christian should possess, a consistency of virtue that Gregory calls stability (*stabilitas*).[49] One achieves stability by obediently submitting one's will to God and letting God govern the soul. Reason knows the truth through the contemplation of God's goodness, and the rational will embraces this truth unconditionally. The soul then participates in God's virtue, gaining the power to overcome and indeed elevate man's carnal nature, so that he might become "spiritual in the flesh."[50] The soul with stability stands as a citadel (*arx*);[51] its intention is unified and fixed in God;[52] its self-discipline, a solid fortress against mutability, whether it be temptations of the flesh, or the distressing assaults of worldly events. To capture this ideal, Gregory employs a wide range of words in addition to *stabilitas* and *stare*. *Soliditas*, *arx stationis*, and *arx mentis* all evoke the firmness and unassailable strength of the soul. The verbs *inhaerere*, *figere*, *permanere*, *perseverare* suggest the soul's unity with God, and the permanence of that attachment.

Gregory's notion of stability touches upon many ancient beliefs about the working of the universe: a belief in the Platonic and Stoic hierarchy of reason over the sensible appetite and over matter, with all the correlating aspects of this order; a concern for the control of mutability which Gregory shares with Cassian[53] and Augustine;[54] a heavy emphasis

48. *Dial.* 2.16.4–5 (SC 260, 186–88); 2.30.2 (SC 260, 220). See Cracco's discussion of the oneness of the saint with God in "Ascesa e ruolo dei *Viri Dei*," 285.

49. Stability is briefly noted by Dudden, *Gregory*, 2:276; Weber, *Hauptfragen*, 226; and by Dagens, *Saint Grégoire*, 169.

50. *Mor.* 5.34.61 (CCL 143, 261).

51. The image of the soul as a citadel goes back to Pl. *Rep.* 8.560.b, and is found in Cic. *Tusc.* 1.10.20; Aug. *civ.* 14.19; and Cassian *inst.* 12.3.2.

52. This unity of intention is illustrated especially by Helcana in *In lib.1 Reg.* 1.61 (CCL 144, 87), who symbolizes the monk; for A. de Vogüé, "Renoncement et désir: la définition du moine dans le Commentaire de Grégoire le Grand sur le premier livre des Rois," *CollCist* 48 (1986): 54–70.

53. Cassian speaks of the stability of the heart, of the soul that clings to God, remaining fixed in him and heavenly things (*inhaerere*, *figere*), see *conl.* 1.8; 6.4; 6.9–12; 7.3; 7.6; *inst.* 2.10.2. *Instabilis*, *instabilitas* designate spiritual ills. See A. de Vogüé, "Persévérer au monastère jusqu' à la mort," *CollCist* 43 (1981): 337–65 for Cassian's use of *stabilitas* and related words. Cassian believed the mind should be hard so that it could withstand all that hits it; see P. Rousseau, "Cassian, Contemplation and the Cenobitic Life," *JEH* 26 (1975): 117; also Owen Chadwick, *John Cassian*, 2d ed. (Cambridge, 1968), 155f.

54. Augustine speaks of the creature clinging to God and overcoming change, and of

on obedience and humility which is especially cenobitic.[55] Further, Gregory echoes the goals of Stoic philosophers and those Christians who adapted Stoic thought in his desire that the soul should achieve a balance (or *constantia mentis*) through self-control and moderation.[56] He stresses that true stability is internal: the monk is bound to God by the "chain" which is Christ; he no longer needs the iron chain binding him to his home.[57]

Viewing life as a hierarchical continuum of spirit and flesh ideally ordered from above, Gregory follows Augustine and preaches: as the soul in the body is the life of the flesh, God, who truly vivifies all things, is the life of the soul.[58] Rational orderliness emanates from God to the soul, and from the soul to the body, assuring self-control and subjugation of man's carnal nature. This harmonious order within man is replicated in the larger concord of society and in the rhythms of the world in general. A cosmic principle fashions an intimate and felicitous order: a management of heavenly government (*superni moderaminis dispositio*) guarantees

---

gaining true satisfaction from adhering to God, *civ.* 12.1; 14.13; *conf.* 10.6.8; 10.40.65. *Stabilitas* appears in Aug. *retract.* 1.13 and *vera relig.* 6.5. He stresses man's participation in God, *civ.* 12–14, and this is the core of Gregory's idea of stability. Augustine mentions *constantia*, *civ.* 14.8, and sees the mind as a citadel, *civ.* 14.19. Augustine also speaks of the soul being upright, *civ.* 14.11, and for Gregory being upright is part of possessing stability. Ladner notes that the idea of being upright has a long tradition and is a common topos; see his "The Anthropology of Gregory of Nyssa," *DOP* 12 (1958): 68, n. 32. See also Charles Morel, "La *rectitudo* dans les Homélies de Grégoire le Grand sur Ezechiel," in Fontaine et al., eds., *Grégoire le Grand*, 289–95. Morel traces the idea *status rectus* back to Minucius Felix, Lactantius and Cyprian and notes usage by Jerome, Augustine, and Cassiodorus of related ideas of *rectitudo*.

55. See Pierre Miquel, "De la stabilité," *CollCist* 3 (1974): 313–22. The Desert Fathers could use *stability* to refer to an inner strength, gained apart from locality. Agathon warns monks not to travel from place to place, but to develop the strength to remain anywhere; cf. Rousseau, "Spiritual Authority," 393. Cassian's *perseverantia* corresponds to the two kinds of *stabilitas* found later in the monastic *Rules* attributed to the Master and Benedict: a stability that guards against apostasy and checks the wandering of monks (*gyrovagi*) who have no fixed abode or commitment to a rule; de Vogüé, "Persévérer au monastère," 345. See also J. Leclercq, "Eloge de la stabilité," *CollCist* 47 (1985): 259–66, for a brief history of stability as it pertains to monastic life.

56. The ancient Greeks termed this self-control and moderation (σωφροσύνη). See Helen North, *Sophrosyne* (Ithaca, 1966), esp. 269, 312ff.; Michel Foucault, *L'usage des plaisirs* and *Souci de soi*, vols. 2 and 3 of *Histoire de la sexualité* (Paris, 1984), esp. 2:76–103; 3:59ff.; 72–89.

57. *Dial.* 3.16.9 (SC 260, 334): "'Si seruus es Dei, non te teneat catena ferri, sed catena Christi.'" Cf. Thdt. *h.rel.* 26.10, cited by de Vogüé, "Persévérer au monastère," 360–61.

58. *HEz.* 2.5.9 (CCL 142, 282): "Anima itaque in corpore uita est carnis, Deus uero qui uiuificat omnia, uita est animarum." See also *Dial.* 4.5.7 (SC 265, 36–38); *Mor.* 9.50.76 (CCL 143, 510). Cf. Aug. *lib. arb.* 2.16.41; *civ.* 13.2.

all things be at peace with themselves when obedience is maintained.[59] Gregory writes of this harmony and peace in his exegesis of Job 9:4: "Who has resisted him and had peace?" [*Quis restitit ei et pacem habuit?*]

> For he who marvelously created all things ordered all creation so that it would harmonize with itself. Where the Creator is resisted, the peace of harmony is dissipated, since things cannot be ordered which lose the management of heavenly government. For the things that are subject to God remain in tranquillity, and those that have been abandoned to themselves bring disorder and confusion upon themselves since they cannot find in themselves that peace from above which they reject in the Creator.[60]

As the prime cause of mutable creation (*causa causarum*), God alone stands absolutely as true being and existence. Only God's immutable perfection offers the peace and respite from change that all mutable creatures seek.[61] Obedience to God communicates this perfection in a downward chain of command, so to speak. If man is willing to be possessed (*possideri*) by God, he gains possession of his body and will be at peace with himself.[62] God will rule his soul directly, unhindered by man's selfish will. And because the body is connected to the soul, the body will rise through its association with the soul governed so perfectly by God. Sin and physical mutability will be checked, and man will enjoy tranquillity, becoming part of the larger concord of the universe and of human society.

59. Cf. Aug. *civ.* 13.2. This Platonic conception of hierarchical order is found generally among the early Fathers, as noted in chapter 1, nn. 6–7. See also R. Buckenmeyer, "Augustine and the Life of Man's Body in the Early Dialogues," *AugSt* 3 (1972): 131–46; and Robert O'Connell, *Augustine's Early Theory of Man* (Cambridge, Mass., 1968), 146ff. Gregory's emphasis on participation is inseparable from his concern for obedience, and here Gregory echoes the call for unconditional obedience found in the Desert Fathers, the *RB* and *RM*. See de Vogüé, "Les Vues de Grégoire le Grand sur la vie religieuse," 32ff. See also Rousseau, "Spiritual Authority of the Monk-Bishop," 391f.; and Henri Delhougne, "Autorité et participation chez les Pères du cénobitisme," *RAM* 45 (1969): 369–94; and 46 (1970): 3–32. Delhougne deals with Basil and the Desert Fathers and refers to participation politically, as sharing decisions. Finally, see Jean Leclercq, "Pour l'histoire de l'obéissance au moyen âge," *RAM* 41 (1965): 125–43.

60. *Mor.* 9.5.5 (CCL 143, 458): "Qui enim cuncta mirabiliter creat, ipse ut creata sibimet conueniant ordinat. In quo ergo conditori resistitur, pacis conuentio dissipatur quia ordinata esse nequeunt, quae superni moderaminis dispositionem perdunt. Quae enim subiecta Deo in tranquillitate persisterent, ipsa se sibimet dimissa confundunt; quia in se pacem non inueniunt, cui uenienti desuper in auctore contradicunt."

61. *Mor.* 5.34.63 (CCL 143, 262–63): "Stare ergo, solius creatoris est per quem cuncta non transeuntem transeunt et in quo aliqua ne transeant, retinentur. . . . Per humanitatis quippe dispensationem transire habuit; per diuinitatis uero potentiam quia ubique praesens est, stare." For God as absolute being, see: *Mor.* 16.37.45 (CCL 143A, 825); *Mor.* 16.43.55 (CCL 143A, 831). See also Aug. *civ.* 12.8, and *conf.* 1.1.1.

62. *Mor.* 8.6.8 (CCL 143, 386): "Quietus homo possidere carnem potuit si bene ab auctore conditus, possideri uoluisset."

The ideal, prelapsarian Adam possessed this stability, and the Resurrection will bring its return, a *soliditas resurrectionis*,[63] where "the glory of the Resurrection will absorb the mortality of the flesh and in clinging to the spirit, the flesh will be preserved by it for all eternity, even as the spirit itself is preserved in God by clinging to him."[64] Stability was the true purpose for which man was created.[65] God alone was his proper place (*locus*), in whom man found his true self and homeland (*patria*).[66] Contemplative vision had a fixity and a unity of intention, a silence and quiet that fulfilled every spiritual yearning.[67] The Fall teaches that only God "suffices" and can give man true happiness.[68]

Adam's ability to remain fixed in God imbued him with a moral continuity. He could stand "upright" morally by participating in God's goodness: both "standing firmly" and "standing erect."[69] In this state of

63. *Mor.* 8.33.56 (CCL 143, 425).

64. *Dial.* 4.3.2 (SC 265, 24): "ipsam mortalitatem carnis gloria resurrectionis absorbeat, et inhaerendo spiritui caro seruetur in perpetuum, quia et ipse spiritus inhaerendo seruatur in Deum."

65. *Mor.* 8.10.19 (CCL 143, 395): "Ad hoc namque homo conditus fuerat ut stante mente, in arcem se contemplationis erigeret, et nulla hunc corruptio a conditoris sui amore declinaret. Sed in eo quod ab ingenita standi soliditate uoluntatis pedem ad culpam mouit a dilectione conditoris in semetipsum protinus cecidit. Amorem uero Dei, ueram scilicet stationis arcem deserens, nec in se consistere potuit, quia, lubricae mutabilitatis impulsu, infra se per corruptionem proruens, etiam a semetipso dissensit."

66. *Mor.* 8.19.35 (CCL 143, 406). In an exegesis of Job 7:10 ("Neque cognoscet eum amplius locus eius"), Gregory writes, "Locus quippe hominis, sed non localis, ipse scilicet conditor exstitit qui hunc ut in semetipso consisteret creauit." Cf. Aug. *conf.* 1.18.28; 3.6.11; 5.2.2; 7.10.16.

67. *Mor.* 8.10.19 (CCL 143, 395); *Mor.* 4.28.54 (CCL 143, 198); "Hoc quietis silentium homo conditus habuit, cum contra hostem suum liberum uoluntatis arbitrium accepit. Cui quia sua sponte succubuit mox de se, quod contra se perstreperet, inuenit, mox in certamine infirmitatis tumultus repperit; et quamuis in pace silentii ab auctore fuerat conditus hosti tamen sponte substratus, clamores de pugna tolerauit." The idea of *quies* is also found in Cassian, *inst.* 2.12.2; 2.17.1; *conl.* 3.8; 6.3; esp. *quies cellae* in 4.12. See *Vitae patr.* 5.2 (entire). See also Jean Leclercq, "*Otia monastica*. Etudes sur le vocabulaire de la contemplation au Moyen Age," *StAns* 51 (Rome, 1963): 13–26. Dagens, *Saint Grégoire* (144) notes *quies* and the classical tradition, citing Seneca's *brev. vit.* 18.1–19.2, which Leclercq had also noticed. See also the idea of silence in Augustine's *conf.* 9.10.23ff. (the vision at Ostia), and Grover A. Zinn, Jr., "Silence, Sound and Word in the Spirituality of Gregory the Great," in Fontaine et al., eds., *Grégoire le Grand*, 367–75.

68. *Mor.* 26.44.79 (CCL 143B, 1325–26), *Mor.* 18.54.93 (CCL 143A, 955), *Mor.* 12.3.4 (CCL 143A, 630); cf. Aug. *conf.* 9.10.24.

69. Gregory also uses words from earlier patristic tradition to describe Adam's prelapsarian condition (e.g., *innocentia, integritas, justitia*). For this tradition, see L. Onings, "Adam," *DS* 1:187–95. See also Norman P. Williams, *The Ideas of the Fall and Original Sin* (London, 1938), passim; and on the Plotinian influence on Augustine's idea of the soul's fall, which is echoed in Gregory, see Robert O'Connell, "The Riddle of Augustine's *Confes-*

uprightness (*status suae rectitudinis*),[70] both the internal mutability of sin and the external mutability of death might be checked.[71] Indeed, Adam's original stability gave him the promise of conquering time and change,[72] so that he would have gone to heaven without dying.[73] In contrast to Adam's pristine stability, the rest of creation suffered change and decay. But after the Fall, man must suffer the mutability of death and sin as just punishment for his desertion of stability in God.[74] Sin, death, suffering, and change are unnatural states man endures in a discordant universe. Man could have been changeless, good, and immortal, had he remained in obedience and harmony with God.

The memory of man's pristine stability should direct his life, for stability remains man's true vocation even after the Fall. He can regain stability and harmony with the greater cosmos through self-discipline and humble submission to God, particularly through obedience to the authorities and institutions that now represent God on earth. Thus, the social implications of such obedience to God are at the center of Gregory's concerns. Man must be a part of the larger order; he must participate in God and share a common life of charity in the body of Christ. For Gregory, self-sufficient autonomy is the true evil, the fatal mistake of seeking to stand in oneself (*stare in semetipso*). Both the devil and man illustrate

---

sions: A Plotinian Key," *IPQ* 4 (1964): 327–72. Plotinus writes of the soul's instability in *Enn* 4.8f.

70. *Mor.* 26.44.79 (CCL 143B, 1325–26).

71. *Mor.* 11.50.68 (CCL 143A, 625): "Fixum etenim statum hic habere non possumus ubi transituri uenimus; atque hoc ipsum nostrum uiuere, cotidie a uita transire est. Quem uidelicet lapsum primus homo ante culpam habere non potuit quia tempora, eo stante, transiebant. Sed postquam deliquit, in quodam se quasi lubrico temporalitatis posuit; et quia cibum comedit uetitum, status sui protinus inuenit defectum. Quam tamen mutabilitatem non solum exterius, sed interius quoque homo patitur, dum ad meliora exsurgere opera conatur. Mens etenim mutabilitatis suae pondere ad aliud semper impellitur quam est, et nisi in statu suo arcta custodiae disciplina teneatur, semper in deteriora dilabitur." Cf. *Mor.* 14.15.17 (CCL 143A, 707–8).

72. *Mor.* 11.50.68 (CCL 143A, 624–25); and *Mor.* 25.3.4 (CCL 143B, 1232): "Primus uero homo ita conditus fuit, ut manente illo decederent tempora, ne cum temporibus ipse transiret. Stabat enim momentis decurrentibus, quia nequaquam ad uitae terminum per dierum incrementa tendebat. Stabat tanto robustius quanto semper stanti artius inhaerebat."

73. *Mor.* 4.28.54 (CCL 143, 198): "Sic namque immortalis est conditus, ut tamen si peccaret et mori posset; et sic mortalis est conditus ut si non peccaret, etiam non mori posset; atque ex merito liberi arbitrii beatitudinem illius regionis attingeret in qua uel peccare, uel mori non posset." Cf. Aug. *civ.* 12.21; 13.19.

74. Cf. *Mor.* 5.34.63 (CCL 143, 262); and *Mor.* 12.15.19 (CCL 143A, 640); *Mor.* 11.50.68 (CCL 143A, 624–26); *Mor.* 25.3.4 (CCL 143B, 1231).

this, for each tried to find sufficiency in himself (*sufficere ad se*), desiring to be on his own (*ad semetipsum*).[75] In his pride, the devil sought to imitate God's power, and man desired to be like gods (Gn 3:5).[76] One should not be like the devil, who was loathe merely to participate in God's greatness. Seeking instead his own private and asocial majesty (*privata celsitudo*), the devil was rightly deprived of sharing in God's majesty,[77] and he fell "beneath himself." This concept informs the curious incident in the *Dialogues* of Bishop Datius. When the bishop spends a night in a house haunted with squealing pigs and mice, he denounces the devil: "It serves you well, wretched one. . . . You were the one who said, 'I will place my seat in the clouds and will be like the Most High' [Is 14:14]. Behold, your pride has made you like pigs and mice: since you wished to imitate God undeservedly, you now imitate beasts deservedly."[78] As the devil has been degraded, so has man. Losing his true self, man is "laid beneath himself" through sin and change[79]—little wonder that he, too, will often imitate the beasts.

The rejection of participation in God can easily lead to social presumption as well. After the devil tried to escape subjection, he sought power over others. Consequently, he became an enemy not only to God but also to his peers, for his actions destroyed charity and concord.[80] Humility and obedience to God are directly linked with charity toward others and the greater harmony of society. When Gregory condemned John IV's claim to be ecumenical patriarch, he likened him to the devil in Isaiah 14:13–14 (quoted above) who spurned the social joy (*sociali gaudio*) of the angels in desiring to set himself up alone above others.[81] The true joy of ruling is found only in serving others, in mitigating their physical discomfort, and in offering the firm but gentle sustenance that can stabilize a tender, uncertain soul. To swagger in glory over another is abominable: power should be undertaken only to profit others.[82]

75. *Mor.* 34.21.40 (CCL 143B, 1761–62); *Mor.* 29.8.18 (CCL 143B, 1446–47).

76. *Mor.* 29.8.18 (CCL 143B, 1446–47).

77. *Mor.* 34.21.40 (CCL 143B, 1762). "Celsus nimirum esset, si ei qui ueraciter celsus est, inhaerere uoluisset. Celsus esset, si participatione uerae celsitudinis contentus fuisset. Sed dum priuatam celsitudinem superbe appetiit, iure perdidit participatam."

78. *Dial.* 3.4.2 (SC 260, 272).

79. *Mor.* 26.44.79 (CCL 143B, 1325–26); *Mor.* 8.10.19 (CCL 143, 395); *Mor.* 26.17.28 (CCL 143B, 1285–86).

80. *Reg. Past.* 3.23 (PL 77, 89–92); *HEv.* 2.27.1–2 (PL 76, 1205–6); *HEz.* 1.8.7 (CCL 142, 105); cf. *In lib. I Reg* 2.12 (CCL 144, 126–27).

81. *Ep.* 5.39 (CCL 140, 316).

82. *Reg. Past.* 2.34 (PL 77, 34): "Unde cuncti qui praesunt, non in se potestatem debent ordinis, sed aequalitatem pensare conditionis; nec praeesse se hominibus gaudeant, sed prodesse."

Gregory's view of the Fall as a loss of stability and his emphasis of stability in his treatment of the holy man reveal his ambivalence about power. Though power could be greatly tainted by delusions of self-elation on the part of the powerful, and thus be chillingly dangerous, power could nevertheless be put to good ends. Gregory believed fervently that authority and prestige should be founded on inner merit, rather than brute force or outward social status. While such attitudes are traditional, an examination of historical conditions around Gregory helps explain why Gregory found stability to be such a compelling spiritual concept and placed it at the very core of his thought. Gregory's was an age of usurpation, where the strong arrogated what powers, wealth, and privileges they could, even in the Church. The flurry of honorary titles found in Gregory's correspondence (*excellentissimus, gloriosissimus, magnificus, illustris, clarissimus*) implies a society at once beset with rapid political change and social mobility and yet determined to contain such instability with minute distinctions of rank and privilege—as if such labels of status could keep each in his proper place and so stabilize society.[83]

Of course the political and social fragmentation proved irreversible. With the Lombard occupation of Italy, the Papacy lost control of the whole Picene patrimony, and parts of the Samnite, Sabine, and Apulian patrimonies as well.[84] Representatives of the Byzantine government could not be trusted to rule justly or effectively. The *magister militum*, Theodore, ruled Sardinia as duke and petty tyrant, exacting illegal taxes and generally oppressing the population.[85] Gregory sought help from the Emperor in Constantinople, but to little avail. Gregory's problems with the exarch of Ravenna were particularly frustrating. The exarch, Romanus, detained the bishop of Orta in Tuscany, allowing that church to decay.[86] He also refused to permit peace with the Lombards, though unable to send troops south against them. Gregory was thus forced to assume responsibility for defending Rome against the Lombard, Ariulph.[87] Meanwhile, the praetor of Sicily tried to restrict the travel of bishops to Rome, an unjust assertion of power aimed at lessening their ties to the pope.[88] Some officials could be bribed to tolerate paganism, and others attempted to extend their power by subjecting the clergy to secular

83. T. S. Brown, *Gentlemen and Officers* (Rome, 1984), 128–38, esp. 131ff. The fluidity with which Gregory applies such terms reveals that the rank system was breaking down.

84. Richards, *Consul of God*, 127.

85. *Ep.* 1.47 (CCL 140, 61); *Ep.* 1.59 (CCL 140, 70).

86. *Ep.* 1.32 (CCL 140, 38–39).

87. *Ep.* 2.4 (CCL 140, 92); *Ep.* 2.27 (CCL 140, 113–14); *Ep.* 2.28 (CCL 140, 114); *Ep.* 2.39 (CCL 140, 123–25).

88. *Ep.* 1.70 (CCL 140, 78–79); *Ep.* 7.19 (CCL 140, 470); *Ep.* 11.24 (CCL 140A, 894–95).

courts.[89] Gregory complained that he met plunderers daily, often enduring their depredations for charity's sake.[90] Angered by what he saw,
Gregory denounced Italy's dukes and princes as "lions" pillaging the
provinces, seizing booty with furious greed.[91]

Within the Church, irregularities were just as common. Members
jockeyed for power, prestige, and social status. To elevate his authority,
the archbishop of Ravenna, John III, presumed to wear the *pallium* (a tri-
angular woolen vestment) at solemn processions and audiences with the
laity in violation of the wishes of the bishop of Rome.[92] John also encouraged the use of *mappulae*, the white linen saddle cloths exclusive to the
Roman clergy.[93] In Catania, deacons wore *campagi*, a style of sandal worn
exclusively by Roman deacons.[94] Elsewhere niceties of dress, formerly
marks of the senatorial aristocracy, were taken over as status symbols by
the Church.

On a more concrete level, usurpation in the Church echoed that of
secular society. Officials of the Church were not above usurping funds or
land,[95] and bishops sometimes turned greedy eyes toward the property
of orphans[96] and monks.[97] Gregory warns often against simony,[98] and
chastens those such as Maximus of Salona who used force to win elec-
tions.[99] Clearly, the danger loomed large of treating the Church like private property, as Natalis did when he tried to give sacred vessels to his
relatives.[100] In the same vein, Gregory rebukes those motivated by private
whims and grudges.[101] Many who entered the Church found it difficult
to forget the family left behind.[102] Or if they succeeded in this, instead

---

89. *Ep.* 5.38 (CCL 140, 312f.); *Ep.* 11.24 (CCL 140A, 894–95); *Ep.* 11.58 (CCL 140A,
964).

90. *HEz.* 1.11.6 (CCL 142, 171).

91. *HEz.* 2.6.23 (CCL 142, 312).

92. *Ep.* 3.54 (CCL 140, 200–203), *Ep.* 5.15 (CCL 140, 280–81); *Ep.* 6.31 (CCL 140, 403–
4), *Ep.* 5.61 (CCL 140, 363).

93. *Ep.* 3.54 (CCL 140, 203).

94. *Ep.* 8.27 (CCL 140A, 548).

95. *Ep.* 4.11 (CCL 140, 228–29); *Ep.* 4.8 (CCL 140, 224); *Ep.* 1.9 (CCL 140,11).

96. *Ep.* 11.25 (CCL 140A, 895–97).

97. *Ep.* 4.8 (CCL 140, 224).

98. E.g., *Ep.* 5.16 (CCL 140, 282–83); *Ep.* 5.62 (CCL 140, 365f.); *Ep.* 9.136 (CCL 140A,
687); *Ep.* 11.28 (CCL 140A, 916); *Ep.* 11.49 (CCL 140A, 948); *Mor.* 32.20.38 (CCL 143B, 1657–
58); *HEv.* 1.17.13 (PL 76, 1145–46).

99. *Ep.* 4.20 (CCL 140, 238).

100. *Ep.* 2.18 (CCL 140, 104).

101. Cf. *Ep.* 2.41 (CCL 140, 129–30).

102. Cf. *Mor.* 32.21.41 (CCL 143B, 1658–59). See *Mor.* 1.4.5 (CCL 143, 27), where large
families are associated with greed and ambition for estates.

they "gird[ed] themselves for dangerous and great labors, to cross seas, attend courtrooms, assail princes, burst into palaces, attend litigious crowds of people, and defend earthly patrimony with painful care."[103] Such "hypocrites" and "hirelings" had merely applied their avarice and ambition to create new and glorious careers for themselves in the Church.[104] They might extend the wealth and power of the Church in the world, but they sorely misunderstood the true nature of her advancement.

Viewing these trends with deep disillusionment, Gregory envisions a purified Church. Ideally, the Church should be set apart from secular society by the absence of personal and familial ties of patronage and favoritism, by a rejection of the obsession with worldly status and private wealth that makes such patrimonial social organizations successful. True charity goes beyond one's natural love of kin.[105] Indeed, the devil can even use one's beloved family and friends as "ladders" to assault the "citadel" of the soul.[106] Furthermore, social rank is false in the external world, for it is determined by circumstance, not by one's inner worth and merit.[107] But God will judge "not by prerogatives of rank, but by works of merit."[108] Therefore, the Church should be purified of considerations of external rank and personal motivation. Gregory asserts that he does not act from "private grudges."[109] With God's help, Gregory "defends no one from personal love." He "keeps to the rule of justice" and "puts aside respect for any man's person."[110]

The Church, however, is not without orderly degrees of distinction. If hierarchical order keeps peace and tranquillity in secular affairs, how much the more must it exist in the Church to avoid discord and confusion? But the principle of rank in the Church is that external status corresponds to internal merit, as in the angelic hierarchy. Peace will be secured, Gregory believes, "if nothing is yielded to power [*potestas*], but all to justice [*aequitas*]."[111] Hypocrites are so despicable precisely because they mock this precious correlation of status and merit.

Gregory distrusts those who seek power to escape subjection rather

---

103. *Mor.* 31.12.20 (CCL 143B, 1565).
104. *Mor.* 31.12.20 (CCL 143B, 1565); *HEv.* 1.14.2–3 (PL 76, 1128–29).
105. *HEv.* 2.27.1 (PL 76, 1205).
106. *Mor.* 3.8.12 (CCL 143, 121–22); *Ep.* 5.44 (CCL 140, 333).
107. *Mor.* 25.1.1 (CCL 143B, 1230).
108. *Ep.* 1.75 (CCL 140, 84).
109. Cf. *Ep.* 6.26 (CCL 140, 397–98).
110. *Ep.* 2.17 (CCL 140, 103).
111. *Ep.* 9.215 (CCL 140A, 775).

than to serve others; such men only imitate the devil. Power may be right-fully assumed only for the service and perfection of others. The carnal, when swollen and exalted by power, invariably try to injure the good.[112] The satanic delusion of self-sufficiency destroys both self and society, for it is a perversion, a wrongful freedom from authority and servitude. All too often freedom to follow one's desires entails a selfish and arrogant disregard of others, a denial of the interdependence of all members in society. Gregory describes this as "the enslaved freedom" (*captiva libertas*) of following one's own will, a notion he contrasts with the "free servi-tude" (*libera servitus*) that the devil (and man) once enjoyed obeying God.[113]

Gregory envisions hierarchical order primarily as the union of Christ with his members. Christ is the head of all Christians. The faithful, who are his body, execute his commands in joyful obedience, for Christ rightly speaks on man's behalf. A second analogy, more deeply embedded in Gregory's mind, is less easily discerned: that of parent and child. God is the true parent, and all good Christians are his obedient children. If Christians love their earthly kin too dearly, they are in danger of being separated from the true parent of the heart,[114] for love of kin often causes the "secularism" polluting the Church. Thus Gregory teaches that Chris-tians must learn to "hate" their relations, as Christ ordered in Luke 14:26: "If any man comes to me and does not hate his father, and mother, his wife and sons, his brothers and sisters, and even his own life, he cannot be my disciple."[115] The community or "family" of Christ should supplant blood ties. Gregory's ideal Christian is like the child Samuel in 1 Kings 3: he obeys the contradictory commands of his lord without question, now rising, now returning to lie down as his master wills. Samuel's absolute obedience exemplifies the ideal of perfect obedience and self-abnegation found in the Desert Fathers and Cassian. Such total obedience is also commanded of monks in the *Regula Magistri* and *Regula Benedicti*.[116] The individual will must be extinguished and offered up in a sacrifice of obe-dience to God and to the superior placed above the Christian by God.

This stark command of obedience had become the essence of monas-ticism by Gregory's time, but the command still evoked resistance. To live

112. *Mor.* 8.23.39 (CCL 143, 410).
113. *Mor.* 34.21.40 (CCL 143B, 1761–62); see also *Mor.* 4.36.71 (CCL 143, 215–16).
114. *Mor.* 7.30.40 (CCL 143, 365).
115. *Mor.* 7.30.41 (CCL 143, 365).
116. See André Borias, "Le Christ dans la Règle de saint Benoît," *RBen* 82 (1972): 109–39; A. de Vogüé, "Les Vues de Grégoire le Grand sur la vie religieuse," esp. 34–35; idem, *La Communauté et l'abbé dans la Règle de saint Benoît* (Paris, 1961); Philip Rousseau, *Ascetics, Authority, and the Church* (Oxford, 1978).

under the will of another was the lot of the slave. The Christian command of obedience overturned the classical ideal of the citizen as manly and self-determined, and it also challenged Germanic values that distinguished clearly between slaves and free men. The Christian's stiff neck of pride will chafe under the yoke of obedience for the will resists submission. But it is precisely this intransigence of the carnal man, the old man, that must be eradicated through grace. Obedience destroys individual will, even individual discretion:

> For true obedience does not inquire into the intention of superiors nor does it examine their commands, since he who submits every judgment of his life to an elder rejoices only in this: to perform anything commanded him. For whoever has learned perfect obedience does not know how to judge, since he considers obedience to orders the only good.[117]

Through obedience to another, one needs neither to judge nor to examine the decisions of one's superiors, but simply to execute them happily. Through obedience to another, one finally overcomes one's own will, transcending the selfish autonomy that destroys social harmony. Indeed, obedience is of such merit that it can earn the recompense of experiencing God in contemplation.[118] Harmony with God first depends upon brotherly concord, as the story of Cain and Abel has traditionally taught Christians.

Submission to another is a sacrifice of the will, and it is the surest way of overcoming one's own will[119] and removing the obstacles that prevent union with God. Obedience is better than the sacrifice of rams (cf. 1 Sm 15:22–23) because one offers up the pride of one's own will and immolates oneself with the sword of commandment: obedience appeases God more quickly than offering the flesh of another, for it is an offering of oneself.[120] Such sacrificial obedience is the hallmark of the holy man, who stands as

---

117. *In lib. I Reg.* 2.125 (CCL 144, 187): "Vera namque oboedientia nec praepositorum intentionem disculit nec praecepta discernit: quia, qui omne uitae suae iudicium maiori subdidit, in hoc solo gaudet, si, quod sibi praecipitur, operatur. Nescit enim iudicare, quisquis perfecte didicerit oboedire: quia hoc tantum bonum putat, si praeceptis oboediat." Quoted by de Vogüé, "Les Vues de Grégoire le Grand sur la vie religieuse," 34. De Vogüé sees an echo of the last line with Colomban, *Reg. Mon.* 9; Hier. *Ep.* 125.15; see also de Vogüé, "Ne juger de rien par soi-même. Deux emprunts de la Règle colombanienne aux Sentences de Sextus et à Jerome," *RAM* 49 (1973): 129–34.

118. *In lib. I Reg.* 2.129 (CCL 144, 189).

119. *Mor.* 35.14.28 (CCL 143B, 1793): "'Vir oboediens loquitur uictorias' (Prv 21:28). Vir quippe oboediens uictorias loquitur, quia dum alienae uoci humiliter subdimur, nosmetipsos in corde superamus." Also *Mor.* 32.20.37 (CCL 143B, 1656–57); *Mor.* 32.21.43 (CCL 143B, 1660); *Mor.* 32.22.46 (CCL 143B, 1663–64).

120. *Mor.* 35.14.28 (CCL 143B, 1792–93); see also *In lib. I Reg.* 2.126–27 (CCL 144, 187–88); cf. *In lib. I Reg.* 6.31–32 (CCL 144, 568).

an example to the rest of the Church. St. Benedict, Gregory's favorite servant of God, teaches and exemplifies this perfect obedience.

The hierarchical order of obedience is not just a model for the Church. The cohesion and unity of such a corporate order has much to offer society as a whole. Although every man is equal by nature in the sight of God, because of man's Fall, social equality has been lost; diversity of status reflects man's sinfulness.[121] The observance of the hierarchical order imposed on man as punishment disciplines and educates the soul.[122] By God's dispensation, a hierarchical order subordinates barbarians to Romans, slaves to free men, women to men, and so on.[123] Those who are more carnal than others must be treated accordingly. For instance, it is permissible to coerce peasants and to subject those of lower status to corporal discipline and other prejudicial treatments.[124] As subjects live sinfully, so they are nearer to brute beasts than rational men and rightly should be broken with fear.[125] Correspondingly, those of higher status must be treated according to their refinement. Impoverished citizens of high birth were granted "pigments" and "more delicate articles of commerce" in recognition of their status.[126]

The political and social implications of maintaining such a right order emerge in Gregory's letter to Brunhilda (*Ep.* 8.4):

> For it is fitting, most excellent daughter, that you allow yourself to be subject to the Lord. For by submitting the neck of your mind to the fear of the omnipotent God, you also solidify your dominion over subject na-

121. *Reg. Past.* 2.6 (PL 77, 34); *Mor.* 21.15.22 (CCL 143A, 1082); cf. Aug. *civ.* 19.15; Ambr. *Ep.* 37.8.

122. *Reg. Past.* 2.6 (PL 77, 34); *Mor.* 21.15.22 (CCL 143A, 1082). This Platonic and Aristotelian notion of order has a long history, both before and after Gregory. But in Gregory this notion of order becomes interwoven with the idea of the corporate Church as Christ's body, so that its unity is based on the complementary functions of members in the Church. On Gregory's hierarchical thinking and its political applications, see esp. two articles by R. A. Markus, "Gregory the Great's Europe," and "Papacy and Hierarchy," in *From Augustine to Gregory the Great: History and Christianity in Late Antiquity*, Variorum Reprints CS 169 (London 1983), XV:21–36; XVII:1–50. In XV:23, n. 8, Markus gives the *locus classicus* of hierarchy in Arist. *Pol.* 1.1252b4, 1255a1–b10.

123. Markus notes how dismayingly often this theme appears in Gregory's correspondence, citing *Ep.* 11.4 (MGH 2, 263) [*Ep.* 11.4 (CCL 140A, 862–63)]; *Ep.* 13.34 (MGH 2, 397) [*Ep.* 13.32 (CCL 140A, 1034)].

124. Cf. *Ep.* 9.205 (CCL 140A, 764) where pagan slaves are to be "uerberibus cruciatibusque . . . castigare," if freedmen, directed to penitence and confinement, that "cruciatus saltem eos corporis ad desideratam mentis ualeat reducere sanitatem." Also, *Ep.* 4.26 (CCL 140, 245), where pagan peasants are to be taxed heavily to hasten conversion; *Ep.* 3.37 (CCL 140, 183), where a Jew is to be punished corporally for having Christian slaves.

125. *Mor.* 21.15.23 (CCL 143A, 1082).

126. If we can trust Io. Diac. *vita Greg.* 2:26, 28. See Richards, *Consul of God*, 96–97.

tions, and by subjecting yourself to the service of the creation, you bind your subjects more devotedly to you in servitude.[127]

Just as a hierarchy is extended from God through the soul to the body, so an analogous chain links God, ruler, and people, or abbot and disciples, or any superior and inferior. The superior becomes responsible for the behavior of the inferior, and so must possess strict control of himself in order to control his subordinates. The waywardness of a superior will invariably undermine younger ones, for there is no one to check their pleasure.[128] Rebellion against God thus travels downward. But, as Gregory suggests to Brunhilda, goodness and obedience are also transmitted to others in the corporate unity. In general, we make the good of others our own through love in the concord of the community.[129]

The emotional ties that develop from hierarchical order supplant those found in the ordinary world. What our modern age might interpret as paternalism is the proper and precious bond that secures Gregory's cherished goal of social concord. Responding to a fierce rebuke received from Anastasius, bishop of Antioch, Gregory writes that he does not marvel at Anastasius's "imperial" language, "since love [amor] and power [potestas] have the greatest kinship with each other; for both presume in a princely way, and both always speak with authority."[130] Love encompasses the power and authority to influence the beloved. The feelings securing social harmony are reciprocal, but not identical, because human society can never possess equality. The love of a servant, son, and wife for the dominus will differ; this is only natural.[131] By divine dispensation different ranks exist so that "the inferiors show reverence [reverentia] to the more powerful, while the more powerful bestow love [dilectio] upon their inferiors." These complementary affections create "one unity and concord from diversity."[132]

Because the superior is responsible for others, he must be especially virtuous. Gregory sees the ruler as a basileus, which he interprets as meaning "base of the people." He bears the people, controls their actions, and is stabilized by holding them.[133] Rulers must surpass others in virtue, as their rank does.[134] As the ruler is the head of his subjects, when

127. *Ep.* 8.4 (CCL 140A, 518–19).
128. *Mor.* 2.15.27 (CCL 143, 76).
129. *Reg. Past.* 3.10 (PL 77, 63).
130. *Ep.* 7.24 (CCL 140, 479).
131. Cf. *Mor.* 34.21.40. (CCL 143B, 1761–62).
132. *Ep.* 5.59 (CCL 140, 357–58).
133. *Mor.* 9.16.25. (CCL 143, 475–76).
134. *Reg. Past.* 2.3 (PL 77, 28).

he is weak, the members lack proper vigor. Just as soldiers depend on their commander, and sheep upon their shepherd, the ruler must be pure and fit, or his subjects might be led astray. He cannot have the "dust" of sin blinding his vision.[135] This clearsightedness is required of all leaders, especially bishops and other *rectores*. Even secular property holders are responsible before God for the souls of peasants (*rusticos*) in their charge.[136] Those who intercede for the people must be pure that they may be assured of the "friendship of God" through the "merit of their lives."[137] Rulers cannot be defective lest their mediation for others fail.[138]

As a ruler's purity is helpful to the greater whole, so his sin damages the greater whole. The consequences of the personal sins of a ruler are as vast as his power. Because of his own sins, Gregory believes the exarch of Ravenna will not take up arms against Agilulf.[139] Gregory suffers such adversities because he has sinned and offended God. He loses the peace the republic secured with the Lombards; Agilulf attacks, grain runs short in Rome.[140] Because priests are wicked, the whole empire suffers the cruelties of the barbarians.[141] The stability of society is inextricably tied to the personal virtue of its rulers. When good rulers communicate virtue downward, society prospers. When bad rulers communicate their sin, the whole social body suffers. But the ties between subject and ruler are bidirectional: the merits of ruler and people are so connected that the weakness of one will wound the other.[142] The interdependence of members of the social body produces a corporate personality whose unity echoes the delicate interconnections of body and soul, and the cosmos as a whole.

According to Gregory's hierarchical thinking, the saint clings to and is possessed by God. Through the saint's obedience and love he is elevated, participating in God's virtues. In turn, his body can be transformed through its intimate connection with the soul, making him virtually spiritual in the flesh. Since perfection ultimately depends on obedience, Gregory alerts his audience continually to the real enemy of peaceful union with God: the desire for self-assertion and power, for freedom from obedience to authority and for liberation from other people.

135. *Reg. Past.* 2.7 (PL 77, 39).
136. *Ep.* 4.23 (CCL 140, 241).
137. *Ep.* 1.24 (CCL 140, 22.).
138. *Reg. Past.* 1.11 (PL 77, 24f.).
139. *Ep.* 2.25 (CCL 140, 111).
140. *Ep.* 5.36 (CCL 140, 304–7); *Ep.* 2.38 (CCL 140, 123).
141. *Ep.* 5.37 (CCL 140, 308).
142. *Ep.* 7.7 (CCL 140, 455–56).

Gregory sets the proud desire of power and self-sufficiency opposite the true love of the saint, for love necessarily implies a humble obedience to authority and a concord with others.[143] Through humility, obedience, and love, one becomes greater than oneself; one participates in God and is gathered into the larger corporate order of Christ's body. This is the source of the saint's wonderful power.

143. Cf. *HEz.* 1.8.7–8 (CCL 142, 105–6).

· IV ·

SOLIDITAS CARITATIS

In a letter to Adeodatus, bishop of Numidia, Gregory reflects upon the power of love to unify men: "[S]ince our mind is one with you, and yours is one with us, we are present to one another through all things, while we see each other in a mind made one through love."[1] The body of Christ is bound so intimately that each member responds to the joys and pains of the others, a sensitivity recalling the intricate connection of body and soul in man himself, or even the mysterious sympathy between the natural world and man.

> Through this disparity in diversity the same members both rejoice in the joys of others, though afflicted themselves, and they waste away at the sorrows of others, though happy themselves. For as the teacher of the Gentiles witnesses, if one member suffers, the other members suffer with him, and if one rejoices, all rejoice with him [1 Cor 12:26]; I do not doubt that you groan for our trouble, as it is certain we rejoice in your peace.[2]

As the Christian joins with others in the body of Christ, so he shares their joys and sorrows. Just as the Christian can be one with God through stability, so too will he be one with his brother through the solidity of charity. This true concord is the sine qua non of the Church and Christian

---

1. *Ep.* 3.48 (CCL 140, 193): "quia animus noster uobis uesterque nobis unitus est, uicissim nobis per omnia praesentes sumus, dum nos unita per amorem mente conspicimus." For other passages on unity between men, see: *Ep.* 8.31 (CCL 140A, 554); *Ep.* 9.223 (CCL 140A, 794–97); *Mor.* 30.9.31 (CCL 143B, 1511–12); *Ep.* 6.19 (CCL 140, 389); *Ep.* 6.56 (CCL 140, 429); *Ep.* 6.57 (CCL 140, 430); and *Ep.* 5.35 (CCL 140, 302–3). On charity, see V. Nugent, "The Concept of Charity in the Writings of Saint Gregory the Great," (Ph.D. diss., Catholic University, Washington, D.C., 1951); E. Marin, *San Gregorio I, papa della carità* (Rome, 1951). I have learned most from Patrick Catry, "L'Amour du prochain chez saint Grégoire le Grand," *Stud Mon* 20 (1978): 287–344.

2. *Ep.* 2.40 (CCL 140, 127–28). Cf. Rufin. *Gr. Naz. orat.* 2.3.

society. Thus two axes of participation tie the Christian to a larger corporate order: a vertical axis links him with God; a horizontal axis joins him to other men. One continuous love embraces God and man, yet this love assumes analogous and complementary forms. The active life of service to neighbor has a breadth (*latitudo*) that widens (*dilatare*) the soul, even as the contemplative life has a height (*altitudo*) that raises (*suspendere, erigere*) the soul.[3] One is "lifted high in love of God, and joined together in love of neighbor" (*in Dei amore suspendere, sed etiam proximo in caritate sociare*).[4] Both loves carry man beyond himself. In *Pastoral Rule*, Gregory teaches ministers the importance of balancing this dual relationship:

> Let the ruler [*rector*] be near each one in compassion, and lifted above everyone in contemplation, so that he may both transfer to himself the weaknesses of the other through the inner depths of his mercy, and also transcend himself seeking the invisible through the highness of his contemplation, lest in seeking the heights, he despise the weakness of his neighbor, or in meeting the weakness of his neighbors, he lose desire for the sublime. . . .[5]

Rising upward to glimpse the invisible world in contemplation, the ruler also reaches out to embrace those near him, taking on their weaknesses and bending to them in mercy. The *rector*'s success in contemplation depends upon his compassion for others: love of God and neighbor are complementary and interdependent. And the more the Christian is drawn beyond himself in such charity, the more he becomes like Christ:

> We draw nearer to him, who is over everything, when in compassion for our neighbor we set ourselves even lower than we are. In corporal affairs, no one reaches high offices, unless he is drawn upward; but in spiritual things it is certain that the more we are drawn downward by compassion, the more truly we approach the heights.[6]

To be like Christ, the Christian must be drawn beyond the boundaries of himself. Charity demands that one give of one's self in sympathy with others.[7] This gift of self becomes the foundation of all goodness, just

---

3. *HEz.* 2.2.15 (CCL 142, 235–36); *HEz.* 2.7.5 (CCL 142, 319). Also, *Mor.* 6.37.56 (CCL 143, 326); *HEz.* 1.12.10 (CCL 142, 188); *Mor.* 7.15.18 (CCL 143, 345).

4. *HEz.* 2.7.5 (CCL 142, 319).

5. *Reg. Past.* 2.5 (PL 77, 32). "Sit rector singulis compassione proximus, prae cunctis contemplatione suspensus, ut et per pietatis viscera in se infirmitatem caeterorum transferat, et per speculationis altitudinem semetipsam quoque invisibilia appetendo transcendat, ne aut alta petens proximorum infirma despiciat, aut infirmis proximorum congruens, appetere alta derelinquat (2 Cor 12:3)."

6. *HEv.* 2.39.10 (PL 76, 1301).

7. *Mor.* 20.36.70 (CCL 143A, 1055).

as Christ's sacrificial gift is the surest sign of his goodness and oneness with the Father.

Gregory's understanding of charity is the key to his understanding of all the virtues. Charity is the "root," "source," "mother," and "guardian" of all virtues.[8] Often Gregory speaks of their interconnection and interdependence:[9] all virtues are branches springing from the single root of charity. Some, and perhaps all, virtues can be seen as multiple facets of charity.[10] Charity is patience and humility,[11] and especially concord. It unites the dissociated, joins what is diverse, and sets right what is wrong.[12] This virtue of charity, too, is ultimately founded in Gregory's idea of participation in a hierarchical order. Through love, one participates in God and in the corporate body of Christ, creating a harmony and concord throughout the cosmos, the Church, and society, and in the Christian himself. In Gregory's opinion, the devil fears nothing but this charity and harmony, "the humble love we bestow in turn on one another," for such concord is the one thing men have that the devil has lost forever.[13] The loss of charity brings the destruction of social order with the advent of quarreling and anarchy.

In transcending himself in charity, the Christian finds stability in the concord of the larger body of Christ. Charity is a type of stability, *soliditas*,

8. *HEv.* 2.27.1 (PL 76, 1205); *Ep.* 7.28 (CCL 140, 486); *Mor.* 1.26.37 (CCL 143, 45); *Mor.* 10.6.9 (CCL 143, 541); *Ep.* 9.223 (CCL 140A, 795); *Ep.* 6.61 (CCL 140, 434); also *Reg. Past.* 3.9 (PL 77, 59), where charity is identified with patience; *Reg. Past.* 3.23 (PL 77, 92), where charity is the internal root of stability. See Catry, "L'Amour du prochain," 305. In a complementary way, *Mor.* 31.45.87 (CCL 143B, 1610): "Ipsa namque uitiorum regina superbia cum deuictum plene cor ceperit, mox illud septem principalibus uitiis, quasi quibusdam suis ducibus deuastandum tradit."

9. See chapter 1, nn. 59–60.

10. In seeing all virtues as originating in charity, Gregory follows Augustine's modification of the Stoic doctrine of the unity and interconnection of virtues. Augustine deemed Stoics to be too perfectionist in holding that the absence of one virtue meant the absence of all virtues and so deemphasized their interdependence; cf. John P. Langan, "Augustine on the Unity and the Interconnection of the Virtues," *HThR* 72 (1979): 81–95, and Marcia L. Colish, *The Stoic Tradition from Antiquity to the Early Middle Ages*, II: *Stoicism in Christian Latin Thought through the Sixth Century*, Studies in the History of Christian Thought, ed. Heiko Oberman (Leiden, 1986), 35:257–62. Yet Gregory is more Stoic in his emphasis on their unity, being influenced by Ambr. *off.* 2.8.43; and Cassian *inst.* 5.1ff.; *conl.* 5.16. See R. Gillet, introduction to Grégoire le Grand, *Morales sur Job* I–II (SC 32), 90–105, discussing not only Cassian's influence but also parallels with Gr. Nyss. *virg.* 16 and 4; and *or. dom.* 4.

11. *Reg. Past.* 3.9 (PL 77, 59); *Mor.* 21.21.33–34 (CCL 143A, 1089–91); *Mor.* 27.46.76 (CCL 143B, 1389–90). For further citations, see Catry, "L'Amour du prochain," 338–403, 407–8.

12. *Ep.* 9.223 (CCL 140A, 794–95). See also: *Ep.* 7.27 (CCL 140, 486), *Ep.* 6.61 (CCL 140, 434). Catry notes that "radix omnium bonorum est charitas" is found in Aug. *Serm.* 350.1 (PL 39, 1534), "L'Amour du prochain," 305, n. 91.

13. *HEz.* 1.8.7 (CCL 142, 105).

a firmness and enduring strength that is the true sign of election.[14] Through participation in the body of Christ, the individual gains the stability he lacks on his own. True participation, however, demands humility and obedience, for only by denying one's selfish will and becoming submissive to God and the larger corporate order does one share in the blessings of earthly peace and heavenly salvation. Through the Church, one can at last approach the ideal of being spiritual in the flesh. Granted, the Church has her carnal as well as spiritual members and must bear this imperfect mixture of wheat and chaff until Judgment Day; nevertheless only the proud condemn her for this.[15] For while the body suffers imperfection on earth, Christ, the Head of the Church, reigns in heaven, triumphant in perfection. By participating in his body on earth, the Christian can begin to partake of Christ's heavenly perfection, wherein alone is found true stability. The concord of the Church, embracing and reconciling spiritual and carnal sides of existence, is therefore a macrocosmic model of that harmony which the Christian hopes to replicate in his own life.

Unity with others is so important for Gregory that a man's salvation cannot be separated from that of his neighbor. Christians must seek friends to accompany them on the road to God. If one goes to the forum or the baths, he takes a friend, Gregory observes. (Like Augustine, Gregory spent his life among a circle of friends; it is difficult to imagine him ever alone, even in prayer.) If one enjoys this pleasant "earthly companionship," Gregory continues, so should he "take care not to journey alone" to God.[16] Even our prayers become "more powerful" for ourselves when we pray also for others, and the penitent is "heard more quickly . . . the more devoutly he intercedes" for his friends.[17] Charity is most perfectly the concern for the salvation of another, the prayers offered in intercession for their sins, a willingness to lay down one's life for one's friends (cf. Jn 15:13).[18] For this reason, the stability of charity—and not miracles—serves as the true sign of holiness and election.[19] Noting that the dazzling feats of the reprobate often overshadow the humble virtues of the holy, Gregory comments:

> Indeed, the proof of holiness is not to make miracles, but to love others as oneself; moreover, to believe truths about God, and to think better

14. *HEz.* 2.5.22 (CCL 142, 292).
15. *Mor.* 26.41.76f. (CCL 143B, 1322–23).
16. *HEv.* 1.6.6 (PL 76, 1098).
17. *Mor.* 35.11.21 (CCL 143B, 1787).
18. *HEv.* 2.27.2 (PL 76, 1206).
19. *Ep.* 11.36 (CCL 140A, 928); *HEz.* 2.5.22 (CCL 142, 292).

things of one's neighbor than of oneself. For true power is in love, not in the showing of miracles. . . . It is not miracles, but charity alone that indicates true servants of God. Therefore, the witness of heavenly discipleship is the gift of brotherly love.[20]

In these days distant from the Church's persecution, charity should inspire faith. The purpose of miracles therefore is to gain souls, Gregory writes Augustine of Canterbury in *Epistles* 11.36.[21] Their true end is the salvation of others. Indeed, miracles can be dangerous, tempting the soul to pride and private interest. They can be counterfeit by reprobates desiring human praise and power over others—the old devilish tyranny.[22] Miracles must be viewed from the correct perspective, that is, from a spiritual point of view. The greatest miracle of all, therefore, is not the resurrection of a dead body but the resurrection of a soul dead in sin.[23] To convert a sinner by preaching the word of God, to help him with tears and prayers, fulfills the commands of charity, and this is the true miracle. The body rises only to die again; the soul rises to live forever.

How can charity win as many souls as miracles? This is the question Gregory confronts in the *Dialogues*, and his answer lies in the didactic role of the holy man. To be sure, miracles gain souls, but the man of God leads souls to salvation in more subtle ways as well. Being both the servant of God and of his neighbor, the holy man stands at the intersection of the vertical and horizontal axes of participation in God and society. Indeed, his holiness is defined by this location. He manifests God to his neighbor, and he intercedes with God for his neighbor. The holy man exemplifies the virtues of the soul stable in God, teaching the lessons of obedience that secure participation in God and in Christ's body. The unification of the Christian with God and neighbor focuses especially on the Mass, and implicitly promotes the Church as an institution. Ultimately, the saint's mission is to direct attention to the vital role of the bishop and of the Mass in obtaining both salvation for Christians and concord for society, for the sacrifice of the Mass integrates the Christian into the corporate body of Christ. The holy man is like John the Baptist, whose function was to point

20. *Mor.* 20.7.17 (CCL 143A, 1016): "Probatio quippe sanctitatis non est signa facere, sed unumquemque ut se diligere, de Deo autem uera, de proximo uero meliora quam de semetipso sentire. Nam quia uera uirtus in amore est, non autem in ostensione miraculi . . . [For because Christ said in Jn 13:35] 'si dilectionem habueritis ad inuicem,' aperte indicat, quia ueros Dei famulos non miracula, sed sola caritas probat. Testimonium ergo superni discipulatus est donum fraternae dilectionis." Also, *HEz.* 1.10.35 (CCL 142, 162); *Mor.* 34.22.43f. (CCL 143B, 1763–64). Cf. Cassian, *conl.* 15.2.

21. CCL 140A, 925–29.

22. Ibid., also *HEz.* 1.9.8 (CCL 142, 127).

23. *Dial.* 3.17.7 (SC 260, 340).

to Christ the Messiah and to remind his followers that "He [Christ] must increase, but I must decrease" (Jn 3:30; cf. Mt 3:11–12).

Even though Gregory is thoroughly steeped in the traditions of the Desert Fathers, he has modified considerably their conception of the holy man by focusing on the Mass, prayer, and penance.[24] The Mass itself symbolizes the obedience man must offer God, even as it is the ritual means of joining man with the body of Christ. The Eucharist is the *hostia*, Christ offered as sacrificial victim in humility and submission to God. As Christ is offered vicariously for man, so each Christian must imitate Christ's obedience in his own life. But since the Mass and other forms of intercession are effective only insofar as one participates in Christ's body, the holy man's primary duty is to inspire those virtues essential to such participation, namely obedience to the authorities, rules, and institutions that represent Christ on earth. As servant of God and neighbor, the holy man cannot spend all his time rapt in contemplation. Instead, he returns to serve his feeble brothers, teaching and rebuking them, inspiring them with his example and interceding for their sins. Exemplifying an active charity, he devotes himself to gaining the obedience that will secure the salvation of others.[25]

The holy man's perfect obedience to God and his ministry of turning others to obedience make him a saint; he is "one with God," much as Christ was one with the Father, humbly doing God's will, in the Gospel of John. This oneness in turn lends the saint extraordinary powers, which range from simple acts of kindness to astonishing displays of authority over spirits from the underworld. Gregory illustrates how such powers enable the holy man to lead others and to inspire their obedience in his consideration of Christ's power over demons and man's participation in such power through obedience to God:

24. Cf. P. Brown, "The Rise and Function of the Holy Man in Late Antiquity," *JRS* 61 (1971): 80–101, reprinted in idem, *Society and the Holy* (Berkeley and Los Angeles, 1982). Gregory's holy man is no longer on the margin bridging Church and society, but rather at the core of the established Church. Also, Philip Rousseau, *Pachomius: The Making of a Community in Fourth-Century Egypt*, Transformation of the Classical Heritage, vol. 6 (Berkeley, Los Angeles, and London, 1985). Pachomius succeeded in creating an alternative community, but Gregory's saint seeks reform within the existing structure. Raymond Van Dam, *Leadership and Community in Late Antique Gaul*, Transformation of the Classical Heritage, vol. 8 (Berkeley, Los Angeles, and London, 1985), provides useful comparisons with Gregory's situation: sacred and secular goals are more harmoniously united in the aristocratic Gallic bishop and holy man; see esp. 142f., 204f.

25. Gregory's devotion of a short but entire chapter of the *Dialogues* (2.36) to the fact that Benedict wrote a rule for monks "remarkable for its discretion and in clear language" places Benedict's teaching and his composition of a Rule for the salvation of others on par with the miracles recounted in other chapters; see A. de Vogüé, "The Mention of the Regula Monachorum at the End of the Life of Benedict," *CistSt* 10 (1985): 7.

Therefore we must be subject to him willingly, for all opposing forces are even subject to him unwillingly. By this we will be stronger than our enemies the more we are made one with the Creator of All through humility. What marvel is it then, if certain elect can work many wonders while in the flesh, and often even their dead bones live with many miracles?[26]

Becoming one with God through humility, the saint recaptures the stability in God that Adam lost long ago. Clinging to God in perfect obedience, the saint can work wonders while alive; when he is dead, his relics can perform miracles. His example of obedience teaches his weaker brothers the path they too must follow.

And this obedience works wonders. Even the submission to another holy man can be the source of miracles. The disciple Libertinus returns a boy to life with the application of his master's sandals and a diligent prayer in his name. His humility worked a miracle, Gregory says: "He could display his master's power when he remembered his master's name. For when he returned to humility under his master's name, he could do what his master did."[27] Conversely, when a disciple performs a miracle at Benedict's command, Benedict humbly attributes it to the obedience of his disciple, rather than to himself.[28] *Virtus*, the power to perform miracles, flows only through lines of humility and obedience.[29] Pride and self-sufficiency sever the connection, both with God and with holy men more powerful than oneself.

Gregory's understanding of the holy man is based very much upon the Pauline image of the body as the temple of the Holy Spirit. As a temple of God, a man shares in God's power and so transcends the normal limits of humanity. In an anthropology that occurs also in his description of Christ's incarnation, Gregory envisions the body of the holy man as the external temple of God. The soul of the holy man adheres to God so tightly and is dominated by God so completely that his spirit actually speaks through the human vessel. The saint's powers (*virtutes*) are in ef-

26. *Dial.* 3.21.4 (SC 260, 354).
27. *Dial.* 1.2.7 (SC 260, 30).
28. *Dial.* 2.7.3 (SC 260, 158).
29. In discussing Gregory's *Dialogues* and Benedict's *Rule*, Catry makes an interesting point: Gregory argues that if one desires to receive the spirit, one must cultivate humility, but the Rule scarcely speaks of the spirit, saying rather, seek humility, and the spirit will do the rest—a more passive position. See Catry, "L'Humilité, signe de la présence de l'Esprit: Benoît et Grégoire," *CollCist* 42 (1980): 301–14. See also Antoine Vergote, "Une approche psychologique de l'humilité dans le Règle de saint Benôit," *CollCist* 42 (1980): 112–35, which explores the mystical meaning of humility to appease God's judgment: to humble oneself is to gain the peace of a child at the breast of its mother—which Vergote considers a universal symbol for desire of God.

fect divine strengths contrasting with the weakness (*infirmitas*) of the sinner. In *Dialogues* 1.9.9, Gregory describes the reverence due these awesome holy men because of their great intimacy with God:

> Peter, we must consider how much fear should be shown holy men, for they are temples of God. And when the holy man is provoked to anger, who else is aroused to anger than he who dwells in his temple? Therefore the wrath of the just must be feared the more it is evident that he is present in their hearts who has the power to inflict whatever vengeance he wishes.[30]

Any challenge to the holy man's authority risks invoking the wrath of God himself, for the holy man allows us to know the will of God in this life. Since we cannot "see God," we must "see him in his servants."[31]

What is it about the saint that lends him this preeminence in authority and charity? To begin with, he is detached and unmoved by the temptations that torment other men. Like the Stoic sage, he looks at the world with the assurance and mastery born of a serene tranquillity and equanimity. In *Dialogues* 2.35.3, Gregory describes Benedict's vision of "being above it all," of being lifted far above the world by an "inner light" so that he gains a true perspective of the world: "the whole world, collected, as it were, in a single ray of light, was brought up before his eyes."[32] Contemplation enlarges and expands the mind in God until it "stands man above himself," and "above the world." As the mind's inner powers unfold, everything in the world seems very small and manageable: "Absorbed as he [is] in God, he can see all that lay beneath God without dif-

---

30. *Dial.* 1.9.9 (SC 260, 84): "Qua in re, Petre, pensandum est, quantus sit sanctis uiris timor exhibendus; templa enim Dei sunt. Et cum ad iracundiam sanctus uir trahitur, quis alius ad irascendum nisi eius templi inhabitator excitatur? Tanto ergo metuenda est ira iustorum, quanto et constat quia in eorum cordibus ille praesens est, qui ad inferendam ultionem quam uoluerit inualidus non est."

31. *HEv.* 2.30.10 (PL 76, 1226).

32. *Dial.* 2.35.2f. (SC 260, 236–38): "omnis etiam mundus, uelut sub uno solis radio collectus, ante oculos eius adductus est." On the sources for Benedict's vision: O. Casel, "Zur Vision des heiligen Benedikts" in *Studien und Mitteilungen zur Geschichte des Benediktiner-Ordens* 38 (1917): 345–48, argues that the vision is influenced by Hellenistic treatises on stars and apotheosis; A. Schaut, "Die Vision des heiligen Benedikts," in *Vir Dei Benedictus* (Munster, 1947), argues the vision is that of Gregory himself; T. Delforge, "Songe de Scipion et vision de saint Benoît," *RBen* 69 (1959): 351–55, examines the parallels in Benedict's and Scipio's vision; and Pierre Courcelle, "La Vision cosmique de saint Benoît," *REAug* 13 (1967): 97–117, demonstrates that Macrobius's commentary on the Dream of Scipio is the source of Benedict's vision. The narrowness of the soul, the vision of the world as a little sphere seen from above are themes in Neoplatonic tradition, as well as the Stoic tradition of Chrysippus and Cicero. See also Vincenzo Recchia, "La visione di s. Benedetto e la 'compositio' del secundo libro dei *Dialoghi* di Gregorio Magno," *RBen* 82 (1972): 140–55, and Pierre Hadot, *Exercices spirituels et philosophie antique* (Paris, 1981), 29ff.: for Stoics, detachment is carried ideally to the point of indifference, or *apatheia*.

ficulty." Seeing the world from God's point of view, Benedict apprehends earthly life as it truly is, quite insignificant relative to God's greatness. Always guided from within, Benedict, like other holy men, does not succumb to the blandishments and anxieties of the external world.

Sharing the strength of God's spirit, the saint prevails against the troublesome mutability of the flesh because he possesses those upright virtues ascribed to man before the Fall: *integritas, impassibilitas, immortalitas*. Abbot Equitius dreams of being made a eunuch and awakens with his body a "stranger to temptation, as if he had no sexuality in his body."[33] Some have sacrificed themselves on the altar of the heart, and they have become true martyrs in self-denial.[34] Bishop Andrew is safe within the citadel of continence (*arx continentiae*), and King Hermangild stands secure on the summit of the mind (*in magno mentis culmine stabat securus*) despite physical torture.[35] Sometimes the saint's body is invulnerable to harm. Servants of God can drink poison unaffected; fire parts before them, rather than devours them.[36] After death the saint's body need not decay nor putrefy; instead, wounds of torture are healed,[37] and bodies smell sweet.[38]

This conquest of the flesh enables a participation in God unobstructed by interference from the body. Unencumbered by the confusion of the world and liberated from bodily weakness, holy men obtain direct access to the truth, as Adam once did. Saints can even know God's thoughts "insofar as they are one with him."[39] Such knowledge explains diverse mysteries of life hidden in the realm of the spirit, and the holy man's possession of this knowledge greatly increases his authority and power over others. The saint can prophesy the future and foretell the collapse of a kingdom so that a malevolent king might moderate his ways.[40] He can foretell one's demise,[41] and so spare a sinner the terror of sudden death. This respite allows a sinner to repent and prepare properly for the true life. But the saint can also force the wicked to savor God's vengeance all the more slowly, beginning their punishment here on earth.

---

33. *Dial.* 1.4.1 (SC 260, 38).

34. *Dial.* 3.26.9 (SC 260, 372). See A. C. Rush, "Spiritual Martyrdom in St. Gregory the Great," *ThS* 23 (1962): 569–89.

35. *Dial.* 3.7.1F (SC 260, 278ff.); 3.31.3 (SC 260, 386).

36. *Dial.* 2.3.4 (SC 260, 142); *Dial.* 3.5.1ff. (SC 260, 272ff.); *Dial.* 1.6.1f. (SC 260, 64).

37. *Dial.* 3.13.1f. (SC 260, 300–302).

38. *Dial.* 4.15.5 (SC 265, 62); *Dial.* 4.28.3f. (SC 265, 96f.).

39. *Dial.* 2.16.3 (SC 260, 186). Gregory cites 1 Cor 6:17 rhetorically: "Qui adhaeret Domino, unus spiritus est?"

40. *Dial.* 2.15.1ff. (SC 260, 182–84).

41. *Dial.* 4.27.3ff. (SC 265, 88ff.).

Being one with God, the holy man possesses impressive *discretio*, that powerful tool for healing souls. Discerning the true quality of souls hidden beneath the heavy blanket of the flesh, the servant of God can strip away the visible carnal covering that so often deludes lesser human beings. He can recognize the devil despite his clever disguises, and he can unveil hypocrites who masquerade as the elect.[42] He can read secret thoughts, as Benedict read the silent grumblings of murmurers.[43] Because he can read souls so clearly, the servant of God is an excellent spiritual physician. He can diagnose the troubling secret sin expressed in bizarre behavior and differentiate between the various causes of illness. He can advise each soul according to need—principles Gregory illustrates in his *Pastoral Rule* and in his severe chastisement of the dying monk Justus.[44] Above all, the man of God employs his discretion so that everyone under his charge maintains discipline and virtue.

The vision of the servant of God not only penetrates the secrets of souls present to him but also discerns objects and events across time and space. Remote vision allows him to see infractions of discipline at great distances. The saint can perceive if food or wine is taken in violation of the rule, even if the offenders are traveling in distant lands.[45] He can also communicate with others directly across time and space by appearing in visions and dreams. The monks know how Benedict wishes them to build a chapel because he has sent his orders in a dream.[46] Like God, who is everywhere present in his entirety, the servant of God can also seem omnipresent and inescapable. Subjects must always expect to be outmaneuvered; their best course of action is to learn humility and obedience. No secrets can be hidden from the servant of God, and this should warn Christians who think they can evade his searching eye.

Although the holy man's primary concern is the spiritual well-being of others, he also has compassion for their physical needs, for he is the instrument of God's compassion in the world and the suffering of others cannot be ignored. The saint's power extends over physical circumstances, making life safer and easier for others. Nature obeys the holy man as God's representative and displays a certain sympathy with him. The natural world can mourn the death of God's servant and obey his word, so that it seems to be animate, even though inanimate.[47] Streams change

---

42. *Dial.* 2.30.1ff. (SC 260, 220ff.); *Dial.* 3.14.1f. (SC 260, 302f.).
43. *Dial.* 2.19.2f. (SC 260, 196f.).
44. *Dial.* 4.57.9–11 (SC 265, 188–90).
45. *Dial.* 2.16.1–2 (SC 260, 184–86); *Dial.* 2.12.2 (SC 260, 176).
46. *Dial.* 2.22.2f. (SC 260, 202f.).
47. E.g., *Dial.* 2.37.1ff. (SC 260, 243).

their channels, a plague of caterpillars turns and marches out of the garden at the holy man's command.[48] To be sure, demons often use the natural world in their schemes to complicate man's life, and they are often
behind the natural obstacles man faces. But with God's power, the saint
can expose the demons' schemes. When demons are recognized, the
saint wins a minor battle with the forces of disorder, and once-immovable
rocks move with ease.[49]

More impressive, the holy man's power reaches into the next world
to help save others: he has power over the souls of the dead.[50] He is often
called upon to change the status of those already dead, to return souls to
life or lay them to rest, by correcting irregularities that obstruct eternal
happiness. Gregory tells of a young monk, too close to his parents, who
leaves the monastery without permission and dies on arriving home. His
body will not stay buried but is hurled up every night, until Benedict forgives the monk his sin and orders him reburied with the Host.[51] In a parallel example, the ghosts of two nuns lurk about a nunnery until Benedict
sends an oblation to be offered during the holy sacrifice of the Mass.[52]

The servants of God may even have the power of returning the dead
to life, like Benedict who raises a boy after assiduous prayer.[53] Implicitly,
all resurrections offer a second chance, for the soul is returned to a state
in which redemption is again possible. Sometimes Gregory explicitly
notes this second chance. When Bishop Fortunatus raises Marcellus from
the dead, he is able to live more virtuously, thanks to the prayers of his
patron.[54] The tears of the priest Severus redeem a sinner from a region of
darkness and fire. But his tears of intercession do not stop there, for he
offers to help the sinner do penance for his sins.[55] Working in the liminal
region between life and death, the men of God direct souls one way or
the other as circumstances warrant, though they are obviously happiest
when guiding souls to the region of light.

The acts of holy men have a symbolic importance to the Christian
community; they are certain, if fragile, dikes set against floods of demonic disorder, reassuring man of God's mercy in checking the fury of
evil forces.[56] The saints' power over demons is an index of the progress

48. *Dial.* 3.9.2–10.1.3 (SC 260, 288–290); *Dial.* 1.9.15 (SC 260, 88).
49. *Dial.* 2.9.1 (SC 260, 170).
50. *Dial.* 2.23.1ff. (SC 260, 204ff.).
51. *Dial.* 2.24.1 (SC 260, 210–12); see also *Dial.* 2.23.1f.(SC 260, 204–10).
52. *Dial.* 2.23.5 (SC 260, 208).
53. *Dial.* 2.32.1ff. (SC 260, 226ff.).
54. *Dial.* 1.10.18 (SC 260, 110).
55. *Dial.* 1.12.2–3 (SC 260, 114).
56. Cf. *Dial.* 3.28.5 (SC 260, 376).

of good against evil; as the devil flees in terror before the virtues of holy souls,[57] for a brief moment at least, order and harmony return. The power to heal those afflicted with physical or mental illnesses exemplifies the holy man's power to set right the chaos inflicted by demons.[58] Because of their extraordinary discernment, holy men can recognize, name, and exorcize demons, purging God's people of diabolical pollution. Curses are similarly effective. A curse from the man of God can make a brutal Goth narrow the path of his destruction.[59] The saint's charisma, his commanding holiness, can make him invulnerable to the murderous intentions of barbarians. Sanctulus goes free when his executioner is paralyzed for daring to raise his arm "against God." He is released from paralysis only after Sanctulus has exacted a promise from him not to kill Christians.[60] In addition to reining in devils and barbarians, the holy man can restrain heretics and common criminals. Heretics may cut out the tongues of Catholic bishops, but the bishops continue to speak the truth, as before.[61] A thief who attempts to steal a sheep is caught in the very act; as he walks over the grave of a saint, his feet seem to take root and he is paralyzed.[62]

Using his divine powers, the holy man secures order in the Church and community, and he looks to the stability and harmony of monastic life as the model for all Christian experience. Consequently, Gregory shows special concern for reinforcing the patterns of monastic experience. When the holy man's vengeance is aroused against the disobedience of monastic life, his vengeance usually allows amendment. Or should a brother die suddenly in sin, his misfortune becomes a lesson inspiring others to obedience and repentance. The young monk who disobeys his holy master is likely to have his punishment meted out with miracles, like Benedict's cellarer. When the niggardly cellarer refuses to distribute oil in a famine, Benedict commands him to throw the oil jar out the window; the jar does not break, and the astounded cellarer is chastened and contrite.[63] When Gregory lets the sinful monk Justus die a lonely death, unreconciled to his brothers and unsanctified by burial in holy ground, the motives of his vengeance are laudatory: he wishes to purify the monk's soul by such a painful death.[64] While saints vent their

57. *Dial.* 3.20.3 (SC 260, 350).

58. Cf. Sofia Boesch Gajano, "Demoni et miracoli nei *Dialogi* di Gregorio Magno," in *Hagiographie, cultures et sociétés iv–xii siècles* (Paris, 1981), 271f.

59. *Dial.* 1.10.15 (SC 260, 106); *Dial.* 3.26.2 (SC 260, 366).

60. *Dial.* 3.37.10–19 (SC 260, 418–24).

61. *Dial.* 3.32.1–4 (SC 260, 390–92).

62. *Dial.* 3.22.1–4 (SC 260, 356–58).

63. *Dial.* 2.28.1–2 (SC 260, 216–18).

64. *Dial.* 4.57.11 (SC 265, 190).

anger freely against the devil, with men they seek to reform and save souls through a righteous zeal that inspires discipline and obedience. Holy men work tirelessly to achieve discipline and hierarchical order in the monastery and the Church, for only such concord offers the genuine stability found in Christ's body and reproduces the greater harmony of the cosmos.

To teach others proper discipline, the holy man exerts himself to perform miracles that protect souls from harm or nurture their advancement. Nonnosus supplies his monastery with oil through prayer, lest the monks be corrupted by working in the outside world.[65] When Benedict prays over an empty oil cask until it overflows, it is to shame the niggardly cellarer for his disobedience and lack of faith.[66] The saint bestows miracles freely upon others to strengthen their discipline and lackluster faith. Anxious to promote the salvation of others, the servant of God not only prays for others in compassion but even suffers for the sins of others, as Gregory felt he himself did.[67] If need be, the servant of God will risk his life to bring about order and harmony. Benedict keeps the path of discipline straight, turning neither to the right nor to the left, even though his personal safety is hostage to malevolent forces.[68] Moses, an earlier man of God, offered his life as a sacrifice for the sins of his people (cf. Ex 32:7) and yet released the scourge of his discipline to chastise and so save his people.[69]

The holy man points the way to the next world, even as Christ showed the way to the Father. To know the mind of God makes the holy man a peerless source of information about the other world and how to get there. Benedict's discussion of the other world with deacon Servandus allows him a foretaste of the heavenly food they cannot yet fully enjoy.[70] The final book of the *Dialogues* is a compendium of the answers holy men have given about the world beyond: what heaven and hell are like, why relics have power, whether souls enter heaven immediately or only after the Last Judgment. Detailed practical questions are raised and answered: how one can be purified to enter heaven, whether prayers release one from hell, if burial in sanctified ground helps one who dies in sin. In *Dialogues* 4.57.1, Peter poses the fundamental question, the core of the entire work: "Can there be anything which is able to benefit the

---

65. *Dial.* 1.7.5–6 (SC 260, 68–70).
66. *Dial.* 2.28.1–29.2 (SC 260, 218–20).
67. Cf. *Ep.* 7.30 (CCL 140, 490); *Ep.* 5.46 (CCL 140, 340); *Ep.* 5.39 (CCL 140, 316).
68. *Dial.* 2.3.3–5 (SC 260, 140–42).
69. *Mor.* 20.5.14 (CCL 143A, 1012–13).
70. *Dial.* 2.35.1 (SC 260, 236).

souls of the dead?" Gregory answers yes: the sacrifice of the Mass. In the end, holy men point back to the Church, specifically to the sacrifice of the Mass, as the most potent aid to salvation. The Mass is the true miracle performed every day, the concrete evidence of Christ's charity for man and the very vehicle of man's unification with Christ's body.

For all his powers, Gregory's holy man remains human, emphatically so. Benedict always "lives with himself" (*habitare secum*);[71] that is, he preserves self-collection by keeping a close watch on all his thoughts and deeds, always imagining himself trembling before his Judge. This form of self-judgment, which appears in Gregory's other works, especially the *Moralia* and *Homilies on the Gospel*, instills humility by forcing man to recall his sinfulness and humanity before the Divine Judge. When Gregory speaks of the saints' gift of prophecy, he speaks as well of the withdrawal of prophecy to safeguard the humility of God's servants: when the spirit leaves them, they "discover what they are on their own."[72] The servants of God may know God's thoughts insofar as they are one with him. But as they are not completely unified with God, his thoughts remain to some extent obscure.[73] Holiness depends on the intensity of one's participation in God; and God may occasionally withdraw his grace to keep the holy man humble.

Gregory's saints are not without their moments of spiritual embarrassment. Some congratulate themselves too precipitously for conquering demons.[74] Bishop Andrew might fancy himself secure in the citadel of continence, yet he is still seduced by a demon to give his housekeeper an affectionate pat on the back. He confesses and mends his ways.[75] Saintly Isaac, so perfect in abstinence, contempt of the world, prophecy and prayer, nevertheless is blameworthy for being lighthearted and silly.[76] Even the prophet Elijah had to use a chariot in ascending to heaven, showing that "even holy men have need of others."[77] Unlike Ambrose, who develops an elaborate allegory to explain David's outrageous behavior in the Old Testament, Gregory freely admits the sins David committed from lust for Bathsheba.[78] Gregory's servant of God is one with him, clinging to God to be elevated. But his saint is like Paul, who

---

71. Pierre Courcelle, "*Habitare secum* selon Perse et selon Grégoire le Grand," *REA* 69 (1967): 266–79, examines the long tradition of this idea.

72. *Dial.* 2.21.4 (SC 260, 200): "cognoscant quid sint de semetipsis."

73. *Dial.* 2.16.3–4 (SC 260, 186–88).

74. *Dial.* 3.33.3–5 (SC 260, 394–96).

75. *Dial.* 3.7.1–10 (SC 260, 278–84).

76. *Dial.* 3.14.10–11 (SC 260, 310–12).

77. *HEv.* 2.29.5 (PL 76, 1216).

78. *HEv.* 2.34.16 (PL 76, 1256); cf. Ambr. *apol. Dav.* esp. 12.9–19.

descended from the third heaven to consider the needs of the flesh and give advice to his weaker brothers about marriage.[79] Even Gregory's saints have their imperfections, despite their holiness. This perfection in imperfection affects how the saint mediates with God for the salvation of his fellow man. All men share human weakness; yet because man is weak, God can be strong in him (cf. Heb 5:2).

Throughout the *Dialogues* Gregory often considers the line between human and divine power in the saint. What can a saint do through his own virtue; what with additional prayer?[80] Do saints always obtain what they desire? Can prayer be of help for predestination? Gregory keeps a careful balance between human merits and divine intervention. Sometimes saints achieve wonders on their own merit and by their own will. The sheer speed at which Benedict frees a prisoner from bonds shows he worked the miracle with his own power.[81] At other times miracles are the result of prayer. Benedict prays before bringing a boy back to life, and Gregory remarks, "It is clear, Peter, that this miracle was not in his power, since he prostrated himself in prayer in order to be able to do it."[82] The saint's own power has limits, and there are also limits to what he can achieve through prayer. Saints do not always obtain what they desire. Because of her greater love, Scholastica's prayer is heard in preference to that of her brother, the holy Benedict.[83] The saint's prayer cannot contravene predestination; predestination is instead fulfilled through the saint's prayer.[84]

In short, Gregory recognizes the limits imposed on the saint. Prayer extends his efficacy, but there are limits to prayer as well. As noted earlier, the Mass is the vehicle through which the saint's intercession becomes most effective. Benedict has a wayward boy buried with the Host, and has the Mass offered for sinful nuns that their bodies might rest in peace. When Agapitus is asked to cure a dumb invalid, he does so by celebrating the Mass and placing the Host on the invalid's tongue.[85] Gregory praises the sacrifice of the Mass for the great benefits it brings to the soul even after death, and tells of the Masses he ordered to be offered for the sinful

79. *Dial.* 3.17.9 (SC 260, 342).

80. *Dial.* 2.30.2 (SC 260, 220–22).

81. *Dial.* 2.31.4 (SC 260, 226): "ipsa miraculi celeritate indicat quia ex potestate acceperat habere quod fecit." By *merit*, Gregory means gifts given to man that then are credited as his own.

82. *Dial.* 2.32.4 (SC 260, 228): "Liquet, Petre, quia hoc miraculum in potestate non habuit, quod prostratus petiit ut exhibere potuisset."

83. *Dial.* 2.33.4 (SC 260, 232–34).

84. *Dial.* 1.8.5 (SC 260, 74).

85. *Dial.* 3.3.1–2 (SC 260, 268–70).

monk, Justus, to liberate his soul from punishment.[86] Of course, Masses also help the living. While at Mass, Bishop Cassius sees visions of the future. A wife frees her imprisoned husband from chains on the day she has the Mass offered for him. Through the Mass, Bishop Agatho saves his ship and crew from a storm.[87]

In particular, the Eucharist mediates between human and divine realms, joining both halves of reality:

> For who of the faithful doubt that at the very moment of the sacrifice, at the voice of the priest, the heavens open and choirs of angels are present at the mystery of Jesus Christ: the highest is united with the lowest, heaven is joined to earth, and a oneness is made from invisible and visible.[88]

The Eucharist is the most important and the most potent form of mediation for it symbolizes a healing of all the divisions caused by the Fall: high and low, invisible and visible, interior and exterior, God and man. The Eucharist becomes the pivotal point of cosmic rest. The daily sacrifice of the Mass recapitulates Christ's sacrifice and reconciliation of the cosmos and offers man the opportunity of sharing concord and harmony through union with Christ's body. It fixes man and the sacrifice he offers firmly at the cosmic center.

According to Gregory's sacramental theology, only the holy sacrifice of Christ benefits souls after death,[89] for it alone saves us from eternal death.[90] This focus on the Mass redefines the role of the holy man and even the sense or degree of sanctity people need to possess. Because the Eucharist is so highly effective, personal sanctity becomes relative rather than absolute, a mixture of perfection and imperfection. Access to the holy is more open because every Christian can replicate the sacrifice of the Mass in his own heart and can make an offering of himself with the sacrifice on the altar. Every Christian can participate in the miracle of the Mass and share in the charity and stability of Christ's body, the Church.

All Christians need to have masses offered for their neighbors and must intercede for them with their prayers. In the Mass man's two axes of participation in God and in neighbor meet. Salvation is in a sense com-

---

86. *Dial.* 4.57.8–17 (SC 265, 188–94).

87. *Dial.* 4.58.1–2 (SC 265, 196–98).

88. *Dial.* 4.60.3 (SC 265, 202): "Quis enim fidelium habere dubium possit ipsa immolationis hora ad sacerdotis uocem caelos aperiri, in illo Iesu Christi mysterio angelorum choros adesse, summis ima sociari, terram caelestibus iungi, unum quid ex uisibilibus atque inuisibilibus fieri?"

89. *Dial.* 4.57.12–17 (SC 265, 190–94).

90. *Dial.* 4.60.2 (SC 265, 200): "Haec namque singulariter uictima ab aeterno interitu animam saluat. . . ."

munal, because the prayers and offerings of others are so much a part of one's own salvation. Yet the focus on the Mass also intensifies personal responsibility. As Gregory says, it is a safer course to do for ourselves while living what we hope others will do for us after our death.[91] "[I]f we offered ourselves to God as a victim (*hostia*) before death, we would not need the Saving Victim after death," the *Dialogues* close.[92] In a typically Gregorian balance, the Christian must both offer sacrifices for others and make them on his own behalf. The saint aids the salvation of others, but everyone is bound to strive for the holiness he can enjoy in stability and unity with God.

Gregory's men of God are guides to the spiritual world, servants laboring to save souls by teaching others the obedience necessary to secure participation in God. Their own union with God exemplifies the stability Adam once possessed in Eden. In this, the saint closely approaches the ideal of being spiritual in the flesh. As such, the holy man has reversed fallen man's condition of being carnal in the mind. That pitiful condition is our next topic of consideration.

91. *Dial.* 4.60.1 (SC 265, 200).
92. *Dial.* 4.62.3 (SC 265, 206): "et fidenter dico quia salutari hostia post mortem non indigebimus, si ante mortem Deo hostia ipsi fuerimus."

· V ·

LUBRICA MUTABILITAS

"And like a flower, he springs forth and is cut down; he flees like a shadow, and never remains in the same state" (Jb 14:2).[1] Human life is fragile and precarious, beset by a troubling instability. The flesh blooms and decays; life is fleeting and chilled by the shade of sin. Battered to and fro, man is subject to alien forces. Demons buffet him with alternating temptations, like the cloud blown by the winds of an unclean spirit in Job 36:28. "[H]ither and thither he pushes them and calls them back, as often as his temptations in their hearts alternate with the breezes of suggestions."[2] Baffled by the frailty of his own body and mind, man cannot silence even the merest whisper of temptation. Like a stream running downhill, life flows only toward death, weighed heavily with sin.[3]

Weakened by his fallen condition, man is invariably slack, careless, and misdirected. Sin is a kind of sickness in which everything is inverted and imbalanced. Instead of enjoying stability and constancy, a life of temperance balanced to preserve a just mean, the sinner finds himself overwhelmed by his own mutability. Constantly changing, he often plunges into uncontrollable extremes. His virtues easily exceed moderation and become vicious perversions: authority becomes arrogant zeal; humility, spineless fear.[4] Even the very "remedies" he applies to restore the balance

---

1. *Mor.* 11.50.67 (CCL 143A, 624). Leonhard Weber sees transitoriness as the pathos of the human condition, *Hauptfragen der Moraltheologie Gregors der Grossen* (Freiburg in der Schweiz, 1947), 122–23; for Claude Dagens, it is "externality," *Saint Grégoire le Grand* (Paris, 1977), 165ff.

2. *Mor.* 27.9.15 (CCL 143B, 1340). See also *Mor.* 11.44.60 (CCL 143A, 619–20), where man is a leaf blown by alternating temptations (cf. Jb 14:25), and *Mor.* 12.7.10 (CCL 143A, 634–35), where the mind is a sea of waves, rising in anger and resting in grace.

3. *HEz.* 1.2.6 (CCL 142, 20).

4. *Mor.* 8.6.9 (CCL 143, 387).

of his life become vicious "wounds," further blighting his life.[5] The sinner's life alternates in continual excess as he strives to find a balance point: sloth and overwork, fasting and feasting, freezing and roasting, sleepiness and restless vigilance.[6] Bewildered by his own inconstancy, he becomes a mystery to himself. He knows what he is today, but who can predict tomorrow?[7]

To Gregory, life is bittersweet, as water is both fresh and salty.[8] Good is always blemished with evil; life is inevitably disappointing. Being so cursed with ambivalence, life is a trial,[9] a dangerous pilgrimage[10] amid alternations of prosperity and adversity:

> If we consider the journey of this life truthfully, we find nothing firm nor stable in it. But just as the traveler walks at one time through the plains, at another time through rocky terrain, so without fail now prosperity, now adversity befall us in this life; they so alternate they become confused with each other in the end.[11]

Life changes constantly, overwhelming man with confusion and fear. One moment he is blessed with good fortune; the next moment, he suffers misfortune. He wonders whether God is "coming" or "going,"

5. *Mor.* 8.32.53 (CCL 143, 423–24): "Quot enim solatia ad uiuendi usum quaerimus quasi tot nostrae aegritudine medicamentis obuiamus. Sed ipsum quoque medicamen in uulnus uertitur, quia exquisito remedio paulo diutius inhaerentes, ex eo grauius deficimus quod prouide ad refectionem paramus."

6. *Mor.* 8.32.53 (CCL 143, 423). Cf. Ambr. *bono mort.* 3.12; Dionys. Exig. *Gr. Nyss. hom. op.* 14.

7. *Mor.* 25.8.21 (CCL 143B, 1245). Cf. Aug. *epist.* 130.2.4.

8. *Mor.* 12.7.10 (CCL 143A, 634): "Qua in re uigilanter intuendum est quod uita praesens, uidelicet quousque anima moratur in corpore, mari comparatur et fluuio. Aqua enim maris amara est, fluminis dulcis. Et quia hic uiuentes modo quibusdam amaritudinibus afficimur, modo autem dulcedine tranquilli ac mites inuenimur, praesentis uitae decursus comparatione exprimitur maris et fluminis." The principle of alternation is noted but not discussed in detail by Robert Gillet, introduction to Grégoire le Grand, *Morales sur Job I–II* (SC 32, 56) and by Jean Leclercq, *The Spirituality of the Middle Ages*, trans. The Benedictines of Holme Eden Abbey, Carlisle, vol. 2 of Louis Bouyer et al., *A History of Christian Spirituality* (New York, 1961), 11.

9. *Mor.* 8.6.8 (CCL 143, 386): "Ipsa ergo hominis uita temptatio est, cui ex semetipsa nascitur unde perimatur. Quae etsi semper ex uirtute succidit quod ex infirmitate generat, semper tamen ex infirmitate generat quod ex uirtute succidat."

10. For life as a rugged road or a journey to our *patria*, see *Mor.* 23.24.47 (CCL 143B, 1179–80): "Via quippe est uita praesens, qua ad patriam tendimus; et idcirco hic occulto iudicio frequenti perturbatione conterimur, ne uiam pro patria diligamus. . . ." Also, *HEv.* 1.11.1 (PL 76, 1115); *HEv.* 1.1.3 (PL 76, 1079); *Ep.* 9.218 (CCL 140A, 782).

11. *Ep.* 3.51 (CCL 140, 196): "Si uitae istius cursum ueraciter attendamus, nihil in eo firmum, nihil inuenimus stabile. Sed quemadmodum uiator modo per plana, modo per aspera graditur, sic nobis utique in hac uita manentibus nunc prosperitas, nunc occurrit aduersitas, denique alternis sibi succedunt temporibus et mutua se uice confundunt."

whether heaven or hell will be his final fate.[12] Such sorrows of mutability come from Adam's rejection of stability in God. Because man has moved the "foot of his will" from the "stability of his standing," he slides beneath himself into corruption, impelled by the "slippery mutability" of the present life.[13] Such mutability causes disharmony and strife, making man perilously insecure.[14] The "waves of mutability" are too great for him to bear.[15] Pushed by mutability, he falters, as if trying to stand on slimy gravel beneath a rushing river.[16]

Gregory shares Augustine's view of man as a pilgrim and prodigal son;[17] but perhaps more than did Augustine, Gregory sees man as the devil's prisoner, a helpless victim of his own body's weakness before the

12. *Mor.* 9.13.20 (CCL 143, 470–71).

13. *Mor.* 8.10.19 (CCL 143, 395): "Ad hoc namque homo conditus fuerat ut stante mente, in arcem se contemplationis erigeret, et nulla hunc corruptio a conditoris sui amore declinaret. Sed in eo quod ab ingenita standi soliditate uoluntatis pedem ad culpam mouit a dilectione conditoris in semetipsum protinus cecidit. Amorem uero Dei, ueram scilicet stationis arcem deserens, nec in se consistere potuit, quia lubricae mutabilitatis impulsu, infra se per corruptionem proruens, etiam a semetipso dissensit." For the Fall as a loss of stability, see *Mor.* 8.10.19 (CCL 143, 395); *Mor.* 26.44.79 (CCL 143B, 1325–26); *Mor.* 11.43.59 (CCL 143A, 619). F. Homes Dudden notes man's loss of stability in the Fall; see *Gregory the Great* (London, 1905), 2:380–81. Franz Lieblang mentions mutability; see *Grundfragen der mystischen Theologie nach Gregors des Grossen Moralia und Ezechielhomilien* (Freiburg im Breisgau, 1934), 32. See also Weber, *Hauptfragen*, 228.

14. This pattern of flux is called variously "mutabilitas alternantium motionum," *Mor.* 24.11.32 (CCL 143B, 1211); "alternans mutabilitas," *Mor.* 25.6.10 (CCL 143B, 1236); "mobilitas humanae mentis," *Mor.* 27.9.15 (CCL 143B, 1340); "diuersitas animae," *Mor.* 5.34.62 (CCL 143, 262); "motus uarietatis," *Mor.* 8.6.8 (CCL 143, 386); and man is said "alternantis desiderii motu uariari," *Mor.* 8.10.19 (CCL 143, 395–96).

15. *Mor.* 11.50.68 (CCL 143A, 625); also *Mor.* 9.33.50 (CCL 143, 491). Cf. Cassian *inst.* 2.14.

16. *Mor.* 20.14.36 (CCL 143A, 1029): "Glarea namque est uita praesens, quae indesinenter ad terminum suum ipso defectu mutabilitatis, quasi impulsu fluminis ducitur. Super glaream itaque habitare, est fluxui uitae praesentis inhaerere, et ibi intentionem ponere, ubi gressum nequeat fixe stando solidare." Cf. Dionys. Exig. *Gr. Nyss. hom. op.* 14. See also *HEz.* 1.2.6 (CCL 142, 20), and *Mor.* 11.50.68 (CCL 143A, 625): "Fixum etenim statum hic habere non possumus ubi transituri uenimus; atque hoc ipsum nostrum uiuere, cotidie a uita transire est. Quem uidelicet lapsum primus homo ante culpam habere non potuit quia tempora, eo stante, transiebant. Sed postquam deliquit, in quodam se quasi lubrico temporalitatis posuit; et quia cibum comedit uetitum, status sui protinus inuenit defectum."

17. Gregory does follow Augustine's view of the Fall in *civ.* 12–14; the influence of other works is more subtle. He borrows the distinction between *utor* and *fruor* (cf. *conf.* 2.5.10–11; 3.8.16; *doctr. christ.* 1.22.20ff.), and the Plotinian theme of the soul's fall from unity in God to a dispersion or "scattering" of itself on the many objects of the world (cf. *conf.* 2.1.1ff.; 2.20.18; 4.7.12; 7.10.16; 10.29.40). Augustine's view of the Fall is important for understanding Gregory; see esp. Peter Brown, *Augustine and Sexuality*, Center for Hermeneutical Studies, protocol 46 (Berkeley, 1983), and Margaret R. Miles, *Augustine on the Body* (Missoula, Mont., 1979); for the legacy of Neoplatonism to the Christian tradition's view of man, see A. H. Armstrong, "Neoplatonic Valuations of Nature, Body and Intellect," *AugStud* 3 (1972): 35–41.

fatal temptation of pleasure. For Gregory shares in a long tradition that viewed the control of pleasure as the basis of man's moral identity.[18] Like many before him, Gregory sees the "appetite for pleasure" as the central curse of mutability.[19] The compelling pull of the unconscious mind for gratification of its desires can easily come to dominate the human personality and destroy man's self-discipline. Consequently, Gregory's anthropology is never far removed from the problem of pleasure and its signal expression in sexuality. Man's internal equilibrium has been disrupted by the Fall; his very constitution has changed. Body and soul are now at war with one another. "The pleasure of the flesh weakens the soul,"[20] Gregory writes, and so, too, "the strength of the spirit weakens the body."[21] The friendship of body and soul is compromised when the appetite for pleasure runs riot and tyrannizes man's reason.

Gregory is keenly aware of how the appetite for pleasure can pervert man's life. Bewitched by pleasure, man becomes bound to the external world and to its transient delights, which tease the senses. Feeling only the burning urgency of the moment, he can no longer postpone the gratification of his desires. Blind to the future, he neglects planning or discipline and so loses control of his life and his heavenly course. As the volatile hungers of the body usurp the powers of the soul for their own wicked designs, the sinner loses all self-control. Without self-restraint, his life degenerates into a restless odyssey driven by the base passions of his animal nature: the lusts for sex, food, money, power, and praise. The addiction to pleasure also causes the sinner to lose his proper sense of place. Selfishly, he fancies himself—not God—as the center of his world.

18. Michel Foucault's *Histoire de la sexualité*, 3 vols. (Paris, 1984), treats this problem through the third century A.D. Foucault distinguishes between classical Greek philosophy, which held an ideal of temperance (σωφροσύνη) permitting the moderate and controlled exercise of passions as a sign of the mastery of self, which defined good citizenship, and late-antique and Christian philosophy, which viewed passions as threatening and moved to prohibit them, eventually defining morality as self-renunciation. Gregory seems to do both. Temperance and the balanced soul are extremely important, yet virtue is also self-renunciation. See also Pierre Hadot, *Exercices spirituels et philosophie antique* (Paris, 1981); Jackie Pigeaud, *La Maladie de l'âme* (Paris, 1981), esp. 243–371; and Helen North, *Sophrosyne* (Ithaca, 1966), esp. 312–86.

19. Selective examples of this frequent theme include Ambr. *Isaac*, 1.12; 6.52; 7.61; *bon. mort.* 3.10; *hex.* 8.31; Aug. *conf.* 4.16.30; 10.31.43; Cassian *conl.* 10.6; 12 (entire). See also Herbert Musurillo, "The Problem of Ascetical Fasting in the Greek Patristic Writers," *Traditio* 12 (1956): esp. 42ff.; Anthony Meredith, "Asceticism—Christian and Greek," *JThS*, n.s. 27 (1976): 313–32; P. Resch, *La doctrine ascétique des premiers maîtres égyptiens du quatrième siècle* (Paris, 1931), 91–133. For the classical roots of the Christian antipathy to pleasure, see J.C.B. Gosling and C.C.W. Taylor, *The Greeks on Pleasure* (Oxford, 1982), esp. 429ff.; and Foucault, *Histoire de la sexualité*, vol. 3, *Souci de soi*, esp. 72ff.

20. *Mor.* 4.27.49 (CCL 143, 193).

21. *Dial.* 3.24.3 (SC 260, 362–64). Cf. *Vitae patr.* 5.10.17.

Whereas Benedict's vision, with God as his center, lifted him far above the world and its blandishments, the sinner, seeing only himself, forgets God and ignores others. Still worse, even as he arrogates God's position, he may seek power over his peers. Because of pleasure seeking, the sinner becomes separated from his true identity as a rational social creature. The harmonious equilibrium of body and soul having been destroyed, the greater concord of social relations also vanishes; for in losing reason and self-control, man loses charity as well. Bound to the body and his own needs, the sinner becomes incapable of understanding a truly spiritual way of life with others.

In Gregory's view, true social order must begin with control of the body by each individual. Through asceticism, the sinner can recover the right perspective on life, learning the proper balance of body and soul and recognizing his proper relationship with God and neighbor. While much of the world seems out of control, caught in the whirlwind of the devil's disasters, the Christian can meet and defeat the enemy in the mastery of his own body and in the conquest of pleasure. This struggle for self-control is a symbolic condensation of a larger effort to structure and resolve greater tensions, which run like a fault line through the universe: the oppositions of high and low, light and dark, inner and outer, male and female. The dangerous carnal side of life can be neutralized, at least in part, and reintegrated when regulated strictly and subject to reason. Even further, carnal life can be purified when pain replaces pleasure, though not everyone can attain this level of sacrifice.

Gregory writes about sin from his experience as a monk and an ascetic, deeply influenced by Cassian and the tradition of desert monasticism. While Augustine's writings are never far from his mind, Gregory always reads them alongside Cassian and Ambrose.[22] Gregory places a heavier burden on the body than Augustine did, and Gregory's view of life in the world is generally bleaker. Unlike Augustine, for whom sensation was an aspect especially of the soul,[23] Gregory associates sensation primarily with the body, and the body becomes the vector of the external world. Leaving behind Augustine's preoccupation with the inner divisions of man's will, Gregory tends to see sin arising from a conflict of

---

22. On the distinction between the theology of sin in Ambrose and Augustine, see Andrew Lenox-Conyngham, "Sin in St. Ambrose," *Studia Patristica* (to appear). Ambrose speaks of the inclination to sin inherited from Adam as *lubricum deliquendi*, which man always bears with him. However, the guilt of original sin (*culpa, reatus*) is removed by baptism. Gregory follows the sharp tension of body and soul found in Ambrose and in Cassian. For Cassian, see Owen Chadwick, *John Cassian*, 2d ed. (Cambridge, 1968), 94–95; also R. Gillet, introduction to *Morales sur Job I–II* (SC 32, 89–102).

23. Miles, *Augustine on the Body*, 9–39.

body and soul, and his interpretation of sin exalts monastic life and justifies asceticism. Unless man submits himself to the rigorous discipline
of monastic life, his appetite for pleasure may well run out of control.
Obedience to monastic rule and submission to a superior are always the
implicit ideal of personal reform. Although Gregory can integrate and accommodate varying degrees of secular involvement *pro bono ecclesiae*, the
monastic life is preferable *pro bono sui*. In Gregory's mind, the important
distinction always lies between the purity of a monastic life and the pollution of a secular vocation. The Christian is safest and most prudent
dedicating himself to the eradication of pleasure, to a return to the promise offered Adam of becoming "spiritual in the flesh."[24]

In contrast, worldly life shades imperceptibly into unlawful behavior.
Secular life is provocative and hazardous. Few can preserve moderation
and temperate use of the world, discharging only necessities, because the
Fall has predisposed man to be "carnal in the mind."[25] Secular life accepts
involvement in the world, opening the door to carnal delights. Once
opened, this heavy door is all but impossible to close. Caught up in family ties and political squabbles, secular people luxuriate in the pleasure
and power of worldly vocations and so commit great evils against others.
A good count like Theophanius is very rare.[26] More typical is the duke
Theodore, whose oppressive rule in Sardinia provoked Gregory's caustic
criticism.[27] Just struggling to get by in the world exposes the soul to un-
avoidable dangers; few are disciplined enough to weather its trials.

Man's Fall is the reason that worldly life has become so dangerous
and deeply flawed, the reason that pleasure seems so unmanageable and
monastic discipline so desirable. While Augustine saw pride and self-
love as the primary sin, with sensuality as a secondary result, Gregory
views pride, self-love, and pleasure as closely related. Man rejects God
in order to pursue the selfish pleasures of the body found in the external
world.[28] Thus the desire for pleasure and a craving for autonomy are inseparable.[29] Following "love of self" instead of "love of God,"[30] man
wanted to be on his own that he might pursue his desires "unhindered

24. *Mor.* 5.34.61 (CCL 143, 261). See also Aug., *civ.* 14.15.
25. *Mor.* 5.34.61 (CCL 143, 261). Cf. Aug. *civ.* 14.15.
26. *Dial.* 4.28.1f. (SC 265, 96–98); *HEv.* 2.36.13 (PL 76, 1273–74).
27. Cf. *Ep.* 1.46–47 (CCL 140, 60–61); *Ep.* 1.59 (CCL 140, 70–71).
28. *Mor.* 34.21.40 (CCL 143B, 1761–62); see also *Mor.* 29.8.18 (CCL 143B, 1446); *Mor.*
8.10.19 (CCL 143, 395); *Mor.* 26.44.79 (CCL 143B, 1325–26).
29. In this Gregory seems to pass over the distinctions made by Augustine, for whom
the desire to be separate from God clearly preceded the appetite for pleasure; cf. *civ.* 14.13ff.
30. *Mor.* 34.21.40 (CCL 143B, 1761–62); see also *Mor.* 29.8.18 (CCL 143B, 1446); *Mor.*
8.10.19 (CCL 143, 395); *Mor.* 26.44.79 (CCL 143B, 1325–26).

by consideration of God."[31] Believing he could find satisfaction in himself (*sufficere ad se*),[32] he wanted the power and authority to arrange his life solely to gratify his own desires. But to seek this kind of power and control is to imitate God, who alone has the right to "arrange the order of the world" and "command obedience from others."[33] Like the devil, a man who rejects his proper role of obedience and participation in God[34] violates the hierarchical order of the universe that is divine law. Since the sinner "lives for himself," "feed[ing] upon pleasures of the flesh," he is rightly reproached for his "idleness" and failure to serve God as he ought.[35]

To his own misfortune, man has lost the true satisfaction found in stability with God. In turning from contemplation of God, man lost his spiritual perception. He could no longer "see [God's] face" and talk with him directly; he lost the intimacy of the "festival of [God's] love."[36] Now carnal perception overwhelms the delicate spiritual senses, so that man suffers a dreadful moral blindness without access to the truth and light of God. Adam "lost his eyes,"[37] falling into a "night of error" and the "darkness of sin."[38] Reason is blinded and this allows the pleasures of the body to prevail. In Gregory's opinion, "[man] is never seized by the pleasures of sin unless he is first weakened through voluntary darkness of

31. *Mor.* 34.21.40 (CCL 143B, 1761–62); see also *Mor.* 29.8.18 (CCL 143B, 1446); *Mor.* 8.10.19 (CCL 143, 395); *Mor.* 26.44.79 (CCL 143B, 1325–26).

32. *Mor.* 34.21.40 (CCL 143B, 1761–62); see also *Mor.* 29.8.18 (CCL 143B, 1446).

33. *Mor.* 29.8.18 (CCL 143B, 1446). Cf. Cass. *conl.* 13.12. See also Norman P. Williams's discussion of this common tradition, *Ideas of the Fall and Original Sin* (London, 1938), 360ff.

34. While Gregory probably takes his views of man's sinfulness as an inversion of right order from Augustine, the parallel with Eastern thought should also be noted, especially with Dionysius the Areopagite, see Ronald F. Hathaway, *Hierarchy and the Definition of Order in the Letters of Pseudo-Dionysius* (The Hague, 1969), 45, citing Dionysius's notion of justice from *d.n.* 8.7 (896f.), and arguing it is epitomized by the definition of Proclus *In R.* 2.146.21–23: "It is evident then that the form of justice is each of the souls doing its own things (αὐτοπραγία), as well as order in each soul, but that the form of injustice is doing the things of others and disorder." Dionysius's definition of hierarchical order and justice is best seen in letter 8, translated by Hathaway (140–50). This idea of justice is of course strong in Plato, cf. *Rep.* 4.427C–445D.

35. Cf. *HEv.* 1.19.2 (PL 76, 1155).

36. *Dial.* 4.1.1f. (SC 265, 18f.); *Mor.* 8.18.34 (CCL 143, 406).

37. *Mor.* 9.33.50 (CCL 143, 491): "Ad hoc homo conditus fuit ut bonum, quod Deus est, uidere potuisset; sed qui stare ad lucem noluit, fugiendo oculos amisit, quia quo per culpam coepit ad ima decurrere, eo caecitatem pertulit ne intimum lumen uideret."

38. *Mor.* 35.17.43 (CCL 143B, 1804): "Homo namque quasi dies ex conditione claruit, quia hunc auctor suus ingenitae innocentiae splendore respersit. Sed sponte sua ad peccati tenebras lapsus, quia ueritatis lucem deseruit, quasi in nocte se erroris abscondit, quia alias dicitur secutus umbram." And *Mor.* 13.44.49 (CCL 143A, 694): "Tunc uero homo suum lectulum in tenebris strauit quando lucem iustitiae persuasori callido consentiendo deseruit"; also *Mor.* 4.1.4 (CCL 143, 166).

mind. For he first becomes blind in the mind and afterwards enslaves himself to damnable pleasures."[39]

Gregory wishes that the "pleasure which seizes man to sin" would perish, that the "dangerous weakness of mind which blinded man even to the darkness of consenting to sin" would pass away.[40] With sensory perception replacing true spiritual understanding, man lives in error, subject to the mistakes and misapprehensions that account for sin. Like the child born in a dark prison, man has neither memory nor experience of the wonderful invisible things of another life.[41] No longer in God's presence, man is in exile and yet so blind that he mistakes his exile for his home.[42]

In blinding man's reason, the Fall also subverted his discipline and self-control. Turning from God, his true "place," man lost his discipline and focus.[43] Now scattered and dispersed (*spargeri, dilabor*), his soul runs freely toward the lowest things (*decurrere ad ima*).[44] Man's involvement with pleasure leads him to forget God utterly. Surrounded by a myriad of bewildering objects, he seeks satisfaction in the sheer variety of things—in constant change.[45] Restless and dissipated, man lacks the tranquillity necessary to know God and secure his identity in stability.[46] The sinner is no longer rational, moral, strong, nor manly. Falling "lower

39. *Mor.* 4.13.25 (CCL 143, 180). This is a complicated exegesis of Job 3:3, "Pereat dies in qua natus sum et nox in qua dictum est: conceptus est homo." Gregory interprets "man" to refer to his fallen condition, "infirmitas." He observes: "Homo ergo in die nascitur sed in nocte concipitur, quia nequaquam a delectatione peccati rapitur nisi prius per uoluntarias mentis tenebras infirmetur. Ante enim caecus in mente fit et postmodum se reprobae delectationi substernit. Dicatur ergo: 'Pereat dies in qua natus sum et nox in qua dictum est: Conceptus est homo'; id est pereat delectatio, quae in culpa hominem rapuit: pereat incauta mentis infirmitas, quae usque ad tenebras praui consensus excaecauit. Homo enim dum blandimenta delectationis caute non perspicit, etiam in noctem nequissimae perpetrationis ruit. Sollerter ergo uigilandum est ut cum blandiri culpa incohat, ad quantum interitum mens trahatur, agnoscat."

40. Ibid.

41. *Dial.* 4.1.1f. (SC 265, 18f.).

42. *Mor.* 7.2.2 (CCL 143, 335): "Homo namque ad contemplandum auctorem conditus, sed exigentibus meritis ab internis gaudiis deiectus, in aerumnam corruptionis ruens, caecitatem exsilii sustinens, culpae suae supplicia tolerabat et nesciebat. Ita ut exsilium patriam crederet et sic sub corruptionis pondere quasi in salutis libertate gauderet."

43. *Mor.* 8.19.35 (CCL 143, 406).

44. *Mor.* 9.33.50 (CCL 143, 491), and *Mor.* 26.44.79 (CCL 143B, 1326).

45. *Mor.* 26.44.79 (CCL 143B, 1326): "Et quia ad Deum solum appetendum facta est, omne autem quod infra appetit minus est, iure ei non sufficit quod Deus non est." *Mor.* 26.44.79 (CCL 143B, 1326): "Hinc est quod huc illucque spargitur; et ab unaquaque re, ut diximus, fastidio impellente remouetur. Delectationis uidelicet auida, quaerit quo pauset, unum uero quem sufficienter habere poterat amisit. Vnde nunc per multa ducitur, ut quia qualitate rerum non potest, saltim uarietate satietur." Cf. Aug. *conf.* 2.1.1; 2.1.4 and passim.

46. Cf. *Mor.* 33.37.63 (CCL 143B, 1727).

than himself,"[47] he becomes emotional and changeable, bestial, weak, and soft. Sin defaces his image-likeness to God.[48]

Ultimately, sin brings a loss of self-knowledge,[49] as man falls beneath himself, and the powers of his discretion languish and fade away. Without proper discretion, man cannot judge his own sinfulness, and the very moment man withdraws his conscience from severe self-judgment, he begins to slide on "slippery ground."[50] The sinner is blind and deaf to his own failings, and eventually pride hardens his heart. He does not confess and repent of his sins, which would remove the evils that separate him from God. For Gregory, who believes so deeply in penitence, this loss of the powers of repentance may be man's greatest punishment. Not only has the sinner forfeited virtue and stability, he is also bereft of means to expiate his sins. He is excluded from the "light of understanding" given only to the humble, and so he persists all too easily in his errors.[51]

Following Augustine, Gregory views sin as externality, a turning away from the interior contemplation of God toward the external world of the flesh and changeable pleasures. Yet Gregory differs from Augustine in stressing the very externality of the process of sin itself. Even the cause of sin is external, for the devil and the flesh bear most of the guilt. Although man is proud, his reason is relatively blameless: he fell instead "from the wickedness of another."[52] Envious of God's chosen creature, the old enemy, the devil, made "war" on man in paradise,[53] trying his loyalty to God, tempting him with the "coin of deception" and the "money of sin."[54] Still the Fall was also God's test of man's obedience,[55] which, alas, he failed. Man did allow the devil to draw him away from God to the external pleasures of the flesh, but only after his reason had been compromised. First the devil suggested sin, then Eve—that is, the flesh—took pleasure. Adam, the rational mind, was seduced to consent to pleasure. Pride appears especially in the final stage, when man has the

47. *Mor.* 26.44.79 (CCL 143B, 1325): "Recta mens staret, si non se in umeris motibus fluxa mutabilitate prosterneret." *Mor.* 8.10.19 (CCL 143, 395): "infra se per corruptionem proruens. . . ."; see also *Mor.* 26.17.28 (CCL 143B, 1285–86).

48. *HEv.* 1.17.10 (PL 76, 1144); cf. Gregorio Penco, "S. Gregorio e la Teologia dell'immagine," *Benedictina* 18 (1971): 41f.

49. *Mor.* 20.14.37 (CCL 143A, 1029). See Pierre Courcelle, *Connais-toi toi-même de Socrate à Saint Bernard*, (Paris, 1974), 1:208–9, noting the influence of Origen and Augustine on this theme in Gregory.

50. *Mor.* 11.39.52 (CCL 143A, 616).

51. *Mor.* 25.12.30 (CCL 143B, 1256).

52. *Mor.* 4.3.8 (CCL 143, 169).

53. *In lib. I Reg.* 1.1 (CCL 144, 55)

54. *Mor.* 4.35.69 (CCL 143, 214).

55. *Mor.* 35.14.29 (CCL 143B, 1793–94).

audacity to defend his sin.[56] Gregory discerns a chain of sin, moving inexorably from the outside inward. The devil and the flesh are the beginning of sin; rational consent of the will and pride come later, as the result of earlier corruption. Certainly, both body and soul bear responsibility for sin, but since sin originates with the devil's attack on the body, the body labors under a heavier burden of guilt.

Man's sin renders him an outlaw: a traitor, a deserter, and a fugitive.[57] In retributive justice, God redresses man's rebellion by permitting the illegitimate rebellion of man's own servant, the flesh. Now the independence of the flesh from rational control mocks man's own desire to be free from God. Following Augustine, Gregory explains:

> For if the spirit is dutifully pressed down under God, the flesh is not illegitimately raised above the spirit. Indeed, the spirit has dominion over the flesh committed to it, as long as it recognizes the law of legitimate servitude to the Lord. For if it despises its Creator in pride, it lawfully undergoes battle from the subject flesh. Whence that first disobedient man, as soon as he sinned in pride, covered his shameful parts. Since the spirit attacked God insolently, soon it was attacked by the flesh insolently. Since it was unwilling to be subject to its Creator, it lost its right to dominate the flesh which it used to rule.[58]

The punishment of the Fall is part of the steady rhythm of retributive justice that is the very foundation of cosmic order. Since man has broken the law of subordination that guarantees justice and right order, he must

56. *Mor.* 4.27.49 (CCL 143, 193). Four stages of sin appear also in *Reg. Past.* 3.29 (PL 77, 109). Three stages appear in *HEv.* 1.16.1 (PL 76, 1135); *Ep.* 11.56a.9 (MGH II, 343). Suso Brechter has noted parallels with Aug. *de serm. dom.* 1.34 (PL 34, 1246), where there are three stages of sin, "Die Quellen zur Angelsachsenmission Gregors des Grossen," in *Beiträge zur Geschichte des alten Mönchtums* 22 (Münster, 1941), 108. But Augustine also stresses Adam's proud defense and refusal to repent (*civ.* 14.13–14). No chronological argument can be made to justify this as an evolution of Gregory's thought. The differing stages are best seen as variations determined by Gregory's exegetical and pastoral concerns.

57. *Mor.* 8.32.52 (CCL 143, 423): "homo Deum peccando dereliquit"; *Mor.* 9.33.50 (CCL 143, 491): "Ad hoc homo conditus fuit ut bonum, quod Deus est, uidere potuisset; sed qui stare ad lucem noluit, fugiendo oculos amisit. . . ."; *Mor.* 35.17.43 (CCL 143B, 1804); *Mor.* 13.44.49 (CCL 143A, 694); *Mor.* 8.19.35 (CCL 143, 406): "Quem nimirum locum tunc homo deseruit cum, seductoris uerba audiens, a Conditoris amore discessit. Sed cum omnipotens Deus redimendo se homini etiam corporaliter ostendit, ipse ut ita dixerim, fugitiui sui uestigia subsequens, ad retinendum quem amiserat hominem locus uenit."

58. *Mor.* 26.17.28 (CCL 143B, 1286); cf. *Mor.* 9.5.5 (CCL 143, 458). Augustine also sees reciprocal punishments, *civ.* 14.17; consent to pleasure makes man captive, *in psalm.* 58.2.11. Enslavement to the flesh, sin, and the devil are traditional ideas going back as far as Irenaeus; see Williams, *Ideas of the Fall*, 244; Hastings Rashdall, *The Idea of Atonement in Christian Theology* (London, 1919), 243, who cites Iren. *haer.* 5.1.1 and 3.22.2. The idea is carried through Tert. *apol.* 2.1. Augustine emphasizes the dominion of the devil as a juridical sentence; cf. *trin.* 13.15.

suffer injustice and disorder as a consequence. Now the world is topsy-turvy, with flesh the master, and reason the slave. Neither performs its proper function. With justice gone, disharmony and tension replace the tranquillity of right order, when things were "ordered by heavenly government."[59] Because of the Fall, the body rightly dominates the soul and pleasure becomes irresistible. If man thought he wanted this mutability, God has granted it to teach him a lesson, changing man's guilt (*culpa*) into his punishment (*poena*).[60] The mutability man sought willingly, he is now forced to bear unwillingly,[61] and he is trapped in the temporal world of pleasures that he preferred to God.[62] No longer God's cherished son, man finds himself "set opposite God" (cf. Jb 7:20) because of his pride.[63] He has become God's "enemy," and the devil's "slave," his unwilling captive in the kingdom of sin.[64] Servitude to the devil is servitude to the flesh, to mutability and corruption manifest internally as sin, externally as death.[65] It is also enslavement to the capricious changes and importunate needs of the physical body.

Gregory attributes to the body a power of its own, a stubborn autonomy quite independent of man's will in its voracious appetite for pleasure. Sexual pleasure, the most obvious symptom of man's appetite, is simply the least manageable pleasure, and its rebelliousness is the fitting punishment for man's proud rejection of God.[66] Appropriately, pride and lust manifest the same contumacious autonomy, one internally, the other externally. With pride the heart is "erected secretly" with an "inward swelling of the heart." Lust is an "open lapse of the body" that happens "in public."[67] This is why proud men so often swell with lust: the sinful

59. *Mor*. 9.5.5 (CCL 143, 458).

60. *Mor*. 9.5.5. (CCL 143, 459).

61. *Mor*. 8.6.8 (CCL 143, 386). Cf. Aug. *civ*. 14.14.

62. *In lib. I Reg*. 5:83 (CCL 144, 470).

63. *Mor*. 8.32.52 (CCL 143, 423).

64. Ibid.; cf. *Mor*. 17.30.46 (CCL 143A, 877): "Ipse namque diabolus in illa nos parentis primi radice supplantans, sub captiuitate sua quasi iuste tenuit hominem qui libero arbitrio conditus, ei iniusta suadenti consensit." Servitude to God is the freedom to do good, servitude to the devil, the compulsion to do evil; see *Mor*. 4.36.71 (CCL 143, 215), and *Mor*. 26.14.23 (CCL 143B, 1281–82). Cf. Cassian *conl*. 1.12; Aug. *in psalm*. 58.2.11.

65. *Mor*. 11.50.68 (CCL 143A, 625): "Quam tamen mutabilitatem non solum exterius, sed interius quoque homo patitur, dum ad meliora exsurgere opera conatur. Mens etenim mutabilitatis suae pondere ad aliud semper impellitur quam est, et nisi in statu suo arcta custodiae disciplina teneatur, semper in deteriora dilabitur. Quae enim semper stantem deseruit, statum quam habere potuit amisit. Vnde nunc cum ad meliora nititur quasi contra ictum fluminis conatur. Cum uero ab intentione ascendendi resoluitur, sine labore reducitur ad ima."

66. Cf. Aug. *civ*. 14.15.

67. Cf. *Mor*. 26.17.28 (CCL 143B, 1285): "quia dum eos spiritus quasi in altum erexit,

impulse within is displaced to the external man. "God sees inwardly what puffs up the mind, and for this reason permits outwardly what deflates him."[68] The body manifests the spirit's depravity as punishment for its sin. This link of pride and sexual pleasure, and of body and soul, explains why Adam covered his genitals after he sinned: after the spirit inflated, so did the flesh.[69]

Sexuality reminds man of his fall from grace, as the most vivid expression of his desire to separate himself from God and pursue the transient world, which only decays and dies. In sexuality, one witnesses most poignantly the autonomy (and anarchy) of the body. As Augustine recognized, neither sexual arousal nor impotence could be dictated by rational control.[70] Because the body seems to act on its own, the flesh has its own capacity for pleasure, quite apart from reason and quite at odds with the will. Unruly and unpredictable, sex is a disorderly corner of man's life, resistant to rational organization. The irrationality of sex especially symbolizes the whole unconscious realm that generates the appetite of pleasure,[71] all the greedy, irreverent, curious, and embarrassing impulses of man's lower nature. Representing this darker, primitive side of humanity, sexuality connects man with the beasts and throws man "beneath himself."[72]

The weakness of man's reason and the consequent erosion of his self-discipline are the primary causes of his sin.[73] To be sure, Gregory distin-

---

caro in infimis mersit. Hii enim prius secreto eleuantur, sed postmodum publice corruunt, quia dum occultis intumescunt motibus cordis, apertis cadunt lapsibus corporis. Sic sic elati iusta fuerant retributione feriendi, ut quia superbiendo se hominibus praeferunt, luxuriando usque ad iumentorum similitudinem deuoluantur." Note the oppositions: *spiritus/caro, altum/infima, secreto/publice, occultis/apertis, cordis/corporis, intumescere/cadere.* Finally the two excesses of flesh and spirit are complementary extremes, *superbia/luxuria.* See Aug. *civ.* 14.17. Gregory takes from Augustine the idea of Adam's punishment through lust but sets it into formulaic oppositions.

68. *Mor.* 26.17.28 (CCL 143B, 1286): "Intus ergo uidet Deus quod mentem eleuat, et idcirco foras permittit inualescere quod deponat."

69. This explanation of pride and lust probably reflects man's psychosomatic unity: the humors causing the swelling (*tumor*) of pride are redirected to cause the swelling (*intumescere*) of the genitals.

70. Cf. Aug. *civ.* 14.23.

71. Cf. Brown, *Augustine and Sexuality*, 31.

72. *Mor.* 8.6.8 (CCL 143, 262); *Mor.* 26.17.28 (CCL 143B, 1285).

73. The notion that sin is weakness is Stoic; see J. M. Rist, *Stoic Philosophy* (Cambridge, 1969), 87f. In *fin.* 4.77, Cicero reports the Stoic view that every sin is a mark of weakness (*imbecillitas*) and instability (*inconstantia*), which Rist sees as the Latin equivalent of ἀσθένια and ἀτονία, states in which the soul lacks proper tension. Gregory's laxity is also the ῥαθυμία or *neglegentia* and *relaxatio* (carelessness, easy temper, slackness, dissolution) condemned in the desert monastic tradition. Evagrius, under the influence of Origen, sets such

guishes between those who sin from "ignorance, weakness, or deliberate intention"[74]: some do not know the good at all; others know the good but are unable to attain it; still others reject the good stubbornly in their pride. Yet such failings are a continuum, for pride is the extreme form of moral blindness that utterly perverts man's rational good intentions. Similarly, says Gregory, sometimes man sins with the eye of discretion blinded first, so that the soul willingly surrenders to the flesh; other times, the mind discerns the right but does not fight hard enough and is overcome while offering resistance. But in both cases, pleasure overthrows reason.[75] Indeed, each sin replicates Eve's seduction of Adam— the subversion of reason by carnal delights. Pleasurable sensations "relax," "loosen," and "soften" the mind's discipline. "[W]hen the flesh is caught up in pleasure, reason is also weakened and bent from its righteousness."[76] After the Fall, man's weakened reason is all the more easily conquered.

The real threat of pleasure is its power to bind man to a lower form of existence in the visible, physical world of the senses; for when reason is defeated, pleasure draws the soul outside to the carnal world. Gregory's exegesis of Job 40:13 demonstrates this degeneration and serves as well as a classic illustration of his basic psychology of sin. The suggestions of the devil are like "pipes of brass." As sweet sounds "attract the interior mind and drag it to exterior pleasures," so the devil's suggestions easily bend the mind from its interior discipline. "Manliness of heart [is weakened] with the flow of pleasure. And when hearing is dragged to delight, understanding is relaxed from the stability of its strength."[77] Once this happens, desire runs unrestrained: "desire is a sin and the punishment of sinning."[78]

Pleasure is a great menace to moral improvement, an excess that un-

---

laxity as the vice opposite the cardinal virtue of *fortitudo*. This theme is also originally Stoic, see Aimé Solignac, "Péchés capitaux," *DS* 12:854.

74. *Mor.* 25.11.28 (CCL 143B, 1253–54): "Sciendum quippe est quod peccatum tribus modis committitur. Nam aut ignorantia, aut infirmitate aut studio perpetratur."

75. *Mor.* 7.28.37 (CCL 143, 361–62).

76. This is Gregory's explanation of Adam's consent to Eve, in *Mor.* 4.27.49 (CCL 143, 193): "Eua delectata est quia carnalis sensus, ad uerba serpentis mox se delectationi substernit. Assensum uero Adam mulieri praepositus praebuit quia dum caro in delectationem rapitur, etiam a sua rectitudine spiritus infirmatus inclinatur."

77. *Mor.* 32.21.40 (CCL 143B, 1659): ". . . Aeris quippe fistulae sonoris aptari cantibus solent, quae admotae auribus dum blandum carmen subtiliter concinunt, interiora mentis in exteriora delectationis trahunt, et dum dulce est quod auribus sonant, uirilitatem cordis in uoluptatis fluxu debilitant. Cumque auditus ad delectationem trahitur, sensus ab statu suae fortitudinis eneruatur."

78. *HEz.* 1.11.24 (CCL 142, 179–80).

dermines the balance of body and soul, allowing the baser inclinations of man to overpower his reason. True virtue lies in temperance and moderation, an inner balance of body and soul that is true health. The Christian must follow the fine line of discretion,[79] discharging only necessities and avoiding pleasure.[80] Like the dove offered for sins, whose neck is partly broken off (Lv 1:15; 5:8), so should man's mind be cut off from carnal pleasure and discharge only the necessities of the flesh.[81] Sin lies in extremes, an excess or defect that occurs when virtues are not held under the "moderation of discretion."[82] As the chords of a lute must be strung neither too tightly nor too loosely, so virtues must be tempered to follow the just mean.[83] Vice is an imbalance and a disease of the soul often displayed in physical maladies as well.[84] When pleasure causes a loss of moderation and temperance, all virtues suffer because their interconnection makes them stand or fall together. Vices enter and take over the soul step by step, for vices are also linked together, like successive plagues of insects that waste the land, one after the other.[85] Sin becomes compulsive and habitual, so that one seems imprisoned and enslaved to the devil. Sin is like a stubborn thistle. One day you uproot it, the next day it returns.[86]

The remedy for this sickness of soul is self-restraint. The proof of love is to show it in deeds, Gregory preaches in his *Homilies on the Gospel* 2.30.1, and this means resisting pleasure:

79. "Linea discretionis": *Mor*. 28.11.26–29 (CCL 143B, 1415–18); "regula": *Mor*. 5.30.53 (CCL 143, 255); *Mor*. 11.49.65 (CCL 143A, 623). See Introduction, n. 59.

80. *Mor*. 20.14.28 (CCL 143A, 1024–25); *Mor*. 30.18.61–63 (CCL 143B, 1532–34); cf. *Mor*. 15.48.54 (CCL 143A, 782–83); and Cassian *inst*. 5.6. For Seneca, pleasures become punishments when they exceed bounds, *epist*. 83.27.

81. *HEz*. 1.7.10 (CCL 142, 89).

82. Cf. *HEz*. 1.5.3 (CCL 142, 58); *Mor*. 2.49.76 (CCL 143, 105); *Mor*. 9.66.106 (CCL 143, 531); *Mor*. 1.34.47 (CCL 143, 51); *HEz*. 1.7.2 (CCL 142, 83–84). Also, *Mor*. 9.25.39 (CCL 143, 483–84); *HEz*. 1.3.8 (CCL 142, 37). See above nn. 4 and 6. The idea that virtue is a mean between extremes goes back to Arist. *Nich. Eth.*, esp. 2.5, but temperance and moderation became especially important to the Stoics and to Ambrose; cf. Cic. *Tusc*. 3.7.15; 4.20.46; 8.16–18; *fin*. 2.14.47; Ambr. *Isaac*. 2.5–6. See also Foucault, *Histoire de la sexualité*, vol. 2, *L'Usage des plaisirs*, esp. 26–76.

83. In this case, abstinence: *Mor*. 1.8.11 (CCL 143, 29–30). In *Mor*. 20.41.78 (CCL 143A, 1061), Gregory likens the interconnection of virtues to the harmony of stringed instruments. Cf. Ambr. *bon. mort*. 7.26; cf. Dionys. Exig. *Gr. Nyss. hom. op*. 14. The lyre image is also employed by Plotinus, *Enn*. 1.4.16; 2.9.18.

84. Sofia Boesch Gajano lists a number of illnesses caused by possession and healed by the relics of their saints, "Demoni et miracoli nei *Dialogi* di Gregorio Magno," in *Hagiographie, cultures, et sociétés iv–xii siècles* (Paris, 1981), 269. Cf. Basil *reg. fus*. 55f.

85. *Mor*. 33.37.65 (CCL 143B, 1728–29). Cf. Cassian *conl*. 13.3.

86. *Mor*. 24.11.30 (CCL 143B, 1209).

We truly love God and keep his commandments if we restrain ourselves from our pleasures. For he who still abandons himself to unlawful desires certainly does not love God, since he contradicts him in his own intentions. . . . Therefore, he loves God truly, whose mind is not conquered by consent to evil delight. For the more one takes pleasure in lower things, the more he is separated from heavenly love.[87]

To love God is to abandon pleasure and let reason reestablish one's stability in God. Because men are "called to be gods" and the "equal of his angels," they should let "no uncleanness pollute [them]" nor "lechery defile [them]," but rather defend their dignity with purity from these and all such vices.[88] Now, after the Fall, man can attain the spiritual understanding he needs only through contemplation and deepest compunction.[89] He must also endure the continual struggle between the *lex carnalis* and the *lex mentis*, as Paul describes.[90] Man becomes a slave of sin, and the devil, the tyrant, oppresses his will with involuntary sin. The devil carries him off violently, as a captive of war. Having once embraced pleasure in paradise, man can no longer stand firm and upright against the devil's attacks:

Whence also in Paradise he [the devil] inflicted upright man with words of flattering persuasion; but man, whom he once led astray to consent, he now drags away, even while man resists, and through violence, he nearly kills the one who has been conquered by the pleasures of his corruption.[91]

87. *HEv.* 2.30.1–2 (PL 76, 1220–21): "Probatio ergo dilectionis, exhibitio est operis. Hinc in Epistola sua idem Joannes dicit: 'Qui dicit, Diligo Deum, et mandata ejus non custodit, mendax est' (1 Jn 4:20). Vere etenim Deum diligimus, si ad mandata ejus nos a nostris voluptatibus coarctamus. Nam qui adhuc per illicita desideria diffluit, profecto Deum non amat, quia ei in sua voluntate contradicit. . . . Ille ergo vere amat, cujus videlicet mentem delectatio prava ex consensu non superat. Nam tanto quisque a superno amore disjungitur, quanto inferius delectatur."

88. Cf. *HEv.* 1.8.3 (PL 76, 1105).

89. *Mor.* 30.5.20–21 (CCL 143B, 1504–5).

90. *Mor.* 9.36.58 (CCL 143, 498–99), an exegesis of Job 9:31 ("Abominabuntur me uestimenta mea.") in which the clothing is the earthly body: "abominabilem facient quia nimirum dum contra mentem membra superbiunt, dum sancti desiderii studia temptationum suarum tumultibus interrumpunt, in ipso suo certamine posita anima agnoscit quantum adhuc a diuinitate despicitur quae correptionem suam plene appetens transire, sed non ualens, foedae puluere cogitationis inquinatur." This is what Paul speaks about in Romans 7:23. Also *Mor.* 9.53.80 (CCL 143, 512): "Plerumque uero contra haec eadem rudimenta spiritalia ex usu ueteri caro submurmurat et mens bella tolerat ex homine quem foras portat." Cf. Ambr. *Isaac.* 2.3; 2.5; 4.3; 7.26.

91. *Mor.* 15.15.19 (CCL 143A, 760): "Vnde in paradiso quoque, stanti homini uerba blandae persuasionis intulit [Gn 3:5f.]; sed quem semel rapuit ad consensum, iam nunc etiam renitentem trahit et corruptionis suae delectationibus deuictum paene uiolenter interficit."

The devil forces man to commit evils against his will, not only in outward deeds, but even in the wayward desires and wicked imaginations
that often steal into the mind. Augustine saw this problem of unconscious desire as a sign of man's fragmented will, as an indication that a
part of man still loved evil. But Gregory presents this conflict as the work
of demons oppressing the rational mind, which otherwise wills the good.
Even man's inmost thoughts fall prey to the "secret suggestions" of demons.[92] Gregory feels very anxious about these loathsome, subversive
desires emerging from the unconscious mind. Evil works might easily be
avoided, but it is exceedingly difficult to rub illicit thoughts from the
mind: "For who can comprehend how many evils we commit each moment through the inconstant motions of our thoughts?"[93] The sinner is
responsible not only for the evil he chooses but also for unconscious
thoughts and inadvertent sins. As God's severity cannot be known, judgment is all the more terrifying. "Even if [sinners] have avoided deeds they
recognize as evil, nevertheless they fear the more those evils they do not
know, and tremble with burning ruin and a more subtle terror."[94] The
only solution lies in supererogatory penance lavish enough to cover the
sins one is not even aware of having committed.

The appetite for pleasure is extremely difficult to manage, not only
because reason has been weakened in the Fall but also because pleasure
itself has become so internal and inescapable, a part of man's very being.
Man "contains within himself the source of his own temptation."[95] Just
as moths spring out of the garment and consume it, so man is a "rotten
thing which consumes itself" (cf. Jb 13:28) in the temptations that issue
from his own flesh.[96] This appetite for pleasure residing in man's very
flesh is inseparable from his nature as a creature generated by sexual intercourse. Because of Adam's sin, all future generations are born with
this capacity or "appetite" for pleasure in the body.[97] Following Augus-

92. Ibid.
93. *Mor.* 24.11.32 (CCL 143B, 1211). Cf. Aug. *conf.* 4.14.22.
94. *Mor.* 24.11.32 (CCL 143B, 1212): "Et si ea quae sciunt numquam se praetermisisse
meminerunt, formidant tamen illa quae nesciunt. . . ."
95. *Mor.* 11.48.64 (CCL 143A, 622): "In semetipso quippe habet homo unde
temptetur."
96. *Mor.* 5.38.68 (CCL 143, 268). Note the associations of the flesh with externality,
corruption, temptation, weight, lowliness, death, and the Old Dispensation: "Tinea autem
de ueste nascitur et eamdem uestem, de qua oritur, oriendo corrumpit. Quasi quaedam
uero uestis animae caro est; sed haec nimirum uestis habet tineam suam quia ab ipsa carnalis temptatio oritur ex qua laceratur."
97. See the remarks of Ferruccio Gastaldelli, "Il meccanismo psicologico del peccato
nei *Moralia in Job* di San Gregorio Magno," *Salesianum* 27 (1965): 565f.; see also his "Prospetti-
ve sul peccato in San Gregorio Magno," *Salesianum* 28 (1966): 65–94.

tine, Gregory believes that Adam polluted (*polluere*) the human race at its root with the infection of sin (*contagio culpae*), and all who succeed him are guilty for they issue from the same mass.[98] The physical body is the vehicle for carrying sin from one generation to the next, and its capacity for pleasure is the visible manifestation of the invisible burden of guilt man bears. Since man is born of a woman subject to sin, he inherits guilt like a child inheriting a parent's physical nature: the branch (*ramus*) of man was corrupted in the root (*radix*), and consequently the healthful greenness will not remain in the rest of the tree.[99]

Following Augustine, Gregory believes sin is transmitted in procreation itself; lust itself is sinful. To the ancient mind, sexual orgasm was an extinction of reason, a suspension of self-control and conscious organization that seemed to adumbrate the death of one's moral identity as well as one's physical being.[100] The intense and ungovernable pleasure of sex is then a stark negation of the discipline and self-possession the Christian needs to reform his life. The moment of conception is clouded with evil. Christians may become sons of God, but they are scarcely *born* holy: "Since we are bound by the very condition of a corrupt nature, we may say with the Prophet, 'For behold, I was conceived in iniquities and in sins did my mother bring me forth' [Ps 50:7]."[101]

Gregory interprets this literally. There is always something of the devil in everyone conceived "out of pleasure of the flesh" (*de delectatione carnis*), meaning that children are subject to corruption because their parents experienced lust in conceiving them.[102] Born with this capacity for sexuality, children are also destined for sexual reproduction by the very physiology of the body. As Gregory explains, we are conceived in sinful lust, polluted by a disease that grows to full term in weak, corrupt bodies

98. *Mor.* 24.2.4 (CCL 143B, 1191): "Omnes uidelicet nos inimica illa persuasio in culpae contagium ab ipsa radice polluerat [Gn 3:5], nullusque erat qui apud Deum pro peccatoribus loquens, a peccato liber appareret, quia ex eadem massa editos aeque cunctos par reatus inuoluerat [Rm 5:11]." Weber gives a thorough discussion of original sin, and argues that Gregory vacillates between creationalism and traducianism; see *Hauptfragen*, 230–33. See also Dudden, *Gregory*, 2:387–90. Gregory follows Augustine in the ideal of a collective sin of all in Adam; see Williams's discussion of Augustine in *Ideas of the Fall*, 365.

99. *Mor.* 17.15.21 (CCL 143A, 864).

100. See Foucault, *Histoire de la sexualité*, vol. 2, *L'Usage des plaisirs*, 131ff.

101. *Mor.* 18.52.84 (CCL 143A, 948). "Nos quippe etsi sancti efficimur, non tamen nascimur, quia ipsa naturae corruptibilis conditione constringimur, ut cum propheta dicamus: 'Ecce enim in iniquitatibus conceptus sum et in delictis peperit me mater mea' [Ps 50:7]."

102. *HEv.* 2.39.8 (PL 76, 1299). Cf. Aug. *pecc. mer.* 2.36. See also Eugene Teselle's discussion in *Augustine the Theologian* (New York, 1970), 316. Two points important for Augustine that Gregory does not emphasize are: (1) carnal delight takes place in the soul, though it could not be experienced without the body; (2) delight is sinful not in itself but because it is a privation of adherence to God.

subject to the same sinfulness. Quoting Job 17:14, Gregory tells us that the worm is our mother and our sister, for we "come into the world out of corruption, and we also live with it."[103]

The body's capacity for pleasure makes it easy for Gregory to associate the body with the devil. The flesh is so stubbornly attached to pleasure, the devil himself seems to be in our body: "Since with guilt punishment is also inherited at birth, we are born with the vice of weakness implanted; and, as it were, we lead the enemy with us whom we conquer with difficulty."[104] Man should consider the body the minion of malevolent forces, for this thought can strengthen discipline and resolve. "Placed in battle, everyone sees more subtly the traps of the enemies the more strictly he disciplines his own body, as an accomplice of the enemies [hostium adiutor]."[105] Yet because the devil has such influence over the body, he seems to hold sway over man's whole personality. The devil, once an external entity, now resides in man's inmost parts, and he is conquered only with special virtues and much effort:

> Indeed, in the beginning when he was created righteous, man did not need such great virtues as he needs now, since if he had wished to remain as he was created, he could have conquered the enemy placed outside him without difficulty. But after the adversary has once invaded man's inmost parts, through man's consent, he is conqueror. Now he is thrown out with great difficulty, who could have been easily repulsed when still the attacker.[106]

The Fall has given the devil possession of man's inmost being. Such helplessness underscores man's need for divine assistance, for the devil is ejected only with diligent penance, confession, works, and, of course, God's grace.[107] Gregory is convinced that devils do enter the human heart (cf. Jn 13:27; 13:2). To reject this is Pelagianism, a denial of man's inborn sinfulness.[108] Original sin gives the devil access to the human heart, which he holds as triumphant conqueror.

103. Mor. 13.45.50 (CCL 143A, 695).

104. Mor. 8.6.8 (CCL 143, 386): "Sed quia cum culpa simul ab origine etiam poena propagatur, inserto infirmitatis uitio nascimur et quasi nobiscum hostem deducimus, quem cum labore superamus. Ipsa ergo hominis uita temptatio est, cui ex semetipsa nascitur unde perimatur."

105. Mor. 31.38.77 (CCL 143B, 1604).

106. Mor. 35.17.43 (CCL 143B, 1805): "In ipsa quippe sua origine in qua iustus homo conditus fuerat tantis quantis nunc opus est uirtutibus non indigebat, quia si stare sicut est conditus uellet, hostem extra positum uincere sine difficultate potuisset. Postquam uero per assensum hominis semel aduersarius ad intima irrupit, laboriosius iam uictor eicitur, qui adhuc impugnans sine labore pelleretur."

107. Cf. Mor. 32.19.34 (CCL 143B, 1655). The devil battles God for Job's soul.

108. Ep. 7.31 (CCL 140, 494); cf. Mor. 32.19.34 (CCL 143B, 1655); Mor. 33.3.6 (CCL 143B, 1674).

Man's subjection to the devil's kingdom is complicated by the nature of his body and mortal life in general. The interdependence of body and soul makes any physical appetite a threat to the soul's equilibrium. As Gregory sees it, the body and soul are a closed system and man possesses only a finite amount of strength and energy. Bodily pleasure necessarily drains strength and power from the rational soul, enfeebling it and making it defenseless against further insults from the body. The body has become the "prison" of man's corruption, whence he cannot escape.[109] Gregory's concept of the weakness and corruption of the body encompasses both the body's appetite for pleasure and its physical changes and needs. Even physical necessities and the lowly pursuits of daily life predispose man to sin, for these belong to the exterior life apart from God. Man's corruption generates not only "moths in the garment of flesh" but also "worms," cares arising from the flesh to gnaw at the soul.[110] Similarly, Gregory interprets the commandment to the Levites to shave (Nm 8:7) as an image of the wastes (*superflua*) that the flesh always produces, which the spirit must cut with the "razor of anxiety."[111] Gregory explains the failure of contemplative vision by reference to this dead weight of necessity and lowly cares:

> Since "the body, which is the way of corruption," still "weighs down the soul" [Wis 9.15]. It does not have the power to cling long to the light of day, which it sees in a glimpse. For the very weakness of the flesh drags the soul down, even as the soul transcends itself. Still panting, the soul is dragged back to think of necessities and the lowest things.[112]

No clear line can be drawn between the physical needs and inconveniences we suffer from our mortal bodies and the darker impulse to sin. The intimate connection of body and soul causes the soul to react quickly and instinctively to changes in the physical body. Simply having a body one needs to care for and being forced to attend to a whole category of "necessary things" (*necessaria*) become a large part of man's corruption. To have hunger and thirst, to need warmth, to suffer disease—such phenomena are themselves the "scourges of sin" (*flagella peccati*), bitter punishments reminding us of our fallen state.[113] All such needs are

---

109. *Mor.* 9.57.86 (CCL 143, 517); and *Mor.* 8.23.39 (CCL 143, 410).
110. *Mor.* 5.38.68 (CCL 143, 268–69).
111. *Mor.* 5.33.59 (CCL 143, 260): "Semper enim caro superflua generat quae semper spiritus ferro sollicitudinis recidat."
112. *Mor.* 8.30.50 (CCL 143, 421).
113. *Mor.* 13.32.36 (CCL 143A, 688): "Aestu enim et frigore, fame sitique turbari, morbis affici, quandoque etiam exstingui, quid sunt haec aliud quam flagella peccati?" See also *Mor.* 4.34.68 (CCL 143, 211–12); *Mor.* 8.32.52–53 (CCL 143, 423); *Mor.* 11.50.68 (143A, 624–25); *Mor.* 4.26.47 (CCL 143, 192).

not merely irksome, but actually dangerous, because the gratification of a legitimate need inadvertently offers the opportunity of pleasure.

Since the sinner's reason is blinded, he lacks the discernment (*discretio*) necessary to distinguish between necessity and pleasure, virtue and vice. Consequently, ordinary life in the body becomes an exasperating trial. Need and desire are notoriously deceitful and confusing. Both are forms of deprivation, and in Gregory's mind "every longing unfulfilled is a punishment."[114] One is dependent upon something one lacks, perhaps something one will never obtain, and this neediness can generate anxiety and overreaction. And economic conditions may exacerbate this distress. When resources are finite, when food, clothing, and warmth are in short supply, as they were for many in Gregory's time, fear of a future of gnawing emptiness impels people to hoard goods. Such pressures further undermine man's fragile self-control.

In such ways, life in the body clearly pulls man from God. Because physical needs open the door to desire and compulsive habit, they are a large part of the curse of mutability man suffers because of the Fall. These dangerous needs arise from man's embodiment, as we experience the body in our fallen state. The body, made of the lowest matter, tends to return to the nothingness of its origin; all its needs and passions are degenerative changes adumbrating death. In contrast, before the Fall, Adam participated in God, enjoying the hope of physical and moral constancy. In paradise, Adam apparently did not have a body subject to the needs and changes we associate with the body and life in this world, even though he felt temptation in the flesh.

Gregory, like Augustine, was unable to remain indifferent to the suffering and imperfection of mortal life. The discomfort and inconvenience of hunger, thirst, and other physical necessities had to be interpreted as punishments and disciplines to educate the elect, for life was not meant to be so flawed and painful. Thus after the Fall, man's whole life degenerated, becoming a mirror image of what life should be. One could even say that man "died" after eating the forbidden fruit of paradise (cf. Gn 2:17), Gregory believes. Man's "way of life" changed "so that afterwards he should live in pain, although he had been created to live happily in joy."[115] In losing virtue and self-possession, man also lost the happiness

---

114. *Mor.* 9.27.42 (CCL 143, 485).
115. *Ep.* 6.14 (CCL 140, 383): "Sed sciendum est quia mors duobus accidit modis: aut absentia uiuendi aut a qualitate uiuendi. In hoc ergo quod comedendo uetitum eius anima mortua dicitur, non absentia uiuendi sed a qualitate uiuendi, ut postmodum uiueret in poena, qui ad hoc creatus fuerat, ut beate uiueret in laetitia." Also, *Ep.* 7.31 (CCL 140, 493), another exegesis of Genesis 2:17.

a life of virtue brings. He is doomed to the pain of living in a mutable body in a changeable world.

At heart, Gregory desires nothing more than to free himself of this numbing carnal life that "lulls one to sleep."[116] Yet through his own experience, he comes to understand a great paradox: life on this earth can be transformed and accepted as a sacrificial burden bringing one closer to God. Though scarred with a fault line of oppositions, life can be made whole again. By embracing life in the body with humility and by governing it with discretion, the Christian can be reformed to an even greater beauty. The body becomes a particular focus of Gregory's spirituality, for his distinctive emphasis on trial and remedial suffering finds its center in man's carnal existence. Through life in the body, man comes to know himself and his Creator, to understand what it means to be human and, by contrast, to glimpse something more of divine perfection. The very mutability of life is both a curse and a blessing, a profound paradox that offers Gregory a logic of asceticism.

116. *Mor.* 25.7.18 (CCL 143B, 1242–43).

· VI ·

THE LOGIC OF ASCETICISM

To snare a lioness, Gregory tells us, one digs a pit and baits it with a sheep.[1] Then one tunnels further, joining the first pit to a second with a hidden cage. Tempted by food, the lioness will leap into the first pit; then, seeking security from terrors above her, she will follow the tunnel to hide away. But alas, she finds herself trapped in the cage. Soon she will be lifted out of the pit, her violent temper contained by the bars of her prison. And so it is with man. Craving to feed the desires of his flesh, he falls into the pit of self-deception and soon wanders to "the prison of his own corruption." The hand of redemption lifts him from death, but he finds himself still caged, bound by his own corruption, as though by sturdy bars. Yet these bars prove to be a healthy discipline, for man now lives restrained from exercising his liberty.[2] Such is Gregory's ambivalence about the body and man's earthly life: a paradoxical logic of asceticism makes the corruption of the body both man's punishment and his salutary discipline.

For Gregory, man's very embodiment is troublesome. Because the body connects man with the exterior world, it is the mediating link between the soul and a world so full of temptations. Gregory generally sees the body as an external object covering the internal soul: a "house,"[3] "tabernacle,"[4] "garment,"[5] "vessel of clay,"[6] "prison of corruption," or "prison

---

1. *Mor.* 9.57.86 (CCL 143, 517–18).

2. Ibid.; see *Mor.* 9.57.87 for a second exegesis where man falls from pride. After sin, he is barred by the cage of humility and knowledge of his own weakness, but then he is restored through pardon.

3. *Mor.* 15.46.52 (CCL 143A, 780–81); *Mor.* 21.2.4 (CCL 143A, 1065–66).

4. *Mor.* 15.30.36 (CCL 143A, 770–71).

5. *Mor.* 9.36.58 (CCL 143, 498–99); cf. also *Mor.* 9.53.80 (CCL 143, 511–12).

6. *Mor.* 3.7.9 (CCL 143, 119).

of man's own punishment."[7] The flesh is the visible house (*domus carnis*), the soul the invisible indweller (*habitator*) looking out the windows or doors of the house, which are the senses.[8] While Gregory may occasionally see the soul as diffused throughout the body, with the diverse senses unified and governed by reason,[9] he generally presents the relationship of body and soul as a trenchant duality, thus heightening the tension between the true inner life of the soul and the delusory wandering of the body.

Even as embodiment is problematic, man's sensation lies at the root of his predicament. Along with the angels, man once enjoyed spiritual senses that linked him to the ineffable perfection of the invisible world. But because of the Fall, carnal senses have come to overshadow those spiritual perceptions. Yet only the spiritual senses can afford man a glimpse of the eternal world, which is "discerned without sight, heard without doubt, taken up without motion, touched without body, and held without place."[10] When God speaks, man inwardly discerns a distinct and powerful inspiration or illumination from God. His "heart is taught [God's] Word, without words or syllables, because his power is known by a certain inward uplifting."[11] He feels "full to overflowing,"[12] his mind is suddenly "illuminated" by a bright light,[13] the "palate of [his] heart" savors "an inward sweetness."[14] Spiritual perception yields perfect understanding, allowing man to grasp God's message instantaneously and completely, undistorted by carnal obstacles, so that his words seem to be "seen" rather than "heard."[15] Spiritual senses are paradoxically opposite yet similar to carnal senses, an interior hearing needs no words, an inner sight perceives the incorporeal. The body is a mirror reflecting yet distorting supernal realities.

Sensory existence is symptomatic of the imperfection of earthly life; things are inverted and topsy-turvy because man has become bound to

---

7. *Mor.* 8.23.40 (CCL 143, 411); *Mor.* 9.57.86 (CCL 143, 517); and *Mor.* 8.23.39 (CCL 143, 410): "Carcere homo circumdatur, quia plerumque et uirtutum prouectibus ad alta exsurgere nititur, et tamen carnis suae corruptione praepeditur."

8. *HEz.* 2.5.9–10 (CCL 142, 282–83); *HEv.* 1.9.1 (PL 76, 1106); *Mor.* 15.46.52 (CCL 143A, 780–81); *Mor.* 21.2.4 (CCL 143A, 1065).

9. *HEz.* 2.5.9 (CCL 142, 282).

10. *Mor.* 5.34.62 (CCL 143, 262).

11. *Mor.* 28.1.2 (CCL 143B, 1396): "de uerbo eius sine uerbis ac syllabis cor docetur, quia uirtus eius in intima quadam subleuatione cognoscitur." See also *Mor.* 30.5.19 (CCL 143B, 1504); *Mor.* 35.3.4 (CCL 143B, 1776–77).

12. *Mor.* 28.1.2 (CCL 143B, 1396).

13. *Mor.* 30.5.19 (CCL 143B, 1504).

14. *Ep.* 9.15 (CCL 140A, 576).

15. *Mor.* 28.1.2 (CCL 143B, 1396–97).

the body. For Gregory, the five senses belong to the body and are useful only in establishing contact with the present external world.[16] The door of the outward court in Ezechiel 40:20 leads to the court of the present life, in which "everything done corporally is also seen corporally."[17] The sinner's knowledge is limited to what reaches the soul through bodily senses, and carnal perception is always a kind of "touching" dependent upon delusive physical images.[18] Gregory argues that the soul is invisible and "in no way is affected by the pleasure of carnal things" except through the senses.[19] In providing knowledge of the visible world exterior to the rational soul, the senses are inadvertently gateways to sin. Sight, hearing, taste, smell, and touch are roads through which the soul or mind travels outside and falls to lusting after things outside its own substance.[20] Ideally, the soul should remain inside the house of the flesh, refusing to pay attention to importunate messages carried by the body's senses. The soul of the righteous man is like a "dove at the windows" (Is 60:8) that refuses to go outside or even look outside with longing. One should station a "doorkeeper outside the house," lest thieves enter and smite the master of the house in the groin (cf. 2 Sm 4:5–7). The entrance of the mind must be fortified with virtue, lest evil spirits enter the soul and attack virtue with delights of the flesh.[21]

In large measure, the carnal senses account for the mutability that defines earthly life. Not only do they carry knowledge of the changeable exterior world to the soul, but contact with the body and changes in one's mortal state affect the soul's varying emotions and dispositions,[22] making rational control all the more precarious. Furthermore, the senses themselves cause a disturbing instability because man is continually changing his attention to follow the stimuli of eyes, ears, or touch. All constant thought or purpose is lost,[23] and man becomes "dissimilar" to himself,

---

16. Cf. HEv. 2.36.4 (PL 76, 1268).

17. HEz. 2.7.2 (CCL 142, 316).

18. Mor. 5.34.61 (CCL 143, 261): "peccando factus est etiam mente carnalis ut sola cogitet quae ad animum per imagines corporum trahit."

19. Mor. 21.2.4 (CCL 143A, 1065–67). See also Mor. 15.30.36 (CCL 143A, 770–71); Mor. 15.46.52 (CCL 143A, 781); HEz. 2.5.9 (CCL 142, 281–82).

20. Mor. 21.2.4 (CCL 143A, 1065–67).

21. Mor. 1.35.49 (CCL 143, 50–51). To Gregory the body was an imperfect organ of the mind; cf. Ad Leand. 5 (CCL 143, 6–7).

22. Mor. 5.34.62 (CCL 143, 262): "Sed quamuis incorporea sit anima, quia tamen corpori inhaeret, ex ipsa sui qualitate agnoscitur quae carnis loco retinetur. Quae dum obliuiscitur scita, cognoscit incognita, meminit obliuioni mandata, hilarescit post tristia, addicitir post laeta. Ipsa sui diuersitate indicat quantum a substantia aeternae incommutabilitatis distat, quae semper ut est, idem est. . . ."

23. HEz. 2.5.10 (CCL 142, 283).

his soul becoming "scattered" and "dispersed," whereas man should be "disciplined" and "collected." Connection with the outside world is so dangerous that even looking at the world carelessly can be fatal, for it can give rise to temptation the mind is ill-equipped to check. David chanced to lay eyes on Bathsheba and so began to desire her.[24] It is as if "death comes through the windows and enters the palace" (Jer 9:21), when such desire comes through the bodily senses and enters the mind.[25]

Sin thus arises from the body's mutability—from its appetite for pleasure, from the needs that lead to excess in pleasure, from sensory existence that draws man toward the world—but sin can also arise from the mind. For sometimes there is a conflict in the soul, and the body only executes the shameful deeds concocted in the mind.[26] Occasionally, Gregory sounds like Augustine, viewing pleasure and sin as capacities of the soul and recognizing the goodness of the body.[27] The soul is by definition mutable, for it is created ex nihilo. The flesh by nature is one thing, and the corruption of the flesh another.[28] Thus Gregory distinguishes between the flesh and the sinful desires that pollute it. "A garment mixed with blood shall be burnt," he writes, citing Isaiah 9:5. To "mix garments with blood is to pollute the body with carnal desires."[29] Too, Gregory recognizes that simply feeling temptation is different from gratifying a de-

24. *Mor.* 21.8.13 (CCL 143A, 1074–75).

25. *Mor.* 21.2.4 (CCL 143A, 1065–67).

26. *Mor.* 21.9.14 (CCL 143A, 1075). Claude Dagens also distinguishes two explanations of temptation, but he sees only one psychology of sin, and it is highly internal; see *Saint Grégoire le Grand* (Paris, 1977), 206f.; Ferruccio Gastaldelli, "Il meccanismo psicologico del peccato nei *Moralia in Job* di San Gregorio Magno," *Salesianum* 27 (1965): 564f. also emphasizes interiority. But see Pierre Boglioni, "Miracle et nature chez Grégoire le Grand," in *Cahiers d'études médiévales*, I: *Epopées, légendes et miracles* (Montreal and Paris, 1974), 44f. on Cassian's influence on the role of demons in sin.

27. See Margaret Miles, *Augustine on the Body* (Missoula, Mont., 1979), passim, and her *Fullness of Life: Historical Foundations for a New Asceticism* (Philadelphia, 1981), esp. 37–62, where she documents Augustine's affirmation of the body. Augustine emphasizes the goodness of the body and the unity of man as body and soul, *util. ieiun.* 4; *doctr. crist.* 1.24.24; *in euang. Ioh.* 27.5; *civ.* 15.7.2; *contin.* 12.26. Concupiscence, carnality, and pleasure are activities of the soul, not the body; cf. *civ.* 14.1ff. Despite Gregory's indebtedness to *civ.* 14, he does not follow Augustine's emphasis here. Augustine also warns against an asceticism that itself becomes carnal by being too centered on the body; the right attitude is neutrality or nonchalance, *vera relig.* 20.40; *mor.eccl.* 1. This position is also that of Plotinus according to R. T. Wallis, *Neo-Platonism* (New York, 1972), 83f. See also Robert O'Connell, *St. Augustine's Early Theory of Man, A.D. 386–391* (Cambridge, Mass., 1968). Gregory rejects nonchalance and is closer to the East. If asceticism is problematic, the danger is pride and excess, too much of a good thing.

28. *Mor.* 14.56.72 (CCL 143A, 744). In refuting Eutychius's views on the resurrection, Gregory asserts: "in sacro eloquio aliter caro dicitur iuxta naturam atque aliter iuxta culpam, uel corruptionem." The resurrected flesh will be in this form of natural goodness.

29. *Mor.* 9.36.58 (CCL 143, 498).

sire. The burden of corruption makes man suffer thoughts of temptation unwillingly, and this is human, but it is devilish to consent to them. Sin is in the body, which is subject to corruption; man should not let it reign (cf. Rom 6:12).[30] Here Gregory uses *flesh* not to refer to the body, but as a synecdoche for man's mortal condition. To be carnal means simply to prefer what is human to what is divine, what is temporal to what is eternal, and visible to invisible.[31] Viewing pleasure as a capacity of the soul, Gregory says the thought of sin is a pleasure, even if no external deed is executed.[32]

Gregory sees two patterns of sin, one more external, the other more internal. Sometimes man sins because he feels the press of desires in his body, or he chances upon something in the world that piques his imagination. At other times, the soul is pierced by the mere memory of sin or the thought of some new delight, images arising only from the vast stretches of the mind. Gregory follows Cassian's belief that concupiscence is rooted in the body, though this does not exclude the birth of desire from thoughts, imagination, and memory.[33] And like Cassian, Gregory's psychology of sin emphasizes the interconnection of body and soul: both will be tormented in hell because both are involved in and tainted by sin.[34] Though the body is the source of pleasure, the soul consents to it, for "the flesh cannot be delighted without the soul."[35] However, Gregory places the greater blame on the body, not so much because sin has physical sources, but because sin is exterior,[36] an involvement with the temporal visible world, which stands in opposition to God. Carnal life, whether perceived through the senses or merely remembered in the mind, is still an external life. The soul, representing the interior side of man, is always in better stead. The soul connects man with the invisible

---

30. *Mor.* 21.3.7 (CCL 143A, 1068–69).

31. *Mor.* 15.61.72 (CCL 143A, 797–98); *Mor.* 16.10.15 (CCL 143A, 807–8); *HEz.* 1.8.13 (CCL 142, 108).

32. *Mor.* 9.55.83 (CCL 143, 513–14).

33. See M. Foucault, "Le Combat de la chasteté," *Communications* 5:35 (1982): 20.

34. *Mor.* 16.14.19 (CCL 143A, 809–10); *Dial.* 4.30.4–5 (SC 265, 102).

35. *Ep.* 11.56a (MGH II, 343): "Et cum caro delectare sine anima nequeat. . . ." On the authenticity of Bede's text of Gregory's writing to Augustine of Canterbury, see Paul Meyvaert, "Bede's Text of the *Libellus Responsionum* of Gregory the Great to Augustine of Canterbury," "Bede and Gregory the Great," "The Registrum of Gregory the Great and Bede," "Bede and the *Libellus Synodicus* of Gregory the Great," all in *Benedict, Gregory, Bede and Others*, Variorum Reprints, CS 61 (London, 1977); see also his "Le *Libellus Responsionum* à Augustin: une oeuvre authentique de S. Grégoire," in Jacques Fontaine et al., eds., *Grégoire le Grand* (Paris, 1986), 543–50.

36. See Dagens, *Saint Grégoire*, 165–70 and 187–90.

world of the spirit, and it is also the source of the reason and discretion that resist the attack of vice rising from the flesh.

In the end, Gregory departs from Augustine's psychology of sin, though he at times uses Augustine's words. While Augustine carefully separated body and soul, affirming the goodness of the body and locating sin in the will and the soul, Gregory tends to view sin as arising from the conflict of soul and body, reason and sensation. For Augustine, sensation comes from the soul's recognition of stimuli; for Gregory, the senses really belong to the body and are gateways linking the soul with the external world of pleasure. Where Augustine sees a paradoxical distance, Gregory sees connections: the body is the source as well as the symbol of man's carnal life; *flesh* denotes both the body and mortal human life. For Augustine, carnality is a state of mind, and the flesh, man's mortal condition. But by setting spirituality in opposition to the body, Gregory causally links them. This interdependence supplies a warrant for asceticism, both because of the physical connection of body and soul through humors and, perhaps more important, the rhetorical opposition of pleasure and self-renunciation Gregory preaches to reform his flock.[37] If the pleasure of the body can be controlled or checked, Gregory believes the soul will rebound in a reciprocal way. Seeking "heavenly desires," the convert should "renounce carnal pleasures [and] crush all earthly desires with the restraint of heavenly discipline, so that he longs for nothing which pleases the flesh, while his soul fears nothing which kills carnal life."[38] When liberated from carnal impulses, the soul is free to soar in heavenly desire.

Gregory's psychology of sin is the product of a monastic culture and is peculiarly Eastern in flavor.[39] It would be wrong to see Gregory as merely simplifying Augustine's position, for Gregory writes from such different assumptions and experience. The wisdom of the desert monastic tradition offers truths about the athlete's training that are the bittersweet fruits of experience more than of theory. If the conflict between flesh and spirit seems often reduced to a blunt conflict between body and soul, this is much the common sense of ascetical experience. Gregory often ignores distinctions that may have seemed to him purely academic,

37. In anthropological terminology, the physical connection is metonymic; the rhetorical relation, metaphoric.

38. *HEv.* 1.11.1 (PL 76, 1115).

39. In addition to the usual influences of Cassian, the Desert Fathers, and Ambrose, Gregory might have been influenced by Hier. *adv. Iovin.* e.g. 1.7; 1.16; 1.49; and Sextus, *Sententiae*, e.g., 231 on sexual pleasure.

departing from paradoxes that may have seemed more like contradictions than mysteries. For those who have undertaken the solitary struggle for perfection, the body *is* the soul's mortal enemy. Like the lioness, the body must be caged and disciplined. It makes little difference to distinguish between the body's instrumental function and its ontological value: in practice, corruption is corruption.

From this premise of the pollution of the flesh, Gregory reevaluates earthly life and relationships. The dangers of pleasure must be strictly controlled, above all through the minute regulation of sexuality.[40] Sexual expression betrays the fidelity one owes God in both body and soul, for participation in God embraces the whole human personality. The body of the Christian enjoys a kind of physical unity in his stability in the body of Christ—so much so that the Christian himself, Christ's spouse, commits a form of adultery and disloyalty in possessing earthly loves. A life defined by ties of the flesh is tainted by the prideful autonomy that pulls one away from participation in God, a selfishness that tends to fragment the human community which is Christ's body. Sexuality inevitably leads one toward the self-centered individualism of the family, with its web of ties to the secular world, its numerous burdens and anxieties. In contrast, the religious community possesses the tranquillity needed to realize man's highest vocations: contemplation, charity, and continence.

Carnal marriage thus stands in opposition to monastic life. In the *Dialogues*, Gregory tells of the young widow Galla, who rejected a second marriage to serve God in the convent at the church of St. Peter the Apostle. The widow is praised, because "it is better to be wed to God in a spiritual marriage, which begins in grief, but ends in eternal joys, than to submit to a carnal marriage, which always begins in happiness, but reaches the end with grief."[41] The nun or monk makes a sacrificial offering of the self to God, but the earthly spouse serves only his or her own lust and weakness.[42] To forgo earthly marriage makes one worthy of having an eternal spouse in heaven.[43]

Gregory's advice to Augustine of Canterbury shows a measured ambivalence toward the flesh, revealing how the threat of sexual pleasure can be neutralized by confining it to strict conditions. This letter also pro-

40. See esp. Jean-Louis Flandrin, *Un Temps pour embrasser: Aux origines de la morale sexuelle occidentale (VIe–XIe siècle)* (Paris, 1983), 48–49 and 69–71; and Pierre Payer, *Sex and the Penitentials: The Development of a Sexual Code, 550–1150* (Toronto, 1984), 19–36. Regulation focused on the liturgical seasons and on female physiological cycles.

41. *Dial.* 4.14.1 (SC 265, 56).

42. This is why the offering of Caterius is rejected; see *Dial.* 3.26.9 (SC 260, 372); *Ep.* 11.18 (CCL 140A, 887).

43. *Dial.* 3.14.1 (SC 260, 302).

vides a good example of the two levels of mutability and sinfulness Gregory perceives: the neutral needs and changes of the flesh, which man unwillingly endures, and the carnal passions of the flesh, which are clearly sinful. Pregnant women may be baptized because it is not the fruitfulness of the flesh but the pleasure of conception that is sinful. Menstruation is no sin, as it occurs naturally; yet it is part of the mutability human nature suffers because of sin, and so humanity bears this result of sin unwillingly. Therefore, if menstruating women wish the sacrament, they are not to be condemned; but if they abstain, they are to be commended. The sexual dreams of men are also a part of the mutability inflicted unwillingly, unless the mind and the will consent to such fantasies, in which case penance must be undertaken.[44]

Sex within marriage is similarly problematic. Like fruitfulness of the flesh, marital intercourse is not a sin in itself, but the pleasure of intercourse is. Because lust is present, even lawful intercourse is sinful. Referring to the law of the Old Testament that ordered people to bathe before entering sacred places (Lv 15:16), Gregory explains:

> We do not consider marriage a sin. But since the very licit mingling of married people cannot come about without lust of the flesh, one should stay away from the entrance to a sacred place because lust itself can in no way be without sin.[45]

In the *Dialogues*, a woman who enters the church in defiance of this rule is possessed by devils so irascible they even attack the priest who attempts to help her, for it is not in his power to help her.[46] Mere human beings are powerless to overcome the realm of demonic forces unleashed by sexual pleasures. One can contain these malevolent forces only by observing strict rules of practice and obeying the authorities who set these rules for our protection. Discipline and obedience are necessary medicines for man's fallen nature.

Because of the Fall, man is forced to suffer the weakness of the body even as he strives for spiritual perfection. His life will always be flawed with imperfection. Man is both captive and free: free because his mind still loves righteousness, and captive because the mind is bound against its will to enjoy carnal pleasure.[47] Because sin so involves man's bodily nature, as long as man has flesh he will never be without sin: "there is no

---

44. *Ep.* 11.56a.8 (MGH, II, 338).

45. *Ep.* 11.56a.8 (MGH II, 340). Also, *Mor.* 32.20.39 (CCL 143B, 1658). Note the parallels with Augustine's views on the ends of marriage in Eugene Teselle, *Augustine the Theologian* (New York, 1970), 316.

46. *Dial.* 1.10.2–3 (SC 260, 94).

47. *Ep.* 11.56a (MGH, II, 342–43).

one who passes through life without sin, so long as he bears the flesh of corruption."[48] Sin only truly ends when the resurrection takes away the corruption of the mortal body and replaces it with an immutable body of perfect stability, the "firmness of the Resurrection" (soliditas resurrectionis): "Certainly then sin will be completely taken away from humanity when our corruption is changed through the glory of incorruption."[49] The perfect spiritual perception will return, and the body's suffering and need will end. Until then the body and soul are locked in warfare, as if heaven and hell have been shut up together.[50]

Gregory correlates the body so strongly with pleasure and sin that the culpability of reason is moot. Though he views reason and will as essentially good, they are hopelessly impotent in the absence of strong discretion and discipline. Like bread baked under ashes (cf. Hos 7:8), "our intention is by nature well made to rise to God, but from evil ways of life, lust enters in immediately to press us down toward the world."[51] Gregory shares with many early writers this Neoplatonic belief in the essential goodness of the rational soul. Unlike Augustine, Gregory is not preoccupied with the problem of gratuitous evil, of how man could know the good, yet deliberately choose to sin. Evil occurs when reason is debilitated—corrupted and relaxed by pleasures and cares of the flesh, so that misapprehension and misjudgments take place. Sin is "error," the mistakes of faulty understanding.[52] Virtue is attained when reason is purified and liberated from the bonds of the flesh, so that the rational soul can remain hard, taut, and disciplined within its citadel. For Gregory, spiritual reform will be directed at subjugating the flesh, for this will release the natural good of reason and reestablish its proper dominion over man's personality.

In contrast, Augustine found spiritual reform much more difficult and mysterious, a long healing of the will, effected not through spiritual exercises (although these can be useful), but through God's enigmatic intervention in man's will. Only grace could reform Augustine's sinner, for whom knowledge and reason are of no avail. But Gregory trusts in reason

48. *Mor.* 17.15.21 (CCL 143A, 864): "Sed ecce nonnulli per donum spiritus adiuti contra infirmitatem suae carnis eriguntur, uirtutibus emicant, signorum quoque miraculis coruscant; nullus tamen est qui sine culpa uitam transeat, quousque carnem corruptionis portat."

49. *Mor.* 8.33.56 (CCL 143, 425).

50. *Mor.* 10.10.16 (CCL 143, 549).

51. *Mor.* 32.10.12 (CCL 143B, 1637): "Ex natura quippe bene condita est nobis intentio, quae surgat in Deum; sed ex conuersatione nequiter assueta inest uoluptas, quae praesens premat in saeculum." See *Mor.* 20.14.28 (CCL 143A, 1024–25), where good intentions are simply overwhelmed.

52. This idea is reminiscent of the Greek idea of ἁμαρτία ("missing the mark").

and believes God has ordered the universe with a rational plan that presumes man's exercise of the mind. Like Eastern Christians with their emphasis on *paideia*, Gregory focuses on education, on enlightening the mind darkened by sin. Reform depends upon knowledge and the restoration of rational control, and this comes about through the removal of forces external and alien to the true man. The "rust" of sin must be purged.[53] The worms, the moths, and the asps—impulses from outside the real man—must be eradicated. Similarly, the demons who wound man with temptations must be conquered.[54]

At times, these external forces, the demons, moths, and worms, seem to dwarf man in a cosmic drama of good and evil. Indeed, the struggle for self-control and discipline of the body is part of the larger question of man's control of his destiny. Just how much power does man have to shape his life? How effective are self-control and discipline in determining what happens to man in this life and the next? The devil looms large in the commission of sin, a measure of how greatly Gregory believes man is helplessly oppressed by his sinful unconscious nature. The devil is the tyrant enslaving man, but above all he is the enemy warring against mankind in particularly underhanded ways. He is the great deceiver laying traps for his victims, a hunter who ambushes his prey while they are least aware of danger.[55] Changing form at will, he tailors his temptations to fit the individual weaknesses of his subjects.[56] Man is constantly battered by the assaults of demons, as the *Dialogues* show us. But if Gregory feels the presence of demonic forces very keenly, he is weighed equally with respect for positive supernatural powers. Angels defend man from the adversary, surrounding him in the battle as mountains surround a valley (cf. Jb 39:8).[57] God's grace often protects man from evils, from external disasters and internal temptations.

At times, in describing man's sobering powerlessness, Gregory sounds more deterministic than Augustine. Not only does man seem merely a pawn in the battle of cosmic forces for the loyalty of his soul, but God has predestined everything from eternity. The drama of life unfolds inexorably as written by God, which explains how the typology of the Old Testament can foretell the future. Something in the future can be described as already passed, "since whatever is in the future outwardly

---

53. *Mor*. 3.14.27 (CCL 143, 132).

54. Boglioni, "Miracle et nature," 49ff., and Sofia Boesch Gajano, "Demoni et miracoli nei *Dialogi* di Gregorio Magno," in *Hagiographie, cultures et sociétés iv–xii siècles* (Paris, 1981), 267.

55. Cf. *Ep*. 9.219 (CCL 140A, 785–86); *Mor*. 32.16.28 (CCL 143B, 1651–52); and *Mor*. 32.21.40 (CCL 143B, 1658–59); most of this chapter discusses the devil.

56. *Mor*. 33.15.31 (CCL 143B, 1700).

57. *Mor*. 30.19.64 (CCL 143B, 1534–35).

in act, is already done inwardly in predestination."[58] Sometimes our own lives are witnesses to events long foretold, and we feel the uncanny truth ourselves. "We see the evils of the world we heard long ago would come; the very misfortunes of the earth have become like the pages of books to us."[59]

God's choice in man's election is clearly felt, and his action in abandoning man is freely confessed. Where Augustine's God passively permitted man to turn away, Gregory's God actively forsakes man—a conclusion Gregory deduces from Augustine's more scrupulous formulations. And in describing God's rejection of man, Gregory uses some of the same verbs that characterize man's rejection of God in sin: *deserere*, *recedere*, *relinquere*. God's "mercy so accomplishes the mystery of divine work that anger is still joined to it, in order that the Secret Judge may look upon some and redeem them, and desert others and ruin them. . . ."[60] Man's will is impotent, one way or the other: "Just as no one resists his bountiful gift in calling, so no one can stop his justice in deserting."[61] God's passivity is also a form of action. He forsakes sinners by withdrawing (*recedere*) from them and not intervening to save them.[62] He hardens Pharaoh's heart by "not softening it with grace."[63] God does not "fashion the minds of the wicked to sin"; he simply "does not liberate them from sin."[64]

Following Augustine, Gregory fully appreciates man's helplessness before divine grace: "from the grace of the omnipotent God we can indeed attempt good works, but we cannot complete them if he does not aid what he commands."[65] Man can accomplish nothing without preve-

58. *Mor.* 28.5.14 (CCL 143B, 1406): "Quod idcirco a Domino iam quasi praeteritum describitur, quia quicquid foras futurum est in opere, intus iam factum est in praedestinatione." Also *HEz.* 1.10.25 (CCL 142, 157).

59. *Ep.* 3.29 (CCL 140, 175).

60. *Mor.* 29.2.4 (CCL 143B, 1437): "Sed cum diuini operis mysterium sic misericordia peragat, ut tamen et ira comitetur, quatenus occultus arbiter alios respiciens redimat, alios deserens perdat, quia cognouimus quomodo per incarnationem suam electos illuminet, audiamus nunc quomodo reprobos damnet."

61. *Mor.* 11.9.13 (CCL 143A, 592): "sicut nemo obsistit largitati uocantis, ita nullus obuiat iustitiae relinquentis."

62. *Mor.* 11.9.12 (CCL 143A, 591): "Neque enim humanam mentem debellando destruit sed recedendo, quia ad perditionem suam sufficit sibi dimissa."

63. *Mor.* 11.9.13 (CCL 143A, 592); *Mor.* 31.14.26 (CCL 143B, 1569); *Mor.* 29.30.60 (CCL 143B, 1476–77).

64. *Mor.* 29.30.60 (CCL 143B, 1476–77).

65. *HEz.* 1.9.2 (CCL 142, 123). This is Gregory's exegesis of Ezechiel 2:2: "'Et ingressus est in me spiritus, postquam locutus est mihi, et statuit me super pedes meos.' Ecce diuina uox iacenti prophetae iussit ut surgeret. Sed surgere omnino non posset, nisi in hunc omnipotentis Dei spiritus intrasset, quia ex omnipotentis Dei gratia ad bona opera conari qui-

nient and subsequent grace.[66] Even Mary Magdalene was inspired inwardly through the spirit of compunction to repent of her sins by the very one who received her tears and forgave her transgressions outwardly.[67]

Furthermore, God's grace is unpredictable and perplexing. One can repent, but still be unable to free himself from sin. Some long to leave their prison of sinful habit, but they are unable to escape.[68] To underscore man's dependence on God's will, Gregory can make God seem very harsh in his justice. God may scorn man's pitiful pleas to change his dispensation. Isaac's prayers for Esau are unanswered, "for he did not find a place of penitence, although he sought it with tears, since lamentations bear no fruit, which desire with groans what must be lost."[69] Tears cannot redeem what God has rejected, and his justice can have a bitter edge. So God said through Solomon to reprobates lingering in sin, "I too will laugh at your ruin" (Prv 1:26).[70] Even those who seem to be chosen should never feel secure from God's scorn, because one can never predict God's surprises. Some may be borne along peacefully by God's mercy, only to be swept away suddenly.[71] Who would have expected Judas to fall and a thief to be saved? Gregory asks.[72] Although God's ways are hidden and mysterious, they are never unjust.[73] It is simply not for man to ask why we suffer, nor to question God's dispensation: to do so is to "contend with God."[74] In fighting God's dispensation, man only fulfills it.[75]

Human life is planned from eternity, unfolding like the pages of a book. However reverent and beloved of God, man still has no control over the spectacular changes of fortune God has ordained. Such views might be expected to discourage human activity, leading Gregory to the same impasse the monks of Hadrumentum faced in Augustine's time.[76]

---

dem possumus, sed haec implere non possumus, si ipse non adiuuat qui lubet." Cf. Aug. *conf.* 10.29.40. This sense of man's passivity is particularly strong in *HEz.*, written after Gregory's first years in the papacy, when he seems most frustrated by the loss of contemplative life.

66. *HEz.* 1.10.45 (CCL 142, 167): "Ad bona quippe assurgere perfecte non possumus, nisi nos spiritus et praeueniendo eleuet et subsequendo confortet." Also, *HEz.* 1.9.2 (CCL 142, 123–24).

67. *HEz.* 1.8.2 (CCL 142, 102–3).

68. *Mor.* 11.9.12 (CCL 143A, 592).

69. *Mor.* 11.9.13 (CCL 143A, 593).

70. *Mor.* 9.27.42 (CCL 143, 485).

71. *Mor.* 25.5.6 (CCL 143B, 1233–34).

72. *Mor.* 25.8.19 (CCL 143B, 1243–44).

73. *Mor.* 25.15.33 (CCL 143B, 1258–59).

74. *Mor.* 11.49.66 (CCL 143A, 623–24); *Mor.* 9.15–16.22–23 (CCL 143, 472–73).

75. *Mor.* 6.18.28 (CCL 143, 304–5).

76. Cf. Peter Brown, *Augustine of Hippo* (Berkeley and Los Angeles, 1969), 398ff.

But instead Gregory follows the Council of Orange (529), which modified Augustine's position to admit the cooperation of man's free will.[77] "Our evils are purely our own, but our goods are both God's and our own," Gregory asserts confidently.[78] More important is Gregory's sense of the providential order that admits this cooperation and other forms of human activity. "Even the predestination itself to the eternal kingdom is so arranged by the omnipotent God that the elect attain it from their own effort."[79] Prayers, penance, masses, intercession, works—all are forms of human effort mediating with the divine. The human effort God foresees does not diminish man's freedom to act, and thus for Gregory there is no conflict between predestination and the cooperation of the human will. God's plan *is* absolute, the perfect work of an omnipotent Creator, owing

77. Gregory's doctrine of grace and free will has been thoroughly treated by Leonhard Weber, *Hauptfragen der Moraltheologie Gregors des Grossen* (Freiburg in der Schweiz, 1947), 174–93, and by F. Homes Dudden, *Gregory the Great* (London, 1905), 2:393–400. Dagens (*Saint Grégoire*, 272f., 446f.) discusses the charges of semi-Pelagianism made by Friedrich Loofs, *Leitfaden zum Studium der Dogmengeschichte* (Halle-Saale, 1906), and takes up as well the general critique of Harnack. Following the canons of the Council of Orange, Gregory ignores the harsher aspects of Augustinianism. All goodness originates with God, and we have not received God's grace as a result of any merits of our own; see *Mor.* 18.40.63 (CCL 143A, 929); *Mor.* 23.6.13 (CCL 143B, 1153–54); *Mor.* 20.4.11 (CCL 143A, 1009). Grace liberates free will from bondage to sin and inspires it to do good. But man's will cooperates and he can be given some credit; see *Mor.* 16.25.30 (CCL 143A, 816): "Superna ergo pietas prius agit in nobis aliquid sine nobis ut, subsequente quoque nostro libero arbitrio, bonum quod iam appetimus agat nobiscum, quod tamen per impensam gratiam in extremo iudicio ita remunerat in nobis, ac si solis processisset ex nobis. Quia enim diuina nos bonitas ut innocentes faciat, praeuenit, Paulus ait: 'Gratia autem Dei sum id quod sum' [1 Cor 15:10]. Et quia eamdem gratiam nostrum liberum arbitrium sequitur, adiungit: 'Et gratia eius in me uacua non fuit, sed abundantius illis omnibus laboraui.' . . . Non enim diceret 'mecum' si cum praeueniente gratia subsequens liberum arbitrium non haberet. Vt ergo se sine gratia nihil esse ostenderet, ait: 'Non ego.' Vt uero se cum gratia operatum esse per liberum arbitrium demonstraret, adiunxit: 'Sed gratia Dei mecum.'" See also *Mor.* 33.21.40 (CCL 143B, 1710): "Bonum quippe quod agimus, et Dei est et nostrum; Dei per praeuenientem gratiam, nostrum per obsequentem liberam uoluntatem." *Mor.* 24.10.24 (CCL 143B, 1204): "Quia praeueniente diuina gratia in operatione bona, nostrum liberum arbitrium sequitur, nosmetipsi nos liberare dicimur, quia liberanti nos Domino consentimus." And *Mor.* 18.40.63 (CCL 143A, 929): "Ex cuius nimirum aspiratione gratiae, quia uirtutum opera protinus in corde generantur; ut ex libero quoque arbitrio subsequatur actio, cui post hanc uitam retributio aeterna respondeat. . . ." See also *Mor.* 24.7.13 (CCL 143B, 1196–97); and *HEz.* 1.9.2 (CCL 142, 124). Gregory's ideas of grace are closest to those of Cassian; see esp. *conl.* 13.6–18, and Owen Chadwick, *John Cassian,* 2d ed. (Cambridge, 1968), 110–36.

78. *HEz.* 1.9.2 (CCL 142, 123–4): "Sed sciendum est quia mala nostra solummodo nostra sunt; bona autem nostra, et omnipotentis Dei sunt, et nostra, quia ipse aspirando nos praeuenit ut uelimus, qui adiuuando subsequitur ne inaniter uelimus, sed possimus implere quae uolumus. Praeueniente ergo gratia et bona uoluntate subsequente, hoc quod omnipotentis Dei donum est fit meritum nostrum."

79. *Dial.* 1.8.5 (SC 260, 74): "Nam ipsa quoque perennis regni praedestinatio ita est ab omnipotente Deo disposita, ut ad hoc electi ex labore perueniant. . . ."

nothing to his creatures. But God's absolute power is forever a rational power; ultimately God's plan is accessible to human reason and reconciled with human activity. As God has disposed the universe with a harmony and order accessible to reason, so he has ordered man's salvation.

By God's ordinance the universe is so arranged to educate man that he might eventually return to God. Catching man's attention with brilliant paradoxes, God offers lessons to all having the vision to grasp them. In the reciprocal justice that governs life, the body actually becomes a vessel of discipline that can safeguard and improve the health of the soul. To become "carnal in the mind" after the Fall means that the mind has grown heavier and defiled through an inescapable involvement with the flesh. But more than this, it means that the body becomes more important spiritually. The body can suffer in ways the soul alone cannot; physical suffering encompasses the whole of man, and this is what Christ redeemed.[80] Physical suffering reaffirms Christ's humble work, his willingness to bear the weakness of human flesh. To Gregory, Christ's humanity is especially evident in his suffering, because his interior reason remained perfect and immutable. Imitation of Christ must be especially an imitation of his Passion.

Even though reason is man's better half, paradoxically the body makes man special to God. Man's fall from grace is a *felix culpa*, although Gregory does not use this term. Man is a perfect combination of spiritual and carnal existence, so that he might eventually return as he had fallen. The body becomes the reason for and the instrument of man's redemption. Angels cannot be excused for their sins, for they have no mixture of flesh to hold them in bonds. But because man bears the weakness of the body and because the devil tempted him through the body, God has pitied man and offered him redemption:

> For the angel is only spirit, but man is spirit and flesh. Therefore, when the Creator took pity on him to redeem him, it was fitting that he ought to bring back what had sinned out of weakness; and it was also fitting that he should reject the apostate angel all the more strongly, the more

---

80. This ability of the body to suffer and perfect the soul is illustrated in an exegesis of the candlestick of beaten gold (Ex 25:31, 37:71) as a symbol of Christ and his body in *HEz.* 1.6.8 (CCL 142, 71): "Ex auro ergo mundissimo ductile candelabrum fuit, quia et peccatum non habuit, et tamen eius corpus per passionis contumelias ad immortalitatem profecit. Nam iuxta uirtutes animae quo percussionibus potuisset proficere, omnino non habuit. In membris autem suis, quae nos sumus, cotidie percussionibus proficit, quia dum nos tundimur et afficimur ut eius corpus esse mereamur, ipse proficit." Assuming human nature without sin, Christ did not have the qualities to be perfected through suffering. It is through the suffering of his members, namely we Christians, that his body "makes progress daily through beatings."

[the devil] fell from the strength of stability and bore no weakness from the flesh. . . .[81]

Man sinned through the weakness of the flesh and deserves mercy because of it. Now the Redeemer will "bring back" to himself the flesh that sinned. In a paradoxical reversal, the mutability that caused man's Fall becomes the very means of his restoration: "Indeed, the human soul would not fall if it were not changeable; and banished from the joys of paradise, if it were not changeable, it would never return to life."[82]

The paradox of man's mutability is matched by further paradoxical acts of divine justice to educate man. As noted earlier, God's retribution gives man exactly what he wants, so man is forced to reap the whirlwind of his own foolish desire for change in the catastrophic mutability of his own mind and body.[83] The corruption of the flesh becomes man's punishment, and this mutability and corruption become an inescapable weight man must bear. Yet while corruption becomes punishment, in turn, punishment is converted to a cure. If man suffers his burdens in sacrificial obedience to God, if he can be disciplined by this punishment, he can at last be restored to God.

> Because we have followed the flesh through the sight of the eyes, we are tortured by that very flesh which we preferred to God's commands. We suffer sorrow, torture, and death in it daily so that by a marvelous dispensation the Lord might convert the cause of sin into a means of punishment; so that the severity of punishment might arise from the same source as sin, so that man might be disciplined to life by the bitter suffering of that very flesh by whose prideful delight man drew near death.[84]

If man fell through his capacity for change and his emotions, then he shall be restored by that same sensitivity. But now man will reverse his Fall: instead of feeling pleasure in his flesh, he will feel penitence.[85] Self-indulgence and gratification will be replaced by suffering and sacrifice. "If we sin much through the delights of the flesh, we are purged by the

81. *Mor.* 4.3.8 (CCL 143, 168–69).

82. *Mor.* 25.6.10 (CCL 143B, 1235): "Humana quippe anima in lapsum non caderet, si mutabilis non fuisset; quae a paradisi quoque gaudiis expulsa, si mutabilis non esset, ad uitam minime rediret." See also *Mor.* 29.10.21 (CCL 143B, 1448).

83. *Mor.* 9.5.5 (CCL 143, 459); *Mor.* 8.6.8 (CCL 143, 386).

84. *Mor.* 24.4.7 (CCL 143B, 1193): "Et quia per oculorum uisum carnem secuti sumus, de ipsa carne, quam praeceptis Dei praeposuimus, flagellamur. In ipsa quippe cotidie gemitum, in ipsa cruciatum, in ipsa interitum patimur, ut hoc nobis mira dispositione Dominus in poenam uerteret, per quod fecimus culpam; nec aliunde esset interim censura supplicii, nisi unde fuerat causa peccati, ut eius carnis amaritudine homo erudiretur ad uitam, cuius oblectatione superbiae peruenit ad mortem."

85. Cf. *HEv.* 1.2.8 (PL 76, 1085), *HEz.* 1.5.2 (CCL 142, 57–58).

afflictions of the flesh,"[86] Gregory writes to Venantius, warning him not
to bemoan the torments of the gout they both suffer. Through suffering
God can even recall men from their own disastrous inclinations. When
God "keeps them busy outwardly in suffering scourges and burdens, he
hides them from receiving the darts of the enemy inwardly."[87]

Man's harmony and right relationship with God are restored when
the things he desires are turned to affliction: through the scourge he is
brought back to peace with God.[88] Man is purged through suffering,[89] returning to "eternal joys through temporal losses."[90] The *flagella peccati* are
turned to *flagella disciplinae*, and "God chastens every son he receives"
(Prv 3:12; Heb 12:6).

As the wounds of mutability cure sin, temporal suffering brings eternal joys. This logic of antithesis also explains God's pedagogic motives
for allowing man to fall in the first place: evils are instrumental in teaching the good by contrasts, which is the best method of instruction. Augustine well understood how God could teach through vexation (*per mo-
lestias*).[91] If the master teaches with contrasts, the rhetor does so in
speaking, and the preacher in ministering to souls.[92] Such is also the practice of medicine, curing with like and unlike remedies, often "wounding
to heal."[93] God uses these methods in Holy Scripture.

86. *Ep.* 11.18 (CCL 140A, 887).

87. *Mor.* 33.19.35 (CCL 143B, 1705–6).

88. *Mor.* 3.9.15 (CCL 143, 124). The paedeutic and remedial function of life in the body
and of suffering is found in Origen, *hom. 1–14 in Ezech.* 12; *princ.* 2.10.6; see Jean Daniélou,
Origen, trans. Walter Mitchel (New York, 1955), 277ff. Augustine also speaks of the Divine
Physician allowing afflictions and temptations to restore the soul to full health; cf. *quaest.
Simpl.* 83. q. 82.3 (PL 40, 99), cited by Rudolph Arbesmann, "The Concept of 'Christus Medicus' in St. Augustine," *Traditio* 10 (1954): 21, n. 98. The painful results of sin are positive
suffering in Maximus the Confessor; see Lars Thunberg, *Microcosm and Mediator* (Lund,
1965), 166–71; 413–15. Thunberg sees not only Gregory's *flagella dei* as parallel to Maximus,
but also Theodoret of Cyrus, for whom simply the ascetic practices of monks are κόπος and
πόνος; see Pierre Cavinet, "Théodoret et le monachisme syrien avant le Concile de Chalcé-
doine," in *Théologie de la vie monastique* (Paris, 1961), esp. 117 ff. The dialectic of pleasure and
pain found in Gregory is ultimately part of the Stoic mentality, which sees world economy
as a pattern of contrasts; see J. M. Rist, *Stoic Philosophy* (Cambridge, 1969), 37–54. The extreme position is the Epicurean model of suffering torture in Phalaris's bull and finding it
sweet: "Quam suave est, quam hoc non curo!"—Cic. *Tusc.* 2.7.17.

89. *Mor.* 24.11.33–34 (CCL 143B, 1212–13); *Mor.* 3.14.27 (CCL 143, 132).

90. *Mor.* 26.16.26 (CCL 143B, 1284): "Quia enim ad aeterna gaudia redire non possumus, nisi per temporalia detrimenta. . . ."

91. *En. 17 in Ps. 118*, 2, cited by Brown, *Augustine of Hippo*, 237, n. 1.

92. For the importance of antithesis in rhetoric, see Quint. *Inst.* 9.3.81–86. Cicero's
parad. also shows the importance of paradox and antithesis in the classical tradition. See
Dagen's discussion of the connection between rhetoric and Gregory's preaching, *Saint Grégoire*, 124–34.

93. *Mor.* 26.47.87 (CCL 143B, 1330).

It must be noted especially that God moderates the words of Sacred Scripture mercifully, now terrifying us with harsh threats, now refreshing us with sweet consolations. He mixes terror with comfort and comfort with terror, so when each is tempered around us through the wonderful art of teaching, we should not become carelessly secure or desperately fearful.[94]

Indeed, all of God's dispensation is an economy of antithesis and paradoxical contrast to teach such lessons. For instance, the devil's fall teaches the other angels by what strength they should remain fixed in God; for man, the vengeance of God visited on the reprobate exists to teach the elect good behavior.[95] Even the punishments of the damned in hell will increase the joys of the elect in paradise: against a black background red or white is more clearly perceived.[96]

This dialectic converts thesis to antithesis, showing the complementarity of opposites. God's justice is transformed to his mercy, and he brings good out of evil. Desiring man's advancement,[97] God challenged man's humility by requiring him to refrain from good, namely, from eating of the tree in paradise.[98] Man disobeyed and was punished in God's "strict justice,"[99] but from that justice comes an even greater mercy:

> If indeed [God] permitted evils to come about by his strict judgment, nevertheless he mercifully foreordained from these evils what good he would make from punishments. For what is a greater sin than that

94. *Mor.* 33.7.14 (CCL 143B, 1684–85).
95. *In lib. I Reg.* 4.9 (CCL 144, 300).
96. *Mor.* 33.14.29 (CCL 143B, 1698–99). The origin of such ideas is Stoic, "that things go by contraries, that there cannot be pleasure without pain; that the existence of local pain, even to the good, is justified by the 'economy' or necessary arrangement of the world"; see Rist, *Stoic Philosophy*, 50. Rist cites Gellius 7.1 and Plut. *Stoic. repug.* 105E in *Stoicorum Veterum Fragmenta*; see also E. Vernon Arnold, *Roman Stoicism* (Cambridge, 1911), 207ff. The mentality of contraries and antitheses is taken up in the early Church by Athenagoras, Tatian, Irenaeus, Clement, and others, and reinforces the paradoxical structures of Paul, themselves Stoic in inspiration; see Michel Spanneut, *Le Stoïcisme des Pères de l'Eglise de Clément de Rome à Clément d'Alexandrie* (Paris, 1969), 378–79. Gregory seems most influenced by Augustine; see *civ.* 14.11, where good cannot exist without evil, and God permits evils to make good use of them. This sense of order through contraries is strong in *civ.* 11.18; 14.11; *enchir.* 13.4; 14.4; *gen. ad litt.* 11.11.15; *in euang. Ioh.* 27.10; *conf.* 10.28.39; *mus.* 6.11.30. Apart from Augustine's works, Gregory could have found such ideas in Tert. *anim.* 8 and *adv. marc.* 1.16, where even man is composed of contraries; and in Philo. See H. A. Wolfson, *Philo*, 2 vols. (Cambridge, Mass., 1947), 1:332–42. For the fullest treatment of this idea, see Leo Spitzer, *Classical and Christian Ideas of World Harmony* (Baltimore, 1963). This pattern of contraries is part of the larger pattern of polarity described by G. E. R. Lloyd, *Polarity and Analogy* (Cambridge, 1966), 48ff. and passim. The contraries of good and evil, black and white, are found in the Pythagorean table of opposites in Arist. *meta.* A5.986a.22ff.
97. *Mor.* 35.14.29 (CCL 143B, 1793–94).
98. *Mor.* 35.14.29 (CCL 143B, 1793–94); cf. Aug. *civ.* 13.20.
99. *In lib. I Reg.* 4.10 (CCL 144, 300–301).

through which all of us die? And what is a greater good than that through which all of us are freed from death? Indeed, if Adam had not sinned, it would not have been necessary for our Redeemer to take our flesh from the Virgin. . . . Therefore, when God was about to be born a man for sinners, he, being omnipotent, foresaw the good he would make from that evil whereby all were to die, and that the good would conquer that evil.[100]

After the strict judgment of the Fall comes the mercy of the Redemption, proof that God's goodness surpasses evil. The magnitude of the Redemption is such that Gregory inquires, "Who would not be willing to suffer worse evils than not to have so great a Redeemer?"[101] Man has learned much from the Fall. Defying God, he lost control of his servant the flesh, so that "the shame of his disobedience would redound upon him, so he would learn when defeated what he lost when proud."[102] But he learns through adversity. Gregory echoes the spirituality of Hebrews 9:13–28 and especially 5:8–9: "Son though he was, he learned obedience through adversity; and when perfected he became the source of eternal salvation for all who obey him."

The psychology of this dialectical mentality is intricate. Pain heightens joy and pleasure, the good is appreciated all the more fiercely when evil is most depraved. The effect is profoundly dramatic, aesthetic, and rhetorical: tension is increased deliberately to make the catharsis of reprieve all the more intense and memorable. The beauty of the universe lies in this harmonious composition of high and low notes, of good and evil, pleasure and pain, well-being and sickness. Without sin there would be no redemption; health means nothing unless sickness schools us in misery (this last applies especially to Gregory, who was chronically ill). Gregory can thus explain the role of suffering and evil with satisfying certitude: they are a necessary part of man's experience of the good.

The final goal is self-control and mastery of one's life.[103] By confront-

100. Ibid.
101. Ibid.
102. *Mor.* 26.17.28 (CCL 143B, 1286–87): "Et quia auctori suo esse subditus noluit, ius carnis subditae quam regebat amisit, ut in seipso uidelicet inoboedientiae suae confusio redundaret, et superatus disceret, quid elatus amisisset." Similarly, *Mor.* 24.7.14 (CCL 143B, 1197): "Sed quia diuino munere redemptus homo iustitiam recepit, quam dudum conditus amisit, robustiorem se iam contra blandimenta callidae persuasionis exercet, quia experimento didicit quantum oboediens esse debeat praecepto. Et quem tunc culpa duxit ad poenam, nunc poena sua restringit a culpa, ut tanto magis delinquere metuat, quanto cogente supplicio et ipse iam quod perpetrauit accusat." Cf. *Mor.* 25.3.4 (CCL 143B, 1231–32); *Mor.* 11.43.59 (CCL 143A, 619).
103. Cf. Sen. *dial.* 1 (*de providentia*, 4.6; 1.6; 2.4), 7 (*de vita beata*, 27.3); *epist.* 75.17–18; 85.28; 9.3–5; 31.11; 63.1; 66.20ff. See M. Spanneut, "Le Stoïcisme dans l'histoire de la patience chrétienne," *MSR* 39 (1982): 101–5.

ing evil and experiencing the worst, the Christian can face the future with confidence and tranquillity. The devil cannot break the soul of the holy man who knows how to bear suffering with *aequanimitas*. At last the devil is conquered with man's patience. Evil dissolves before man's *fortitudo*, his courage and strength to endure suffering. Each "wound inflicted in [the devil's] cruelty" furnishes an opportunity of victory for the holy man.[104] To control one's reaction to suffering and temptation is to be master of all the possible disasters the devil can devise. Even the darkest moments of trial are somehow triumphant with man's defeat of evil.

The Christian should not merely tolerate ambivalent situations, but expect them. To embrace the good, one must conquer the evil; and to conquer evil, one must endure it. Sometimes one even seeks out the challenge in order to prove one's strength to deepen one's soul, one's *magnanimitas*. "There is no palm of victory without the toil of battle," Gregory writes in *Dialogues* 3.19.5.[105] Herein lies stability, for Gregory's dialectic embraces a wide variety of experience and integrates many different feelings into the mosaic of life. The negative and positive aspects of life become inseparable and interdependent, unified in a pattern of puzzling complexity and haunting ambivalence.

104. *Mor.* 23.1.1 (CCL 143B, 1143–4).
105. SC 260, 348.

· VII ·

THE MEDIATOR OF GOD
AND MAN

The theological disputes of late antiquity had a sharp and bitter edge. Partisan camps marred the Church's tranquillity with their contentious zeal and unsavory tactics. Much was at stake, for, just as today, theological positions could encapsulate a world view and a political outlook. Yet the extent and the intensity of engagement in these debates is surprising, if the anecdote told by Gregory of Nyssa is an accurate reflection of the times. He could scarcely buy bread or visit the baths without being lectured on theological niceties by eager shopkeepers and attendants.[1]

By the sixth century the theological climate was perhaps more subdued, but no less tangled. The disputes about the Trinity provoked by Arius had been adjudicated by the Council of Nicaea in 325, but, ironically, Arianism always seemed latent in the Eastern empire, and even came to flourish among Germanic tribes in the West. These Trinitarian controversies in turn spurred interest in the nature of Christ. Although Christological heresies—Apollinarianism, Nestorianism, and Monophysitism—were primarily Eastern phenomena, the West had intervened at a crucial moment with Leo's *Tome* at the Council of Chalcedon in 451. The next century brought stormy reactions to Chalcedon that confounded imperial efforts to secure harmony.

For his part, Gregory bore the inauspicious legacy of Justinian. Surrounded by a court of Monophysite sympathizers, Justinian had obtained a condemnation of the Three Chapters[2] at the Fifth Ecumenical

1. Gr. Nyss. *deit.*, cited by A. H. M. Jones, *The Decline of the Ancient World* (London, 1966), 329.
2. That is, certain works of Theodore of Mopsuestia, Theodoret of Cyrus, and Ibas of Edessa.

Council in 553. The settlement satisfied no one. The papacy agreed very reluctantly to this rejection of allegedly Nestorian writings, since the synod did reaffirm Chalcedon. But this very affirmation alienated Monophysites in the East, who grew increasingly autonomous. Meanwhile, in the West, where few had deemed the Three Chapters as dangerous in the first place, protests rang out, especially from bishops in Africa, Illyricum, and Dalmatia. All northern Italy seceded for a time. While the church under the metropolitan of Milan did reestablish relations with Rome about 570–573, Gregory later had to detach a number of Istrian and Venetian bishops from their loyalty to the Patriarch of Aquileia.

In his own time, Gregory upheld the orthodox position, steering a steady course around the problems posed by Arianism, Monophysitism, and the dispute over the Three Chapters. Indeed, he displays little interest in the kind of technical speculation one finds in such "professional" theologians as Athanasius or Gregory Nazianzen. Gregory reiterates Chalcedonian formulas,[3] and perhaps his traditionalism has led historians to overlook the finer points of his Christology.[4] However, in Gregory's distinctive pattern of thought, there are idiosyncratic emphases and departures from prevailing tradition.

Structurally, Gregory's is a Christocentric spirituality, for the remedies and reversals of Christ are the archetypes of the larger paradoxical order Gregory sees throughout the universe. Christ explains how and why life is ordered as it is: how carnal life can be transformed and elevated; how the flesh can be returned to its true partnership with the spirit. Man, his body, his active service to neighbor, even the worldly power of the Church can be renewed and revivified because Christ reverses the unfortunate order resulting from man's Fall. The carnal realm can be exalted, though this exaltation comes dialectically through humility and sacrifice: triumph comes through suffering temptation and physical tribulation. Here again one sees the dialectical ambivalence charac-

3. Gregory's tendency to balance the human and divine sides is Chalcedonian, and he follows closely the Christology of Leo's *Tome* (= *ep.* 28) and his sermons. Two sets of Leo's sermons or *Tractus* survive, edited in CCL 138 and 138A, indicated by roman and arabic numerals from which I will cite. While deacon, Gregory probably wrote a letter on the Three Chapters for Pelagius II to the bishops of Istria (MGH *Ep.* 2 *App.* 3 (3), 449–67); an article by Paul Meyvaert on the subject is forthcoming. On Gregory's support of orthodoxy, see Jaroslav Pelikan, *The Emergence of the Catholic Tradition (100–600)*, vol. 1 of *The Christian Tradition: A History of the Development of Doctrine* (Chicago and London, 1971), 335–57.

4. Little has been written on Gregory's Christology beyond F. Homes Dudden, *Gregory the Great* (London, 1905), 2:324–47; Claude Dagens, *Saint Grégoire le Grand* (Paris, 1977), 166, 176, 255, and passim. Much of Gregory's Christology and soteriology is part of a Christian tradition shared by all writers; only the particularities of interpretation that can be traced to certain writers will be noted.

teristic of Gregory's thought. Carnal and spiritual realms are reunited in Christ, yet man is never free to celebrate this reunion, for fear always balances hope. Though the economy of salvation proves again that all power rests in God's hands, nevertheless man's efforts must be continual and assiduous.

In emphasizing the redemptive power of suffering and sacrifice, Gregory may be countering Monophysite tendencies to emphasize Christ's divinity, and also following Leo, who successfully coupled the divinity of Christ displayed in miracles with the humanity of his suffering.[5] Like Leo, Gregory realizes that some have been outraged or scandalized by the Cross.[6] But through his Passion, Christ triumphs: "the more [Christ] endured indignities for men, the more fittingly should men honor him as God."[7] Yet Gregory also anticipates the Christology of the High Middle Ages, with its emphasis on Christ's Passion, in seeing Job as a type of Christ. Job's patience, his profound and deeply human confrontation with the mystery of suffering and evil lend an even deeper hue to Christ's Passion.[8] Thus while Gregory follows neo-Chalcedonian formulas that carefully balance Christ's humanity and divinity, his own predilections and particularly his attachment to monastic values subtly shape his views of Christ. A monk firmly convinced of the value of obedience, Gregory emphasizes Christ's humility and submission to adversity, a sacrifice of will anticipated by Job and recapitulated by every good monk.[9] Like the Desert Fathers, Gregory believes life should be a continual act of penitence and compunction.[10] Man's imitation of Christ's humility and Passion fulfills this imperative; indeed, the core of the New Dispensation is penitence, that sacrifice of self and confession of sinfulness which purifies one's work and makes it acceptable to God.

Sacrifice is the "hinge" joining spiritual and carnal. On one level, sacrifice separates body and soul in death; but on another, it reunites them,

5. In addition to Leo's *Tome*, his sermons on the passion and transfiguration influenced Gregory; cf. Leon. *tract.* LI; LIV–LXI; LXX; *tract.* 62–69. The unity of God and man is especially emphatic in the transfiguration, and this is a Byzantine interest. Art works reflecting Byzantine ties emphasize the transfiguration during this period; see O. G. Von Simson, *Sacred Fortress: Byzantine Art and Statecraft in Ravenna* (Chicago, 1948), 40–68; C. Ihm, *Die Programme der christlichen Apsismalerei vom vierten Jahrhundert bis zur Mitte des achten Jahrhunderts* (Wiesbaden, 1960), 69–74.

6. Cf. *HEv.* 1.6.1 (PL 76, 1095–96); *HEz.* 1.2.11 (CCL 142, 23); cf. Leon. *tract.* LI.3.

7. Cf. *HEv.* 1.6.1 (PL 76, 1096). See also *HEv.* 1.2.1 (PL 76, 1082).

8. On Christ crucified, see Jaroslav Pelikan, *Jesus Through the Centuries* (New Haven and London, 1985), 95–108.

9. See A. Borias, "Le Christ dans la Règle de saint Benoît," *RBen* 82 (1972): 127ff., on the monk imitating especially the passion of Christ and his obedience to the Father.

10. E.g., *Vitae patr.* 5.3.1–27.

regenerated and transformed. Christ died for all humanity, and in imitation of Christ, man must sacrifice his carnal life, mortifying the flesh and separating his soul from involvement with worldly pursuits. Yet body and soul were rejoined when Christ rose from the dead, foreshadowing the reunion of all bodies and souls in the Resurrection. So even now each man's carnal life can return in a purified form when cleansed with tears of compunction and dedicated to God as a humble offering. Through this separation, purification, and reunion, sacrifice actually reverses the rebellion of the flesh, rejoining it to the spirit. As Christ's sacrifice has purified humanity and opened a channel of grace to elevate man, so this channel is renewed continually in the sacrifice of the Mass and in the offering of oneself in penance. Ultimately, the Christian's transformation becomes tied to the Church, the priest, and the sacraments—a focus on institutions that also informs Gregory's idea of the saint.

Gregory's Christology encourages hope; indeed, he offers several reasons why man should rejoice in his redemption. (But, as we shall see later, Gregory never releases his audience from the fear that balances such hope.) It is surely heartening to see how Christ reveals the inner harmony of cosmic order. Despite all the contraries and oppositions man perceives, he can still recognize the providential hand of God directing his fate. With Christ's advent, the unity and continuity of God's dispensation is at last apparent. God has always desired man's righteousness, and with Christ this can at last be attained. Christ also manifests the unity of God in himself, showing how God's justice and mercy, his severity and kindness, are complementary sides of his concern for man. Creator and Redeemer, Judge and Advocate—all are Christ. Performing contrasting roles, creating and dying, condemning and pardoning, Christ reminds man of God's omnipotence and omnipresence as the divine plan unfolds to save the elect.

The Christian should find consolation here in knowing the varieties of divine concern, for Christ heals the divisions that scar human experience. Man's redemption depends upon the reunion of God and man; his humble participation in God had to be reestablished. Christ accomplishes this, rejoining God and man and reconstituting a divided universe of flesh and spirit. As the Mediator of God and man (*mediator Dei et hominum* [1 Tm 2:5]),[11] Christ restores the cosmos by mediating its dis-

---

11. Patrick Catry notes that Gregory uses *Mediator Dei et hominum* over fifty times in his exegetical works to refer to Christ, but one finds only one usage in *In lib. I Reg.*, which

parate halves. Every level of creation, from the most secret recesses of the human heart to the furthest extremities of the physical world, is touched and healed. Christ reconciles the irreconcilable: spirit and flesh, high and low, heaven and earth, God and man. As Mediator, he is both Teacher and Redeemer, Priest and Victim; each pair represents a carnal and spiritual polarity. Christ is a midpoint gathering and reconciling every contrariety:

> Being mortal and unrighteous, we were a great distance from the Righteous and Immortal One. But the Mediator of God and Man appeared between us, the mortal and unrighteous and the Immortal and Righteous One, sharing mortality with men, and righteousness with God. Since through our depths we were so far away from the heights, he joined in himself the lowliness and highness together, and this became for us a way of return, for he joined our depths with his heights.[12]

The contrarieties of mortal and immortal, righteousness and unrighteousness, highness and lowness are canceled out in Christ, who makes remedies of opposites. Christ creates a new equilibrium that restores man to his rightful position and returns him to his true spiritual identity.

This restoration begins by reversing man's Fall. The humility of Christ becomes central to all the reversals of redemption. He is the Second Man whose humble submission to suffering reverses the pride and disobedience of the first man, Adam.[13] Christ teaches humility and the necessity of submission to God. Reversing the devil's pride with humility, Christ is "the goodness born on earth to unite those whom evil had separated from us."[14] While the devil and the first man sought power and self-sufficiency, proud mistakes separating them from God, Christ's humility reestablishes the proper hierarchy of subordination, and so recaptures unity with God through his obedience. With awesome sympathy for man, Christ deliberately rejected the power of majesty in his divinity and chose instead to endure suffering in the flesh with patience and hu-

---

suggests Claude of Ravenna may have substantially edited the text; "L'Amour du prochain chez saint Grégoire le Grand," *StudMon* 20 (1978): 299, n. 62.

12. *Mor.* 22.17.42 (CCL 143A, 1122): "Longe quippe distabamus a iusto et immortali, nos mortales et iniusti. Sed inter immortalem iustum et nos mortales iniustos apparuit Mediator Dei et hominum mortalis et iustus, qui et mortem haberet cum hominibus, et iustitiam cum Deo; ut quia per ima nostra longe distabamus a summis, in seipso uno iungeret ima cum summis, atque ex eo nobis uia redeundi fieret, quo summis suis ima nostra copularet."

13. *Mor.* 3.14.26 (CCL 143, 131).

14. *Mor.* 27.15.29 (CCL 143B, 1352).

mility.[15] Through Christ, through the imitation of such humble and right-eous virtue, man's true likeness to God can be restored.[16] Man becomes a "new creature" and the "old has passed away" (cf. 2 Cor 5:17).[17]

Through Christ's humility man rises, as he is elevated by clinging to God. Christ demonstrates that man can regain stability and reclaim his proper inheritance. Although man is both spirit and clay, he can now con-quer the devil, who is pure spirit. The devil may be higher ontologically, but man is higher morally, so "rightly does humble dust now conquer the proud spirit."[18] Now man gains power over the spiritual world. He will sit in judgment of the angels; he can free souls from torment after the grave through his prayers.[19] Flesh rises above spirit, because spirit con-descended to bear the flesh.

In order to restore man's true spiritual inheritance, Christ needs to heal the human condition by supplying what is wanting. A reciprocal ex-change between Christ and mankind allows each side to acquire the qual-ities of its opposite. This complementary exchange, effected by Christ's redemption, is a variation of the traditional *communicatio idiomatum*.

> For [Christ] was made flesh to make us spiritual. He mercifully lowered himself to raise us; he departed [from heaven] to admit us; he appeared visible to show us the invisible; he suffered scourges to cleanse us; he bore rejection and derision to free us from eternal reproach; he died to vivify us.[20]

God and man bear the outline of Christ, but, like images in a mirror, they are reversed—what the divinity does can bring the equal and op-posite effect in man. As each takes on an aspect of the other, the transfer of energy is balanced, so to speak. Through the mediation of Christ, who

---

15. *Mor.* 20.36.69 (CCL 143A, 1054); *Mor.* 34.23.54 (CCL 143B, 1770–71).

16. *In lib. I Reg.* 2.106 (CCL 144, 176); cf. *Mor.* 18.48.79 (CCL 143A, 942–43); *HEz.* 1.2.19 (CCL 142, 28–29); cf. Gregorio Penco, "S. Gregorio e la teologia dell'immagine," *Benedictina* 18 (1971): 42–44.

17. *Cant.* 4 (CCL 144, 6).

18. *Mor.* 32.24.51 (CCL 143B, 1669): "Sed quia supernorum spirituum conditor ter-renum corpus assumpsit, recte iam superbientem angelum humilis puluis uincit. Inhaeren-do quippe uerae fortitudini uires accipit, quas transfuga spiritus, cum semetipsum sequi-tur, amisit. . . . homo ad summa conscendat; quod in illa celsitudine subuecta caro permanet, a qua tantus ipse spiritus sine fine proiectus iacet. Sed loca mentium mutauit ordo meritorum. Sic sic superbia meruit deici, sic humilitas exaltari, quatenus et caelestis spiritus erigendo se tartarum toleret, et terra humilis sine termino super caelos regnet."

19. *Dial.* 2.23.6 (SC 260, 208–10).

20. *HEz.* 2.4.20 (CCL 142, 272): "Caro enim factus est ut nos spiritales faceret, benigne inclinatus est ut leuaret, exiit ut introduceret, uisibilis apparuit ut inuisibilia monstraret, flagella pertulit ut sanaret, opprobria et irrisiones sustinuit ut ab opprobrio aeterno libera-ret, mortuus est ut uiuificaret."

is both divine and human, power is transferred across the boundary between divinity and humanity. Spiritual becomes carnal, making carnal spiritual. This complementary exchange remedies differences and restores balance, cleanses and heals man to restore his spiritual health. Christ is the Physician whose remedies of likeness and unlikeness provide what is lacking: "our Physician, coming from above and finding us oppressed with much cold, applied like and unlike remedies. To men he came as man, but to sinners he came as a righteous man. He agreed with us in the truth of his nature, but he differed from us in the power of his righteousness."[21]

Christ becomes the remedy of likeness in being human, for this unity with man allows him to transfer qualities to mankind. Yet Christ is also the remedy of unlikeness, for he supplies the warm righteousness necessary to cure man's cold sin. This opposition and inner unity is the fundamental structural pattern of the Redemption, and indeed of the larger cosmos.

More precisely, Christ reestablishes man's spiritual health by redirecting man's use of the flesh from sin to righteousness, not only in conquering temptation but also in suffering pain. In the context of Gregory's suspicion of the body, this use of the flesh for salvation is highly paradoxical. Christ's humility is so great that he chooses suffering in the flesh as the primary means of expiating man's sin. When Job sits on the dunghill in Job 2:8, Gregory interprets this as symbolic of the Incarnation, when the Redeemer takes on the flesh to suffer the "pain of his Passion" amidst the "contempt of his people."[22] For Gregory, who so identifies the flesh with weakness and pollution, even bearing the flesh is a great con-

---

21. *Mor.* 24.2.2 (CCL 143B, 1189): "Veniens ergo ad nos desuper medicus noster, tantisque nos inueniens languoribus pressos, quiddam nobis simile, et quiddam contrarium apposuit. Ad homines quippe homo uenit, sed ad peccatores iustus. Concordauit nobis ueritate naturae, sed discrepauit a nobis uigore iustitiae." See also *Mor.* 24.2.2ff. (CCL 143B, 1189ff.); *HEz.* 1.2.9ff. (CCL 142, 22ff.). For Christ as Physician, see Adolf Harnack, *Medizinisches aus der ältesten Kirchengeschichte* (Leipzig, 1892), 4:136ff. Harnack notes medical imagery is particularly strong in Tert. (esp. *anim.*) and in Or. *Cels.* See also G. Dumeige, "Le Christ médecin dans la littérature chrétienne des premiers siècles," *RAC* 48 (1972): 115–41, an article with much on Origen. Medical imagery is also strong in Augustine; see Rudolph Arbesmann, "The Concept of 'Christus Medicus' in St. Augustine," *Traditio* 10 (1954): 1–28; and his "Christ the *medicus humilis* in Saint Augustine," in *Augustinus Magister* (Paris, 1955), 2:623–29. Augustine speaks of the humility of the Divine Physician, who heals the tumor of pride in man. See also Erich Dinkler, *Die Anthropologie Augustins* (Stuttgart, 1934), 128ff. See also: M. E. Keenan, "Gregory Nazianzen and East Byzantine Medicine," *BHM* 9 (1941): 8–30; Arthur S. Pease, "Medical Allusions in the Works of St. Jerome," *HSPh* 25 (1914): 73–86. Theodoret of Cyrus also employs medical imagery; cf. *affect.*, *h.e.*, as does Cic. *Tusc.* 4.10.22f. and passim.

22. *Mor.* 3.19.34 (CCL 143, 137).

descension and sacrifice for God. For Christ's divinity to assume corruptible flesh is to be "shod" with the "skin of dead animals."[23] Like a
vulture, Christ descends to the carcass of dead humanity and becomes
himself the prey.[24] But Christ chooses to bear the "scourges of man's mortal nature" to remove man's sins.[25]

Yet the strength of this paradox shows how deeply Gregory rejoices
in the redemption of the flesh and the return of its true inheritance. As
bearer of man's corruptibility, the flesh represents man's sinfulness, the
means by which the devil holds him captive. With his death, however,
Christ atones for man, so setting him free through his Passion.[26] Christ
purifies the flesh through suffering: the "rust of sin could not be cleansed
except by the fire of torture"; his "blood cleanses the stain of our guilt."[27]
What man has made "an instrument of sin," Christ converts to the "arms
of righteousness";[28] that is, the flesh Adam used for pleasure and sin
Christ now converts to righteousness by suffering human weakness. The
very power of sinless divinity suffering the flesh now tempers it to immutability: "from the tribulation of suffering Christ strengthened the assumed flesh for the glory of the Resurrection."[29] Made "hard" through
the Resurrection, the flesh becomes "durable like brass."[30] At last, the
true inheritance of incorruptibility is restored to the flesh. No longer need
the flesh obstruct spiritual vision. Now the flesh can be disciplined to
endure the troubling mutabilities of daily life.

Man regains his true inheritance because Christ's sacrifice discharges
the claims of both the devil and God against man. Through his Passion,
Christ frees man from the power of Satan, giving himself over to Satan's
rage to be spat upon, beaten, pierced, and crucified.[31] Gregory does believe that the devil has a legal claim to enslave man for his voluntary sin,
and that this claim cannot be abrogated until some recompense is made.[32]
Christ's sacrifice takes away the guilt that binds man in the devil's thrall.[33]

23. Cf. *HEv*. 1.7.3 (PL 76, 1101).
24. *Mor*. 18.34.54 (CCL 143A, 921–22).
25. *Mor*. 3.14.26 (CCL 143, 131).
26. *Mor*. 3.18.33 (CCL 143, 136–37).
27. *Mor*. 3.14.27 (CCL 143, 132): "Rubigo quippe uitii purgari non potuit nisi igne tor-
menti. . . . sed cruore proprio reatus nostri maculam tersit."
28. *Mor*. 3.18.33 (CCL 143, 137).
29. *HEv*. 2.34.6 (PL 76, 1249).
30. Cf. *HEz*. 1.4.3 (CCL 142, 49); *HEv*. 2.34.6 (PL 76, 1249).
31. *Mor*. 3.16.29 (CCL 143, 133–34).
32. *Mor*. 17.30.46 (CCL 143A, 877–78). See Aug. *trin*. 13.15; Ambr. *epist* 72.8; *Isaac*
1.3.10; and *epist*. 41.7, where the blood of Christ is a ransom paid to the devil. Gregory is
not so explicit, but still the devil as well as God is satisfied by Christ's sacrifice.
33. *Mor*. 17.30.46 (CCL 143A, 877–78).

The devil loses claim over his kingdom when Christ, the Second Man, reverses the Fall of the first man.[34] Matching deceit with deceit, Christ frees man by tricking the devil into overstepping his authority. Christ becomes a "fishhook": his humanity is the bait, his divinity the hook, and Leviathan is snared.[35] Because the devil is proud, he cannot understand Christ's humility and so believes he tempts and kills a mere man.[36] But in inflicting a sinless man with death, the devil loses his rights over man from his "excess of presumption."[37] Christ conquers the devil's kingdom of sin, liberating captives from the devil's tyranny. Order is reinstated when man returns to serve God, his true master.

Man's predicament with God must be rectified as well, for every sin offends God and demands its recompense. Though deeply indebted for his sins, man alone cannot make satisfactory compensation. For this reason, Christ takes on suffering and death in payment of man's sins.[38] Though perfect himself, he deigns to take on the punishment and chastisement due man's iniquities. This sacrifice of his unjust suffering substitutes for man and propitiates God's wrath. As both a rational creature and a sinless one, only Christ could be man's substitute.[39] His sacrifice atones for man's sin because he has suffered the punishment that cleanses and removes man's transgressions.[40]

With the defeat of the devil and the propitiation of God's wrath, the order of creation is not only restored but even regenerated for the better. All things are made anew in Christ,[41] and the established hierarchical or-

---

34. *Mor.* 3.14.26 (CCL 143, 131).

35. *HEv.* 2.25.8 (PL 76, 1194): "In hamo autem esca ostenditur, aculeus occultatur. Hunc ergo Pater omnipotens hamo coepit, quia ad mortem illius unigenitum Filium incarnatum misit, in quo et caro passibilis videri posset, et divinitas impassibilis videri non posset. Cumque in eo serpens iste per manus persequentium escam corporis momordit, divinitatis illum aculeus perforavit." See also *In lib. I Reg.* 1.5.10 (CCL 144, 422). The fishhook image is Gregory of Nyssa's, coming to Gregory through Rufinus, *symb.* 16; cf. Jean Rivière, *Le Dogme de la rédemption après saint Augustin* (Paris, 1930), 94; Gustaf Aulén, *Christus Victor,* trans. A. G. Herbert (New York, 1969), 68.

36. *Mor.* 17.30.47 (CCL 143A, 878); *Mor.* 2.22.41ff. (CCL 143, 84ff.); cf. *Mor.* 3.20.38 (CCL 143, 139).

37. *Mor.* 17.30.47 (CCL 143A, 878). From Irenaeus we have the notion of the devil overextending his authority; cf. *haer.* 3.32.2. See also Hastings Rashdall, *The Idea of Atonement in Christian Theology* (London, 1919), 243.

38. *Mor.* 3.14.27 (CCL 143, 132): "Venit itaque sine uitio; qui se subiceret sponte tormento, ut debita nostrae iniquitati supplicia eo reos suos iuste amitterent, quo hunc a semetipsis liberum iniuste tenuissent."

39. *Mor.* 17.30.46 (CCL 143A, 877–78).

40. Cf. *Mor.* 17.30.46 (CCL 143A, 877–78).

41. *Mor.* 31.49.99 (CCL 143B, 1618–19). After explaining that the Mediator came to restore the number of fallen angels with men, Gregory continues: " 'Proposuit in eo, in dispensatione plenitudinis temporum, instaurare omnia in Christo, quae in caelis, et quae in

der of spirit and flesh is inverted. Not only is man exalted as the devil is laid low, but man's relationship with the angels changes as well. In Christ, man is made equal to the angels—indeed, human nature is exalted above them.[42] The highest and the lowest are united because man is taught to ascend by condescending to suffer, a union symbolized in the Mass.[43] The angels can no longer despise man for his carnal life, for it is precisely through Christ's condescension to bear the flesh that man becomes even more righteous than they.

While Gregory's soteriology is traditional, even punctilious, the very smoothness and polish of his treatment warrant study. Whether discussing the process of salvation itself, the activities of Christ, or the two natures of Christ, Gregory constructs a distinctive balance and complementarity between carnal and spiritual realms. Their elaborate reconciliation through Christ redounds to the benefit of the carnal realm, for it is elevated and strengthened through its association with the spiritual.

Salvation entails a balance of human and divine activities, an equilibrium between God and man, and, correspondingly, between human and divine natures in Christ. Salvation involves both human and divine action, for the just God demands that man perform righteous acts, while the merciful God accepts man's deeds because Christ has won God's favor. Thus Christ has two roles: to teach man righteousness and to die vicariously for man. Christ desires that this lesson of his redemption not be lost: "[He] came in the flesh not only to redeem us by his Passion but to teach us by his way of life, giving an example to those who follow him."[44] Christ knows both redeeming and teaching are necessary, so he does not offer one without the other.[45] Consequently, those whom Christ "teaches by living," he "redeems by dying."[46] Christ is both Teacher and Redeemer, but the two roles are one and the same: Christ's sacrifice is both man's redemption and his instruction. Christ sacrifices himself to

---

terra sunt in ipso' [Eph 1:9–10]. In ipso quippe restaurantur ea quae in terra sunt, dum peccatores ad iustitiam conuertuntur. In ipso restaurantur ea quae in caelis sunt, dum illuc humiliati homines redeunt unde apostatae angeli superbiendo ceciderunt." Cf. *Cant.* 4 (CCL 144, 7). Christ brings more than a recapitulation of the universe and a return to beginnings, as is found in the Greek Fathers; see Gerhart B. Ladner, *The Idea of Reform* (New York, 1959; repr. ed. 1967), 154ff. Gregory's reform is *ad melius*, not only because creational order is reworked, giving man a higher place, but because reform comes about through the remission of sins, a most wonderful act of grace.

42. *HEz.* 1.8.23 (CCL 142, 144).
43. *Dial.* 4.60.3 (SC 265, 202).
44. *Reg. Past.* 1.3 (PL 77, 16); cf. Leon. *tract.* 67.5; 45.2; 63.1.
45. *In lib. I Reg.* 1.10 (CCL 144, 61); see also *HEv.* 1.18.4 (PL 76, 1152).
46. Ibid.

propitiate the wrath of the Father, so God becomes more mercifully disposed to mankind. Yet Christ also teaches man to become righteous, following his example of sacrifice. Through this imitation of Christ, man is purified and becomes acceptable to God. A true mediator, Christ brings reconciliation by looking both upward to God and downward to man.

Christ's sacrifice brings about reconciliation by tempering both parties, God and man. Christ becomes the Mediator who reproves or accuses both God and man (cf. Jb 9:33: "There is no one that may be able to accuse both, who can extend a hand against both").[47] Gregory pictures Christ as shaking his fist toward the heavens and toward man. The Mediator of God and man succeeds in accusing or reproving both (*arguere*), being righteous and yet a man; sinless, yet suffering punishment for sin:

> He reproved man so that he would not sin, and he resisted God so that he would not strike man dead. He offered an example of innocence, and he undertook punishment of evil. Therefore, he reproved both by his suffering, since he both corrected the sin of mankind by inspiring righteousness, and he tempered the wrath of the Judge by dying. He shook his fist against both, since he offered examples to men which they could imitate, and displayed works in himself to God by which God could be placated toward men. . . . He taught the guilty righteousness by the same means he placated the angry Judge.[48]

Through his innocent suffering, Christ dies vicariously for man's sins and he placates God's wrath against man. Yet through this sacrifice, he leaves behind an example of perfection for man to imitate that he might stand before God in righteousness. Both actions are necessary. Christ must first soften the relentless justice of severity, obtaining the mercy that will render human actions acceptable to God. Gregory explains how such mercy is a precondition of meritorious action:

> Behold, [man] confesses the evil he has done, but the good that he ought to offer God in compensation he cannot find, since the power of human action is ineffective for the cleansing of sins, unless his mercy in sparing man render it effective, and the justice of the righteous judge not press him down. For this reason it is correctly said by the Psalmist, "Your

47. *Mor*. 9.38.60 (CCL 143, 499–500).
48. *Mor*. 9.38.61 (CCL 143, 501): "Redemptor quippe humani generis, mediator Dei et hominis per carnem factus, quia iustus in hominibus solus apparuit et tamen ad poenam culpae etiam sine culpa peruenit et hominem arguit ne delinqueret, et Deo obstitit ne feriret, exempla innocentiae praebuit, poenam malitiae suscepit. Patiendo ergo utrumque arguit, qui et culpam hominis, iustitiam aspirando, corripuit et iram iudicis moriendo temperauit. Atque in utrisque manum posuit, quia et exempla hominibus quae imitarentur praebuit, et Deo in se opera quibus erga homines placaretur, ostendit. . . . Manum ergo suam in ambobus posuit quia unde reum recta docuit, inde iratum iudicem placauit."

mercy is better than life" [Ps 62:4], since however innocent it seems, our life still does not free us in the strict judgment of God, if the gentleness of his mercy does not free it from the guilt of its debt.[49]

Christ's sacrifice shifts the cosmic balance to win mercy for man. Through Christ, the guilt of man's debt is paid. Now God may accept man's work and penance, even though strict justice has decreed that "no prayer of man's can obtain indulgence [nor] any work prove righteousness." But "for whom no prayer of man sufficed, the mercy of the Redeemer did not fail."[50]

Christ's work is necessary, but so is man's. Both the individual Christian and Christ act in complementary ways in salvation. Christ redeems mankind corporately, and yet the Christian must imitate this redemption individually.[51] Christ is part of mankind and acts for the whole, while the individual replicates Christ's sacrifice to participate in the larger body of Christ. The corporate action of Christ is primary, but individual action is also enhanced. By winning God's mercy, Christ makes human actions count. Indeed, Christ's redemption is ineffective (*non ualet*) without man's corresponding efforts.[52] Man must imitate the pattern of Christ's life and behave as Christ did.[53] To be a "new creature" in Christ means imitating his Resurrection. As in the Resurrection, the body will be strengthened and elevated through its connection with the spirit, so now that transformation should begin: "just as then we will have nothing pas-

49. *Mor.* 8.31.51 (CCL 143, 422): "Ecce fatetur malum quod egit, sed bonum quod Deo in recompensationem debeat offerre non inuenit; quia ad abluendam culpam quaelibet humanae actionis uirtus infirma est, nisi hanc misericordia parcentis foueat, et non iustitia recte iudicantis premat. Vnde recte per psalmistam dicitur: 'Melior est misericordia tua super uitam' [Ps 62:4]; quia quamlibet uideatur innocens, apud districtum tamen iudicem nostra nos uita non liberat, se ei reatus sui debitum misericordiae benignitas non relaxat."

50. *In lib. I Reg.* 1.2.48 (CCL 144, 148).

51. In the terms of structural anthropology: metaphor balances metonym, the paradigmatic association balances the syntagmatic chain. Yet the two become joined.

52. *In lib. I Reg.* 4.136 (CCL 144, 366).

53. For Christ as Illuminator in Gregory, see Franz Lieblang, *Grundfragen der mystischen Theologie nach Gregors des Grossen Moralia und Ezechielhomilien* (Freiburg im Breisgau, 1934), 44ff. For the tradition of Christ as Illuminator and example of man, see Henry E. W. Turner, *The Patristic Doctrine of Redemption* (London, 1962), 29–46. This theme is found especially in the Apostolic Fathers and later recurs freely; cf. Ambr. *c. Aux.* 28; *in psalm.* 43.46; *virg.* 3.24; esp. *in psalm.* 40.1 and *in psalm.* 20.33, where Christ's life is an example teaching righteousness, an idea found in Aug. *vera relig.* 16.32, and *ep.* 9.4, where Augustine believes the sole reason for the Incarnation is the need to supply an example of behavior for man. Later in life Augustine emphasizes the sacrifice of Christ; see Ladner, *The Idea of Reform*, 153–66, for the Christology of the mature Augustine. The notion of Christ as an example is particularly important to the Greek Fathers in their Logos theology. See Rashdall's remarks in *The Idea of Atonement* on Clement of Alexandria (224ff.), Irenaeus (243ff.) and Origen (258ff.).

sible in the body, so now we should have nothing passible in the heart."[54]
But to imitate Christ is not simply to conquer temptations and passions.
It requires especially a willingness to share in his suffering. In an exegesis
of 1 Sm 9:24 ("Behold what is left, set it before yourself"), Gregory writes:

> Indeed, it is left, since Christ did not fulfill everything for us. To be sure,
> he redeemed everyone through the Cross, but it is left that he who
> strives to be redeemed and reign with him should be crucified with him.
> Clearly, he [Paul] saw what remained who said, "If we suffer with him,
> we shall also reign with him" [2 Tm 2:12], as if he said, "What Christ
> accomplished is not effective for him unless he fulfills what remains."
> Blessed Peter the Apostle said this: "Christ suffers for you, leaving be-
> hind an example for us that we should follow his footsteps" [1 Pt 2:21].
> Paul, for this reason, said: "I fill up those things which are wanting in
> the Passion of Christ in my body" [Col 1:24].[55]

Man must "activate" Christ's redemption. He must complete Christ's
work in his own actions, taking up the sufferings of Christ in his own life,
or Christ's redemption will not work for him. And it is in the sacrifice of
the Mass that the Christian meets Christ's sacrifice in ordinary life. The
Good Shepherd laid down his life for his sheep, Gregory quotes John
10:11–12. He died "so that he could change his body and blood in our
sacrament and satisfy the sheep he redeemed with the food of his
flesh."[56] Man activates the sacrifice of the Mass by replicating it internally:
"that the sacrament of our Lord's Passion may not be inactive in us, we
ought to imitate what we take."[57] Through the ritual drama of the Mass,
the Christian offers himself along with the offering of bread and wine:

54. *Cant.* 4 (CCL 144, 6–7): "Ait apostolus: 'Si qua igitur in Christo noua creatura, uet-
era transierunt' [2 Cor 5:17]. Et scimus, quia in resurrectione nostra ita corpus spiritui ad-
nectitur, ut omne, quod fuerat passionis, in uirtute spiritus adsumatur. Is ergo, qui deum
sequitur, imitari debet cotidie resurrectionem suam: ut, sicut tunc nihil passibile habebit in
corpore, ita nunc nihil passibile habeat in corde; ut secundum interiorem hominem iam
noua creatura sit, iam quidquid uetustum sonuerit calcet, et in uerbis ueteribus solam uim
nouitatis inquirat."

55. *In lib. I Reg.* 4.136 (CCL 144, 366): "Remansit quidem, quia non omnia nostra Christus expleuit. Per crucem quippe suam omnes redemit; sed remansit, ut, qui redimi et reg-
nare cum eo nititur, concrucifigatur. Hoc profecto residuum uiderat, qui dicebat: 'Si con-
patimur, et conregnabimus.' [2 Tm 2:12] Quasi dicat: 'Quod expleuit Christus, non ualet
nisi ei, qui id quod remansit adinplet.' Hinc beatus Petrus apostolus dicit: 'Christus passus
est pro uobis, nobis relinquens exemplum, ut sequamur uestigia eius' [1 Pt 2:21]. Hinc Paulus ait: 'Adinpleo ea, quae desunt passioni Christi, in corpore meo.'" [Col 1:24].

56. *HEv.* 1.14.1 (PL 76, 1127).

57. *Mor.* 13.23.26 (CCL 143A, 683): "Vt ergo in nobis sacramentum dominicae passionis non sit otiosum, debemus imitari quod sumimus et praedicare ceteris quod
ueneramur."

> We must immolate ourselves to God in contrition of heart whenever we
> offer the Mass, since we who celebrate the mysteries of the Lord's Pas-
> sion ought to imitate what we do. For then the Victim will be truly of-
> fered to God for us, when we offer ourselves as victim.[58]

To make the sacrifice of the Mass truly effective, the Christian must
offer himself in penitence and obedience as a burning sacrifice to God.
Each life is offered inwardly on the altar of the heart at the same time the
Holy Victim is offered on the outward altar of the Church on behalf of all
Christians. Through such imitation of the sacrifice of Christ, the individual truly participates in the body of Christ: he continues Christ's Passion
in his body, he follows his footsteps in good works, and he offers his
whole life as a sacrifice in penitential contrition.

This reciprocity of human and divine action expresses the justice, or
aequitas, governing the world: retribution restores the equilibrium and
balance. Salvation is grace, but man must imitate Christ's sacrifice as repayment for his work on man's behalf.[59] This is only just and fair. Each
sinner, purchasing the price of his redemption (*sumere pretium suae re-
demptionis*), confesses, praises, and preaches as much as he is able.[60]
Through the redemption, man becomes Christ's "debtor," where he was
once indebted to the devil because of sin.[61] Now freed, man must repay
his liberator, and he discharges his debt in works by imitating Christ.

In this balance of divine and human activity in salvation, Christ has
reconciled God's justice and his mercy. Christ satisfies the harsh demands of God's justice against man through his sacrifice as a perfect man.
Yet he also displays mercy by acting as a teacher of a new way of life that
justifies man before God. Gregory hopes fervently to bring man to righteousness, and the imitation of Christ holds this extraordinary potential
for man, though few, if any, can reach such perfection. Some men, however, might become like Job, as he stood upright before God and shook
his fist, reproaching (*arguere*) God on the basis of his own good deeds, a
position Gregory admits sounds "very disagreeable." But he recalls God's
admonition to Isaiah as he explains this meaning of *arguere* in Job's lament (Jb 9:33):

58. *Dial.* 4.61.1 (SC 265, 202): "Sed necesse est ut, cum hoc agimus, nosmetipsos Deo
in cordis contritione mactemus, quia qui passionis dominicae mysteria celebramus, debemus imitari quod agimus. Tunc ergo uere pro nobis Deo hostia erit, cum nos ipsos hostiam
fecerit." Cf. Leon. *tract.* 50.3: "quod celebrare optamus imitemur"; *tract.* 70.4.

59. Cf. Leon. *tract.* 67.5.

60. Ibid.

61. *HEv.* 2.25.9 (PL 76, 1195).

Indeed, through Isaiah he admonishes man, saying, "'Cease to do evil, learn to do well. Seek justice. Relieve the oppressed. Judge for the fatherless. Defend the widow [Is 1:16–17]. And then come and accuse me,' says the Lord." For whom we accuse, we oppose with the authority of reason. And why is it that the Lord, admonishing us to do holy deeds, adds, "Come and accuse me," except that he clearly points out how much trust he has in good acts, as if he had openly said, "Do right, and confront my judgment, not with groans for pardon, but with the confidence of authority." Whence John said, "If our heart does not reprehend us, we have confidence towards God" [1 Jn 3:21].[62]

Through good works, man can enjoy a trust or security (*fiducia*) with God. God will have "good faith" in us, as if he were entering into a legal contract. Good works possess a merit that is self-evident: God will acknowledge the righteousness of such good works because his whole dispensation is surely in concert with the "authority of reason." With good works, man may stand before God without fear, for God will acknowledge his merit. The very justice of the universe assures that man's work will gain some hearing with God. Such moments of confidence, however, are rare in Gregory's works and help illuminate the stronger and deeper currents of penitence and fear. For who could hope to be as righteous as Job?

62. *Mor.* 9.38.60 (CCL 143, 500).

· VIII ·

THE GOD-MAN AND THE NEW DISPENSATION

Christ is the grain of wheat, of whom John wrote: "Unless the grain of wheat falls to the earth and dies, it will remain alone" (Jn 12:24). Christ dies to "sanctify" us, and yet his flesh is also the "food" for those hungry for eternal knowledge.[1] As Redeemer, Christ dies to atone for man's sins and restore a disordered universe. But even the example of his life on earth illuminates man, teaching him righteousness and virtue. This duality of Christ's mission, redeeming and teaching,[2] is reflected in the duality and reciprocity of his two natures. Christ's power to save comes from his humanity as well as his divinity.[3] For Gregory, this means that God remains God in all power and virtue while deigning to make himself *visible* as man.[4] In fact, Christ remains so much God that Gregory says that Christ became incarnate not simply as man but as God-Man. Gregory likens the Son to a wall surrounding the elect: inwardly he is God, outwardly he is God-Man (*Deus-homo*).[5] Clearly, the perfection of Christ's earthly life far transcends that of mere men, who inevitably fall from grace.

1. *HEv.* 1.8.1 (PL 76, 1104).
2. Cf. Leon. *tract.* 63.1, where Christ both ransoms and instructs man.
3. *Mor.* 17.30.46 (CCL 143A, 877–78); *Mor.* 24.3.5 (CCL 143B, 1192).
4. *Mor.* 34.23.54 (CCL 143B, 1770–71); also *HEv.* 2.30.9–10 (PL 76, 1226–27). This notion of remaining God and becoming visible as man is found in Leon. *tract.* 26.1; cf. *Tom.* 2 and 4; *tract.* LI.1; LI.3; LI.6; XXIII.2; XXII.1. Also, Hilary, *Trin.* 9.14; cf. J. McHugh, "The Exaltation of Christ in the Arian Controversy" (Ph.D. diss., Pontifical Gregorian University, 1959), n. 1214. Michael Frickel notes the influence of Hilary, *Deus totus ubique simul* (Freiburg im Breisgau, 1956), 78, and passim. The emphasis on the divinity of Christ is also found in the early Augustine, who too may have been influenced by Hilary; see Tarsicius van Bavel, *Recherches sur la Christologie de Saint Augustin* (Fribourg, 1959), 123.
5. *HEz.* 2.2.5 (CCL 142, 228): "Murus enim nobis intus est Deus, murus uero foris est Deus homo."

To explain Christ's perfection, Gregory usually applies dualistic images suggesting an internal divinity inhabiting an external humanity, as if Christ were a man whose humanity consists in his flesh, his body, and his emotions, while his divinity functions as the animating spirit.[6] Here Gregory goes farther than Leo, who was wary of expressing the union of Christ's natures as one in which "the One was the indweller, and the other the dwelling."[7] While part of the neo-Chalcedonian tradition, Gregory's views are shaped by the tension he perceives and the harmony he desires between body and soul in man. Generally, Gregory places the two natures of Christ in a side-by-side relationship. They are separate, unmixed and unconfused, yet united in one person.[8] The divine nature of the Logos inhabits a human nature that expresses natural mutabilities such as hunger, ignorance, and pain. Christ does not, however, take up sinfulness of the flesh. Born from the Virgin, he has not inherited the "pleasure of the flesh" that leads man to sin.[9] In assuming this "clean" flesh, his divinity is not diminished, for his majesty could not bear injury.[10] Nor is his humanity consumed by his divinity, since Christ had to assume all he would save.[11]

Gregory's dualistic images are concrete and straightforward, derived almost exclusively from the pericopes he interprets. Christ is the lamp the woman uses to search for the lost drachma, her lost image-likeness to

6. Augustine also states that one can compare the two natures in Christ to that of a soul in the body on condition that one discards all thought of a material mixture in which one or the other element loses its integrity; see *epist.* 169.2.7 and *epist.* 137.30.11; cf. van Bavel, *Recherches*, 49. Yet the comparison of the unity in Christ with the unity of body and soul in a human being is the starting point for Arian, Apollinarian, and even Nestorian Christologies; see Aloys Grillmeier, *Christ in Christian Tradition*, trans. John Bowden, 2d rev. ed. (Atlanta, 1975) 1:457 and on Chalcedon in general, 1:520ff.; also Jarislav Pelikan, *The Emergence of the Catholic Tradition*, vol. 1 of *The Christian Tradition* (Chicago, 1971), 226–78.

7. Leon. *tract.* XXIII.1. Such metaphors were associated with Nestorianism; see Pelikan, *Emergence of Catholic Tradition*, 1:251–255; and ironically with Athanasius, whose tendency was toward a logos-sarx Christology, see Aloys Grillmeier, *Christ in Christian Tradition*, trans. J. S. Bowden, 1st ed. (New York, 1965), 215–19.

8. Cf. Leon. *Tom.* 3; *epist.* 124, 5–6.

9. *Mor.* 11.52.70 (CCL 143A, 626), and *Mor.* 17.30.46 (CCL 143A, 877–78): "Sed quis esset homo sine peccato, si ex peccati commixtione descenderet? Proinde uenit propter nos in utero uirginis Filius Dei, ibi pro nobis factus est homo. Sumpta est ab illo natura non culpa." See also *Mor.* 2.22.41 (CCL 143, 84–85): "apparuit in carne qui in peccati contagione ex carnis nil habebat infirmitate." The idea that Christ was born of a virgin without original sin and without the weakness for pleasure is found of course in many Fathers; e.g., Tert. *carne.* 16; Hil. *trin.* 10.25; Ambr. *in Ps 118.* 6.21; and Aug. *pecc. orig.* 2.29.48; and Leon. *Tom.* 3, *tract.* XXIII.1; XXII.1–3.

10. Cf. Leon. *Tom.* 4, *tract.* XXIII.2. Cf. Hil. *trin.* 9.38; cited by McHugh, "Exaltation of Christ," 9.

11. *Mor.* 2.23.42 (CCL 143, 85).

God (Lk 15:8–9).[12] The Logos is the flame illuminating the lamp, and this is Christ's divinity. The clay urn is the humanity, the assumed flesh. Like pottery, the assumed flesh is tempered by fires of suffering and so strengthened for the glory of the Resurrection.[13] Christ is also the Word who has assumed flesh in Mary's womb, being "one thing from his Father [and] another thing from the Virgin."[14] He is eternal and impassible from his Father, and yet temporal and passible from his mother.[15] Christ has inherited a divine nature in the Word from his Father and a human nature in the flesh from his mother, and they are united in his person.

Yet exactly how are they united? As these several images suggest, the flesh, Christ's humanity, is the external container of the invisible God. Christ assumes (*assumere*) the flesh, taking it up (*suscipere*) like a garment or a cloak.[16] This outward humanity both disguises and reveals Christ's divinity, a paradox evident in Gregory's exegesis of Song of Songs 2:9 ("Behold he stands behind our wall, looking through the windows, looking through the lattices").[17] Christ stood behind the wall, showing his humanity and hiding his divinity. But as one who looks through windows and lattices is partly seen as well as partly covered, so there was sometimes unmistakable evidence of his internal divinity in the miracles he performed, even though his divinity was hidden by the humiliation of human suffering.[18] As Wisdom built her house in Proverbs 9:1, so the

12. *HEv.* 34.6 (PL 76, 1249). "Et quia imago exprimitur in drachma, mulier drachmam perdidit, quando homo, qui conditus ad imaginem Dei fuerat, peccando a similitudine sui conditoris recessit. Sed accendit mulier lucernam, quia Dei sapientia apparuit in humanitate. Lucerna quippe lumen in testa est: lumen vero in testa, est divinitas in carne. . . . Quia enim testa in igne solidatur, ejus virtus sicut testa exaruit, quia assumptam carnem ad resurrectionis gloriam ex passionis tribulatione roboravit."

13. Ibid.

14. *Mor.* 18.52.85 (CCL 143A, 948–49). Cf. Leon. *epist.* 31.2.

15. *Mor.* 18.52.85 (CCL 143A, 948–49). Here Gregory is refuting the Nestorian claim that Christ is two persons: Christ consists of two natures, or things (*aliud*) in one person. Yet Gregory's own dualism should be noted: "Non purus homo conceptus atque editus, post per meritum ut Deus esset accepit, sed nuntiante angelo, et adueniente Spiritu, mox Verbum in utero, mox intra uterum Verbum caro, et manente incommutabili essentia quae ei est cum Patre et cum sancto Spiritu coaeterna, assumpsit intra uirginea uiscera ubi et impassibilis pati, et immortalis mori, et aeternus ante saecula temporalis posset esse in fine saeculorum . . . Et quamuis ipse aliud ex Patre, aliud ex uirgine, non tamen alius ex Patre, alius ex Virgine, sed ipse est aeternus ex Patre, ipse temporalis ex matre. . . ."

16. *HEz.* 2.1.9 (CCL 142, 215): "Quid enim uestimentum eius est, nisi corpus quod assumpsit ex Virgine?" Gregory stresses that this does not make Christ less real: "Nec tamen aliud eius uestimentum est, atque aliud ipse. Nam nostrum quoque uestimentum caro dicitur, sed tamen ipsi nos sumus caro, qua uestimur." See also *Mor.* 2.23.42 (CCL 143, 85), where the "forma servi tegeret" the divinity. Cf. Aug. *agon.* 25.27; *in evang. Ioh.* 27.5; see van Bavel, *Recherches*, 35 and 64f.

17. *HEz.* 2.1.15 (CCL 142, 220).

18. See Hil. *trin.* 9.51; and Grillmeier, *Christ in Christian Tradition*, 2d ed., 1: 396.

Wisdom of God created a body, by the soul's mediation, in the womb of the Virgin. The body is the temple of the house of Wisdom, Gregory explains, so the Son of God and Man is both the "temple inhabited" and the "inhabitor of the temple."[19]

In passages with such dualities, Gregory appears to neglect the human soul of Christ. However, in one instance, Gregory explains the mediation of Christ's human soul more fully. From a curious passage in Job 39:18 ("When time shall be, she raises her wings and scorns the horseman and his rider"), Gregory explains how the Logos can inhabit the flesh through the mediation of the human soul. A tripartite image explains the Incarnation: a horse (*equus*), a mounted horseman (*eques*), and lastly a rider (*ascensor*) mounted upon the horseman. Perhaps the rider sits upon the shoulders of the horseman, as will be understood in the later Middle Ages. Gregory interprets the horse as Christ's body, the horseman his soul, and the rider the Logos. Gregory further explains the image:

> Then he [the rider, the Word of God] mounted the horseman when, by creating himself for divine worship, he subjugated a human soul riding its own flesh. Indeed, divinity took up flesh by mediation of the soul and through this he held the whole horseman at once, since in himself he drew together not only that which was ruled, but that which ruled.[20]

The Logos rules a human soul, which in turn rules a tranquil human body, posing no opposition from carnal desires.[21] As mediator, the soul takes orders from the divine Logos and transmits them to the flesh. Technically, the free will and separate mind of Christ exist because his submission to God is voluntary. Yet the soul is so perfectly obedient and subject to the Logos that it ceases to have its own identity. However, this is the very ideal of stability everyone should attain. Man is to emulate Christ's mind clinging (*inhaerere*) to the divine nature in total obedience,[22] even as the soul of Adam was supposed to have clung to God. Christ

19. *Mor.* 33.16.32 (CCL 143B, 1701): "Sapientia quippe domum sibi condidit, cum unigenitus Dei Filius in seipso intra uterum uirginis mediante anima, humanum sibi corpus creauit. Sic quippe corpus Vnigeniti domus Dei dicitur, sicut etiam templum uocatur; ita uero, ut unus idemque Dei atque hominis filius ipse sit qui inhabitat, ipse qui inhabitatur." Cf. Leon. *Tom.* 2, where the same image is used without the notion of indwelling.

20. *Mor.* 31.23.42 (CCL 143B, 1578–79). This image illustrates the *anima mediatrix* found in Aug. *epist.* 137 and *epist.* 140. See van Bavel, *Recherches*, 33–34. In Augustine, the soul of Christ is more connected to God than to the body, which is clearly the case for Gregory as well. See Aug. *in evang. Io.* 23.6; also Ambr. *Isaac* 8.66, which may have inspired this image, and *incarn.* 5.37–39, for the emphasis of Christ's divinity. For the tradition of *anima mediatrix*, see Grillmeier, *Christ in Christian Tradition*, 2d ed., 1: 286, 379–80, 404, 410–11, 466.

21. Cf. Leon. *epist.* 35.3; cf. Grillmeier, *Christ in Christian Tradition*, 2d ed., 1: 535.

22. *Mor.* 3.16.30 (CCL 143, 134–35).

recaptures the relationship of obedience and stability in God that man lost in the Fall. He also anticipates the new man's participation in God through contemplation and humble submission to divine teachings.

In explicating the subtleties of the Incarnation, Gregory sees Christ's two natures not only as distinct,[23] but also as complementary opposites. Christ is both Creator and contingent being, master and servant.[24] Christ is both the Creator and the work created, the builder of the temple and the temple.[25] In the form of God, Christ is equal to the Father; in the form of a servant, less than the Father.[26] As a divine being, he "stands" immutably; as a created man, he "passes" and undergoes changes.[27] As God, he gives all things; as man, he receives all things at the hand of the Father.[28] He is fully God and fully man, as human redemption necessarily demands both.

Gregory associates the redemptive death with Christ's humanity, and the righteousness that purifies and expiates sins with his divinity. Through his human nature, Christ is "capable of dying," through his righteousness he is "capable of purifying."[29] The relationship between the internal divinity and the external humanity is dialectical, so that the divinity conquers through the humanity. But this relationship is also circular and self-contained: Christ ordains inwardly in his divine nature all he is to suffer outwardly in his human nature;[30] and what he assumes in his human nature he conquers in his divine nature.[31] Christ undergoes temptation, suffering, and death in the flesh to overcome these weak-

23. Leo stresses the distinction of Christ's natures and the retention by each of their proper character, cf. *tract*. XXV.2; *epist*. 35.2; *epist*. 124.5–6.

24. This dualism of Christ as God and man follows rules of exegesis for Christ in Aug. *trin*. 1.7.14; *in evang. Ioh*. 78.2; *trin*. 1.10.20; cf. van Bavel, *Recherches*, 106.

25. *Mor*. 18.52.85 (CCL 143A, 948–49).

26. *Mor*. 30.21.66 (CCL 143B, 1536): "Incarnatus itaque Dominus qui in forma Dei aequalis est Patri, in forma serui minor est patre, qua minor est etiam seipso" [Phil 2:6f.]. Cf. Leon. *tract*. 27.1.

27. *HEv*. 1.2.6 (PL 76, 1084): "Transire namque humanitatis est, stare divinitatis. Per humanitatem quippe habuit nasci, crescere, mori, resurgere, de loco ad locum venire. Quia ergo in divinitate mutabilitas non est, atque hoc ipsum mutari transire est, profecto ille transitus ex carne est, non ex divinitate. Per divinitatem vero ei semper stare est, quia ubique praesens, nec per motum venit, nec per motum recedit."

28. *Mor*. 2.37.60 (CCL 143, 97): "Redemptor noster per hoc quod Deus est cum Patre dat omnia; per hoc uero quod homo est a patre accipit inter omnia." Cf. Leon. *epist*. 124.7.

29. *Mor*. 17.30.46 (CCL 143A, 878). Cf. Leon. *Tom*. 3.

30. *Mor*. 3.16.30 (CCL 143, 134–35).

31. *Mor*. 14.55.69 (CCL 143A, 741): "unus idemque Deus et homo mortem, quam ex humanitate pertulit, ex diuinitate superauit." This is true not only for death but for all human frailties. See *HEv*. 1.16.1 (PL 76, 1135): "Justum quippe erat ut sic tentationes nostras suis tentationibus vinceret, sicut mortem nostram venerat sua morte superare."

nesses of the flesh with his divinity. His wounds are self-inflicted to win mercy for others.[32]

Gregory's explanation of Christ's activities should be viewed in the context of *stabilitas*, for therein lies Christ's perfection as man. In Christ, the flesh can at last be conquered because his soul rests under the complete and absolute control of the Logos. Because of this adamantine stability, Christ can undergo every temptation from the devil, yet the devil "[is] not able to unsettle the mind of the Mediator of God and man with temptation. For he so condescended to take upon himself all things externally so that his mind, clinging inwardly to his divinity, nevertheless could remain unshaken."[33] The human soul of Christ clings to the divine Logos and thus is possessed by God. Passions cannot gain dominance in his human soul since it is so completely subjugated to the Logos.

Not only is temptation external, but suffering and the human limitation of ignorance also remain separate from the Logos and the soul it dominates. The Logos directs and indeed foresees all. When Christ is asked about the hour and day of judgment, or other such questions, he in fact knows the answers, but "makes himself not know this."[34] Through the power of his divinity, Christ is omniscient, but he displays ignorance from the desire to present an "appearance of innocence."[35] Consequently, Christ will often speak with our doubts and uncertainties to teach man lessons of patience and humility, though inwardly Christ remains unmoved and totally in control.

> And also if he is said to have groaned sometimes in spirit, he ordained as a divine being how much he would be troubled as a human being. And governing all things immutably, he showed himself mutable for the satisfaction of human weakness. Therefore, remaining unmoved in himself, he ordained whatever he did with a troubled spirit for the display of the humanity which he had undertaken.[36]

32. *Mor.* 3.16.29 (CCL 143, 134).

33. *Mor.* 3.16.30 (CCL 143, 135): "ut tamen eius mens interius diuinitati suae inhaerens inconcussa permaneret." Cf. Leon. *tract.* 68.1, where the Godhead does not actually suffer. Gregory takes this idea and places it in the context of stability.

34. *Ep.* 10.21 (CCL 140A, 852–56): "filius nescire se dicit diem quem nescire facit, non quod ipse nesciat, sed quia hunc scire minime permittat." See also F. Homes Dudden, *Gregory the Great* (London, 1905), 2: 330.

35. *In lib. I Reg.* 3.17 (CCL 144, 212): "Nescire ergo dominum dicitur non ignorantia cognitionis sed praetextu simplicitatis."

36. *Mor.* 3.16.30 (CCL 143, 135): "Qui et si quando turbatus spiritu infremuisse dicitur, ipse diuinitus disponebat quantum ipse humanitus turbaretur, immutabiliter omnibus praesidens et semetipsum mutabilem in satisfactione infirmitatis ostendens. Quietus ergo in semetipso manens, disposuit quidquid pro ostendenda humanitate quam susceperat,

Because Gregory describes Christ as remaining unmoved inwardly by human mutabilities or emotions and intellectual limitations, some modern critics have charged him with Docetism.[37] But this interpretation fails to comprehend Gregory's cultural inheritance, which viewed passions as bestial and mutable, a curse that lowered and deformed humanity, and the charge further ignores Gregory's own ideal of stability. Passion could hardly have been included in a definition of Christ's perfection, unless it were that singular *passio*, suffering, which separated man from involvement in the world. Christ's conquest of the mutabilities that afflict mankind ensures the perfection of the resurrected body and serves as an example of the self-control and stability the Christian should imitate in his earthly life. Apart from these reasons, Gregory also may have been led to emphasize Christ's divinity from his own wariness of Arianism.[38]

This divine and perfect self-control does not in any way minimize the total importance of Christ's humanity. Though Christ's divinity is important in providing the righteousness to propitiate God and defeat the devil, Christ's humanity is equally important. Christ's suffering expiates man's sins and supplies a substitute sacrifice that ransoms man from the devil's power and frees man from God's punishment. Such remediation involves the complementary interaction of Christ's two natures, as Gregory sees it. Although the polarity between Christ's divinity and his humanity is depicted as an internal core and an external covering, the dialectic that allows Christ's divinity to conquer through his humanity creates a compelling synthesis typical of the complementary patterns of Gregory's thought.

On one level, Christ's righteousness is associated with his divinity; it

---

etiam turbulentus fecit." J. Lebreton argues that Stoicism prevents Augustine from recognizing the reality of Christ's sufferings, that the intellectual climate of antiquity was hostile to emotions and displays of weakness; see "L'Agonie de Notre Seigneur," *Revue Apologétique* 33 (1922): 716. Gregory, as most of the other Fathers, betrays the same discomfort with emotions as Augustine.

37. Dudden argues Gregory's Docetism: *Gregory*, 2: 329–35. Lebon refutes him, arguing that the perfection of Christ's manhood does not make Christ less human; see J. Lebon, "Le Prétendu Docétisme de la Christologie de s. Grégoire le Grand," *RecTh* 1 (1929): 177–201. Gregory's beliefs about Christ's emotional life are consistent with those of other Fathers, both Eastern and Western, with the exception of Jerome. The other Fathers had difficulty accepting the possibility of the God-man, but Jerome, from his battles against Apollinarianism, came to appreciate the necessity that Christ be fully human. See Grillmeier, *Christ in Christian Tradition*, 2d ed., 1: 401, and passim; also J. N. D. Kelly, *Jerome* (London, 1975), 38, 59, 81, for Jerome's conflict with Apollinarianism.

38. For an examination of how anti-Arianism resulted in Hilary's stressing Christ's divinity, see McHugh, "Exaltation of Christ."

is the perfection necessary to compensate for man's weakness and the supernatural power competent to restore man's inheritance. In turn, Christ's suffering is associated with his humanity, and such pain is offered as a sacrifice to atone for man's sins. But on a second level, Christ's righteousness is communicated or attributed to his humanity, and his suffering is linked to his divinity. The poles of the original antithesis of divinity and humanity have begun to reverse themselves by sharing aspects of one another. Or, as Gregory describes the effect of this *communicatio idiomatum* much more elegantly, electrum fittingly symbolizes Christ, "a mixture" of gold and silver.[39] As gold is tempered by silver, so manhood and the suffering of adversities tempers the divinity. As silver is made more splendid by gold, so the divinity renders the humanity more glorious with miracles showing forth the power of divinity. Christ's two natures are distinct, yet alloyed: Christ's humanity is elevated by the power of his divinity, while his divinity is humbled by adversity. Both natures share in placating God and correcting man.

In elevating humanity to divinity, Christ further bestows righteousness upon humanity. Both suffering and the conquest of temptation are part of the perfect righteousness that Christ as man offers to God. Assuming the form of man, Christ presents God with the righteousness he demands. He also intercedes on man's behalf and ransoms him.[40] This righteousness is attributed to Christ the man,[41] though technically the Logos is the ultimate source of his righteousness, albeit governing a human soul. Christ displays his perfect manhood before God to intercede on man's behalf.[42] His perfect manhood propitiates God's demand for righteousness from man.[43] And because victory over the devil is attributed to the weakness of humanity, Gregory believes it is written prophetically in Jeremiah 31:22 that "the woman will besiege the man."[44]

In a complementary way, just as Gregory stresses the inward impassibility of Christ and counts it as man's perfection, so he sees all the more strongly the external suffering of Christ and emphasizes God's humility in assuming it. Gregory asserts that Christ did take on the body from the Virgin whereby he might be "impassible and suffer passion, immortal

---

39. *Mor*. 28.1.5 (CCL 143B, 1398); cf. *HEz*. 1.2.14 (CCL 142, 25) where Christ, as *species electri* is tempered from brightness in his divinity, and proceeds to brightness in his humanity; but the immutable nature remains the same in itself, though it renews all things. Note again the implicit emphasis on visibility.

40. *Mor*. 24.2.4 (CCL 143B, 1191).

41. *Mor*. 24.3.5 (CCL 143B, 1191–92).

42. *Mor*. 24.3.5 (CCL 143B, 1192).

43. *Mor*. 24.3.6 (CCL 143B, 1193).

44. *In lib. I Reg*. 1.1.1 (CCL 144, 55).

and die, and though existing before time and remaining forever, be temporal."[45] The Creator became incarnate to free us from everlasting death by his Passion.[46] The loftiness of the divine nature was made low, and strength made weakness, to elevate man.[47] Gregory invites us to think of the gentleness of God who came to free us from sins, to suffer and not to show his power.[48]

But physical suffering is not the only sacrifice Christ makes, for his obedience and service to neighbors are also sacrifices. Christ bears "two crosses," Gregory writes in *Homilies on the Gospel*: one is abstinence, borne in the body, the other is compassion for others, borne in the soul.[49] Whatever the trial, by enduring such sacrifices, Christ conquers suffering through submission, at last revealing his power only at the Resurrection. He alone "trampled the winepress" within which he was trampled, for he conquered that passion which, by his power, he suffered to the end (cf. Is 63:2). He suffered the cross to death, then rose from death in glory.[50] Like Leo, Gregory sees Christ's Passion as inseparable from his triumph and Resurrection.[51]

Christ remains God, yet becomes man, because in the Incarnation divinity is not transfigured; it is made visible.[52] While remaining God—transcendent, infinite, invisible, and purely spiritual—Christ enters a lower physical realm and takes a finite and visible form. Commenting on Paul's idea of *exinanitio* (Phil 2:6–7), Gregory writes:

> For him, to have emptied himself means to have shown himself to be visible from the greatness of his invisibility, so that the form of a servant might cover that which would without limitation penetrate all things by virtue of his divinity.[53]

45. *Mor.* 18.52.85 (CCL 143A, 948): "sed nuntiante angelo, et adueniente Spiritu, mox Verbum in utero, mox intra uterum Verbum caro, et manente incommutabili essentia quae ei est cum Patre et cum sancto Spiritu coaeterna, assumpsit intra uirginea uiscera ubi et impassibilis pati, et immortalis mori, et aeternus ante saecula temporalis posset esse in fine saeculorum. . . ." Similar paradoxes are found in Aug. *trin.* 4.14.16; *serm.* 218.1.1; cf. van Bavel, *Recherches*, 123.

46. *Mor.* 14.54.67 (CCL 143A, 739).

47. *Mor.* 16.30.37 (CCL 143A, 820–21).

48. *HEv.* 1.18.1–4 (PL 76, 1149–53).

49. *HEv.* 2.32.3 (PL 76, 1234).

50. *HEz.* 2.1.9 (CCL 142, 215): "Solus enim torcular in quo calcatus est calcauit, qui sua potentia eam quam pertulit passionem uicit. Nam qui usque ad mortem crucis passus est, de morte cum gloria surrexit."

51. Cf. Leon. *Tom.* 5; *tract.* LI.3; LI.7; LIX.6–7; LXXII.1; cf. also *tract.* LXXI.1.

52. See esp. Leon. *Tom.* 3.

53. *Mor.* 2.23.42 (CCL 143, 85): "ei semetipsum exinanisse, est ab inuisibilitatis suae magnitudine se uisibilem demonstrasse ut serui forma tegeret hoc quod incircumscripte omnia ex diuinitate penetraret."

The invisible and infinite God who sustains all creation with his presence now assumes a visible and finite form. A second use of Philippians 2:6–7 occurs in Gregory's exegesis of Song of Songs 1:2 ("Thy name is like oil poured out"),[54] where he explains that Paul's "emptying out" is what Solomon calls a "pouring out." Like perfume, the divinity of Christ rests in a jar, whose odor or "name" is narrowly confined. In the Incarnation, the immensity of the divinity is poured out externally, making the invisible visible, and the perfume of God's name is made known among men. The "emptying out" (*exinanitio*, *kenosis*) thus signifies a change from infinitude and invisibility to finitude and visibility.[55]

Insofar as the Incarnation is a change from invisibility to visibility, it bears a special association with teaching.[56] God corrects and transforms man through the examples of Christ's life, offering a visible model of the righteousness man needs:

> For sinful man could not be corrected except through God. However, he who corrected had to be seen, to offer an example for imitation that past lives of evil might be changed. But God could not be seen by men. For this reason, God was made man, so that he could be seen. Therefore, the righteous and invisible God appeared as a visible man like us, so that while he would be seen from likeness, he could cure from righteousness; and while he agreed with us in the truth of his nature, he could cure our sickness from the power of his medicine.[57]

Above all, through the Incarnation God became visible in order to teach man righteousness. Yet this teaching of the incarnate Christ remains inseparable from his suffering and redemption, for this is the example of righteousness taught. To have become visible is but the first sign

54. *Cant.* 21 (CCL 144, 23). Cf. Hil. *in Ps 118*. 4. *Kenosis* is also a renunciation of the *forma dei* and an acceptance of the *forma servi*, preserving divine virtues and changing only the *habitus*: cf. *trin.* 9.38. This tradition goes back as far as Tertullian; cf. Grillmeier, *Christ in Christian Tradition*, 2d. ed., 1: 396.

55. See Henry E. W. Turner's chapter on the tradition of Christ as Illuminator: *The Patristic Doctrine of Redemption* (London, 1962), 29–46, in which this kind of *kenosis* of visibility/invisibility is characteristic. See also Franz Lieblang, *Grundfragen der mystischen Theologie nach Gregors des Grossen Moralia und Ezechielhomilien* (Freiburg im Breisgau, 1934), 44ff. The idea of Christ as Teacher and Illuminator is very strong in Ambrose; see F. Homes Dudden, *The Life and Times of Ambrose* (Oxford, 1935), 2: 604–5.

56. Another theme found in Leo; cf. *tract.* XXIII.5.

57. *Mor.* 24.2.2 (CCL 143B, 1189–90): "Vitiosus enim homo corrigi non poterat nisi per Deum. Videri autem debuit qui corrigebat, ut praebendo imitationis formam, anteactae malitiae mutarent uitam. Sed uideri ab homine non poterat Deus; ergo homo factus est, ut uideri potuisset. Iustus igitur atque inuisibilis Deus, apparuit similis nobis homo uisibilis, ut dum uidetur ex simili, curaret ex iusto; et dum ueritate generis concordat conditioni, uirtute artis obuiaret aegritudini."

of God's compassion. God could have saved man in some other way, but instead he chose to reveal himself and to undertake the suffering of our wounds.[58] The true marvel is that Christ's incarnate Passion provides man with a living example of the humility and sacrifice he offers God on man's behalf:

> For this, the only begotten Son of God took on the form of our weakness; for this, the invisible not only appeared visible, but even despised; for this, he bore mockeries and insults, derisions and disgrace, suffering and torments, namely, that the humble God could teach man not to be proud. Therefore, how great a virtue is humility, when Christ, who was great beyond measure, was made small, even unto suffering, in order to teach this virtue truly?[59]

All Christ's life—not just his death upon the Cross—is exemplary of his Passion, his humility and sacrifice. Gregory presents the Incarnation as inseparable from the Redemption, for Christ's entire life was indeed a sacrificial offering of himself and his righteous innocence to atone for man's sins.[60] Gregory explains that Christ's work of intercession was prefigured in Job's continual sacrifices (Jb 1:5), where Christ represents implicitly both Priest and Victim:

> Job does not cease to offer sacrifice continually since our Redeemer offers a holocaust continually for us, in presenting his Incarnation to the Father continually on our behalf. Indeed, this same Incarnation is an offering for our purification, and when he shows himself as man, he intercedes and washes away men's crimes. And the mystery of his humanity offers a perpetual sacrifice since he purifies even things which are eternal.[61]

---

58. Cf. *Mor.* 20.36.69 (CCL 143A, 1054–55) and *Mor.* 34.23.54 (CCL 143B, 1770–71).

59. *Mor.* 34.23.54 (CCL 143B, 1770–71): "Ad hoc namque unigenitus Dei Filius formam infirmitatis nostrae suscepit, ad hoc inuisibilis, non solum uisibilis, sed etiam despectus apparuit, ad hoc contumeliarum ludibria, irrisionum opprobria, passionum tormenta tolerauit, ut superbum non esse hominem doceret humilis Deus. Quanta ergo humilitatis uirtus est, propter quam solam ueraciter edocendam is qui sine aestimatione magnus est, usque ad passionem factus est paruus?"

60. *Mor.* 1.24.32 (CCL 143, 42–43); *Mor.* 24.2–3.4–5 (CCL 143B, 1190–92); *Mor.* 22.17.42 (CCL 143A, 1121–22). For Irenaeus and Tertullian there could be salvation directly through the Incarnation apart from the death of Christ; cf. Hastings Rashdall, *The Idea of Atonement in Christian Theology* (London, 1919), 250. Ambrose stressed the saving efficacy of both Christ's life and his death; see Dudden, *Ambrose*, 2: 606f. Augustine is significant for his emphasis on Christ's suffering and redemptive sacrifice; see Gerhart B. Ladner, *The Idea of Reform* (New York, 1959; repr. ed., 1967), 153ff; A. Krueger, "Synthesis of Sacrifice According to Saint Augustine" (Ph.D. diss., Santa Maria ad Lacum, 1950), esp. 68–99.

61. *Mor.* 1.24.32 (CCL 143, 42): "Cunctis diebus Iob sacrificium offerre non cessat, quia sine intermissione pro nobis holocaustum Redemptor immolat, qui sine cessatione Patri suam pro nobis incarnationem demonstrat. Ipsa quippe eius incarnatio nostrae emundationis oblatio est cumque se hominem ostendit, delicta hominis interueniens diluit. Et hu-

Christ's Incarnation is a sacrifice for man's purification, just as his suffering is. His Incarnation mediates continually with God as a sacrifice interceding for mercy toward man. The Incarnation and Redemption converge in being sacrifices, just as Christ's roles as Teacher and Redeemer are complementary expressions of his sacrifice.

Christ's sacrifice joins his humanity and divinity: his condescension and suffering become righteousness both as God and man. For the Christian, this translates into a moral imperative to offer one's life as a sacrifice to God in continual penitence and humility, even as Christ is offered again and again in the Mass.[62] For Gregory, the Redemption, the Mass, and man's penitence are inextricably linked as manifestations of sacrifice. Marvelously, through man's offering of himself, his carnality is overcome and he advances toward righteousness. At last, the divine plan is fulfilled through Christ and the dispensation of penitence he brings.

Christ culminates a continuous historical process aimed at attaining man's righteousness (iustitia), his obedience to God's commands. God first created and then redeemed man to bring him to this righteousness: "since the generosity of our Creator's goodness did not fail, even against the darkness of sin, God first created man powerfully for righteousness, but afterwards he recalled man even more powerfully from error by redemption."[63] Before the Law, Adam turned his back on God in sin. Yet God did not desert man, but instead sent his Law to recall man to righteousness. Still man failed. Now, after the Law (in the New Dispensation of Christ), man may still turn his back on God in sin, but God continues to invite man's return through penitence.[64] Only in the New Dispensation can man meet God's commands. The "heavy commandments of the Law, . . . could not be borne when they were held carnally; [the Holy Spirit] shows how they are bearable for us through spiritual understanding. . . . The weight of the commandments of the Law he turns back by the power of confession."[65]

The New Dispensation recapitulates the goal of iustitia found in the

---

manitatis suae mysterio perenne sacrificium immolat quia et haec sunt aeterna quae mundat." For Augustine, Christ is both priest and sacrifice; see Krueger, "Synthesis of Sacrifice," 109–10.

62. Gregory's emphasis on the Mass and Christ's sacrifice may be influenced by Augustine; see Krueger, "Synthesis of Sacrifice," 100–163, as well as Leon. tract. LVIII.3; LI.3; LXX.4; tract. LXVI.3; cf. also, tract. XLII.5.

63. Mor. 35.17.43 (CCL 143B, 1804).

64. Reg. Past. 3.28 (PL 77, 105); an exegesis of Isaiah 30:20–21: "And thy eyes shall see thy teacher, and thy ears shall hear the word of one admonishing thee behind thy back." See also HEv. 2.31.3 (PL 76, 1228–29).

65. HEv. 2.33.8 (PL 76, 1244–45), an exegesis of Exodus 17:12, where Aaron and Hur hold up Moses' arms to assure victory over Amalek.

Old, yet where the Old Dispensation failed to inspire obedience through fear, the New succeeds through love and repentance, through compunction, as Gregory might say. Where the Law simply commanded obedience, Christ came "through grace, since he taught by exhibiting the presence of his mercy."[66] Bringing the Holy Spirit, the spirit of love, he revivified man dying of sin under the Old Law.[67] The crucial distinction between the Old and the New Dispensations is a love of good and a hatred of evil, which inspires good works and repentance of sin.[68] Significantly, the New Dispensation of grace is just as much a law as the Old Dispensation—indeed, it is more so. Christ gives man laws and precepts to obey, just as the prophets gave the people laws in the Old Dispensation. But the New Dispensation is more strict and demanding, for it forbids not merely sinful acts, but even sinful thoughts. It judges more harshly than the Old Dispensation.[69]

Yet the New Dispensation perfects the Old through confession and repentance.[70] Now the Law is interpreted spiritually, so that man can and indeed *must* keep it. The very opportunity of cleansing one's life of sin makes confession necessary and obligatory. Penitence constantly renews man's obedience to the Law; it is a path of continual return to God. The Christian's progress toward God may be full of digressions, but he is always headed in the right direction. He who was "unwilling to stay" returns; he who "disdained to stand" in righteousness can now "rise again after sin."[71] In his grace and mercy, Christ not only redeemed man through his death but also gave man a New Law he could keep through confession. At last, man can attain righteousness, even if he is erring and pitifully imperfect. Through repentance, the Christian can capture the

---

66. *HEv.* 2.31.3 (PL 76, 1228–29).

67. *Mor.* 9.40.63 (CCL 143, 502). For Ambrose also, the New Dispensation brought the gift of repentance; cf. *paenit.* 1.12.54. Christ's crucifixion earned forgiveness of man's sins; cf. *paenit.* 2.2.9–10. Gregory shares the deep sense of penitence found in *Vitae patr.* 5.3 (entire); 6.4 (entire); 7.22 (entire).

68. Cf. *In lib. I Reg.* 2.106 (CCL 144, 176).

69. *Mor.* 22.18.44 (CCL 143A, 1123–24); *HEv.* 2.40.3 (PL 76, 1304).

70. On penitence in Gregory's time, see Pierre Adnès, "Penitence," DS 13: 958–66; Karl Baus et al., *The Imperial Church from Constantine to the Early Middle Ages*, trans. Anselm Biggs, vol. 2 of *History of the Church* (New York, 1969), 678, 681–84; Paul Galtier, *L'Eglise et la rémission de péchés aux premiers siècles* (Paris, 1932); idem, *De Poenitentia* (Rome, 1956), esp. 109–52; and J. Tixeront, "La doctrine pénitentielle de s. Grégoire le Grand," in *Bulletin d'ancienne littérature et d'archéologie chrétienne* (Paris, 1912), 241–58. Because the demands of public penitence were so great in the early Church—e.g., continence and various mortifications of the flesh—it tended to be postponed until one's deathbed. But with the Desert Fathers, a certain form of private confession to one's *abba* became an element of monastic discipline. Gregory encourages this monastic tradition, extending it to confession to the preacher. Penitence is not officially numbered among the sacraments until the second half of the eleventh century.

71. *HEv.* 2.33.8 (PL 76, 1245).

"inheritance of the just," for Christ wills "[that] the kingdom of heaven, which is not earned by our merits, may be seized by our tears."[72]

Gregory's soteriology preserves a salubrious balance of hope and fear. Gregory recognizes Christ's vicarious justification of man, but also stresses man's need to do his own part to activate this sacrifice. The New Dispensation gives man the capacity to act, to feel repentance and do good works. With grace man responds to God in a way impossible under the Old Dispensation of fear; he can now "render" and "pay back" God's gifts with worthy works.[73] Because works are only meritorious when performed in love, the Holy Spirit has given man an ability to act, a capacity that was wanting in the Old Dispensation. Now the sinner can "pay back" the price of his redemption, offering confession and praise as well as works in compensation.[74] The New Dispensation, to extend Gregory's legal metaphor, restores man's solvency, allowing him to expunge or repay his debts, even permitting him to earn credit.

Yet ultimately the New Dispensation recapitulates much of the form of the Old. The emphasis on the strict judgment of God remains, though now it is internalized as self-judgment and penitence. In one way, fear is mitigated because judgment is partly put in man's control. Man can punish his own sins and by this payment remove the need for God's vengeance.[75] In so many words, an account is kept in which man always attempts to make sufficient penance for the sins he has committed, for at the Last Judgment those who are "debtors" will have to pay "every last penny."[76] Precisely because self-judgment is put in man's control, the burden of penitence becomes more severe and a source of keen anxiety. The Christian must be absolutely certain he has discovered every sin and performed penance sufficient to expunge his sins. Man's responsibilities thus increase under the New Dispensation of penitence.

Paradoxically, Gregory collapses the distance between the Old Dis-

---

72. HEv. 1.20.15 (PL 76, 1169): "Recogitemus ergo, fratres charissimi, mala quae fecimus, et nosmetipsos assiduis lamentis atteramus. Haereditatem justorum, quam non tenuimus per vitam, rapiamus per poenitentiam. Vult a nobis omnipotens Deus talem violentiam perpeti. Nam regnum coelorum rapi vult nostris fletibus, quod nostris meritis non debetur."

73. Mor. 9.41.64 (CCL 143, 503): "Respondere homo tot beneficiis debet; sed tamen respondere metuens non ualet quia humani generis conditorem qui adhuc seruiliter formidat, procul dubio non amat. Nam tunc solum Deo uera obsequia reddimus cum eum propter amoris fiduciam non timemus; cum nos ad bona opera affectus, non metus dirigit; cum malum nostrae menti iam non placet etiam si licet."

74. Mor. 13.23.26 (CCL 143A, 682–83); Mor. 33.12.24 (CCL 143B, 1694); Mor. 9.43.95 (CCL 143, 524); Mor. 12.51.57 (CCL 143A, 662–63).

75. Mor. 4.15.27 (CCL 143, 181), citing 1 Cor 11:31: "Si nos metipsos diiudicaremus, non utique a Domino iudicaremur."

76. Mor. 15.33.39 (CCL 143A, 773).

pensation of justice and fear and the New Dispensation of mercy and grace. Grace and penitence become an ever stricter law, just as the sacrifice of the New Dispensation becomes the perfect form of righteousness satisfying the demands of the Old Dispensation. One new law now prevails, recapitulating the old, uniting justice and mercy. Man's fate alternates between carnal and spiritual poles of God's justice and mercy, which Gregory reconciles in an ambivalent balance. Christ reconciles the justice and mercy of God throughout time, revealing the essential unity of the divine dispensation in calling man to righteousness; yet Gregory leaves man suspended about his fate and God's intentions, God's "merciful justice" and "just mercy," his harshness and softness. Christ is the Creator, the Logos, who becomes the Redeemer, and the Redeemer who becomes the Judge as well as man's Advocate.[77] God has guided man every step of the way, yet whether his justice or mercy will prevail is never certain. As Redeemer, Christ came like the dove,[78] collecting and sparing man "through gentleness."[79] He came first not to judge but to suffer.[80] As man's Advocate, Christ never ceases in his intercession.[81] He displays his Incarnation continually before the Father, as a sacrifice, seeking great patience for us. He succors man faithfully in his battles and trials.[82] The Lord is like the woman patiently bearing in her womb the child conceived in sin. He bears sinners even though they resist him; daily he calls them "mercifully" through his Gospel.[83]

But while Christ teaches man, praying for his sins and bearing with him patiently, man himself must act, or a severe and terrifying judgment will fall in proportion to his recalcitrance. For if Christ first comes in humility, he comes again in terror, demanding in strictness what he ordered in gentleness (districtio, mansuetudo): what was given in gentleness will be exacted with scourges (mansuetudo, verbera); what were sweet commands will become bitter in judgment (blanda, aspera).[84] The Creator and

---

77. The Creator becomes the Redeemer: *Ep.* 6.12 (CCL 140, 380–81); *HEz.* 2.9.22 (CCL 142, 376–77); *Mor.* 17.33.54 (CCL 143A, 883); *Mor.* 9.11.12 (CCL 143, 464–65); *HEz.* 1.8.22 (CCL 142, 113); *HEv.* 1.3.1 (PL 76, 1086); *HEz* 1.2.19 (CCL 142, 29); *Ep.* 11.36 (CCL 140A, 928); *HEz.* 1.11.6 (CCL 142, 172); cf. *Mor.* 30.25.73 (CCL 143B, 1541–42). The Redeemer becomes the Judge: *Mor.* 17.33.54 (CCL 143A, 883–84); *HEv.* 2.29.11 (PL 76, 1219); *HEz.* 1.7.20 (CCL 142, 96); *Mor.* 10.31.53–54 (CCL 143, 576–77). Our Advocate is also our Judge: *HEv.* 2.28.9 (PL 76, 1209–10).

78. *HEv.* 2.30.6 (PL 76, 1224).

79. Ibid.

80. *HEv.* 1.18.4 (PL 76, 1152).

81. *Mor.* 28.15.35 (CCL 143B, 1422); *HEv* 2.27.9 (PL 76, 1210).

82. *Mor.* 2.2.2 (CCL 143, 60).

83. *Mor.* 28.15.35 (CCL 143B, 1422); cf. *HEv.* 2.27.9 (PL 76, 1210).

84. *Mor.* 22.18.44 (CCL 143A, 1123): "Erit ergo tunc auctor iudicii, qui nunc est condi-

Redeemer will come in greater severity the less man has been recalled by his gifts to the grace of restoration;[85] and the less sins have been feared, the more severe the judgment.[86] Like the pregnant woman silently bearing the child who was witness to sin, the Lord will one day reveal his burden with pain in the vengeance of judgment (*ultio iudicii*).[87]

Both the ambivalence of Christ's role and the precarious interplay of divine and human activity in redemption intimate the depth of Gregory's uncertainty and anguish. Ultimately everything rests securely in God's hands, as it has always been. Whatever merit man might possess, he is still only a man, and mere dust and ashes can scarcely satisfy the Creator of the universe. The very absurdity of the proposition should comfort us: one can only trust in God's mercy. Citing Job 10:7 ("Since there is no man that can deliver out of your hand"), Gregory explains the logic and rationality that would be manifest in God's forgiving man, when even the just man bows before God's omnipotence. How much more do sinners need his indulgence? Gregory argues as if reassuring himself of the rational order of God's dispensation, perhaps hoping God is listening as well. Job argues his case before God:

> [This is] as if Job had openly said: "What is left for you, except to spare, since no one can resist your power? For as there is no one who can check your punishments by the merits of his own virtue, so let your mercy demand more easily to spare him." Moreover, since we are conceived in sin and born in iniquity, we either commit evils viciously, or even in doing right things sin unintentionally, we do not have the ability to propitiate the strict judge. But since we are not able to display our works as worthy of inspection, it remains that we offer him his own work to propitiate him.[88]

Since God is omnipotent, no man can resist his power, nor have any merit of his own. Man's righteousness is always unrighteousness compared to God. When we offer good works to God we are only offering God his own works. God is alpha and omega, the beginning and the end. The cosmos is a closed system whose final equilibrium rests in God's

---

tor libri, ut tunc districtus exigat quod modo mansuetus iubet. Sic namque cotidie conspicimus quod magistri pueris elementa litterarum blandientes imponunt, sed haec ab eis saeuientes exigunt; et quae dant cum mansuetudine, cum uerbere exquirunt. Blanda namque nunc sonant eloquii diuini mandata, sed erunt aspera in exactione sentienda. Mansueta modo est admonitio uocantis, sed tunc districta uentura est iustitia iudicis. . . ."

    85. *Mor.* 8.19.35 (CCL 143, 406–7); cf. *HEz.* 1.11.25 (CCL 142, 182); *HEv.* 2.29.11 (PL 76, 1219).

    86. *HEv.* 2.39.3 (PL 76, 1296); cf. *HEv.* 2.29.11 (PL 76, 1219).

    87. *Mor.* 28.15.35 (CCL 143B, 1422).

    88. *Mor.* 9.48.73 (CCL 143, 508).

unity. The power to save or damn rests solely with God, for Gregory realizes that only God propitiates himself, be it through accepting man's works or by becoming incarnate in Christ, and so reconciling himself to the world through his self-sacrifice. Gregory sees the universe so ordered that it is only reasonable that God should accept his own propitiation. Gregory turns to Job 10:8 ("Your hands have made me and fashioned me wholly round about. And do You thus cast me down headlong suddenly?"), and interprets Job's words to mean, "Since under just examination what I have done is not worthy of propitiating You, weigh mercifully, lest what You have made should perish." Surely, God would not unjustly (*inique*) spurn what he has mercifully (*benigne*) created;[89] and he who made the world from nothing would never desert unjustly (*iniuste*) that which exists.[90] Or so one hopes.

What comfort these reflections give Gregory is difficult to know. God's mercy applies only to the elect, but, more importantly, God's mercy is never a reason for man to relax but rather an incentive to increase his vigilance. Mercy means God *accepts* man's good works and penitence rather than closing the door against him and allowing him to be damned. Man's new task is to be certain he performs sufficient works and penance to be received by God's mercy. As always, Gregory leaves us with a balance of hope and fear. Man has reason to hope, for surely the Creator would not destroy his creation capriciously, and man is given the opportunity of performing penance for his sins. Yet there must always be fear, for man can never know the extent of God's severity.

89. *Mor*. 26.20.35 (CCL 143B, 1292–93).
90. Ibid.

· IX ·

THE SACRIFICE OF A
CONTRITE HEART

Sacrifice is the core of Gregory's moral theology. Through sacrifice, adversity and suffering yield to triumph, as the "infirmities of [Christ's] Passion were changed into the glory of his Resurrection."[1] So for man, to accept a life of earthly adversity and sacrifice is to anticipate the glorious new life of the Resurrection. In part, Gregory's focus on sacrifice and on the Mass simply reflects general historical trends. Both Augustine and Leo wrote several sermons on Easter that emphasize the sacrifice of Christ. Easter is, of course, the climax of the liturgical year. Christmas, Epiphany, and other celebrations are subordinate to this great drama, and as such are interpreted in relation to the paschal mystery.[2] Of monastic sources, the *Regula Magistri* freely speaks of Christ's Passion and Resurrection. Although the *Regula Benedicti* removes most of this language, perhaps because of the rule's anti-Arian emphasis, monastic profession is still seen as an imitation of the sacrifice of Christ.[3] In Cassian and the Desert Fathers, imitation of the sacrifice of Christ is implicit, even

---

1. Cf. *Mor*. 30.22.67 (CCL 143B, 1536–37), an exegesis of Job 39:5: "Quis dimisit onagrum liberum et uincula eius quis soluit?" Christ takes on humanity, the "wild ass," and frees us from the bonds of our mortal state through his Passion.

2. For the centrality of Easter in the liturgy of the early Church, see Josef A. Jungmann, *The Early Liturgy to the Time of Gregory the Great*, trans. Francis A. Brunner (South Bend, Ind., 1959), 19–39.

3. See A. Borias, "Le Christ dans la Règle de saint Benoît," *RBen* 82 (1972): 109–39. Borias also discusses the *Regula Magistri*, noting its free use of imagery emphasizing Christ's humanity. Borias argues that in the Benedictine Rule the monk's life is offered as a sacrifice on the altar to be taken up with the sacrifice of Christ in the Eucharist (133ff.). See de Vogüé, *La Communauté et l'abbé dans la Règle de saint Benoît* (Paris, 1961), 266–75, for more on obedience and imitation of Christ in the Benedictine Rule. In the *Rule* of St. Benedict sacrificial obedience and humility to the abbot is an imitation of the sacrifice Christ made to the Father.

though the image of the athlete dominates these works.[4] Sacrifice is also of great importance to Origen, who along with Augustine may have influenced Gregory considerably.[5]

To be sure, the theology of the sacrament of the Eucharist had undergone significant changes from the time of Ambrose and Augustine to Gregory.[6] Where Ambrose identifies the mystery (*sacramentum*) with what is signified (*res*), Augustine carefully distinguishes between *res* and *sacramentum*. However, in the period after Augustine this distinction collapses, and Ambrose's theology of the Eucharist comes to dominate theological discourse. We see this world and the next joined even more closely through the mediation of the Mass. Faustus of Riez (d. ca. 490), for instance, focuses attention on the moment of consecration, emphasizing the actual moment when the same Jesus who died at Calvary becomes present upon the altar. Like Faustus, Gregory also stresses the words of consecration as effecting a cosmic transformation that brings the body and blood of Christ into the mouths of the faithful.[7] The Mass itself was slowly changing, with intercessions becoming connected more closely with the Holy Sacrifice: communication with God is especially intense at this moment. The Eucharist was no longer only a thanksgiving (in the original meaning of the word) but especially a sacrifice. Offered as "se-

---

4. E.g., *Vitae patr.* 5.6.16; Mart. Brac. *sent. patr.* 108; Cassian *inst.* 12.8. In Cassian and the Desert Fathers the imitation of Christ's crucifixion is implicit in the notion of compunction as the monk meditates on Christ crucified for his sins. See *vita Pachom.* 7, cited by Irénée Hausherr, *Penthos*, trans. Anselm Hufstader, Cistercian Studies 53 (Kalamazoo, Mich., 1982), 49, n. 59.

5. Cf. Aug. *civ.* 10.3f., where man is reunited to God through sacrifice. From this spiritual embrace, the soul is impregnated with true virtues. In *civ.* 10.5–6 the concord of the Church is a sacrifice: to be many, yet one. Origen's homilies on Genesis, Exodus, and Leviticus especially may have influenced Gregory; he seems to borrow details of imagery. Origen's division of sacrifices *pro peccato* and *pro delicto* (Rufin. *Orig. in lev.* 4.7) is followed by Gregory. Cf. also the sin-offerings allegorized, ibid. 2.4; the sacrifice of turtledoves and pigeons, ibid. 2.1; of repentance, ibid. 3.4; of praise and vows, ibid. 5.7 and 9.1; of obedience and contrite heart, ibid. 4.5; prayer and other virtues, ibid. 9.1 (also Rufin. *Orig. in exod.* 9.4); of weak flesh, ibid. 13.5. Rufin. *Orig. in gen.* 8.8 discusses Abraham's sacrifice of obedience. See also Ambr. *bon. mort.* 3.8 and *Iac.* 6.23, emphasizing the Christian's need to suffer Christ's Passion to be above passions. On Augustine's ideas, see A. Krueger, "Synthesis of Sacrifice According to Saint Augustine" (Ph.D. diss., Santa Maria ad Lacum, 1950), esp. 5–48. For Origen and others, see Frances M. Young, *The Use of Sacrificial Ideas in Greek Christian Writers from the New Testament to John Chrysostom*, Patristic Monograph Series 5 (Philadelphia, 1979).

6. The following discussion is based on the treatment of Johannes Betz, "Eucharistie als zentrales Mysterium" in *Mysterium Salutis: Grundriss heilsgeschichtlicher Dogmatik*, eds. Johannes Feiner and Magnus Löhrer (Einsiedeln, 1973), 4, pt. 2, 229ff.

7. Cf. *Dial.* 4.60.2–3 (SC 265, 200–202).

curity" in exchange for one's petitions, the Eucharist mediates with God for fulfillment of one's prayers.[8] And, as we have seen, Gregory understands the Eucharist, the Holy Victim (*hostia*), as a continuation of the sacrifice of Christ mediating with God for mankind, a sacrifice all Christians are called to replicate in their own lives to reconcile themselves with God.[9] In short, mediation between this world and the next is ever present in a variety of ways.

Gregory's understanding of the Eucharist as Victim adumbrates the physicality of medieval Christianity and the Capernaitic mentality that dominated later Eucharistic controversies. His belief that the offering of the Host called forth reciprocal sacrifice from individual Christians is a tradition still alive today; it is at the very core of Gregory's personal spiritual needs. Gregory works to bring the sacrifice of the Mass into the center of the Christian's life. He speaks of the daily offering of the Eucharist,[10] a practice not common among Christians in the sixth century, with its rigorous attitude toward penance. Gregory also emphasizes confession to the preacher, a move toward private confession that will facilitate more frequent communion.[11]

Yet Gregory's emphasis on the Eucharist also reflects the influence of the monk-bishop in late antiquity.[12] A clerical culture had evolved that saw monastic virtues as prescriptive for the Church in general. The monk's life is a holocaust, the prelate's a sacrifice.[13] The emphasis on sacrifice in monastic life is transferred to the Church at large, along with the essentially monastic view of life as a perpetual act of penitence. The belief in offering Masses may be characterized as another extension of monastic

8. Jungmann, *Early Liturgy*, 303: "we are offering him a precious gift, and surely we can make this gift a security for expecting a gift in return."

9. *Dial*. 4.60.3 (SC 265, 202); *HEv*. 2.37.9 (PL 76, 1279); *Mor*. 13.18.26 (CCL 143A, 683); cf. Ruf. *Orig in lev*. 9.2. See also Henry Ashworth, "The Liturgical Prayers of St. Gregory the Great," *Traditio* 15 (1959):119; Betz, "Eucharistie als zentrales Mysterium," 229–30; Ph. Oppenheim, "Eucharistischer Kult und Messopfer. Ein Beitrag zur Geschichte des Wandels der eucharistischen Frömmigkeit," in *Miscellanea Pio Paschini. Studi di Storia Ecclesiastica* (Rome, 1948), 1:237–68.

10. *Dial*. 4.60.2–3 (SC 265, 200–202). See Cyril Vogel, "Deux Conséquences de l'escatologie Grégorienne: la multiplication des messes privées et les moines-prêtres," Fontaine, et al., eds., *Grégoire le Grand*, 270–71.

11. See Karl Baus et al., *The Imperial Church from Constantine to the Early Middle Ages*, trans. Anselm Biggs, vol. 2 of *History of the Church* (New York, 1969), 2:678, 681–84.

12. Phillip Rousseau, "The Spiritual Authority of the Monk-Bishop," *JThs* n.s. 22 (1971): 380–419; see also his *Ascetics, Authority, and the Church* (Oxford, 1978), esp. 62–67, 130–32, and Cyril Vogel, "Deux conséquences de l'escatologie grégorienne," 271–74.

13. Cf. *HEz*. 2.8.16 (CCL 142, 348–49). The holocaust is the life of the monk; the sacrifice, of the prelate.

practices: like abstinence or alms, they are works or offerings the individual performs to promote his own salvation and that of others.[14] The penitential processions Gregory led are a further expression of this mentality. Through such processions, one makes an offering of repentance to atone for the iniquities that have evoked God's visitation, and one seeks the intercession of those more holy and more powerful. Masses, alms, virtuous acts—all are forms of intercession mediating between man and God, and all are called sacrifices.

Yet even as Gregory was a monk, so too was he a bishop, a preacher and prelate deeply concerned with the salvation of others. As a priest, Gregory may have found special inspiration from Hebrews, the book of the Gospel that deals most fully with Christ as Priest and Sacrifice. Certainly Gregory's writings have many themes in common with Hebrews, which itself reiterates many passages from the Old Testament on priesthood and sacrifice. But Hebrews especially focuses on the role of Christ's sacrifice mediating for man—a mediation Gregory extends to the sacraments—and man's own imitation of Christ.[15] Even more important was Gregory Nazianzen's second *Oration*, which shaped Gregory's *Pastoral Rule*. Gregory Nazianzen saw the priest's mission as "providing the soul with wings," and in this devotion to the salvation of others, the priest imitates Christ.[16] The priest needs to have Paul's magnanimity in being ready to suffer for Christ's sake and be crucified to the world.[17] As "mediator of God and men," the priest needs special purity and likeness to the divine image.[18] The priesthood demands that one present oneself as a "living sacrifice," "the sacrifice of praise and of a contrite heart."[19] As bishop, Gregory must surely have felt the same responsibility to intercede for the sins of his people—even to the point of self-sacrifice, which he attributes to Moses and other "good shepherds."

If we would speak of a world view of the sixth century, such intercession and sacrifices are central. The desire for hierarchical order and the mediation such an order implies are strong in the minds of many of this era, including Dionysius the Aeropagite, Maximus Confessor, John Climacus, and Gregory himself. This heartfelt need for intercession increases the power of the clergy (and of spiritual authorities in general)

14. Gregory's strong emphasis on the value of ascetic practices and on works in general has led to speculations of semi-Pelagianism.

15. E.g., *HEz.* 2.1.16 (CCL 142, 221–22), an exegesis of Hebrews 13:12–14.

16. Rufin. *Gr. Naz. orat.* 2.22–24.

17. Ibid. 2.55–56.

18. Ibid. 2.91.

19. Ibid. 2.95.

over the means of salvation. The bishop or priest performs a special role in the drama of salvation, absolving sins and offering the Mass for Christians. Appropriately, Gregory calls preachers "doors" or "gates" through which the Christian comes to know "true life."[20] Gregory's younger contemporary, John Climacus, will make an astonishing claim for the powers of mediation and intercession, remarking that it was "better to sin against God than against one's father." The spiritual director can reconcile the sinner to God, but there is no one to propitiate one's *abba*.[21] Gregory's immediate social situation also reinforces his concept of sacrifice. Like the holy Job, Gregory has been born into a world of opposing camps of purity and pollution, and he must live among "dragons and ostriches," those grotesque and baleful creatures symbolizing sinners. On more than one occasion Gregory muses that there could have been no Abel without Cain.[22] Gregory often castigates the powerful who oppress the poor, but the disparity between Gregory's moral authority and his actual power against evil men must have been frustrating. While some oppressors could be rebuked, others had to be endured.[23]

A willingness to sacrifice oneself separates the elect from the reprobate: it is the singular quality identifying the true Christian. Christians are a sacrificial people; from the beginning of the world, they have "suffered cruelties." Abel was only the first of many sacrificial lambs.[24] When Saul is converted to become Paul, he changes from an aggressive "rhinoceros" persecuting others into a docile servant willing to suffer for Christ's sake.[25] A clear line can be drawn between secular prelates, with their love of wealth and power, and true bishops who serve God and neighbor. The former are mere "hirelings," seeking reward and scrambling to avoid adversity, whereas the latter are true "shepherds" willing to lay down their lives for their flock.[26] "One is truly glorious, who glories not in temporal power, but in Christ's Passion," Gregory writes.[27] Believing "all who will live godly in Christ suffer persecution" (2 Tm 3:12), Gregory reminds the monk Narses that he would "live less godly, were

20. *HEz.* 2.7.1 (CCL 142, 315); *HEz.* 2.8.2 (CCL 142, 336–37); cf. *Mor.* 28.18.38 (CCL 143B, 1424–25).

21. *Scala parad.* 4.121.

22. *Ep.* 11.27 (CCL 140A, 904); *HEv.* 2.38.7 (PL 76, 1286).

23. Cf. *HEz.* 2.4.3 (CCL 142, 259–60); *HEv.* 1.14.2 (PL 76, 1128); *Mor.* 31.13.22 (CCL 143B, 1566–67).

24. *Mor.* 3.17.32 (CCL 143, 135–36).

25. *Mor.* 31.16–19.30–35 (CCL 143B, 1572–76).

26. *HEv.* 1.14.1ff. (PL 76, 1127ff.).

27. *Ep.* 7.5 (CCL 140, 451).

[he] to suffer less persecution."[28] Those corrupted by secular motives are strangers to the spirit of sacrifice animating God's elect.

In addition to these historical trends, personal experiences seem to motivate Gregory's placing sacrifice and suffering at the heart of the Christian mystery. In a dedicatory letter to Leander of Seville, Gregory explicitly identifies himself with Job. After recounting his digestive ailments, his fears and worries, he writes: "And perhaps it was the plan of Divine Providence that I, one afflicted, should explain the afflicted Job; and that through my scourges, I should better understand the mind of one scourged."[29] Buffeted and stricken by adversities, Job is himself a type of the suffering Christ.[30] But if Gregory suffers, he is recompensed by being allowed to understand Job more completely: a small but significant instance of the balance of justice that steadies the world.

Gregory identifies again with Job, echoing his tribulations, in the closing lines of his commentary on *Ezechiel*.[31] No one will condemn him, Gregory writes, if he ceases work after this sermon. All Romans recognize the growing trials they suffer. Surrounded by swords, they fear imminent death. Some return to the city without hands, while others lie decapitated. Like Job, Gregory "is weary of life" (Jb 10:1); his "harp is turned to mourning," his "organ to the voice of those that weep" (Jb 30:31). Gregory concludes *Ezechiel* with lines that epitomize the main themes of the *Moralia*:

> And why am I daily forced to drink bitter things, when I can hasten to the sweet? What therefore remains except to give thanks with tears amidst the scourges we suffer for our sins? For the Very One who created us is also made our Father through the spirit of adoption whom he has given. Sometimes he nourishes his sons with bread, other times he corrects them with the scourge, since through sorrows and wounds and gifts he trains them for their eternal inheritance.[32]

The tribulations Gregory suffers are bitter draughts he is forced to drink when he longs instead for the sweetness of God. But now, by God's mysterious yet just dispensation, he must suffer both for his own iniqui-

28. *Ep.* 7.27 (CCL 140, 483).

29. *Ad Leand.* 5 (CCL 143, 6): "Et fortasse hoc diuinae prouidentiae consilium fuit, ut percussum Iob percussus exponerem, et flagellati mentem melius per flagella sentirem."

30. *Mor.* praef. 14 and 16 (CCL 143, 19–20, 20–21).

31. *HEz.* 2.10.24 (CCL 142, 397–98).

32. Ibid.: "Et qui cogor cotidie amara bibere, quando possum dulcia propinare? Quid igitur restat, nisi ut inter flagella quae ex nostris iniquitatibus patimur cum lacrimis gratias agamus? Ipse etenim qui nos creauit etiam pater nobis factus est per adoptionis spiritum quem dedit. Et aliquando filios pane nutrit, aliquando flagello corrigit, quia per dolores et uulnera et munera ad hereditatem perpetuam erudit."

ties and for those of others. Amid his inner turmoil he asserts that somehow love *must* overcome suffering: despite the strokes, God still remains
man's Father. God's severity is transformed, at least partly, for his severity
becomes as necessary as his mercy for the training (*eruditio*) of his sons.
His scourges and wounds become equivalent to his gifts and his bread.
Still, ambivalence remains: one accepts and gives thanks "with tears."

Shaken by the sheer momentum of dark forces, Gregory's suffering
is grievous in his own eyes, and that is what matters. He endures chronic
illness; his perilous work depresses his spirit. Now, so near the end of
time, the calamities visited upon Rome seem brutal and unremitting.
Once proud, Rome is now embarrassingly impotent: the noble eagle has
lost her crown of feathers and grown bald in tribulation.[33] In a more ma-
cabre image, Rome is the cauldron set upon the fire in Ezekiel 24:10–
11.[34] First, the cauldron boils with broken bones and seething flesh. But
in the end, the cauldron itself melts and is utterly consumed in apocalyptic fire. The destruction of Rome at last fulfills the sentence pronounced
long ago on the city of Sumeria by the prophet Ezechiel.[35]

Gregory's suffering was acute, but neither the number nor the intensity of the horrors he witnessed can fully explain his feelings. Surely Augustine, Ambrose, Cyprian, and others endured trials as dramatic and
bloody. Rather, Gregory's own raw sensitivity and his brittle vulnerability
account for his powerful and acute reactions. The disorders around him
loom larger than life; they appear relentless and overwhelming. Gregory,
however, faces them with gravity and determination, fearing yet struggling to exert control when he can. Hemmed in and anxious (*angustare,
anxius*), he desires the power to master a painful and chaotic world. That
Gregory has considerable success in this struggle does not seem to soothe
him. On the contrary, it makes him more watchful and troubled for this
very prosperity. This anxious care (*solicitudo*) so characteristic of Gregory's spiritual life is of a piece with the efficiency he imposes on papal
government. Disciplined and fastidious, he desires a right order in government as well as the soul.

Though the desire to assert order upon chaos is universal, the terms
of Gregory's struggle and its resolution are significant. Like Job, Gregory
faces the eternal confrontation between suffering and necessity, rage and
impotence. Gregory struggles to accept God's dispensation as the work
of a loving Father rather than that of a vengeful judge, and this turmoil
emerges obliquely in his exegesis of the angry protests of Job's wife and

33. *HEz.* 2.6.23 (CCL 142, 312).
34. *HEz.* 2.6.22 (CCL 142, 311).
35. *HEz.* 2.6.22 (CCL 142, 311–12).

his friends. When adversity struck, some part of Gregory may have longed to reproach God, as Job did, shaking his fist. He could understand, if not sympathize with, the resentful cry of Job's wife, "Curse God and die!" In rebuking such blasphemy and condemning those who take up arms against God, Gregory strives as well to eradicate any trace of resistance from his own soul, perhaps without being aware how such conflict could be embedded in his own tense and ambivalent mind.

The contrast between those who possess *patientia* and those who display *impatientia* suggests Gregory's inner division. Like Job, some are long-suffering and accept patiently both good and evil from God's hands. Others, like Job's wife and his friends, misinterpret God's actions and rebel imperiously against them. The imagery Gregory uses to describe God also reflects his own inner ambivalence. In the tension and complementarity of God's mercy and severity one sees a division of feeling between fear and love that resolves in a bittersweet synthesis. God will always "mix scourges and gifts,"[36] and "blend comforts with terrors."[37] He will "repel when holding," and "in holding repel."[38] He will be the mother who "beats her child one moment as if she never loved him," and the next moment "loves him as if she had never beaten him."[39] Just as man alternates between rebellious impatience and submissive patience, God alternates between loving man and punishing him.

The roots of this ambivalence are difficult to uncover. In a continuous cycle Gregory's Christian alternates between the rebellion of sin and the sacrifice of obedience. The latter expunges and compensates for the former, but inevitably sin returns, and the cycle of sacrifice must begin again. The Christian must expiate his sins, and he bears a heavy burden, for he carries with him, in his corruptible nature, the guilt of man's Fall. Ultimately, the Christian recognizes that his sinfulness is united with that

---

36. *HEz.* 2.4.3 (CCL 142, 260).

37. *Mor.* 33.7.14 (CCL 143B, 1684). Cf. *BenRegula.* 2.24, where the abbot is said to: "miscens temporibus tempora, terroribus blandimenta, dirum magistri, pium patris ostendat affectum. . . ." The emphasis on the mercy and justice of God is found also in Ambrose; cf. *Cain et Ab.* 2.15; *in psalm.* 108.20.40; *obit. Theod.* 25; *paenit.* 1.16. Ambrose may have been influenced by Philo, for whom God's mercy and justice are always important themes. Dagens notes the importance of the mercy and severity of God in Tertullian; cf. *Saint Grégoire le Grand* (Paris, 1977), 377.

38. *HEz.* 1.1.18 (CCL 142, 14).

39. *HEz.* 1.1.18 (CCL 142, 15): "Sic plerumque paruulo filio delinquenti irascitur mater, reprehendit, increpat, uerberat; sed si hunc in praeceps ire conspexerit, ubi in mortis periculum ruat, manum tendit et retinet, et quae sic irata uerberauerat ac si non diligeret, sic diligendo retinet, ac si irata non uerberasset."

of all mankind and that this very sinfulness occasioned the death of the Redeemer: had man not sinned, Christ need not have suffered.[40] Now the blood that polluted the hands of Christ's murderers becomes an awesome sacrament for the salvation of his elect.[41]

Christ died because of our sins, and what can man offer in compensation?[42] Somehow his offering must restore the mysterious equilibrium of justice that governs the world. Considering that the Creator is made man and pours his blood upon the Cross, man should not find it difficult (*laboriosum*) to make himself a sacrifice.[43] Since we are the more Christ's debtor the more he suffered indignities,[44] any suffering that man endures can never begin to requite the death of the Sinless One. Given Christ's perfect sacrifice, the Christian must never protest against the scourge: it is much less for man to bear wounds than for Christ to have borne human sufferings,[45] and no man should complain.[46] Thus the compensation man renders God entails a dramatic equalization. Not only must man activate his redemption by imitating Christ, he must be willing to match his Passion. Stamped with the image of the Redeemer, he must consider his ways and give his due to Christ.[47]

Like Augustine and Origen, Gregory believes that the whole life of the Christian is a sacrifice. In the *Moralia*, Gregory focuses on the sacrifice of Job's life in obedience to God. Job's name, he explains, means "grieving" (*dolens*), the grieving of the Redeemer's Passion.[48] Virtually every act Job and man perform before God is a sacrifice, an offering to God. There

40. *Mor.* 3.14.26 (CCL 143, 131–32).

41. *Dial.* 4.60.2 (SC 265, 200–202): "tamen in se ipso inmortaliter atque incorruptibiliter uiuens, pro nobis iterum in hoc mysterio sacrae oblationis immolatur. Eius quippe ibi corpus sumitur, eius caro in populi salutem partitur, eius sanguis non iam in manus infidelium, sed in ora fidelium funditur." The polluted and the sacred are two complementary sides of taboo.

42. Gregory's thoughts on this theme may be influenced especially by Ambr. *Iac.* 7.27, 6.23; *Ioseph.* 7.42.

43. *HEz.* 2.9.22 (CCL 142, 376–77).

44. *Mor.* 29.1.1 (CCL 143B, 1434).

45. *Mor.* 30.1.3 (CCL 143B, 1492–93).

46. *Mor.* 29.14.26 (CCL 143B, 1451–52).

47. *HEz.* 2.2.15 (CCL 142, 236).

48. *Mor.* praef. 7.16 (CCL 143, 20–21): "Nam quia beatus Iob uenturi Redemptoris speciem teneat, etiam nomine demonstrat. Iob quippe interpretatur dolens. Quo nimirum dolore uel Mediatoris passio uel sanctae Ecclesiae labor exprimitur, quae multiplici praesentis uitae fatigatione cruciatur." Job's wife typifies the "vita carnalis," *Mor.* praef. 6.14 (CCL 143, 20); his friend Eliphaz, "Domini contemptus"; Baldad, "uetustas sola"; Sophar, "dissipatio speculae" or "speculationem dissipans," *Mor.* praef. 7.16 (CCL 143, 21). Cf. *HEz.* 1.4.1 (CCL 142, 47–48).

are sacrifices of self,[49] life,[50] conversion,[51] obedience,[52] humility,[53] the flesh,[54] carnal life,[55] continence,[56] compunction,[57] fear,[58] tears,[59] works,[60] virtue,[61] contemplation,[62] prayer,[63] and praise.[64]

But it would be well to begin with Gregory's larger perspective and definition of sacrifice, for Gregory differs from earlier fathers. Sacrifice is first an abnegation of carnal life, an immolation of what is sinful so that man might be cleansed and rejoined to God. Yet more profoundly, sacrifice is the obedient return to bear the imperfection of the carnality one has abnegated; a reluctant return to the world and all its temptations in obedience to God's commands of charity. Paradoxically, perfection lies in the recognition of one's imperfection: "quo se ipse imperfectum respicit, inde ad humilitatis culmen perfectior assurgat."[65] The deeper meaning of

---

49. *Mor.* 9.55.84 (CCL 143, 515); cf. *Mor.* 6.37.56 (CCL 143, 325–26); *HEz.* 1.10.11 (CCL 142, 149); *HEz.* 2.8.14 (CCL 142, 347); *HEz.* 2.10.19 (CCL 142, 394ff.); *Dial.* 3.26.4–9 (SC 260, 368–72). See Alfred C. Rush, "Spiritual Martyrdom in St. Gregory the Great," *ThS* 23 (1962): 569–89. Rush argues that for Gregory martyrs in his times were those making sacrifices of themselves to God in their hearts in charity (cf. *HEv.* 2.2.3 [PL 76, 1206]). Cf. Aug. *civ.* 10.3 and 10.6; Rufin. *Orig. in exod.* 13.2.

50. *Mor.* 6.37.56 (CCL 143, 325–26); *Mor.* 35.14.28 (CCL 143B, 1792).

51. *Mor.* 35.8.14 (CCL 143B, 1782); cf. also *Mor.* 35.8.11 (CCL 143B, 1780–81).

52. Cf. *Mor.* 32.3.4 (CCL 143B, 1628–29). Cf. also *Mor.* 9.55.84 (CCL 143, 514–16). See also Aug. *civ.* 10.5.

53. *Mor.* 26.26.47 (CCL 143B, 1302). Aug. *civ.* 10.5.

54. *Mor.* 6.37.56 (CCL 143, 325–26); see also *HEz.* 1.4.4 (CCL 142, 47–48), *HEz.* 2.9.21 (CCL 142, 375). See n. 1 above and *HEz.* 2.10.4 (CCL 142, 381–82). Cf. Aug. *civ.* 10.6; Rufin. *Orig. in exod.* 13.5; Rufin. *Orig. in num.* 9.1.

55. *Mor.* 28.18.41 (CCL 143B, 1427–28). Two types of sacrifice typify the change from the Old to the New Dispensation. Note also in this passage the parallelism of Christ's death and the sacrificial death of the carnal man. The imitation of martyrdom (here of S. Felicitas) involves sacrifice; cf. *HEv.* 1.3.4 (PL 76, 1088–89). See also *HEz.* 1.10.11 (CCL 142, 149); *HEz.* 2.9.2 (CCL 142, 357); *HEz.* 2.10.4 (CCL 142, 381–82).

56. *HEz.* 2.8.19 (CCL 142, 350); and *HEz.* 2.10.4 (CCL 142, 381–82); *Mor.* 6.37.56 (CCL 143, 325–26); *HEz.* 1.4.4 (CCL 142, 47–48); *HEz.* 2.9.21 (CCL 142, 375); and *HEz.* 2.10.4 (CCL 142, 381–82).

57. *HEz.* 2.10.4 (CCL 142, 381–82); *HEz.* 2.10.20 (CCL 142, 395); *HEz.* 2.18.17 (CCL 142, 349); *Mor.* 1.34.48 (CCL 143, 50); and *HEz.* 1.1.15 (CCL 142, 12–13).

58. Ibid. See also *HEz.* 2.8.17 (CCL 142, 349).

59. *Dial.* 4.60.1 (SC 265, 200); *HEz.* 2.8.17 (CCL 142, 349); and *HEz.* 2.8.19 (CCL 142, 350).

60. *Mor.* 6.37.56 (CCL 143, 325–26); see also *HEz.* 2.9.2 (CCL 142, 356–57); *HEz.* 2.10.19f. (CCL 142, 394ff.). Cf. Aug. *civ.* 10.6; Rufin. *Orig. in lev.* 2.4.

61. Ibid.

62. *Cant.* 1.5 (CCL 144, 8).

63. *Mor.* 35.11.21 (CCL 143B, 1787) and *Mor.* 1.34.48 (CCL 143, 50). Cf. Rufin. *Orig. in lev.* 9.1.

64. *HEz* 2.10.4 (CCL 142, 382); *HEz.* 1.1.15 (CCL 142, 12–13); cf. Aug. *civ* 10.3. See also *conf.* passim; Rufin. *Orig. in lev.* 9.1.

65. *Mor.* 5.4.5 (CCL 143, 222). Cf. Pasch.Dum. *lib. geron.* 34.3.

sacrifice is the surrender of the ascetic perfection one would have wished to enjoy. Having been converted to love heavenly realities, man makes a greater sacrifice of will to leave this security of salvation than to depart from the mere carnal shadows he once enjoyed. This level of sacrifice has more dangers, yet it also promises special rewards.

This paradox of perfection in imperfection modifies earlier tradition. In general, fathers before Gregory define perfection according to Pauline thinking, positing the antagonism of flesh and spirit and the superiority of the spirit. The antagonism is reconciled dialectically, with one moving through flesh to spirit. This is the lesson of Martha and Mary, Leah and Rachel (representing active and contemplative lives), letter and spirit, Old and New Dispensations. In contrast, Gregory emphasizes a cyclical return to the carnal element. This return to the carnal is adumbrated in Origen, Cassian, and Augustine, but only very faintly and without affecting the structure of their thought.[66] For Gregory, however, the return to the carnal is integral to his expression of the complementarity of spiritual and carnal. That Jacob finally wins Rachel is less important than that he needs both Rachel for her beauty and Leah for her fruitfulness and that he must alternate continually between the two.[67] Each remedies the deficiencies of the other; both are necessary for the perfect Christian life, poised delicately on the balance point of humility and hope.

Nonetheless, that Gregory views Jacob's return to Leah, to the active life and carnal burdens, as a sacrifice of humility, a paradox of perfection in imperfection, testifies to his residual belief in the ethical antagonism of spiritual and carnal. This fundamental antagonism is especially discernible when Gregory speaks of monastic ideals. The monastic life is a grave that buries man perfectly because it severs all ties with worldly concerns.[68] It is secret and hidden, inward and safe. As we have seen, there

66. The salutary effects of temptation preventing one from spiritual pride are found in Cassian, *conl.* 4.3, 4.12, 4.16. Augustine speaks of Jacob's need to return to Leah, *c. Faust.* 22.51–57. Origen speaks of the need to begin and return to the carnal, *in Matt.* 17.27, as noted by Gerard Caspary, *Politics and Exegesis: Origen and the Two Swords* (Berkeley, 1979), 154. See also Aug. *corrept.* 24; *civ.* 19.1, 19.19; *conf.* 10.65.

67. *HEz.* 2.2.10 (CCL 142, 231–32). See also *In lib I Reg.* 5.179 (CCL 144, 530–31); *HEz.* 1.3.9f. (CCL 142, 37f.); *Mor.* 6.37.61 (CCL 143, 330). Jean Leclercq investigates the tradition of such terms as *quies, otium, vacatio,* which Gregory is changing when integrating them with the active life; see "*Otia Monastica.* Etudes sur le vocabulaire de la contemplation au Moyen Age," *StAns* 51 (Rome, 1963): 13ff. On the mixed life, see Dagens, *Saint Grégoire,* 145–58; Jean Leclercq, *The Spirituality of the Middle Ages,* trans. The Benedictines of Holme Eden Abbey, Carlisle, vol. 2 of Louis Bouyer et al., *A History of Christian Spirituality* (New York, 1961), 10–12; Patrick Catry, "Amour du monde et amour de Dieu chez saint Grégoire le Grand," *StudMon* 15 (1973): 265ff.; Johannes Mehlmann, "Minus quam inter duos caritas haberi non potest," *VD* 45 (1967): 97–103; Vera Paronetto, "Rachele e Lia," *Studium* 62 (1966): 733–40.

68. *Mor.* 6.37.56 (CCL 143, 325–26).

is a security in the complete abnegation of will that one makes in obeying a superior; the sacrifice of one's will far excels the ritual sacrifice of animals.[69] Similarly, one propitiates God the more quickly, the more one "represses the pride of his own will" and "sacrifices himself [with the] sword of rules."[70] In the contemplative life, the Christian is crucified to the world, and the world crucified to the Christian.[71] The contemplative man is like the corpse cast into the sea of the world: because he is dead, the sea disgorges him willingly.[72]

In contrast to the safety and security of the contemplative life, the active life is fraught with danger. For Gregory, the seductions of the world are no mere literary topoi. The temptations of the world, the desire for gratifications other than God, truly are tempting—at least some of them are. Though Gregory's conscious intent is to reject worldly affairs and hold himself far above them, beneath his contempt lies a secret attraction to secular affairs:

> For it is very difficult for the tongues of secular men not to pollute the mind they touch. Very frequently, if we condescend to speak of certain things with them, little by little we become accustomed to this very speech which is unworthy of us, and we even cling to these things with pleasure so that we are no longer willing to relinquish them. We have entered these things against our will, from condescension, so to speak, but it turns out that we move from inconsequential to weighty discussions, from frivolous errors to culpable guilt.[73]

The merest involvement in worldly affairs, here exchanging small talk with men of the world, can imperil the soul. One begins unwillingly, yet soon conscious aims and self-discipline are subverted, and the impulse one has been struggling to subdue makes a shameful reappearance. One finds oneself clinging to the carnal things one wants to reject and partaking of exactly the enjoyment one has abnegated. To his great distress, he is "punished by his former pleasures."[74] Still another danger exists. Some men, before they are fixed and stable in heavenly things, may return inadvertently, through a "numbness" of mind,[75] to the very evils they condemned and fled. They may revert to former evils from desire, rather than condescending to bear their abnegation as a duty.[76] A more subtle

---

69. *Mor.* 35.14.28 (CCL 143B, 1792).
70. Ibid.
71. *Mor.* 5.3.4 (CCL 143, 220–21).
72. Ibid.
73. *Dial.* 3.15.16 (SC 260, 324). Cf. *HEz.* 1.11.6 (CCL 142, 171).
74. *Mor.* 24.11.32 (CCL 143B, 1211–12).
75. *Mor.* 12.52.59 (CCL 143A, 664).
76. *HEz.* 2.1.7 (CCL 142, 213).

rebellion is found in those who mourn for the things they have abnegated.[77] Gregory issues a stern warning: those who leave the world should never return unless they are "firm in hating it."[78]

One finds this same pattern of unintentional self-gratification and the same fear of relapse concerning any aspect of carnal life, be it wielding power in office or simply attending to the daily demands of life. One must always exercise great discretion lest pleasure veil itself as legitimate need, or necessity lead to an abusive excess.[79] One can rejoice in the security of the contemplative life, but one must mourn the active life bitterly, for one can neither control its claims nor obliterate its temptations. The world may be crucified to the Christian, but the Christian is not crucified in the eyes of the world.[80] The grave of the active life is imperfect. It covers the man dead to evil works, but does not shield him from secular life. The active man is the body swallowed by the sea of the world and kept within its grasp, because, unfortunately, he is still alive to some degree.[81]

The sacrifice made in returning to the world will always have two parts. The sacrifice of obedience demands that man give up in part his purity and closeness to God to return to the world in service to his neighbor. This will be the sacrifice of love. But the sacrifice must also include the immolation and purification of one's intentions, because one may possess an unknown, unconscious attraction to the world. One can never act safely in the world without carefully examining one's motives for secret sins and striving to eradicate them. This will be the sacrifice of fear, a recognition that the carnal life still remains.[82]

Ideally, abnegation is to be complete and absolute, an all-or-nothing choice, because spiritual and carnal, contemplative and active sides of life are antagonistic. But on a second level, these opposites become complementary, replicating the Incarnation and Passion of Christ. It becomes a paradoxical sacrifice for man to suffer carnal activities, just as it was a paradoxical sacrifice for God to suffer human things. The opposition of spiritual and carnal lives and Gregory's personal struggle and sacrifice to reconcile them are revealed in his letters. In describing his conversion to monastic life to Leander, Gregory notes that he was displeased with him-

---

77. *HEz.* 2.8.15 (CCL 142, 347–48).

78. *Mor.* 8.47.78 (CCL 143, 442): "Qui enim mundum deserunt, ad exteriora officia prouehi non debent, nisi per humilitatem diutius in eiusdem mundi contemptu solidentur."

79. Cf. *Mor.* 2.48–50.75–80 (CCL 143, 104–8); *HEz.* 1.7.10 (CCL 142, 89–90).

80. *Mor.* 5.3.4 (CCL 143, 220–21).

81. Ibid. Cf. *Mor.* 5.3.4 (CCL 143, 220–21).

82. *Mor.* 9.55.84 (CCL 143, 514–16).

self and inspired with a desire for heavenly things long before he made a formal break with the world and changed his secular habit.[83] At first, he attempted to reconcile his inner vocation and outward duties. He tried to serve the world in appearance only, but found himself so entangled that he became bound also in his mind. Thus, though he began by condescending, he ended by clinging to the world. Filled with great anxieties, he fled to the "haven" of the monastery to anchor and repair what had become the "shipwreck" of his life. Unnerved by the incompatibility of the spiritual and the carnal, the contemplative and the active, he felt a deep need for complete abnegation.

A letter to Emperor Maurice touches on this same problem of incompatibility.[84] Maurice had forbidden anyone engaged in public administration to take ecclesiastical office or enter a monastery. Gregory agrees that one who is in haste to leave secular honors for ecclesiastical office is not wishing to relinquish secular affairs, but merely to exchange them. But Gregory protests the decree, observing, "There are many who are able to live a religious life even in a secular condition; but there are many who cannot in any way be saved with God unless they give up all things." Apparently, some can reconcile the two lives, others cannot.

Shortly after his election to the papacy, Gregory reflects on his state of mind in a letter to Theoctista.[85] He reiterates many familiar themes on the problems of the mixed life, but here his exhortations are posed as lamentations and fears. He seems to have risen outwardly while falling inwardly. Because of the busyness of secular activities, he has lost the joys of inward tranquillity. He was once lifted up upon high places [Is 58:14], treading beneath him the glorious things of the world, but now he is dashed from the summit and caught in a whirlwind of trial. After work, he desires to retreat to his heart, but tumultuous thoughts block his return. He has loved Rachel, but by God's mysterious judgment, been wed to Leah. He longs to sit with Mary and caress the feet of the Savior with his tears, yet he is compelled to serve with Martha. To be sure, there are many who know how to govern (regere) their external advancement so that they do not fall inwardly. They do not become like the sinners who are wheels, falling in the things that are before them, and rising in what they have left behind (Phil 3:13). But for Gregory, this is difficult, for

83. *Ad Leand.* 1 (CCL 143, 1). A certain judgment, mind, or purpose (*animus*) kept him in the world. Precisely what this purpose was has been the object of scholars' speculation, generally with the rather safe conclusion that Gregory probably felt he could be of some benefit to his country or people; cf. C. Dagens, "La 'Conversion' de saint Grégoire le Grand," *RecAug* 15 (1969): 149–62.

84. *Ep.* 3.61 (CCL 140, 209–11).

85. *Ep.* 1.5 (CCL 140, 5–7).

"what the mind has not accepted willingly, it cannot control fittingly and harmoniously."[86]

Among other things, this letter illustrates the central importance of discretion. When exercised with reason and moderation, active and contemplative lives can balance and even reinforce each other. But if discretion is lost, the two lives become incompatible, sharply at odds. In his letter to Theoctista, Gregory says he feels his self-control eroding as his rational will is disregarded. When one is forced to act against one's better judgment, internal conflicts arise to upset the soul's harmony. Thus the theme of the successful mixed life found in Gregory's exegesis is in part wishful thinking, as his letter to Theoctista is doubtless in part apophatic. To justify worldly involvement is daring and dangerous. He ends the letter by citing Job 36:5, as if to console himself: "God does not cast away the powerful, for he himself is powerful." Indeed, the right exercise of power has its special reward.[87] Gregory works out the complementarity of active and contemplative lives with such thoroughness and clarity in order to validate his own worldly involvement. A formula of such mathematical elegance and musical harmony must surely point to a divine Author. Or if not the Author, God cannot fail as a rational Creator to uphold Gregory's arguments.

Guilty and anxious about involuntary as well as voluntary sin, Gregory stresses that worldly activity must be accompanied by the deepest penitence and compunction. The offering of works must always be cleansed first with tears of penitence. Worldly activity can be pursued safely only as a sacrifice of obedience, for here the mysterious judgment of God actually compels man to accept the temptations and gratifications he earnestly desires to renounce for God's sake. Perfection can be found through imperfection because the soul that is stable and governed by discretion has the balance and equilibrium to reverse bad fortune and temptation and turn them to good ends. Yet before the Christian can attain such perfection, he must be converted and reformed, a process that is itself another form of sacrifice.

86. Ibid.
87. Ibid.; see also *Mor.* 26.26.44 (CCL 143B, 1298–1300).

· X ·

REFORM AND THE PREACHER

God does not easily forsake his own creation. Sinners may lie hardened in their torpid indifference, but God reaches out to convert his elect: "now he terrifies them with threats, now with beatings, now with revelations, so that those hardened in deadly security may be softened with healthful fear, so that they may return, even if late, and at least blush with shame that they have been so long awaited."[1]

These ominous threats, beatings, and revelations suggest the fearsome difficulty of reform. Battling himself and the devil in the dull campaigns of daily life, the sinner labors all his life for moral improvement. His conversion is not a single act, but a continuous struggle, an endless cycle of sin, repentance, and virtue. "Excess is followed by correction, correction by penitence, penitence by forgiveness, and forgiveness by gifts."[2] But invariably gifts lead again to excess, and the cycle begins anew. The Christian may progress from fearful servant to loving son, and finally to bride, whose soul is embraced by God.[3] But for all her excel-

---

1. *Mor.* 29.9.20 (CCL 143B, 1447): "Sed quia plus conditor facturam suam non deserit, . . . Cum duras atque insensibiles mentes respicit, modo eas minis, modo uerberibus, modo reuelationibus terret, ut quae pessima securitate duruerant, salubri timore mollescant, quatenus uel sero redeant, et hoc ipsum saltem, quod diu exspectati sunt erubescant."

2. *Mor.* 35.12.22 (CCL 143B, 1788): "Excessum quippe correptio, correptionem paenitentia, paenitentiam uenia, ueniam uero munera subsequuntur."

3. *Cant.* 8 (CCL 144, 10–11); *Mor.* 24.11.28 (CCL 143B, 1207–8); see also *Mor.* 8.8.13 (CCL 143, 391). See esp. Claude Dagens's treatment of conversion, which centers on the interiority/exteriority contrast, *Saint Grégoire le Grand* (Paris, 1977), 247–345. Dagens notes these stages are a tradition from Irenaeus on and sees in the bitter/sweet contrast an echo of Augustine. But on the whole, Dagens sees Gregory closer to Cassian than Augustine when speaking of the soul's conversion. See also Gerhart B. Ladner, "Gregory the Great and Gregory VII: A Comparison of Their Concepts of Renewal," *Viator* 4 (1973): 1–31.

lence, the bride does not enjoy tranquillity. God tries her, as a husband tests his bride, first "consoling her with sweet offerings; then trying her with bitter rebuke." Only after she has been tried and proved, will he "possess her in security." So God tried the Israelites in the desert, alternating love and fierce trials. When they were proved, he led them to the promised land.[4]

Joy and sorrow alternate especially at three stages of the Christian's life: at conversion, midway, and at the end of his pilgrimage, when temptations and assaults from the devil are particularly severe.[5] The heart is grieved with anxiety because the "spirit calls him in one direction, the flesh calls him back in the other; love of a new way of life invites him on one side, the habits of his old wickedness fight on the other."[6] Even so, this worrisome trial is recapitulated in the alternations of daily life, as the Christian feels the ebb and flow of God's grace and wrath in the adversity and prosperity he suffers. He knows God is like the angry yet loving mother alternately beating yet saving her "little delinquent son."[7] From moment to moment, the son must live in uncertainty, yet never yield to despair.

That the Christian's conversion should be so filled with turmoil, with alternations and reversals, is scarcely surprising. Gregory sees reform as the perfection of the rational man through *paideia*, a rigorous education and training that elevates man far above his lower, irrational impulses. In this, Gregory is consistent with the classical heritage of early Christian thought.[8] But the Christian must surpass the rational control prescribed by the ancients, for he must imitate Christ.[9] Sinners must leave behind the "old" man and become the "new" man, must "leave behind what we

4. *Mor.* 24.11.28 (CCL 143B, 1207–8).

5. Ibid.

6. *Mor.* 24.11.26 (CCL 143B, 1206): "Et quis ibi maeror, quae anxietas cordis, quando hinc spiritus uocat, hinc caro reuocat, hinc amor nouae conuersationis inuitat, hinc usus uetustae peruersitatis impugnat; hinc desiderio ad spiritalem patriam flagrat, et hinc in seipso carnalem concupiscentiam tolerat, quae eum aliquo modo etiam inuitum delectat?"

7. *HEz.* 1.1.18 (CCL 142, 15).

8. See Pierre Hadot, *Exercices spirituels et philosophie antique* (Paris, 1981), esp. 25–74; Werner Jaeger, *Early Christianity and Greek Paideia* (Oxford, 1961); idem, *Paideia: The Ideals of Greek Culture*, trans. G. Highet (New York, 1939–1944), 3 vols.; Gerhart B. Ladner, *The Idea of Reform* (New York and Evanston, 1950; repr. 1967), esp. 63–132. Gregory's ideas of reform are especially close to Ambrose in emphasizing rational control of fleshly pleasures, cf. *Isaac* 1.2f., 4.16, 8.79; *bon. mort.* 3.9, 6.25, 7.26; *Iac.* 1.1, 2.5, 3.9–10, 8.37. See also *Vitae patr.* 5.4.14; 5.4.34; 5.4.43; 5.4.45; 5.4.49; 5.5.1ff. and passim; Cassian *conl.* 3.76–77; 4.9; 12.1ff. (on chastity); 10.6; *inst.* 5.18.1–2. On Augustine, see the discussion and citations in Ladner, *Idea of Reform*, 153–283.

9. *HEz.* 1.2.19 (CCL 142, 28–29); *Mor.* 16.33.41 (CCL 143A, 823).

have made ourselves through sinning and abide in what we are made through grace."[10] Conversion is a radical, stunning change that turns the old life upside down. "The earth is overturned" (Jb 12:15) because, like earth inverted by a spade, the sinner's life is completely reversed in conversion.[11] Humility, continence, and generosity replace pride, lechery, and avarice.[12] The Christian recoils from his former habits. The sinner's "hard resistance" turns to "tearful obedience," and

> he willingly bears injuries which he formerly inflicted. Afterwards, he even gives his own when he previously stole from others. After, he tortures the flesh with abstinence, when first he was degenerate, gratifying the flesh through the deadly attractions of sin. After, he even loves his persecutors, when earlier he did not wish to love even those who loved him. Therefore, when the human mind, infused with the divine gift, begins to act against its custom, the earth is overturned since both what stood out is put down, and the face which was first pressed in the depths is now turned upwards.[13]

The carnal life that gratifies the flesh leads as well to cruelty and avarice. Preoccupied with pleasure, the sinner cannot see beyond himself. Charging through life like a self-centered "rhinoceros," he tramples on others.[14] The sinner must sever his attachment to pleasure if his life is to change; he must reject the worldly life that pampers the flesh and embrace instead a spiritual life that accepts tortures of the flesh. The aggressive energy spent indulging oneself and tormenting others must be redirected against one's lower nature, to kill and sacrifice all one's inner evil. The sinner must "exchange the first born of an ass for a sheep,"

10. *HEv.* 2.32.2 (PL 76, 1233): "Relinquamus nosmetipsos quales peccando nos fecimus, et maneamus nosmetipsi quales per gratiam facti sumus."

11. *Mor.* 11.10.14–15 (CCL 143A, 593–594).

12. *HEv.* 2.32.2 (PL 76, 1233–34). See also the "impetus spiritus" and "impetus carnis" in *HEz.* 1.5.2 (CCL 142, 57).

13. *Mor.* 11.10.15 (CCL 143A, 594): "si sancti Spiritus gratia superno munere iuxta uocem praedicantis infunditur, statim terra subuertitur, quia peccatricis mentis duritia ab immobilitatis suae obstinatione permutatur, ut tantum se postmodum praeceptis dominicis flendo subiciat, quantum superbiendo prius contra Dominum ceruicem cordis erigebat. Videas namque quod terra cordis humani, aqua diuini muneris infusa, post libenter iniurias toleret quas prius uehementer irrogabat. Post etiam sua tribuat quae prius et aliena rapiebat; post carnem abstinendo cruciet quae prius satietate carnis per mortifera turpitudinum oblectamenta defluebat; post etiam persecutores diligat quae prius diligere etiam se amantes nolebat. Cum igitur mens humana, diuino munere infusa, contra hoc quod consueuerat agere coeperit, terra subuersa est quia et deorsum missa est, quae prius eminebat; et sursum leuata est facies quae prius in profunda premebatur."

14. The rhinoceros is a type of Paul before his conversion, and the secular prince before he allies himself with the Church. Cf. *Mor.* 31.16.30f. (CCL 143B, 1572f.); *Mor.* 31.2.2f. (CCL 143B, 1549f.).

Gregory writes, referring to Exodus 13:13. "The beginning of an impure life [must be] converted to purity and innocence, so after the sinner has committed deeds the Lord rejects as unclean, he may now set forth behavior he can offer in sacrifice to God."[15]

In offering a life of innocence as a sacrifice to God, the sinner extinguishes and sacrifices his old carnal identity. He "abnegates himself" and "leaves himself behind," embracing a new identity in grace.[16] Thus the raging rhinoceros Saul becomes the humble servant Paul when converted, willing "'to fill up what is lacking of the sufferings of Christ in his own flesh'" [Col 1:24].[17] So, too, the convert learns to bear Christ's crosses in body and mind: in the affliction of abstinence and in compassion for others.[18] Gregory sees the two crosses as interconnected, for a willingness to suffer discomforts in the flesh spiritually transforms the Christian. From the depths of his own suffering, he learns empathy and compassion; true generosity, patience, and kindness awaken. Conversion is certainly a "change of heart,"[19] because the sinner's feelings are reoriented toward others with a new tenderness and respect, but it is a change founded in a different attitude toward the body and life in the flesh. Love of pleasure changes to a willingness to suffer; sacrifice replaces sin.

As one who suffered privately from chronic illness, who endured also the public suffering of famine, plague, and war, Gregory was keenly aware of how adversity and misfortune could transform the personality. Since man must come to know himself before he can know God,[20] the trials of life reveal the raw bones of his true nature and force him to come to terms with himself. Sometimes only misfortune can inspire introspection and a return to God: "after we fail to obtain what we want in this world, after we languish from the impossibility of attaining earthly de-

---

15. *Mor.* 27.18.38 (CCL 143B, 1359): "Asini ergo primogenita oue mutare, est immundae uitae primordia in innocentiae simplicitate conuertere, ut postquam illa peccator egit, quae ut immunda Dominus respuit, ea iam agendo proferat, quae Dei sacrificio imponat."

16. *HEv.* 2.32.2 (PL 76, 1233–34), a sermon on Luke 9:23–27: ("Si quis vult post me venire, abnegat semetipsum et tollat crucem suam quotidie, et sequatur me"): "Tunc ergo nosmetipsos reliquimus, tunc nos ipsos abnegamus, cum vitamus quod per vetustatem fuimus, et ad hoc nitimur quod per novitatem vocamur." Paul is the model of this death and new life: "Exstinctus quippe fuerat saevus ille persecutor, et vivere coeperat pius praedicator. . . . Quia nisi quis a semetipso deficiat, ad eum qui super ipsum est non appropinquat; nec valet apprehendere quod ultra ipsum est, si nescierit mactare quod est."

17. *Mor.* 31.18.33 (CCL 143B, 1574).

18. Cf. *HEv.* 2.32.3 (PL 76, 1234).

19. Cf. *HEz.* 1.10.8 (CCL 142, 148).

20. Cf. *HEz.* 2.5.8–9 (CCL 142, 281–82).

sires, then we call God back to our minds."[21] Retreating from the world, one withdraws to the citadel of the mind. Knowing the dangers of the world and the high price exacted for its pleasures, one grows more reflective, more detached and self-possessed. In detachment and retreat, one is unmoved by the world's pale delights and strong enough to withstand its terrors. Adversity sharpens the mind and makes one more cautious and deliberate, for it gives man the distance needed to see life more clearly. Adversity helps one focus on essentials and discern what truly matters. Material comforts, success, and power are inconsequential; they can easily be lost to the vagaries of fortune. Only the life of the spirit matters, the kindness none can take away, the love that exists eternally and is inexhaustibly delightful.

More than others before him, Gregory stresses how adversity can lead to spiritual transformation.[22] Fire is fanned brighter by the wind,[23] and the grape must be trampled to produce wine.[24] Trials may bend and bruise the Christian, but they can bring out his virtues and spark his renewal by perfecting his mastery of himself. Life in the body and experience of the mysterious and imponderable suffering of the human condition give one a strength and insight denied those whose lives are untroubled and therefore unexamined. Every vice "narrows" the soul, every virtue "expands" it.[25] Adversity "widens" the soul,[26] helping it grow in spiritual subtlety and heavenly desire. "You have enlarged me in tribulation," David wrote in Psalms 4:2, and so it is that the consciences of holy men are enlarged when "pressed outwardly by adversities."[27] Slowly the Christian attains *longanimitas* and *magnanimitas*, a greatness of soul that possesses not only patience and compassion but also equanimity and stability. Reason and discretion govern his life, for reason is cus-

21. *HEv.* 2.36.9 (PL 76, 1272).

22. The interweaving of Judeo-Christian and Stoic attitudes on suffering is illustrated well by the case of Chrysostom; see Edward Nowak, *Le Chrétien devant la souffrance: étude sur la pensée de Jean Chrysostome*, Théologie Historique 19 (Paris, 1973). See also E. Borne, "Sens et non-sens de la souffrance," *Vie intellectuelle* 27 (1957): 5–16; idem, *Le problème du mal*, Initiation philosophique 33, 4th ed. (Paris, 1967); and A. Bremond, "Le moine et le Stoïcien, le Stoïcisme et la philosophie du désert," *RAM* 8 (1927): 26–40.

23. *Mor.* 26.14.24 (CCL 143B, 1282).

24. *HEv.* 1.15.4 (PL 76, 1133).

25. *Mor.* 29.16.30 (CCL 143B, 1454).

26. *Mor.* 29.17.31 (CCL 143B, 1454).

27. *Mor.* 29.17.31 (CCL 143B, 1454): "'In tribulatione dilasti me' [Ps 4:2]. . . . sanctorum conscientia, dilatatur, cum mundi huius aduersitatibus, exterius premitur. Nam cum a praesentis uitae securitate repellitur, intus ad se impingitur, ut ad speranda superna tendatur. Cumque euagari exterius non permittitur, quasi in sinum suum reuocata dilatatur."

todian of the spiritual realm, while the body's dominion is too easily pleasure and selfishness.

Paradoxically, the recovery of spirit and reason comes through "letting go," by sacrificing the will in obedience and accepting all trials and
suffering God sends. In this precept Gregory transforms the doctrine of
constancy familiar to Stoics and joins it to Christian sacrifice. Both doc-
trines seek the triumph of self-control over suffering, but Christianity demands not *apatheia*, but *passio*.[28] We conquer the devil with patience in
suffering, as Job has taught us. The devil's attacks are really opportunities
for victory,[29] if we can be like Job, whose "constancy stood unconquered,
his equanimity unbroken" against the many machinations of the Old Enemy.[30] The mastery of suffering is the key to self-control and to the quality
of one's relations with others. Reason and charity are brothers; selfishness is antisocial and irrational. Sometimes only the harsh experience of
adversity can recall man to reason, purifying him of selfishness and
awakening him to the needs of others. Spiritual reform demands that one
give of oneself, offer oneself as Christ did in sacrifice to God, for the sake
of one's neighbor. Only by this gift of self can the Christian be perfected
and his eternal happiness assured.

Yet because conversion demands self-sacrifice, the offering of oneself
to God and neighbor, man finds in himself a natural resistance to bearing
crosses and laboring along the rocky road of adversity. How sweet are
the attractions of pleasure in comparison to the galling trials he must face!
Loving his comfortable life, the carnal man is not easily extinguished. If
life is dramatically overturned in conversion, it always threatens to revert
to its original pose of self-indulgence, for unconscious desires are notoriously difficult to conquer. "On one side, the desire of the heavenly
country sets him burning; on the other, he bears carnal desires in himself
that somehow delight him, even against his will."[31] The morbid outlines
of selfishness and pleasure lurk beneath the contours of the new self,
often erupting to parade desires long suppressed. Reforming the human
personality calls upon all the resources of self-control and discipline man

---

28. M. Spanneut, "Le Stoïcisme dans l'histoire de la patience chrétienne," *MSR* 39
(1982): 101–5, distinguishes between Stoics who seek autarchy through the conquest of suffering, and biblical traditions that seek to "enlarge the soul" through suffering (conferring
longanimitas, or μακροθυμία), but in Gregory this distinction does not hold. Suffering is both
an opportunity of gaining self-mastery and of improving the soul.

29. *Mor.* 23.1.1 (CCL 143B, 1143–44).

30. Ibid.: "Sed contra tot antiqui hostis machinas stetit inuicta constantia, stetit aequanimitas infracta."

31. *Mor.* 24.11.26 (CCL 143B, 1205–6).

can muster, and even then the only security lies in God's mercy and in penitence, that fortunate insurance against man's predictable relapse. Inward penitence becomes a permanent disposition, inseparable from the discretion and rational self-control that rule man's life. Life is always imperfect, a long circling dance of valor and frailty. The only perfection comes in repentance of one's imperfection, and perseverance in the struggle for virtue, despite one's sins.

But man does not undertake this struggle on his own, without God's grace softening the soul.[32] God reaches man through various media, transmitting his "threats, beatings, and revelations." The "Emperor of heaven" sends letters to his creatures in the Holy Scriptures. For the "welfare of our lives," we should not fail to "read" and "meditate" upon them.[33] Through meditation on the Scriptures the Christian finds the measuring rod (*calamus mensurae*) of moral behavior, so he might discern "how much he advances in spiritual virtue, and how much he remains disjoined from the good works ordered; how much he rises to the doing of good, and how much he lies prostrate in depravity."[34] Scripture is also a "mirror" in which we can see an "inward face" and "recognize our beauty and ugliness."[35] For those who cannot read, art serves as the text, teaching the illiterate what should be worshipped, even inspiring them with the "ardor of compunction,"[36] that burning fire of repentance essential to reform.

Conversion comes not only through study, but especially through the Christian's tremulous sensitivity to the vicissitudes of life. The manifold and perplexing trials man suffers should call him to repentance. Yet all these communications from God would go unnoticed and misunderstood were it not for the preacher, whose role is central to Gregory's program of reform. At heart, Gregory is ever teacher and preacher, preoccupied with the direction of souls. Throughout his writings Gregory continually broaches the fundamental question, What must I do to be

32. This point is stressed by Dagens, noting the importance of predestination, *Saint Grégoire*, 247–51.

33. *Ep.* 5.46 (CCL 140, 339–40). See esp. Patrick Catry, "Lire l'écriture selon saint Grégoire le Grand," *CollCist* 34 (1972): 177–201, for the role of reading scripture and spiritual reform.

34. *HEz.* 2.1.14 (CCL 142, 219).

35. *Mor.* 2.1.1 (CCL 143, 59). See Benedetto Calati, "La 'Lectio Divina' nella tradizione monastica Benedettina," *Benedictina* 28 (1981): 407–38; such reading is part of a scale of spiritual advancement: *lectio, meditatio, oratio, contemplatio, evangelium*. Gregory is noteworthy for stressing the communal aspect of this reading and spiritual growth (Calati, 411ff.).

36. *Ep.* 11.10 (CCL 140A, 874f.).

saved? Exegesis is a powerful tool for teaching sinners. As Gregory explains the adventures of prophets and saints, he exposes the sins of his audience, stirring up their tears of repentance and exhorting them to reform their wicked ways. Thus the theme of preaching arises frequently as a counterpoint to other topics. The later books of the *Moralia*, Gregory's treatment of such figures as Ezechiel, Paul, Samuel, and others, and even the whole of *Pastoral Rule* may be considered Gregory's meditations on his own identity and his relationship with others. If drawn to the serene isolation of contemplation, a deeper need returned Gregory to his friends and disciples to share the secrets of contemplation and ponder the meaning of virtue and sin. Like "a raven thinking of nourishment for his chicks," the teacher flies heavenward in contemplation and "brings back in his mouth the food they are gaping for."[37]

The tie of unselfish love between teacher and disciple is a microcosm of the disinterested charity binding the whole Church as a new family. If the teacher cherishes his spiritual children, they in turn help stabilize their father. In Constantinople, Gregory was tossed by the disturbing "waves" of secular affairs, but the company of his monks provided a "cable to anchor [him] to the shore of prayer."[38] Gregory extends this fundamentally monastic tie of *abba* and disciple to the larger audience of the whole Church, to preacher and sinners. As the whole Church is a new family generated by the spirit, the preacher is a parent of souls. "With great pains and struggles" preachers "give birth to souls in faith and conversation."[39] "Fathers from the vigor of discipline," these true teachers are also "mothers through the bowels of their mercy [who] endure the labors of holy conception and bear their children in the womb of love to be delivered to God."[40] Through them new members of the Church come to life: "the Church's children [are] born through the mouth of the preacher."[41] Correspondingly, bad preaching is like misspent seed, a repellent infertility and pollution.[42]

As often happens with parents and children, bound so closely by ties of love and dependency, a certain merging of identities takes place so that preacher and disciple form a corporate personality. The subject the

37. *Mor*. 30.9.34 (CCL 143B, 1514).

38. *Ad Leand*. 1 (CCL 143, 2).

39. *Mor*. 30.10.42 (CCL 143B, 1520).

40. *Mor*. 30.10.43 (CCL 143B, 1521): "illi ueri doctores sunt, qui cum per uigorem disciplinae patres sunt, per pietatis uiscera esse matres nouerunt. Qui labores conceptionis tolerant, et proferendos Deo filios intra uterum caritatis portant."

41. Cf. *Mor*. 35.20.48 (CCL 143B, 1808–10).

42. *Mor*. 23.15.28 (CCL 143B, 1164–65).

preacher strives to set right is very much a part of him, and he feels his own authority as a form of love for his dependent.[43] Gregory explains Job 39:24 ("he swallowed the earth") by telling us that Paul by exhortation "convert[ed] sinners into his own body."[44] Through the sinner's conversion the bond between preacher and disciple becomes so intimate and indissoluble that they seem to be an organic unity. Similarly, "holy teachers who instruct others in virtue, devour their enemies, when they change them into their own bodies by the power of conversion."[45] The hierarchical and corporate structure of the Church places the preacher implicitly as temporal head of the body of Christians. While the *Dialogues* may recall the intimate world of holy man and disciple described by the Desert Fathers, Gregory's society is in fact more formal and hierarchical. Preachers become the moral and institutional leaders as well as the emotional center of the visible Church.

Preachers are set apart from all others. Certainly some Christians lead holy lives, but very few have this special "gift of preaching."[46] In Gregory's church, the preacher was to carry the Word of God to the many who had neither the education nor the means to study Scripture. His duty was to "enlighten the darkness of others by preaching," and so he deserved the full support and protection of the secular powers.[47] Among monks and other clergy, the preacher was set apart by his office to be a healer of souls. He is the ruler and his flock are his subjects, as we see in *Pastoral Rule*. His words should be received with joy, although some reject

---

43. This is but another example of participation in the harmony of hierarchical order: the lower, more carnal element participates in the identity of the higher, more spiritual and rational element.

44. *Mor.* 31.32.68 (CCL 143B, 1597–98).

45. *Mor.* 34.11.22 (CCL 143B, 1747): "Sancti quippe doctores qui ad uirtutem et alios instruunt, hostes deuorant, dum eos intra corpus suum per uim conuersionis immutant."

46. *Mor.* 27.8.12 (CCL 143B, 1338). Gregory stresses their sacramental character, and sets them above the other orders of the Church in *In lib. I Reg.* 1.52 (CCL 144, 82); 4.209 (CCL 144, 411f.); 4.149–50 (CCL 144, 371–72); 4.205 (CCL 144, 409f.). They combine perfectly both active and contemplative lives, *HEz.* 1.3.9 (CCL 142, 37–38), as noted by C. Dagens, "Grégoire le Grand et le ministère de la parole: les notions d'*ordo praedicatorum* et d'*officium praedicationis*," in *Forma Futuri: Studi in honore del Cardinale Michele Pelligrino* (Turin, 1975), 1054–73. See idem, *Saint Grégoire*, 311–44, where the influence of Augustine and Origen is discussed. Since Rufin. *Gr. Naz. orat.* 2 influenced the *Reg. Past.*, he is also an important influence. On the preacher, see also Robert A. Markus, "Gregory the Great's *Rector* and His Genesis," in Jacques Fontaine et al., eds., *Grégoire le Grand* (Paris, 1986), 137–46; Sofia Boesch Gajano, "La *Sapienza*: Teoria e pratica pastorale nelle opera di Gregorio Magno," in Fontaine et al., eds., *Grégoire le Grand*, 181–89; Vera Paronetto, "Connotazione del 'Pastor' nell'opera di Gregorio Magno: teoria e prassi," *Benedictina* 31 (1984): 325–43; and Vincenzo Recchia, "Il 'Praedicator' nel pensiero e nell'azioni di Gregorio Magno," *Salesianum* 41 (1979): 333–74.

47. *HEz.* 1.7.21 (CCL 142, 96–97).

them through envy.[48] The prestige of the preacher is second to none. The preacher is at the end of a long line of teachers, prophets, and saints. Successor to the Apostles,[49] he continues the work of other holy men who also preached, if only in their exemplary behavior as God's elect, such as Abel, Isaiah, and John. Though the host of God's messengers is diverse, the spirit is the same.[50] Like the saint and the holy man, the preacher is primarily concerned with the salvation of others.

That the preacher's role in the conversion of sinners can hardly be overestimated is a measure of Gregory's pessimism about the motivation and understanding of his audience. The soul, he tells us, "reflects that she understands nothing except through the words of the preacher" (cf. Song 1:15). This understanding must precede the greater "touch of internal grace," which is the "kiss of his mouth" (cf. Song 1:1).[51] Of course the bishop's power of remitting sins means that sinners must turn to him for entrance to heaven;[52] but more than this, Gregory appreciates and stresses the intimate involvement of the preacher in the soul's conversion. Preachers are God's messengers (cf. Mal 3:1), and God "walks in them" (cf. Lv 26:12), "pouring himself into the minds of men through their preaching." Because God reaches the sinner's soul through the torrent of the preachers' words, no man can afford to ignore them unless he is confident of "the grace of compunction" and the "fountain [of his own] wisdom."[53] Preachers not only deliver God's words, they also carry his grace. They are "tents" because his grace is concealed in their hearts (Lam 2:6).[54] The preacher "does business" for God (cf. Lk 19:13). His life is a sacrifice to God; he renders all the "gains" of his work to God.[55]

The human element in preaching is always subordinate to the divine, for it is God's presence that makes the preacher powerful and effective. Preachers must recognize this and be humble, even while they exercise great power over others. To "outward preaching" God must add "inner inspiration."[56] If the Holy Spirit does not fill their hearts, the voices of teachers fall in vain on the "ears of the body" only,[57] and all their exhor-

---

48. Cf. *Mor.* 29.32.76 (CCL 143B, 1488–89).
49. Cf. *Mor.* 27.8.13–14 (CCL 143B, 1339). See Judith McClure, "Gregory the Great: Exegesis and Audience" (D. Phil. diss., Oxford, 1978), 47f.
50. *Mor.* 29.31.68–69 (CCL 143B, 1481–82).
51. *Cant.* 1.15 (CCL 144, 17).
52. *Mor.* 27.12.22 (CCL 143B, 1346–47).
53. *Ep.* 7.27 (CCL 140, 484).
54. *Mor.* 27.11.19 (CCL 143B, 1344–45).
55. *Ep.* 2.40 (CCL 140, 128).
56. *Mor.* 29.26.51 (CCL 143B, 1469).
57. *Mor.* 27.38.64 (CCL 143B, 1381–82).

tations will not change their listeners' ways. The preacher can "deliver words to the ears, but he cannot open hearts."[58] But since the lives of preachers and subjects are so interwoven, the eloquence or ineptitude of the preacher can be God's way of chastening or comforting both preacher and listener. For this reason, both should be humble.[59]

Nevertheless, the preacher's effectiveness is dependent on his power and authority over others, for his subjects must trust him and be receptive and vulnerable. Gregory portrays this power and authority in images of the preacher giving birth to Christians and devouring sinners. The preacher can both create and destroy, and subjects are dependent upon his help for their welfare. The conversion of sinners is very much a healing art, like medicine or modern psychotherapy; conversion heals the soul through self-examination and the power of words.[60] "What is a sinner except the wounded? And what is the preacher except the physician?"[61] As in bodily cures, so in spiritual healing the power of suggestion and a therapeutic alliance can work in the patient's favor. Just as the patient's confidence in the doctor makes the cure more effective, so the physician of the soul is aided in his healing when he has his patient's trust and respect. In Gregory's mind, the sinner's reverence for his preacher could only expedite the cure; his cooperation and docility are great advantages. The "arrow of divine fear" easily penetrates the bowels of the elect, but it finds the proud hard and resistant.[62] The sinner's heart should be vulnerable and soft, so that fear can "pierce" (*transfigere*) it like an arrow, causing the "blood of confession" to "pour from the wound."[63] The preacher wields "the sword of God's word" in his rebuke,[64] and his words are "thorns" piercing the listener's heart with fear of judgment

---

58. *Mor.* 29.23.47 (CCL 143B, 1465–66); *Mor.* 29.24.49 (CCL 143B, 1467).

59. *Mor.* 30.27.81–82 (CCL 143B, 1546–47).

60. At best, this comparison is crude. I am not suggesting that psychotherapy is a substitute for religion, as the ultimate goal of religion, union with the divine, is far removed from the intentions of psychotherapy. Nevertheless, insofar as each aims to change the behavior of individuals through self-consideration, understanding, and effort, there are enlightening similarities. Christian reform should also be compared with Stoic practices outlined by Hadot, *Exercices spirituels*, esp. 57–59.

61. *HEz.* 1.10.17 (CCL 142, 152): "Quid est autem peccator, nisi uulneratus? et quid praedicator, nisi medicus." Cf. Rufin. *Gr. Naz. orat.* 2.16ff. See Adolf Harnack, *Medizinisches aus der ältesten Kirchengeschichte* (Leipzig, 1892), 4:138ff. for the tradition of bishop as surgeon. See also Einar Molland, "*Ut sapiens medicus*: Medical Vocabulary in St. Benedict's *Regula Monachorum*" StudMon 6 (1964): 273–96, discussing how the abbot is to act as a wise physician. Molland cites a work unavailable to me that supplements Harnack: H. J. Frings, *Medizin und Arzt bei den griechischen Kirchenvätern bis Chrysostomos* (Bonn, 1959).

62. *Mor.* 10.14.25 (CCL 143, 555).

63. *Mor.* 7.5.5 (CCL 143, 337).

64. *HEz.* 1.11.5 (CCL 142, 171).

and desire for heaven.[65] Pricked with compunction, tears flow from the sinner's eyes, "as though the blood of the soul ran out in tears."

The match of preacher and subject is crucial. The preacher must use discretion in considering the needs of his subjects that he might approach them in the most effective way: this is the subject of Gregory's *Pastoral Rule* and also part of the tradition of ancient rhetoric as adapted by Christian writers.[66] The preacher considers the needs of his audience and adapts his words accordingly, pondering "what he should say, to whom he says it, when he should speak, in what manner and how long he should speak."[67] The preacher restores his subject to health with words that somehow have the power to evoke changes in the psyche of his listener.[68] Filled with divine inspiration, the preacher's words are powerful indeed, at times numinous and magical. With just a few words he can exorcise demons; his exhortation compares with spells, the "speech of charmers" (*incantantium sermo*).[69] His "bodily words" can carry such grace that they "water the invisible places of the heart, so that it performs the highest commands."[70]

The preacher directs his subject on an inward journey of self-discovery, to find and explore the hidden recesses of the heart. Through education and training, the subject learns to gain control of his life and change his attitudes and behavior, so that he can "perform the highest commands." But since knowledge comes especially through the Christian's own experience, the preacher's duty is to help him understand this process of reform through adversity. Mediating between God and the sinner, the preacher teaches the sinner, helping him interpret the meaning of his trials so that he might be disciplined and improved by them. Every incident seems to tell the sinner more about himself, his unsuspected weaknesses and surprising strengths. Reform comes in slow

65. *HEv.* 1.20.13 (PL 76, 1166).

66. Cf. Rufin. *Gr. Naz. orat.* 2.31ff.; Aug. *doctr. christ.* esp. 3.12.18ff. and 4 (entire).

67. Cf. *HEz.* 1.11.12ff. (CCL 142, 174ff.): "Pensare etenim doctor debet quid loquatur, cui loquatur, quando loquatur, qualiter loquatur, et quantum loquatur." See also *HEz.* 1.11.28 (CCL 142, 183–84), *HEz.* 1.11.16 (CCL 142, 176).

68. See Pedro Laín Entralgo, *The Therapy of the Word in Classical Antiquity*, ed. and trans. by L. J. Rather and John M. Sharp (New Haven and London, 1970), 122ff., and 245ff. According to Laín Entralgo, the ancient Greeks believed one could cure people of evil as if it were a sickness by administering the right words. The disordered mind produces illness; right order could be restored with words producing catharsis and change. See also Paul Rabbow, *Seelenführung: Methodik der Exerzitien in der Antike* (Munich, 1954), 16f., for the Stoic influence on the direction of souls; see 55ff. for rhetorical devices used.

69. *Mor.* 34.10.21 (CCL 143B, 1746–47), where such exhortations do not work for the reprobate.

70. *Mor.* 29.23.48 (CCL 143B, 1466–67).

stages of gestation and growth, as knowledge, discipline, and inner control strengthen to fulfill divine commands:

> But since we conceive divine precepts in our hearts, we do not give birth to them immediately, as if they are already solidly formed by thought. . . . For first the seeds of divine fear received in the womb of the heart are strengthened by meditation so that they might remain. After that, they are fixed with strict concentration of thought, then they grow to reason and discretion, as if formed into distinct limbs. Next, confirmed by the habit of perseverance, they reach the solidity of bones, so to speak. But at last, strengthened by perfect authority, they proceed to be born. . . .[71]

Little by little the Christian grows stronger through reason, discretion, and meditation until finally he is firm and stable.

Since reform is very much a rational process, involving education, judgment, and self-control, conversion begins with enlightenment of the mind. The Christian must first understand the truth before he can recognize how far he has departed from it, a rational judgment that will in turn spur a desire for change. The preacher is especially useful in educating the sinner; he diffuses "the virtues of saints" to "resound in the conversion of a multitude of people."[72] Discussing the preaching of Peter, Paul, and John, Gregory explains that preachers draw their listeners to "interior understanding,"[73] a comprehension of the "inner" spiritual goals of Christianity, which stand in contrast to the external pursuits of the secular world.[74] The preacher teaches by word and by his own example, for the hearts of teachers contain "divine riches [that they] make known outwardly in words and deeds."[75]

To learn is to internalize the knowledge of interior truths, to become "impregnated" with them and "incorporate" them so that these truths become a very part of the subject. The seeds of knowledge are therefore sown by "divine fear" in the womb of the heart, where they might take root in one's inmost being. To prepare the sinner's heart for sowing, the preacher becomes the ox turning the "field" with the "plowshare of his tongue."[76] He then can sow the seeds of understanding and supply the

---

71. *Mor.* 30.10.40 (CCL 143B, 1519).

72. *HEz.* 1.8.1 (CCL 142, 101), an exegesis of Ezechiel 1:24 ("Et audiebam sonum alarum, quasi sonum aquarum multarum") where wings are the virtues of saints, and the waters are the people.

73. Cf. *HEz.* 2.8.14 (CCL 142, 346).

74. Dagens rightly describes the road of salvation as a return to the interior, *Saint Grégoire*, 173–76.

75. *HEz.* 2.8.14 (CCL 142, 346).

76. *Ep.* 8.29 (CCL 140A, 551); *Ep.* 13.43 (CCL 140A, 1048). Cf. Prv 14:4. For other ex-

nourishment for their growth, for his preachings are "drops of rain" to "water souls" and make them grow and eventually "bear fruit" in good works.[77] Following Augustine, Gregory views preaching as food for listeners: preaching nourishes minds hungry for spiritual truth and provides the substance necessary for spiritual growth.[78]

The food of the Holy Scriptures must be digested and absorbed fully in the "belly" of the memory.[79] Since Gregory's is still an oral and rhetorical culture, the emphasis on memory is crucial. Memories of the Psalter, of key passages of the Bible, and the gnomic sayings of the Desert Fathers were to form a living core of knowledge to define and discipline one's life. The Scripture and other holy works must be implanted in the Christian's very marrow, lest he lose his way, for the "evil spirit can steal the word from memory."[80] Only when knowledge and understanding become fixed in the very core of one's being can one begin to change. The truth becomes an internal reservoir affording constant refreshment in meditation and contemplation.

Yet merely to know the standard of truth is useless unless the Christian applies it in his own life. Because most souls resist examining the secrets of their inner lives, the preacher works hard to uncover his subject's sins and bring him to repentance. His office allows him to "persuade, exhort, alarm and preach"[81] that he might awaken the sinner to his own depravity and weakness. Sometimes it is necessary to "open the ear in tribulation" (Jb 36:15), that is, "with scourges and beatings . . . to open the hearing of the heart . . . [which] the prosperity of the world often closes."[82] Even more so than Augustine, Gregory understands how

---

amples of such imagery, see *HEz.* 1.3.4 (CCL 142, 34f.); *Mor.* 7.12.14 (CCL 143, 343–44); *HEz.* 1.2.3 (CCL 142, 18); *Mor.* 16.45.58 (CCL 143A, 832–33); *Mor.* 2.46.72 (CCL 143, 101–2); *Reg. Past.* 1.7 (PL 77, 20). In *Reg. Past.* 2.5 (PL 77, 33), Gregory quotes 1 Corinthians 9:9 and 1 Timothy 5:18, both taken from Deuteronomy 25:4 ("Do not muzzle the mouth of the ox who threshes the grain"), which suggests that the parable of the wheat, the tares, and the threshing floor is associated also with this exegesis.

77. *Ep.* 13.43 (CCL 140A, 1048); cf. *Mor.* 29.23.47ff. (CCL 143B, 1466ff.); *Mor.* 27.8.12ff. (CCL 143B, 1338ff.).

78. Food: *Mor.* 27.12.22 (CCL 143B, 1346–47); also *HEz.* 1.10.6 (CCL 142, 146); milk: *Mor.* 30.13.48 (CCL 143B, 1523–24). See Catry, "Lire l'écriture," 193, who notes also "drinking" the Scriptures imbuing one with a "holy drunkenness." Cf. Cassian *conl.* 12.13; *inst.* praef. 4–5.

79. *HEv.* 1.15.2 (PL 76, 1132); *HEz.* 1.10.2–7 (CCL 142, 145–48).

80. *HEv.* 1.15.2 (PL 76, 1132). Cf. Rufin. *Clement* 26.1. This emphasis on memory (μνήμη) as the foundation of moral change, of changing one's inner disposition or character (διάθεσις), is strong in Basil; see John Eudes Bamburger, "ΜΝΗΜΗ-ΔΙΑΘΕΣΙΣ: The Psychic Dynamisms in the Ascetical Theology of St. Basil," *OCP* 34 (1968): 233–51.

81. *Ep.* 12.1 (CCL 140A, 968).

82. *Mor.* 26.35.64 (CCL 143B, 1315): "Aurem in tribulatione reuelare est auditum cor-

stubborn and resistant the sinner can be, and a certain pessimism about the stubbornness of the human condition influences his emphasis on adversity. Without God's visitation of adversity, sinners too often lack the motivation to change. Feeling comfortable and secure, they become lazy and neglect their moral health. Most learn only through bitter experience, and only in stinging pain do they embrace discipline. The scourge serves to awaken the sinner from the "sleep of sloth" and bring him to a knowledge of himself and his desperate situation.[83] As such, adversity is a desirable trial.

Like Gregory, Venantius of Syracuse suffered from ill health. Gregory admonishes him to be thankful for suffering, explaining how adversity can educate the soul and lead it to conversion:

> [P]resent pain, if it converts the mind of the afflicted, is the end of guilt up to this time. But if it fails to convert the soul to fear of God, it is the beginning of future pain. We must take care, and with the greatest effort of our tears be vigilant for the complete conversion of our minds, lest we pass from torment to torments. We should consider how great the Creator's dispensation of mercy is toward us, which repeatedly strikes us who deserve to die, but does not yet kill us. For God threatens what he will do, and yet he does not do it, so that the pains sent in advance may terrify us, and when we have been converted to fear of the strict Judge, they may hide us from his punishment at the end of life.[84]

Christians should therefore view their present sufferings as punishments for sins whereby they can expiate the guilt of their present lives. Present afflictions are indeed a foretaste of hell, but if sinners are converted to fear of God, they will be spared further punishment and suffering after death.

To the damned, however, with their stony hearts, present suffering is not educative, but only the beginning of worse torments. Some "never even suffer a headache," Gregory observes, "and they are suddenly

---

dis uerberum plagis aperire. Cum enim praecepta despicimus, pia districtione nobiscum agitur, ut flagella timeamus. Aurem itaque cordis tribulatio aperit, quam saepe huius mundi prosperitas claudit."

83. *Mor.* 27.17.33 (CCL 143B, 1355–56).

84. *Ep.* 11.18 (CCL 140A, 887): "poena praesens, si afflicti animum conuertit, finis est culpae praecedentis, si autem ad timorem Domini minime conuertit, initium poenae sequentis. Curandum ergo nobis est et summopere in fletibus tota mentis conuersione uigilandum, ne de tormento ad tormenta transeamus. Considerandum quoque est quanta erga nos dispensatione pietatis agit conditor noster, quod morte dignos assidue percutit et tamen adhuc minime occidit. Minatur enim quod facturus est, nec tamen facit, ut dolores nos percurrentes terreant et conuersos ad timorem districti iudicis ab eius nos animaduersione in termino abscondant." For Seneca, suffering gout teaches endurance of hardships, *epist.* 67.4.

stricken and dragged off to the fires of hell." Scourges thus indicate to the sinner that he is not "forsaken," and he should be "disciplined" by them.[85] Sometimes God "kills to vivify and wounds to heal [cf. Dt 32:39] since for this purpose he inflicts outward beatings so that he may heal the inward wounds of sin."[86] Recognizing that Divine Providence sends misfortune and suffering to convert the soul, Christians should welcome adversity as a salutary correction administered by God in order to turn them toward salvation.

The preacher's words are meant to replicate the visitation of adversity they describe. Like adversity, his words are sharp instruments that inspire the soul with fear. Darts (*iacula*),[87] arrows (*sagittae*),[88] thorns (*spinae*),[89] nails (*clavi*),[90] swords (*gladii*),[91] and knives (*ferrum*)[92] penetrate the soul and pierce it with fear of judgment. God's adversity is above all the whip or scourge (*flagellum*);[93] it is also the knife of tribulation (*ferrum tribulationis*) that lances the wound of sin or excises its poison.[94] Like the plowshare of the preacher's tongue (*vomer linguae*), these cutting instruments serve to sunder the hardness of the sinner's heart.[95] Though stern, the preacher's rebuke is neither destructive nor punitive. Whereas the devil can execute God's judgment with the hammer (*malleus*), the battle-axe (*securis*), and iron weapons (*ferramenta*),[96] the preacher's rebuke is always to be balanced with healing and positive inspiration for change. If

---

85. Ibid.

86. *Mor.* 6.25.42 (CCL 143, 315): "Occidit enim ut uiuificet, percutit ut sanet; quia idcirco foras uerbera admouet ut intus uulnera delictorum curet."

87. God: *Mor.* 15.24.29 (CCL 143A, 766); the preacher: *Mor.* 27.2.4 (CCL 143B, 1333).

88. God: *Mor.* 10.14.25 (CCL 143, 555); the preacher: *Mor.* 34.10.21 (CCL 143B, 1746–47); *Mor.* 29.23.47 (CCL 143B, 1465–66); *Mor.* 31.31.65 (CCL 143B, 1596–97); *Mor.* 33.29.51 (CCL 143B, 1718).

89. *HEv.* 1.20.13 (PL 76, 1166).

90. God: *Mor.* 25.7.18 (CCL 143B, 1242–43); the preacher: *Mor.* 24.16.41 (CCL 143B, 1218–19).

91. God: *Mor.* 15.24.29 (CCL 143A, 766); the preacher: *Mor.* 33.29.51 (CCL 143B, 1718); *Mor.* 34.8.17 (CCL 143B, 1744–45).

92. God: *Mor.* 26.19.34 (CCL 143B, 1291–92); *Mor.* 7.18.21 (CCL 143, 347–48); *Mor.* 10.7.11 (CCL 143, 544); the preacher: *Mor.* 24.16.41 (CCL 143B, 1218–19).

93. An image reserved for God's chastisement, and apparently not applied to the preacher. For *flagella dei* see Gillet, "Grégoire le Grand," *DS* 6:889, who notes that *aduersa, aduersitas, flagella, tentatio, tribulatio,* and *uerbera* appear around six hundred times in the *Moralia*, and one hundred times in remaining works. See also Patrick Catry, "Epreuves du juste et mystère de Dieu: Le commentaire littéral du *Livre de Job* par saint Grégoire le Grand," *REAug* 18 (1972): 125ff.

94. *Mor.* 26.19.34 (CCL 143B, 1291–92); *Mor.* 7.18.21 (CCL 143, 347–48); *Mor.* 10.7.11 (CCL 143, 544).

95. *Ep.* 8.29 (CCL 140A, 551); *Ep.* 13.43 (CCL 140A, 1048). Cf. Prv 14:4.

96. *Mor.* 34.12.23 (CCL 143B, 1748–49).

his words are "thorns," he also carries "myrtle" and "olive oil" to soothe
and comfort his afflicted neighbor.[97] His tongue heals sinner's wounds,
even as the dogs licked Lazarus's sores.[98] When he contemplates heavenly mysteries, the preacher's words may thunder like fearsome "lightning" flashing down from the heavens, but his lightning inspires others,
setting them aflame with love of the heavenly fatherland.[99]

The preacher's rebuke must awaken the stubborn sinner to the severity of God's reprimand, to the catastrophic force of God's omnipotence. If the sinner seeking autonomy attempts to rebel against God, God
unleashes arrows, darts, and swords of rebuke to wreak war upon the
sinner, to defeat his proud and misguided effort to stand on his own.
God's vengeance destroys the weaponry of man's rebellion in sin (*repug-
natio, defensio, bellum contra Dominum*).[100] He "burns the shields with fire,"
"breaks man's bow," and "shatters his arms" in confounding him and destroying the prideful "human defense" (*humana patrocinia*) set up against
him.[101] This terrifying visitation brings havoc and confusion, as if heaven
and hell have been shut up together (cf. Jb 11:10).[102] God's visitation is a
trial by fire, as gold is tried in the furnace (Wis 3:6).[103]

Gregory understands the sinner's instinctive reticence, his desire to
avoid self-analysis and to pretend nothing is amiss. Since sin causes a
loss of self-knowledge, a blinding of the "eye of reason," the erring soul
often cannot discern its own evil.[104] Unless the sinner is forced to acknowledge his own frailties, he is very likely to persist in his muddled
self-delusion. Whether through adversity or the preacher's reproof, rebuke uncovers man's sins and exposes his pitiful weakness. Piercing the
hidden corners of the sinner's soul, adversity exposes precisely those
evils man hopes to hide. Like a candle searching the inward parts of the
belly (Prv 20:27), God's visitation discloses the mysterious depths of the
mind hidden from man's sight.[105] This trial reveals the true man, much to
his confusion and shame.[106] The scourge of adversity cuts through the

---

97. *HEv*. 1.20.13 (PL 76, 1166–67).
98. *HEv*. 2.40.2 (PL 76, 1302–3).
99. *HEz*. 1.5.13 (CCL 142, 64).
100. *Mor*. 33.28.49 (CCL 143B, 1716).
101. *Mor*. 33.28.49 (CCL 143B, 1716–17).
102. *Mor*. 10.10.16ff. (CCL 143, 549ff.).
103. Cf. *Mor*. 23.26.52 (CCL 143B, 1186).
104. *Mor*. 20.14.37 (CCL 143A, 1029).
105. *Mor*. 8.30.49 (CCL 143, 420–21).
106. Typical passages of this frequent theme are: *Mor*. 23.26.52 (CCL 143B, 1186); *Mor*.
23.24–25.48–51 (CCL 143B, 1180–85); *Mor*. 23.1.1 (CCL 143B, 1143–44); *Mor*. 5.16.33 (CCL
143, 240–41); *Mor*. 2.38.63 (CCL 143, 98–99); *Mor*. 9.53.80 (CCL 143, 511–12). Cf. Cassian
conl. 2.4.

flesh to reveal the soft layers of man's weakness along with the bones of his strength.[107]

The preacher who carries God's rebuke in his words is also thorough and formidable. His intimacy with his subjects makes it easy for him to probe their secret weaknesses. The preacher is like Ezechiel digging into a wall and finding a door through which he discovers wicked abominations (cf. Ez 8:8–10). He "lays the heart bare with sharp reproofs" and so "opens" the sinner's hardness of heart so that "secret thoughts" are revealed.[108] Rebuke should destroy man's resistance, humbling the sinner so that he confesses God's power and his own nothingness. Now stripped naked by adversity, the sinner seems to dissolve in fear of judgment, and the last traces of his selfish independence can be destroyed. Even as trial and suffering shake the sinner, the preacher dramatizes the horrors of the reprobate's future. God's justice can be astoundingly severe. Every "step" is "counted," every "trace" is "minutely examined."[109] Nothing is forgotten: God binds all man's sins in a little sack (cf. Jb 14:17) and will hold them hidden until Judgment Day, when he will reveal them publicly, to man's utter shame.[110] The sinner recognizes that God has the power to destroy him utterly, and he begins to fear for the ultimate safety of his soul. Even the perfect man is destroyed by God (cf. Jb 9:22), for whatever purity and righteousness man has is devoured by divine purity.[111] The sinner's proud defenses fail, his heart melts before God's scrutinizing eye, as the clouds are consumed by the sun (cf. Jb 7:9).[112]

Rebuke penetrates the barriers of the sinner's ego, shattering the independence and self-absorption that separate him from God and his fellow man. The mind of man is like a sea God enters.[113] He tramples the waves of sin rising against him,[114] and stirs the dark and murky depths of his mind to the lamentations of penitence. The battle against God ends at last with man's compunction.[115] The sinner's "security" and "self-love" are obliterated, as God crushes the cold, hard shell of selfishness and

107. *Mor.* 23.25.51–52 (CCL 143B, 1184–86).

108. *Mor.* 26.6.7 (CCL 143B, 1271).

109. *Mor.* 21.5.10 (CCL 143A, 1071–72). See Irénée Hausherr, *Penthos*, trans. Anselm Hufstader, Cistercian Studies 53 (Kalamazoo, Mich., 1982), 28ff. The idea of counting every step or trace (*gressus* or *vestigium*) is found in the notion of compunction among the Desert Fathers. Traces (τόποι) were believed to be left in the soul because of sins, and penitence was to wash away and heal these.

110. *Mor.* 12.17.21 (CCL 143A, 641–42).

111. *Mor.* 9.26.40 (CCL 143, 484).

112. *Mor.* 8.17.33 (CCL 143, 405).

113. *Mor.* 29.15.27 (CCL 143B, 1452).

114. Ibid.

115. *Mor.* 33.28.49 (CCL 143B, 1716–17).

complacency. The sinner's pleasure in self-indulgence turns to bitterness, and self-contempt replaces pride.[116] With Job, the sinner trudges to the dunghill of humility and confesses he is but dust and ashes, a mere creature dependent upon God.[117] The pride he took in his accomplishments turns to anxiety as he gazes only upon his sins and trembles at the thought of judgment.[118] Now the soul is cleansed and ready to begin anew.

Yet conversion is a laborious course of uncertain outcome. Once awakened by the preacher and shaken by God's adversity, the sinner must turn to the internal process of reform. Now warmed and thawed from indifference, the sinner comes to know himself and must transform his fear of judgment into an uncompromising zeal for change.

116. *Mor*. 3.33.60 (CCL 143, 152–53); see also *Mor*. 3.7.10–11 (CCL 143, 119–21); *Mor*. 35.6.7 (CCL 143B, 1777–78).
117. *Mor*. 3.33.60 (CCL 143, 152–53). See also previous note, CCL 143B, 1777–78.
118. Ibid.

· XI ·

THE JUST PENITENT

Adversity shakes the sinner to his senses. "The dart of terror pierces and recalls us to our sense of righteousness," Gregory remarks.[1] In Gregory's program of reform, fear serves as the first stage and the very foundation of change, for often only fear of God's judgment repels the Christian from worldly involvement, teaching him "what he should avoid in the world," and "severing him from pleasures of the flesh."[2] Reason returns,[3] and fear gives man seriousness and discipline so that he might restrain his dissolute thoughts.[4] "In fear of the Lord there is strong confidence" because when shaken by tribulation, the Christian learns to rise above the vicissitudes of the world and he becomes stable (*constituere*) in God.[5] Now distanced from the world, he "collects" the attention scattered on worldly delights and withdraws to the inner world of his conscience, the "citadel" and "courtroom" of his mind.[6]

When battered by misfortune, one withdraws instinctively and considers strategies to regain control of one's deranged life. By seeking the cause of one's troubles, by determining what really matters and practicing new behavior, one can minimize exposure to suffering and redirect the course of one's life. Such planning and husbandry of self is very much in the Stoic tradition,[7] and for Gregory such mastery depends on discre-

1. *Mor.* 6.25.42 (CCL 143, 315).
2. *Mor.* 23.25.51 (CCL 143B, 1184–85); *Mor.* 7.27.33 (CCL 143, 356).
3. *Mor.* 2.46.73 (CCL 143,102).
4. Cf. *Mor.* 6.37.58 (CCL 143, 328).
5. *Mor.* 5.16.33 (CCL 143, 241).
6. For self-collection see *Mor.* 31.12.19–20 (CCL 143B, 1564–65); *Dial.* 2.3.5–9 (SC 260, 142–46); *HEz.* 2.5.9 (CCL 142, 281–82); *HEz.* 1.8.13–14 (CCL 142, 108); *Mor.* 22.17.42 (CCL 143A, 1121–22); *Mor.* 15.46.52 (CCL 143A, 780–81); *HEz.*1.11.6 (CCL 142, 171–72); Claude Dagens, *Saint Grégoire le Grand* (Paris, 1977), 211ff.
7. Cf. Pierre Hadot, *Exercices spirituels et philosophie antique* (Paris, 1981), 71–74.

tion, the masterful exercise of reason that both discerns truth and moderates behavior according to the rule.[8] Adversity sharpens discretion,[9] for fear generates the anxious scrutiny and vigilant prudence that must order thought and deed. Adversity gives man strength, patience, and self-possession, Gregory tells his audience, commenting on Job's perfection through God's scourging. Adversity restores self-control:

> Hence the Truth says in the Gospel, "In patience you will possess your souls" [Lk 21:19]. For what is it to possess one's soul, except to live perfectly in everything, and to rule all movements of the mind from the citadel of virtue. Therefore, he who has patience possesses his soul, since from the strength with which he conquered all adversities, he has conquered himself and is made master of himself.[10]

By conquering the trials of adversity man gains knowledge of himself, and with that knowledge comes control of his moral identity.

Gregory sees conversion as a two-stage process of reform that requires a dual sacrifice to God. The sinner begins to be reconciled with God when he first "burns" and "kills" his carnal identity in fear of judgment. Only when purified may he progress to the second stage, in which he is reunited with God, and a new self emerges from the ashes of the old. Cleansed and renewed, the Christian pledges his future life as an offering of loving obedience. For Gregory, reform focuses around compunction, the emotions first of fear and sorrow, and then of joy and love that inspire this two-part sacrifice.[11] As the soul progresses toward perfection, it moves from a lower, outward, carnal compunction of fear to a higher, inward, spiritual compunction of love.[12] These compunctions of fear and love are complementary opposites: each supplies what the other lacks, and they are bound in a complex dialectical relationship in which opposites are attracted and resolve in various compromise formations.[13]

8. See Introduction, n. 60.

9. *Mor.* 8.10.20 (CCL 143, 396–97); *Mor.* 2.46.73–77 (CCL 143, 101–2); 2.50.80 (CCL 143, 108).

10. *Mor.* 5.16.33 (CCL 143, 241): "Hinc in euangelio Veritas dicit: *In patientia uestra possidebitis animas uestras* [Lk 21:19]. Quid est enim animas possidere, nisi perfecte in omnibus uiuere, cunctis mentis motibus ex uirtutibus arce dominari? Qui igitur omnia fortis efficitur, unde sibi et semetipsum uincendo dominatur." Cf. Sen. *de prov.* 4.4.4–5.

11. For a definition of compunction, see Introduction, n. 72.

12. For these two compunctions, see *HEz.* 2.10.20 (CCL 142, 395); *HEz.* 2.9.3 (CCL 142, 358); *HEz.* 2.9.12 (CCL 142, 365–66); *HEz.* 2.10.13–14 (CCL 142, 388–89); *Mor.* 24.6.10 (CCL 143B, 1194–95); *Mor.* 32.3.4 (CCL 143B, 1629); *HEz.* 1.10.11 (CCL 142, 149); *In lib. I Reg.* 5.148 (CCL 144, 509); *Dial.* 3.34.1–6 (SC 260, 400–404); *Ep.* 7.23 (CCL 140, 475–76); *Cant.* 18 (CCL 144, 19–21).

13. Several compromise formations can be distinguished. At a primary level, fear and love are negative, carnal and positive, spiritual opposites, but they "switch charges" so that

To capture the first phase of reform, purgation through fear and repentance, Gregory uses legal and medical imagery. Through rigorous self-judgment and analysis, the soul can be set right with God and so healed of its sin. With his conscience awakened by external adversity, the sinner begins to ponder his situation. As God battles the sinner in his outward rebuke of adversity (or through the preacher's words of chastisement), his visitation is replicated internally in the inner courtroom of the mind. As sinners reel under God's mysterious wrath, they should "retire to the hidden recesses of their hearts" and consider the "eyelids" of God's judgment (Ps 10:5).[14] Examining their consciences,[15] they ponder their deeds; already feeling God's stinging rebuke, they imagine his secret judgment. What sins known and unknown can account for this wrath of God? What evil committed, what good omitted warrants his scourging? In the courtroom of the mind, the inner scales of the human heart serve as counterparts to the external scales (*lanx*) that God holds above man, dispensing his "scourges" as he deems fitting.[16] These "scales of scrutiny in the bosom of interior justice" subject man to trials that measure his merit.[17] While God holds his scales of cosmic justice, the sinner, in the bright light of the interior, weighs his own actions carefully on "scales of discretion,"[18] "scales of the heart,"[19] and "scales of scrutiny."[20] Knowing that the "board will look straight . . . [until] it is compared to the rule,"[21] the sinner measures his actions with meticulous discrimination, setting himself against the standards of righteousness found in the Scriptures and in the lives of saints.

---

fear becomes healthful and sweet, and love becomes painful and wounding. Temporally and hierarchically, fear precedes love, as lesser, lower, and outward progressing to greater, higher, and inward. But this opposition is resolved in a dialectical "alternation" in which each leads to the other: the heights of love depend upon the depths of one's fear; the quality of fearful discernment upon the intensity of one's loving contemplation. Finally, the opposites can be integrated so one never holds love without fear, or fear without love. Active and contemplative lives follow this same pattern.

14. *Mor.* 28.4.13 (CCL 143B, 1403–4).

15. See the explanation of compunction as self-examination in *Mor.* 23.21.41 (CCL 143B, 1175): "Quattuor quippe sunt qualitates quibus iusti uiri anima in compunctione uehementer afficitur, cum aut malorum suorum reminiscitur, considerans ubi fuit; aut iudiciorum Dei sententiam metuens et secum quaerens, cogitat ubi erit; aut cum mala uitae praesentis sollerter attendens, maerens considerat ubi est, aut cum bona supernae patriae contemplatur, quae quia necdum adipiscitur, lugens conspicit ubi non est."

16. Cf. *Mor.* 24.18.44 (CCL 143B, 1221–22).

17. *Mor.* 9.25.39 (CCL 143, 483–84).

18. *Mor.* 3.13.24 (CCL 143, 129–30).

19. *Mor.* 33.35.60 (CCL 143B, 1725–26); cf. Cassian *conl.* 1.20.

20. *Mor.* 9.25.39 (CCL 143, 483).

21. *Mor.* 5.37.67 (CCL 143, 267).

Within this courtroom of internal judgment are all the agents needed to arraign, try, and punish the self-accused sinner: a prosecutor to probe and discover hidden sins, a judge to convict the guilty and deliver his sentence, even an exactor of punishment. For "conscience accuses, reason judges, fear binds him over, and pain tortures him." And this judgment punishes the more certainly, "the more it rages inwardly," since it is not "inflicted by outward forces."[22] To be sure, not all suffering is the result of sin, and charity demands that one not condemn one's neighbor if he suffers, as Elihu taunted Job with mistaken zeal.[23] Yet in practice, the individual sinner cannot afford to be complacent with his own conscience. Knowing God's possible severity, he must scour every corner of his mind in search of sin. The presumption of sin lies with every man.

As both prosecutor and accused, the sinner is torn by opposing identities: the external body and its gratifications fight against the internal soul and its spiritual values. Part of man remains attached to the world, addicted to old passions and selfish desires, and this carnal voice struggles to resist righteousness and reform. While his better side, his spiritual voice, advances rational arguments and judgments of conscience, his sinful side yet fights to seduce reason and dominate his entire self. The conflict is at last resolved when the prosecutor convicts and punishes the accused: "He hates himself as he remembers himself to have been; and through the very one he presently is, he persecutes what he was in the past."[24]

The sinner's examination of conscience repeats the probing scrutiny of God's rebuke. Man's spirit is to be a candle examining his inmost parts for hidden sins.[25] If God and the preacher pierced and probed the sinner's faults, he must repeat this searing examination of conscience. His interior senses must be as teeth tearing the flesh (cf. Jb 13:14),[26] carefully chewing and breaking down every thought and deed, so that he digests the knowledge of his sinfulness fully. To scrutinize one's past deeds with dis-

---

22. *Mor.* 25.7.13 (CCL 143B, 1238): "Nam conscientia accusat, ratio iudicat, timor ligat, dolor excruciat. Quod iudicium eo certius punit, quo interius saeuit, quia uidelicet ab exterioribus non accedit. Vnusquisque enim cum causam huius examinis contra se aggredi coeperit, ipse est actor qui exhibet, ipse reus qui exhibetur. . . ." Aubin treats Christ as the *internus judex*, the judge within, but does not mention this correspondence between God's judgment in heaven which takes place external to man and man's interior judgment of himself; see "Intériorité et extériorité dans les *Moralia in Job* de saint Grégoire le Grand," *RSR* 62 (1974): 117–66.

23. *Mor.* 26.5–6.5–6 (CCL 143B, 1269–71).

24. *Mor.* 25.7.13 (CCL 143B, 1238): "odit se qualem fuisse se meminit, et ipse qui est, per semetipsum insequitur illum qui fuit. . . ."

25. Cf. *Mor.* 8.30.49 (CCL 143, 420–21).

26. *Mor.* 11.33.45 (CCL 143A, 610–12).

cretion is to "rend a mantle" as Job did (Jb 1:20).[27] The sinner tears apart and inspects each shred of sin. Like a horse striking the ground with his foot (cf. Jb 31:21), the sinner smites and scrutinizes the earth of his thoughts with forceful investigation.[28] As God commanded Ezechiel, "Dig through the wall" (Ez 8:8), so must man "pierce through the hardness of his heart with blows of self-examination."[29] He is also like Isaac digging a well in a strange land (cf. Gn 26:18):[30] digging and discarding the soil of his thoughts, he at last finds the water of true wisdom.

Self-examination brings the soul's hidden conflicts to the surface. Should the sinner instead seek to suppress his desires, he will only confound serious change, for reform is impossible if the Christian denies that a part of him is still attracted to earthly delights. Because reform is especially the healing of a sick, imbalanced soul, Gregory uses medical imagery to supplement the legal metaphors of the courtroom. When at last the sinner makes a true confession, the "wound" of sin bursts like a festering boil, exposing the "virus of sin" that has concealed its "poison" within the soul.[31] Just as the ancient physician would bring the illness to a crisis before healing his patient, or just as the modern psychotherapist will reveal unconscious conflicts in order to resolve them, so rebuke first evokes the sinner's resistance and defiance of God, exacerbating the pride and love of pleasure that emboldened him to sin. Bruised by adversity, the sinner resents the attack and impatiently protests the dislocation of his placid life. The contention of self-judgment is a furious conflict between impulses of sin and righteousness, habit and reason. A chain of unconscious custom controls man's destiny as surely as any deterministic fate. But reason frees man and heals his divided identity. Reason restores discipline and bridles the flesh. With self-possession regained, the Christian may anticipate spiritual progress, if God so wills.

This battle of identities is laborious and painful; its resolution, cathartic: "a certain struggle in the soul arises from man's opposition to himself, giving birth to peace with God."[32] Little by little the old identity of sin is sacrificed; having been destroyed by rational judgment, sins must then be punished with penitence. Punishment is the final and necessary step of the conversion, for without it, healing would be incomplete: "Punishment of sins is necessary medicine, so that being pierced

---

27. *Mor.* 2.51.81 (CCL 143, 108–9).

28. *Mor.* 31.27.53 (CCL 143B, 1587–88).

29. *Mor.* 31.27.53 (CCL 143B, 1588); also *Mor.* 31.27.54 (CCL 143B, 1589).

30. *Mor.* 31.27.53 (CCL 143B, 1587–88); cf. Rufin. *Orig. in gen.* 13.3–4.

31. *HEv.* 2.40.1 (PL 76, 1302).

32. *Mor.* 25.7.13 (CCL 143B, 1238): "atque ab ipso homine aduersus semetipsum fit quaedam rixa in animo, parturiens pacem cum Deo."

by conversion, the abscess of guilt may be cleansed with confession and healed with the medicine of affliction."[33] Penitence and confession are "remedies" for the "wound" of sin.[34] As a "remedy of unlikeness," the pain of repentance reverses the pleasure of sinning; as a "remedy of likeness," repentance and compunction "pierce [the soul] with pain," just as temptation and sin "wound" the soul with pleasure, like thorns or goads.[35] Like goads or darts, penitence lances the swollen wound of sin, releasing tears or blood.[36] Gregory may have believed, as others did, that tears of compunction release excessive humors, helping the soul regain balance and self-control.[37] Whatever the physiology, the tears and blood of compunction purify: the "blood of confession cleanses sin"; "tears wash the stains of sin."[38] Gregory also sees compunction as a cleansing fire, a "flame" consuming evil,[39] a "fire of tribulation" burning the rust of sin,[40] and a "burning sorrow" washing the mist of sin in the eye of the mind.[41] In removing sin, compunction also "hides" or "conceals" iniquities, shielding the sinner from God's judgment.[42] This hiding of sins is symbolized by the command in Deuteronomy 23:12–13 that the Israelites carry a stake to dig ditches to conceal their excrement in the desert sand.[43] So must the goad of compunction pierce the soil of the mind that the excrement of man's sins might be buried from God's sight.

Whether presented as cleansing, burning, or concealment, the purification of penitence brings an emotional release that is sublimely pleasurable. Like Augustine, Gregory finds a sweetness in tears. There is "joy in the grief" of compunction, and "sorrows" have a "sweet taste." Unlike

---

33. *In lib. I Reg.* 6.46 (CCL 144, 577–78): "Tria quippe in unoquoque consideranda sunt ueraciter paenitente, uidelicet conuersio mentis, confessio oris et uindicta peccati. . . . Tertia ergo species, id est uindicta, quasi medicina necessaria est; ut apostema reatus, quod conuersione conpungitur, confitendo purgetur, afflictionis medicina sanetur."

34. Penitence: *Mor.* 33.12.23 (CCL 143B, 1693–94); *Mor.* 3.22.43 (CCL 143, 142–43); *HEz.* 1.10.28 (CCL 142, 157); *Mor.* 23.21.40 (CCL 143B, 1174–75); confession: *Mor.* 8.21.37 (CCL 143, 408); cf. *Mor.* 7.4.5 (CCL 143, 337); *In lib. I Reg.* 6.46 (CCL 144, 577–78).

35. Thorn imagery: *Mor.* 20.10.21 (CCL 143A, 1019–20); *Mor.* 20.13.24 (CCL 143A, 1022); *Mor.* 28.1.8 (CCL 143B, 1399–1400); *Mor.* 34.2.3 (CCL 143B, 1734–35); goads: *Mor.* 26.45.82 (CCL 143B, 1327–28); *Mor.* 9.13.20 (CCL 143, 470); *Mor.* 9.34.53 (CCL 143, 494–95); *Mor.* 9.40.63 (CCL 143, 502–3); *Mor.* 33.4.10 (CCL 143B, 1678).

36. *Mor.* 31.27.54 (CCL 143B, 1589); *Mor.* 6.25.42 (CCL 143, 315); *Mor.* 8.24.41 (CCL 143, 412); *Mor.* 27.2.4 (CCL 143B, 1332–33).

37. Peter Brown, *The Body and Society*, chapter 17 (forthcoming).

38. Cf. *Mor.* 7.5.5 (CCL 143, 337–38); *Mor.* 9.55.84 (CCL 143, 514–16); *Mor.* 29.30.62 (CCL 143B, 1478–79); *Mor.* 10.15.29 (CCL 143, 557–58); *Mor.* 16.20.25 (CCL 143A, 813–14).

39. *Mor.* 3.30.59 (CCL 143, 152): "cor nostrum flamma compunctionis concremat ut omne quod in eo est illicitum et operis et cogitationis exurat."

40. *HEz.* 1.5.7–8 (CCL 142, 60); cf. also *HEv.* 2.30.5 (PL 76, 1223).

41. *Mor.* 24.6.11 (CCL 143B, 1195–96).

42. Cf. *HEz.* 1.7.22 (CCL 142, 99); *Mor.* 8.34.57 (CCL 143, 426).

43. *Mor.* 31.27.54 (CCL 143B, 1589).

physical beatings that merely torture and pain, the "wailings of compunction . . . restore when they afflict."[44] Such repentance brings a radical change of heart; it is a "sacrifice of conversion,"[45] painful in destroying the old identity of sin, pleasurable in reuniting man with God. The sinner's perception of himself and of God changes. God was once an Avenger, against whom the carnal protested with impatience at the "severity of his lancing."[46] After conversion, God becomes the loving Father one strives to please. And although the Christian still fears God's judgment, now he is pierced with regret for his sins, for having offended the one he loves. The converted sinner drinks the "wine of remorse," and his "joy turns to tears."[47] God's discipline is accepted joyfully in recognition that God chastens every son he receives (Prv 3:12; Heb 12:6).[48] Instead of resisting God and hating his punishment, the sinner learns to inflict such aggression upon himself, now loving his punishment in order to be healed.[49] The Christian begins to associate himself (sociare se) with God in his own punishment; indeed his punishment is more severe for being in his own hands.[50] The terror he once felt at judgment is now transformed into the power to judge himself. Man comes to "chasten in penitence what was once committed through pride."[51] Sitting on the "dunghill of his heart," the sinner grieves bitter tears. Heaping the dung of his sins before his eyes, he "afflicts himself with lamentations."[52]

The very pain of penitence makes it a punishment, a cure, a discipline, and, above all, a sacrifice reconciling man to God. To be genuine, penitence must offer even a willingness to suffer the painful punishment of sins, for only then does one know compunction is true and deeply felt: affliction is the fruit of the tree of true penitence.[53] Gregory believes that inward compunction is analogous to corporal discipline. The soul is a metaphoric mirror of the body's activities; even as body and soul are united and interconnected. Thus, Gregory explains, Solomon rightly spoke of such chastisements together in Proverbs 20:30 ("The bruise of a

44. Mor. 23.21.40 (CCL 143B, 1175): "Sed hoc inter se utraque haec differunt, quod plagae percussionum dolent, lamenta compunctionum sapiunt. Illae affligentes cruciant, ista reficiunt, dum affligunt. Per illas in afflictione maeror est, per haec in maerore laetitia. Quia tamen ipsa compunctio mentem lacerat, eamdem compunctionem non incongrue disciplinam uocat."

45. Cf. Mor. 35.8.12 (CCL 143B, 1781); Mor. 25.7.16 (CCL 143B, 1240–41).

46. Mor. 20.32.64 (CCL 143A, 1050–51).

47. Mor. 19.30.54 (CCL 143A, 999–1000).

48. Mor. 18.22.35 (CCL 143A, 907–9); Mor. 14.37.45 (CCL 143A, 725).

49. Cf. Mor. 24.24.51 (CCL 143B, 1226); Mor. 24.7.14 (CCL 143B, 1197).

50. Mor. 25.7.13ff. (CCL 143B, 1237ff.).

51. Ibid.

52. Mor. 3.19.34 (CCL 143, 137).

53. In lib. I Reg. 6.46 (CCL 144, 577–78).

wound will cleanse away evil; and beatings will cleanse the innermost parts of the belly"):

> Through the "bruise of a wound," [Solomon] symbolizes the discipline of corporal blows. But "beatings in the more secret parts of the belly" are internal wounds of the mind that come about through compunction. For just as the belly is distended when full of food, so the mind is puffed up when swollen with evil thoughts. Therefore both the bruise of a wound and beatings in the innermost parts of the belly cleanse evil, since not only external discipline washes away sins, but also compunction pierces the distended mind with the punishment of penitence.[54]

Compunction punctures the mind swollen with pride, just as beatings deflate a belly swollen with bad humors. Each is a painful wound that purifies man through punishment.

Most important, these wounds of corporal affliction and spiritual compunction are disciplines; they teach as well as punish. Man learns how to conquer evil by suffering God's purifying trials: "Whoever desires to conquer sins completely, must be eager to bear the scourges of his cleansing humbly, so that afterwards he comes to judgment the more pure, the more the fire of tribulation purges his pollution."[55] Suffering purifies the soul,[56] teaching it to turn away from the evil that has brought the terrible visitation of God's adversity. Physical illness can be especially disciplinary. Sickness can be the result of sin, providing an awesome punishment capable of purging great malice in the heart.[57] If the sinner is beaten severely enough, sooner or later he learns not to return to his wicked ways. This is why to Gregory the Romans of his day seem so particularly hard of heart: they continued to sin, despite God's scourges.[58]

God's pedagogy has an even wider scope, for he has strewn the whole world with many such punishments lest man come to love his pilgrimage and forget his true homeland.[59] God has "hedged your way with thorns" (cf. Hos 2:6), Gregory warns his listeners. God has scattered ad-

---

54. *Mor.* 23.21.40 (CCL 143B, 1174–75): "Per liuorem quippe uulneris, disciplinam insinuat corporeae percussionis. Plagae uero in secretioribus uentris sunt interna mentis uulnera, quae per compunctionem fiunt. Sicut enim uenter cibis repletus extenditur, ita mens prauis cogitationibus dilatata subleuatur. Abstergunt igitur mala et liuor uulneris et plagae in secretioribus uentris, quia et disciplina exterior culpas diluit et extensam mentem compunctio paenitentiae ultione transfigit."

55. *HEv.* 1.15.4 (PL 76, 1133): "Quiquis ergo appetit plene uitia uincere, studeat humiliter purgationis suae flagella tolerare, ut tanto post ad judicem mundior veniat, quanto nunc ejus rubiginem ignis tribulationis purgat."

56. *Mor.* 24.11.34 (CCL 143B, 1213); *Mor.* 14.33.40 (CCL 143A, 722).

57. *HEv.* 1.19.7 (PL 76, 1159); *HEv.* 1.12.7 (PL 76, 1122).

58. *HEz.* 1.9.9 (CCL 142, 128).

59. *Mor.* 23.24.46 (CCL 143B, 1179); cf. Aug. *conf.* 2.2.4; 3.1.1.

versities and trials throughout the lives of Christians, so that beaten and afflicted with serious injuries, "they see in this world's pain that they should have put no trust in the world's delights, and rebuking themselves for their former desires, they turn their hearts to God."[60] The suffering of the world quenches its sweetness, revealing the empty folly of lending the heart to untrustworthy, transient pleasures. This indeed is a discipline of penitence: a self-inflicted chastisement extinguishes man's fatal attraction to pleasure. Every "appetite" and every "wound of pleasure" must be "cleansed by the sharp severity of penitence"; every "lax and dissolute" motion must be chastened by the judgment of "rigid strictness."[61] Gregory sees a symbol of this discipline in Job's scraping the oozing humors from his wounds with a potsherd (Jb 3:8).[62] Man must "wipe away the rottenness of all pleasure" with thoughts of judgment.[63]

Because the world is so "hedged with thorns," the Christian can learn God's discipline by suffering the misfortunes of his life patiently and joyfully:

> "And let this be a consolation to me, that afflicting me with pain, he does not spare me" (Jb 6:10). When the elect know they have committed sins, but upon examination if they find they have suffered no adversities for their sins, they are consumed with the immense force of their terror, and they burn with fear. Agitated, they labor under sinister suspicions lest, safe from retribution of evil in the present, grace has forsaken them forever.[64]

Suffering reassures the sinner that retribution is being exacted in the present. Adversity "purges" the soul, and God is "appeased" when the sinner suffers with "patience."[65] Too happy and peaceful a life on earth is cause for anxiety, lest all punishment of sin be accruing in eternity. For this reason "the elect desire to be stricken with this paternal correction . . . [believing] the pain of the wound is the medicine of salvation."[66]

Through penitence, the sinner acquires the "legal" power to balance his account with God: he should "consider what he owes" and "offer sac-

---

60. *HEv.* 2.36.9 (PL 76, 1271); *Mor.* 30.15.30 (CCL 143B, 1526).
61. *Mor.* 3.29.57 (CCL 143, 150–51).
62. *Mor.* 3.30.58 (CCL 143, 151).
63. Ibid.
64. *Mor.* 7.19.22 (CCL 143, 348).
65. *Ep.* 10.12 (CCL 140A, 839), to Libertinus, expraetor: "Forsitan enim, magnifice fili, aliquid illum in prosperis positus offendisti, unde te clementi amaritudine uult purgari. Et ideo nec temporalis te frangat afflictio nec rerum damna discruciant, quia, si in aduersis gratias referens Deum tibi patientia feceris esse placabilem, et quae amissa sunt multiplicata redduntur et super hoc gaudia aeterna praestantur."
66. *Mor.* 7.19.22 (CCL 143, 348): "Electi . . . feriri paterna correptione desiderant et dolorem uulneris medicamina salutis putant."

rifices" for the expiation of his sins.[67] The sinner's sacrifice averts God's anger, [68] for his penitence atones for his sins while here on earth.[69] Like the sacrifice of the Mass, the sacrifice of compunction performs a continual mediation reconciling man and God. Always available, penitence is also inexhaustible. The Lord "rejoices in man's chastisement,"[70] and man is to continue his offering until he reaches heaven. Penitence reconciles man with God by removing the sin that separates him from his Creator. Man's willingness to submit to God's chastisement compensates for his rebellion in sin, and so restores his right relation of humility before God. This destruction of one's sinful identity is a sacrifice made to God, as the Psalmist says referring to "the sacrifice of a contrite spirit" (Ps 50:19).[71] Imitating Christ, the sinner "empties out" his carnality to become more perfect, even as, conversely, Christ was "emptied out" of the greatness of his divinity in becoming man.[72] The sinner also imitates Christ's crucifixion in the sacrifice he offers "crucifying" his body.[73]

Gregory's method of exegesis brings him to see in the sacrifices of the Old Testament priesthood a foreshadowing of the spiritual sacrifices of repentance in the New Dispensation. This first sacrifice of fear is symbolized by the brass altar that stands outside the temple, in the atrium, to receive burnt offerings of flesh (Ex 39:38–39). For Gregory, this image represents the internal sacrifice for sins the Christian offers on the altar of his heart. Afflicting himself with tears in fear of punishment, the sinner burns his sins in the "fire of compunction."[74] He repents of the evil works he has committed and the good he has neglected, as the offering of two turtledoves ordered in the Old Testament (Lv 5:7) indicates. This "sacrifice of flesh" symbolizes the "twofold groan of penitence," when man "burns with the fire of grief."[75] While the sacrifice of animals atoned for sins in the Old Dispensation, in the New Dispensation one must offer a greater sacrifice, the immolation of oneself in compunction.

67. *Mor.* 24.24.51 (CCL 143B, 1226).

68. Cf. *In lib. I Reg.* 3.92 (CCL 144, 249–50); see also *HEz.* 2.8.19 (CCL 142, 350–51).

69. *Mor.* 8.20.36 (CCL 143, 407); *In lib. I Reg.* 2.150 (CCL 144, 198–99); see also *Mor.* 24.24.51 (CCL 143B, 1226); *Mor.* 2.14.23 (CCL 143, 74); *Mor.* 4.25.46 (CCL 143, 191–92); God forgives the sin lamented in penitence: *Mor.* 33.12.23 (CCL 143B, 1693–94); *Mor.* 4.19.36 (CCL 143, 186); *Mor.* 25.6.8 (CCL 143B, 1234–35); *Mor.* 8.20.36 (CCL 143, 407–8).

70. *Mor.* 9.27.43 (CCL 143, 486); cf. *Dial.* 4.61.1 (SC 265, 202).

71. *HEv.* 1.10.7 (PL 76, 1114).

72. *Mor.* 3.30.59 (CCL 143, 151–52).

73. Ibid.

74. *HEz.* 2.10.20 (CCL 142, 395). See also *HEz.* 2.9.3 (CCL 142, 358); *HEz.* 2.9.12 (CCL 142, 365–66); *HEz.* 2.10.13–14 (CCL 142, 388–89).

75. *Mor.* 32.3.4 (CCL 143B, 1629).

Repentance is cathartic as it draws the soul from fear and sorrow to love and hope. The anxious examination and the grief of repentance slowly dissipate the sinner's feelings of guilt. Released from the burden of anxiety and fear, the Christian feels a new optimism: "When fear has been consumed by a prolonged anxiety and grief, then a certain security is born from the anticipation of forgiveness."[76] Calm returns as conflict is resolved, and the Christian feels purified and cleansed, as if he were a new person with a future of open possibilities. Confession makes man shine in the beauty of righteousness, as if he were in "radiant garments" (cf. Ps 103:2).[77] Cleansed of guilt, man is reborn in the second baptism of penitence.[78] The polluted conscience is renewed;[79] the "robe of innocence" restored.[80] The sinner can be like Lazarus arising from the grave and returning from death to life.[81]

When cleansed of sin and selfish pride, man yearns again for God. The sinner's feelings slowly evolve from fear through sorrow to love and its wound of sweetness, and these new feelings of love flood his soul, kindling his desire for union with God:

> Who first cried that he should not be led to the punishment, afterward begins to cry more bitterly since he is delayed from the kingdom. For the mind contemplates what the choirs of angels, the very society of saints, and the majesty of inward vision of God might be like and it laments more being removed from these everlasting blessings than it cried earlier when it feared eternal punishment. So it happens that when the compunction of fear is perfect it draws the soul to the compunction of love.[82]

Man first cries for fear of the evils that may befall him in punishment. Then he cries the more from love and sorrow for the greater evil, the delayed reward of eternal bliss.[83] The compunction of fear is the first and

76. *Dial.* 3.34.2 (SC 260, 400); also *In lib. I Reg.* 2.92 (CCL 144, 168–69) and *In lib. I Reg.* 3.93 (CCL 144, 250–51).

77. *Mor.* 32.6.8 (CCL 143B, 1634).

78. *HEv.* 1.10.7 (PL 76, 1114); cf. *HEz.* 1.10.29 (CCL 142, 158).

79. *Mor.* 27.18.38 (CCL 143B, 1359–60).

80. *Mor.* 12.6.9 (CCL 143A, 633–34).

81. *Reg.* 4.83 (CCL 144, 336); *Mor.* 4.27.52 (CCL 143, 196–97); *Mor.* 22.10.21 (CCL 143A, 1108).

82. *Dial.* 3.34.2 (SC 260, 400): "qui prius flebat ne duceretur ad supplicium, postmodum flere amarissime incipit quia differtur a regno. Contemplatur etenim mens qui sint illi angelorum chori, quae ipsa societas beatorum spirituum, quae maiestas internae uisionis Dei, et amplius plangit quia a bonis perennibus deest, quam flebat prius cum mala aeterna metuebat. Sicque fit, ut perfecta conpunctio formidinis tradat animum conpunctioni dilectionis."

83. *Ep.* 7.23 (CCL 140, 475–76).

lower spring Caleb gives his daughter, Achsah, to water her land (cf. Jos 15:18); the compunction of love is the higher spring, given last (though mentioned first for honor's sake), a far more excellent gift.[84]

While the first compunction of fear is a sacrifice of obedience immolating the sins of the old man, this second compunction of love is a holocaust tendered by the new man, renouncing the world.[85] Offered to the glory of the Resurrection, this second sacrifice praises God and the kingdom to come.[86] While the altar of brass outside the temple symbolizes the sacrifice of fear, the second altar, the internal altar of gold standing before the ark, symbolizes the sacrifice of love. On this golden altar perfumes burn fragrantly, representing the offering of virtues.[87] Like a pillar of smoke from incense, the compunction of prayer arises from the virtue of love.[88] Contemplation is another virtue offered God. Hearts burning with love, we offer our minds as a "holocaust" to God in contemplation.[89] Monks make the most perfect offering to God, the holocaust of their very lives, "keeping back nothing for themselves, but offering to the omnipotent God their understanding, their speech, their lives, and the property they have received."[90]

In his own distinctive way, Gregory stresses the interdependence and complementarity of the two stages of reform, of fear and love, purification and union. First there is cleansing, then contemplation; first labor, then rest.[91] While he first "labored with groans of sorrow, now he is

---

84. Ibid.

85. An extensive exegesis of the two tables of sacrifice inside and outside the vestibule is in Exodus 40:40. *HEz.* 2.9.2 (CCL 142, 358ff.): "Mensae ergo interioris portae holocaustum habent, quia in uirtutibus Testamenti noui quasi per holocaustum omnia incendimus, quando omnibus quae huius mundi sunt renuntiamus. Mensae uero portae exterioris sacrificium habent, sed holocaustum non habent, quia praecepta legalia decimas offerri iubent, sed dimitti omnia non iubent." See *HEz.* 1.10.11 (CCL 142, 149): "Tunc ergo in nostris mentibus noua fiunt, cum a nobis uetusti hominis uitia transeunt, et tunc uitia uetusti hominis transeunt . . . atque inter uerba Dominica recognoscentes in quantis deliquerint, semetipsos in lacrimis mactare, maerore continuo affici. . . ."

86. *HEz.* 2.10.4 (CCL 142, 382).

87. *HEz.* 2.10.21ff. (CCL 142, 395ff.); cf. *HEz.* 2.10.4 (CCL 142, 382).

88. *HEz.* 2.10.22 (CCL 142, 396); *Mor.* 1.36.54 (CCL 143, 55–56).

89. *Cant* 1.5 (CCL 144, 8).

90. *HEz.* 2.8.16 (CCL 142, 348). Gregory contrasts those still held in the world, who make a sacrifice in good works, and those who have dedicated everything to God, making a holocaust: "Nam sunt quidam qui adhuc mente in hoc mundo retinentur, et tamen ex possessis rebus subsidia egentibus ministrant, oppressos defendere festinant. Isti in bonis quae faciunt sacrificium offerunt, quia et aliquid de actione sua Deo immolant, et aliquid sibimetipsis reseruant. Et sunt quidam qui nihil sibimetipsis reseruant, sed sensum, linguam, uitam atque substantiam quam perceperunt omnipotenti Domino immolant."

91. *Mor.* 6.37.58 (CCL 143, 328–29).

refreshed with the cheer of contemplation."[92] After the mist of sin is burned away by the fire of sorrow, then the eye of the mind is enlightened with flashes of boundless light.[93] Indeed, the success of one's union with God is proportional to one's penitence and rejection of self. "The more we learn what we should fear," Gregory reflects, "the more God gives us something to love."[94] "The more man is displeased with himself, the more he sees what he might love about the omnipotent God in the sacred books";[95] "[the] more he has abased himself in self-contempt, the more he is uplifted by contemplation."[96] In a dialectical movement, the Christian rises in contemplation just as he had lowered himself before in penitence, for he "laments what weighs him down in order to produce what raises him up."[97] Now the Christian is "lifted to joy through tears,"[98] "arriving with many victories of splendid suffering to the summit of love."[99]

Fear and love are two sides of the same coin, another pair of complementary opposites. Just as penitence is a burning fire and contemplation a burst of bright light, Gregory speaks of the compunctions both of fear and of love as burning sacrifices, piercing darts, and stinging wounds. Just as God may wound man externally with scourges to inspire his return, so God wounds man inwardly, piercing him with love for the same purpose.[100] Darts of fear inflict the first wound; darts of love, the second. Like darts of fear, the darts of love "torture" the soul, albeit "sweetly" now.[101] The same pattern of ambivalence appears in Gregory's exegesis of Song of Songs. The kiss bestowed on the bride in Song of Songs "pierces" her soul with love.[102] The wound of love is a sorrow, and the mind that loves the Bridegroom sighs, burns, pants, and is woefully anxious be-

---

92. *Mor.* 5.8.14 (CCL 143, 227).
93. *Mor.* 24.6.11 (CCL 143B, 1195–96).
94. *Mor.* 22.20.48 (CCL 143A, 1127–28).
95. *HEz.* 1.10.45 (CCL 142, 167).
96. *Mor.* 30.19.64 (CCL 143B, 1534–35); cf. *In lib. I Reg.* 1.68 (CCL 144, 93).
97. *Mor.* 31.46.93 (CCL 143B, 1613–14).
98. *Mor.* 5.8.14 (CCL 143, 227).
99. *In lib. I Reg.* 2.2 (CCL 144, 121).
100. *Mor.* 9.53.81 (CCL 143, 512); *Ep.* 7.23 (CCL 140, 475); *Mor.* 6.25.42 (CCL 143, 314–15).
101. *Mor.* 6.25.42 (CCL 143, 314–15). Jean Doignon has demonstrated the parallels between this text and several texts from Aug. *conf.*: 6.6.9–10; 7.1.1–2; 6.7.12; 12.10.10; 7.10.16; 6.11.20. He notes also the influence of Origen on the dialectic of affliction and affection. See "'Blessure d'affliction' et 'blessure d'amour' (*Mor.* 6.25.42): une jonction de thèmes de la spiritualité patristique de Cyprien à Augustin," Fontaine et al., eds., *Grégoire le Grand*, 297–303.
102. *Mor.* 6.25.42 (CCL 143, 314–15), also *Cant.* 1.18 (CCL 144, 19–20): "totiens enim anima osculatur deum, quotiens in eius amore conpungitur."

cause it is denied the presence of the Beloved.[103] When this true love fills the soul, it "tortures it with tears," and the soul is "fed with its own torments."[104] Ill is the health of the heart that does not know the sorrow of this wound. The soul stricken by the "wound of love" is healthier than the soul that remains intact, languishing in its health.[105] The love for God and the longing for the eternal now bruise the soul just as much as fear ever did, but much more exquisitely. The fear of hell is replaced by the anxiety that God is even now distant and may never be quite within one's reach. The pain remains, despite the progression from fear to love; indeed, the yearning of such uncertain promise intensifies the love. The soul is "fed by such tortures"; such "misery is sweet."[106] Remarkably, the bitter sweetness of love and longing for God matches the sweet bitterness of penitence that wounds to heal. Thus the complementary opposites of fear and love each share something of the other, and both are ambivalent.

Indeed, fear and love, penitence and contemplation are closely interwoven. One rises from penitence and the compunction of fear, ascending to contemplate God. Love becomes the "machine" propelling the soul toward the Creator.[107] Contemplative union is both intellectual and emotional, and love itself is knowledge.[108] Love is eminently rational, for the knowledge of love transforms one's life, conferring righteousness and self-control. Unlike mystics such as St. Theresa, Gregory does not distinguish between a stage of illumination and one of union. In *Moralia* 24.12.35, the elect despise the corporeal light of the present, which is the light of the dead darkening their souls (cf. Jb 33.30). In intense mystical language, Gregory explains that the elect instead

---

103. *Mor.* 6.25.42 (CCL 143, 314–15), also *HEz.* 2.3.8 (CCL 242).

104. *HEv.* 2.30.5 (PL 76, 1223).

105. *HEz.* 2.3.8 (CCL 142, 242).

106. Ibid. Cf. also *Cant.* 1.31 (CCL 144, 31); the second wound of compunction of love is sweet compared with the first wound of compunction of sorrow: "Sed dulcedo amoris timentibus absconditur."

107. *Mor.* 6.37.58 (CCL 143, 328–29).

108. *HEv.* 27.4 (PL 76, 1207): "amor ipse notitia est." Extensive work has been devoted to Gregory's views on contemplation; see several articles by A. Ménager: "La contemplation d'après saint Grégoire le Grand," *VS* 9 (1924): 242–81; "La contemplation d'après un Commentaire sur les Rois," *VS Suppl.* 11 (1925): 49–84; "Les Divers Sens du mot *contemplatio* chez saint Grégoire le Grand," *VS* 59 (1939): 145–69, continued in *VS Suppl.* 60 (1960): 39–56. See also G. A. Zinn, Jr., "Silence, Sound, and Word in the Spirituality of Gregory the Great," Fontaine et al., *Grégoire le Grand*, 367–75. Cuthbert Butler, *Western Mysticism* (London, 1922), 91–133; Patrick Catry, "Désir et amour de Dieu chez Grégoire le Grand," *RecAug* 10 (1975): 269–303; Michael Casey, "Spiritual Desire in the Gospel Homilies of Saint Gregory the Great," *CistSt* 16 (1981): 297–314; Dagens, *Saint Grégoire*, 211–15; and esp. Franz Lieblang, *Grundfragen der mystischen Theologie nach Gregors des Grossen Moralia und Ezechielhomilien* (Freiburg im Breisgau, 1934), which is devoted to Gregory's mystical theology.

run back to the splendor of interior clarity, so that they may live where they see by feeling the True Light, where light is not one thing and life another but where the light itself is life [cf. Jn 1:4], where the light so encircles us outwardly that we are filled inwardly, and so fills us inwardly that, being limitless, it encircles us outwardly. Therefore they are illuminated by this light of the living, and they perceive it the more clearly the more purely they live according to it.[109]

Contemplation expands and enlightens the soul with a love that is itself knowledge, for as man draws closer to God in loving union, he grows in the knowledge to reform his life.

The internal truths apprehended in contemplation become the *regulae* the Christian needs to govern his life. Thus discretion and contemplation cannot be separated. Judgment is interlaced with contemplative union, fear becomes again joined to love. From the inward things the soul perceives in contemplation, the soul forms a "rule of judgment" for the outward things it must bear.[110] When a Christian is uplifted inwardly in contemplation, he struggles all the more passionately to conform to the rule he sees above him.[111] The interrelatedness of contemplation and the judgment of discretion explains why teachers are like noisy roosters: they fly up to penetrate invisible things, then crow about them to awaken their flock and reform their behavior (cf. Jb 38:36).[112] Contemplation and discretion are at times interchangeable. One contemplates the meaning of the Holy Scriptures to gain the inner understanding given to man by Christ,[113] or one meditates on the life of Christ, a measuring rod that shows us perfection.[114] So, too, consideration of the lives of the Fathers provides us with a line of discretion (*linea discretionis*) that guides our behavior.[115]

Just as the heights of contemplation depend upon the depths of one's penitence, so does the intensity of contemplation determine the severity of discretion. The more one discerns the "rule of truth" in contemplation, the more one knows how much one has fallen short.[116] The mind rises in contemplation, and yet it discerns all the more clearly that it is not sufficient for that enjoyment.[117] Because contemplation is knowledge of the

109. *Mor.* 24.12.35 (CCL 143B, 1214).
110. *Mor.* 32.1.1 (CCL 143B, 1625–26); see also *Mor.* 35.5.6 (CCL 143B, 1777).
111. *Mor.* 35.5.6 (CCL 143B, 1777).
112. *Mor.* 30.3.11 (CCL 143B, 1498–99).
113. *Mor.* 28.13.33 (CCL 143B, 1420–21).
114. *HEz.* 2.2.7 (CCL 142, 229).
115. *Mor.* 5.11.26–28 (CCL 143, 236–37).
116. *Mor.* 5.30.53 (CCL 143, 254–55); *Mor.* 5.22.56 (CCL 143, 258–9).
117. *Mor.* 24.6.11 (CCL 143B, 1195–96).

light and discernment of the "rule of judgment," a *reverberatio*[118] is implicit, for the knowledge of perfection immediately forces man to recognize his imperfection. Contrasting himself with God, man is astounded by God's brilliance and falls back in awe and terror: he is but dust and ashes compared to God's glory.[119] Isaiah illustrates this reverberation very well. Uplifted in contemplation of God, Isaiah is struck down when he discovers his own sinfulness (cf. Is 6:5).[120] Being displeased with himself, he is quiet and obedient when a seraph purges the pollution of his lips with a hot coal from the altar: "unless he had contemplated the heights of a celestial cleanliness, he would not have found himself guilty," Gregory explains.[121] Truly, men "judge their own darkness" more exactly as the "light" is manifest to them,[122] and "the more they advance in contemplation, the more they despise what they are, and recognize that they are nothing, or almost nothing."[123]

Ideally, man is to cling to God in tranquillity of mind[124] and aim at the stability of eternity. But in practice contemplation is not stable. Man's search for God is a cycle of ascent and descent. *Reverberatio* is inevitable, either because man recognizes his own unworthiness contemplating God or, worse, because temptations strike man down. The mind simply cannot stand long in contemplation; the soul is repulsed because of its own weakness and falls back on itself from the immensity of such great heights.[125] Just as contemplation began with a penitential purgation of carnal impulses, so contemplation is often aborted when these stubborn carnal impulses return to taunt the sinner. Sometimes even the very attempt to be penitent fails, for the mind can be so shaken by the recollection of a sin that it is prompted to do far worse than in its previous slavery to sin.[126] At other times, even in prayer, the mind can be polluted when awareness of a sin returns to accuse the mind.[127] Here the mind loses the

---

118. Dagens notes the idea of *reverberatio* comes from Philo through Augustine; cf. *Saint Grégoire*, 90.

119. *Mor.* 35.5–6.6–7 (CCL 143B, 1777–78).

120. *HEz.* 1.8.19 (CCL 142, 111); cf. Ambr. *Isaac.* 8.77.

121. Ibid.

122. *Mor.* 5.37.67 (CCL 143, 266).

123. *Mor.* 35.2.3 (CCL 143B, 1776).

124. Ibid. and *Mor.* 30.16.54 (CCL 143B, 1528).

125. *HEz.* 1.5.12 (CCL 142, 63).

126. *Mor.* 9.55.84 (CCL 143, 516): "Saepe autem ita mens in culpae recordatione concutitur ut ad perpetrationem illius longe grauius quam prius capta fuerat urgueatur; et deprehensa trepidat seque ipsam uariis motibus impulsa perturbat. Metuit quidem ne uincatur temptationibus sed resistens hoc ipsum quod longo labore certaminis affligitur perhorrescit."

127. *Mor.* 10.15.27 (CCL 143, 556–57).

hope of obtaining what it seeks, since it remembers it is unwilling to fulfill God's commands. Emptied through prayer, the mind may rise, yet suffer *reverberatio* from the very images of the things it considered before the *otium* of prayer.[128] To man's dismay, the sin lamented often returns anyway; the "scars" of man's iniquities ooze again with the "humors" of sin.[129] The stirrings of the flesh and the assaults of various temptations frequently strike down the soul, causing it to descend trembling with fear.[130] All these examples reveal man's innate weakness, for the soul is stunned and forced to descend to carnal realities. Predictably, man's old feelings and thoughts return unwelcome and lamented.

All these reverberations Gregory sees as dark and bitter adversities overturning the light and sweetness of prosperity. The overthrow of contemplation resembles an attack of enemies sneaking into a city, causing disorder and despair.[131] The fear of judgment returns, piercing the soul, like the horror of a vision in the night (Jb 4:13).[132] Fear depresses the soul and makes it feel bitter against itself.[133] The joy experienced in union suddenly turns to penitence and humility, and it seems as if the Lord has "overturned the heavens" (cf. Jb 11:10).[134] But paradoxically, this very knowledge of one's sinfulness perfects the soul in humility, and reinvigorates penitence. The prophet Ezechiel fell on his face before the glory of God, because although man is raised to understand sublimities, he learns the weakness of his condition from the contemplation of God's majesty.[135] Yet this makes him progress in wisdom and humility.[136] Paradoxically, failure in contemplation is turned into success, for man returns to humility in recalling his sinfulness. He can renew the cycle of penitence, contemplation, and reverberation.

It would seem that Gregory's fear of judgment is so strong it often overwhelms contemplation; moments of joy are interludes and moments of respite from continual severity of conscience. The *reverberatio* from contemplation and virtue is, it seems, inescapable. The soul is first pierced

---

128. *Mor.* 10.15.29–30 (CCL 143, 557–59).

129. Ibid.; *Mor.* 9.55.83 (CCL 143, 513–14).

130. Cf. *Mor.* 8.30.50 (CCL 143, 421–22). Passages referring to *reverberatio* by temptation are numerous; for typical cases see *Mor.* 6.25.42 (CCL 143, 314–15); *Mor.* 9.55.84 (CCL 143, 514–16); *Mor.* 5.33.58 (CCL 143, 259–60); *Mor.* 33.23.43 (CCL 143B, 1711–12).

131. *Mor.* 26.45.82 (CCL 143B, 1327–28).

132. *Mor.* 5.30.53 (CCL 143, 254–55).

133. *HEz.* 1.10.45 (CCL 142, 167): "sermo Dei in ore cordis dulcis esse coeperit, huius procul dubio contra semetipsum animus amarescit." See also *Mor.* 35.2.3 (CCL 143B, 1774–75).

134. *Mor.* 10.10.16 (CCL 143, 549).

135. *HEz.* 1.12.4 (CCL 142, 186).

136. *Mor.* 27.37.62 (CCL 143B, 1380).

with love, then pricked by temptation, what Gregory terms "the movement of alternating thoughts" in his exegesis of Psalm 106:26: "They ascend to the heavens and descend to the abyss."[137] Ironically, where the
soul turns to seek a retreat of infinite delight, it often finds instead the
stinging wounds of temptation.[138] Contemplation is all too brief and fragile. It is the silence of only half an hour (Rv 8:1), for tumultuous thoughts
force themselves back into the mind against its will.[139] This temporal alternation serves to resolve the opposition between the spiritual pole of
contemplation and love and the carnal pole of sinfulness and fear.

Just as the cyclical pattern of alternation unites spiritual and carnal
poles, so these poles can also be bridged by hierarchical mediation. While
moments of contemplation are stricken with temptation and sin, accommodations can be made. If the Christian cannot enjoy perfect union in
contemplation with God, he can nevertheless pursue this same goal in
varying degrees. As Dom Guéranger has noted, contemplation is simply
the most intimate relation between God and the soul.[140] A continuum extends from highest vision and union with God to meditation upon lower
levels of perfection, seen in angels, disciples, and saints.[141] No harsh
break exists between contemplating the invisible spirituality and perfection of God and the visible spirituality and perfection manifest in lesser
levels of creation, be it in the examples of holy men or in the life of the
Church. One can mount the *scala considerationis* to God, returning step by
step from visible creation to invisible reality.[142] This continuity of spiritual
and carnal makes movement between this world and the next relatively
easy, and it is accessible to anyone. No one should glory himself in the
singularity of the gift of contemplation.[143]

As there is reconciliation of carnal and spiritual in degrees of contem-

---

137. *Mor.* 9.19.29 (CCL 143, 478).

138. *Mor.* 8.23.40 (CCL 143, 411).

139. *Mor.* 30.16.53 (CCL 143B, 1527); cf *HEz.* 2.2.14 (CCL 142, 234).

140. Dom Guéranger, *Année liturgique* (Temps pascal) III, cited in A. Ménager, "La
Contemplation," 268. Ménager distinguishes five senses of contemplation: consideration of
typology, consideration of mysteries, to believe or have a point of view, to possess highest
vision of God, and to enjoy "l'activité mystique de l'âme." Note that Ménager's distinctions
are hierarchical, moving from lower, more external, and relatively "carnal" pursuits to
higher, inward, and more spiritual activities.

141. *In lib. I Reg.* 1.80 (CCL 144, 99).

142. *Mor.* 15.46.52 (CCL 143A, 781): "Quia ergo rebus uisibilis inuisibilia praestantiora
sunt, carnales quique ex semetipsis pensare debuerunt, atque per hanc ut ita dixerim, scalam considerationis tendere in Deum. . . ." Also *Cant.* 1.9 (CCL 144, 13), where the *gradus
scalae* are the three levels of Sacred Scripture: natural (associated with Isaac), moral (Abraham), contemplative (Jacob).

143. *HEz.* 2.5.18–19 (CCL 142, 289–90).

plation, so the distance between the poles narrows even further, and an integration of hope and fear occurs. The Christian's life should combine the complementary compunctions of love and fear. Even though all virtues, contemplation, and prayer are offered as sacrifices from love, they can never be made without the accompanying sacrifice of fear, penitence, and self-judgment. We beat the spices small (cf. Ex 30:36), like perfumes and spices burnt on the altar.[144] We are to pound good deeds in the mortar of the heart, and sift through them with careful discretion to see if they be without admixture of sin.[145] Works are more pleasing when they have been bruised with self-examination,[146] and a prayer should be offered with each virtue for hidden impurities.[147] Only by returning to tears of fear can the sacrifice one offers of one's life be pure and acceptable to God.[148] Unless fear is present, the offering of love is invalid.

The gifts of virtue offered to God in love are never presented without fear and penitence. The sacrifice of self in love has its mixture of fear even as the longing for God has pain in its tortures and sorrows. The complementary oppositions of love and fear, contemplation and temptation, and virtue and vice resolve in such compromise formations as these, integrating the unsettling contradictions of life. Life is a trial whose moments of perfection are continually overthrown by sin, yet such imperfection is accommodated as a lesson of humility, so making one even more virtuous. If contemplation cannot be absolute, it may be possessed in degrees, and one may make progress. If sin is inevitable, even virtue cannot be performed without repentance of one's sins, and this ensures the acceptability of one's offering. All life mixes failure and success, light and darkness.

The darker side of penitence prevails, yet only because it ensures the bright safety of the soul. Compunction must become a continuous inner disposition for the Christian. Sin is ineluctable, and Gregory can see little relief from the severity of God's judgment. The sinner's internal examination with *discretio* must become every bit as exacting as God's might be, and his compunction must know no end. We "weigh our sins more carefully" when we lament and consider what severity threatens sinners, what reproach, terror, and loathing of God's implacable majesty will be-

144. *Mor.* 1.36.54 (CCL 143, 55–56).
145. Ibid., also *HEz.* 2.10.23 (CCL 142, 397); *Mor.* 9.55.84 (CCL 143, 514–15).
146. *HEz.* 2.10.23 (CCL 142, 397); *Mor.* 1.36.54 (CCL 143, 55–56).
147. *Mor.* 1.35.49 (CCL 143, 51): "Atque holocaustum per singulos filios offerimus [cf. Jb 1:5], cum pro unaquaque uirtute Domino hostiam nostrae precis immolamus."
148. Cf. *HEz.* 2.8.19 (CCL 142, 351); *HEz.* 2.8.17 (CCL 142, 349).

come our lot.[149] Holy men bind themselves more minutely, the more they see themselves examined strictly by the heavenly Judge.[150] And "the more the mind of the elect cling to the internal light, the more subtly they see how virtues ought to be discerned from vices."[151] Like the Desert Fathers, Gregory lives with a vision of himself before God's tribunal, always judging himself with the sharpest *discretio* in fear of future judgment.[152] A Christian can scarcely judge himself too severely, considering he is "the more blameless the more he blames himself,"[153] and knowing as well that he must recompense not only sins but also good works whose purity is uncertain.[154] Because so much of man's sinfulness remains opaque, and because the severity of God's scrutiny is also unknown, the wise sinner should perform more than enough penitence to obliterate any possible error.

Thus Gregory proposes the ideal of the just penitent, who in his actions shuns even what is lawful, and in his penitence laments even the slightest sin with abundant tears:

> For there are many guilty of no sins, and yet they afflict themselves fiercely as though every sin oppressed them. They reject even what is permitted lawfully; they are more than ready to face the contempt of the world; they do not allow themselves anything pleasing, but even cut off the goods permitted them. They despise visible things, and burn for the invisible. They rejoice in weeping and humble themselves in all things. And just as some lament their sinful works, so these lament their sinful thoughts. And so what should I call them, except both just and penitent, who humble themselves in penitence for sins of thought and stand in perseverance of good works?[155]

To insulate himself from the possibility of sin, the just penitent avoids even what is lawful; he lavishes tears of compunction on the slightest

149. *Mor.* 16.29.36 (CCL 143A, 819–20).

150. *Mor.* 21.5.10 (CCL 143A, 1071–72).

151. *Mor.* 33.35.60 (CCL 143B, 1725).

152. *Mor.* 25.7.15 (CCL 143B, 1239–40). Cf. *Vitae patr.* 5.3 (entire), esp. 2–5, 21–23. See Irénée Hausherr, *Penthos*, trans. Anselm Hufstader, Cistercian Studies 53 (Kalamazoo, Mich., 1982), 41, where tears of compunction arise from fears of judgment. The intensity of tears must correspond to the gravity of the fault.

153. *Mor.* 21.5.10 (CCL 143A, 1071–72).

154. *Mor.* 1.36.53ff. (CCL 143, 53ff.).

155. *HEv.* 2.34.5 (PL 76, 1248): "Nam multi et nullorum sibi malorum sunt conscii, et tamen in tanti ardoris afflictione se exerunt, ac si peccatis omnibus coangustentur. Cuncta etiam licita respuunt, ad despectum mundi sublimiter accinguntur, licere sibi nolunt omne quodlibet, bona sibi amputant etiam concessa, contemnunt visibilia, invisibilibus accenduntur, lamentis gaudent, in cunctis semetipsos humiliant; et sicut nonnulli peccata operum, sic ipsi cogitationum peccata deplorant. Quid itaque istos dixerim, nisi et justos et poenitentes, qui se et in poenitentia de peccato cogitationis humiliant, et recti semper in opere perseverant?"

faults, so that his penitence may be more than sufficient. One can never perform too much penance: repentance in excess of one's sin is accounted as merit; but if repentance falls short, the soul can be lost.[156] Gregory frequently expresses his anxiety whether penitence be sufficient or wanting.[157] But if all life is a sacrifice, the Christian can be assured that his actions and thoughts are purified and pleasing to God. Every time he participates in the Mass, he is to offer himself as a sacrifice, along with the offering of the Holy Victim. The sacrifice to God on the altar of the heart enables one to become a martyr even in times of peace.[158] Through compunction all of the Christian's life is offered as a sacrifice to God, in fear and love.[159]

Gregory proposes a pattern of perfection in imperfection that recognizes man's frailty yet never relinquishes hope for his improvement. The virtues of prayer, contemplation, and good works are never complete, but always interwoven with reversals and resistance. Yet the sinner should not lose hope, for perseverance is itself virtuous: at least the weak are seeking perfection. Reform is continual growth and change, never straightforward progress. Everyone fails at times, taking actions that contradict his professed desires. But constancy of intention and perseverance distinguish the elect from hypocrites. The wicked eventually give in to trials and temptations, while the elect persevere to their reward, bearing temptations as sacrifice.[160] The struggles against temptation become virtually as good as purity itself. The persevering soul never fully loses stability in contemplation.[161] If the soul feels unequal to God's footstep, nevertheless the soul loves God the more for being unable to bear his astounding sweetness, for scarcely touching him with uncertain vision.[162] If God is denied the soul, the memory of his sweetness remains as an anchor that stabilizes man's life.[163]

Although the soul is repulsed from contemplation, the desire for God always persists in intention. Man "seeks again after punishment" the face of God he feared after sinning.[164] Nor is discretion lost when virtue

---

156. Cf. *Mor.* 26.10.15 (CCL 143B, 1276).
157. Cf. *Mor.* 35.20.49 (CCL 143B, 1810–11).
158. *Dial.* 3.26.9 (SC 260, 372).
159. Such doublets of sacrifice are found in *HEz.* 2.10.19–23 (CCL 142, 394–97); *HEz.* 2.10.4 (CCL 142, 381); *Mor.* 6.37.56 (CCL 143, 325); *HEz.* 2.8.16 (CCL 142, 348); and *HEz.* 2.9 (CCL 142, 355–77), which contains several pairs.
160. *Mor.* 9.55.83 (CCL 143, 513–14).
161. *Mor.* 10.15.31 (CCL 143, 559–60).
162. Ibid.
163. *HEz.* 1.5.12 (CCL 142, 63): "suauitatis Dei memoria pascitur."
164. *Mor.* 11.43.59 (CCL 143A, 619).

and contemplation fail. On the contrary, temptation strengthens discretion, for a temporary lapse of discretion teaches one how better to distinguish good from evil.[165] The apparent failures of spiritual perfection occasioned by an active life present many opportunities for spiritual advancement. If the listener cannot fully imitate the perfection of his teacher, he both "progresses in things he masters, and in the things he masters not at all, he grows in humility."[166] And though virtue is lost, it continually returns: "the Lord does not cease to love those who wander."[167]

Gregory's exposition of the cycle of contemplation and reverberation and his explication of the complementary sacrifices of fear and love reflect his struggles during and after his conversion. He strove to abnegate himself of carnal impulses and to follow a life of ascetic virtue, yet he always had to fight the unwilling attraction that secular pursuits held for him. To be sure, in the contemplative life one invariably "stumbles at the summit,"[168] but one returns to the journey humbled and wiser. The convert to monastic life endures the fiercest temptations, like the early monks who retired to the desert to fight demons. But those battles were overt and edifying. One can never experience such conspicuous trials in the active life, for the "root of sin" is concealed in its very busyness.[169] In a wholesome way, the tranquillity of the desert retreat or the contemplative life "removes the crowd of anxieties from the pathway of the heart" and uncovers the root of sin.[170]

In the contemplative life, the face-to-face struggle against one's sins is much more dramatic and absolute than in the active life, whose "day of prosperity" conceals temptations and sin. The uncovering of evils by the contemplative is preferable to the plight of the active man, who is subject to the sudden revelation of sin lurking beneath the cloak of goodness and to the anxiety of concealed sins. These burdens of the active life Gregory does not wish to bear; nevertheless, he knows that God has ordained this dangerous life of activity and he must obey humbly. He remains convinced he can still find perfection, for God does not reject the powerful per se. In sum, Gregory creates an order that encompasses

---

165. Cf. *Mor.* 2.50.80 (CCL 143, 108), also *Mor.* 11.49.65 (CCL 143A, 623).

166. *HEz.* 2.6.8 (CCL 142, 300): "In quibus praeualet, proficit, in quibus minime praeualet, ad humilitatem crescit."

167. *Mor.* 30.1.5 (CCL 143B, 1493).

168. *Mor.* 24.11.30 (CCL 143B, 1209–10).

169. Ibid.

170. Ibid.; also *Mor.* 30.16.53 (CCL 143B, 1527–28). This theme of the greater trials found in contemplation is reminiscent of the Desert Fathers, cf. *Vitae patr.* 5.2.16, but is modified by Gregory, due to his own involvement in activity.

both the sins he commits inadvertently as well as the virtue he wills deliberately.

Because the true constancy of the soul is what really matters, as long as the Christian accepts worldly life as a sacrifice of obedience, his salvation can be safeguarded. One is reminded of Augustine, who contemplated a retreat to the desert to fight devils, only to be pressed into service of the Church. Gregory may well have consoled himself with Augustine's reflections on that lost retirement in *Confessions* 10.13.70:

> [But] you forbade me to do this and gave me strength by saying "This is why Christ died for us all, so that those who live may now no longer live for themselves but for him who died for them" [2 Cor 5:15]. Behold O Lord, "I cast all my care on you" [Ps 54:23] so that I may live and "I shall contemplate the wonders of your law"[Ps 118:18].

By God's mysterious order Gregory was also compelled to undertake service for the sake of his neighbor, and he did so with a similar sense of sacrifice and obedience to God's law.

The soul's integrity can remain intact, despite the defilement of secular affairs. Though Count Theophanius spent his days occupied with worldly affairs, his remarkable death revealed that duty more than inclination bound him to the world. He was buried in the odor of sanctity, and it seemed that perfumes replaced the worms of putrid flesh. "I tell you these things," Gregory writes, "that I might show you from a recent example that some may wear secular dress, and yet not have a secular mind."[171] Such sanctity and perfection can be gained only when one has learned to balance the alternations and contradictions of life, so creating a dynamic stability of soul, a *constantia mentis*.

171. *HEv.* 2.36.13 (PL 76, 1273–74).

· XII ·

CONSTANTIA MENTIS

Discretion dispels the gloomy mist of sin, for it points out the narrow road charted between virtue and vice. Life can be transformed through such discernment and self-control. No external evil need affect the Christian, for "if the heart is in God, the bitter will be sweet."[1] The world no longer looks so menacing when one is so well apprised of its dangers; aware of the soft vulnerabilities hidden in the heart, one more easily constructs strong defenses. When so perfected and refined, discretion allows not only man's withdrawal from the world but also his active involvement in it. Internally safe within the citadel of his soul, the Christian can return to the world to serve his neighbor and advance the several causes of the Church. Indeed, it is fitting he do so: he who "builds a solitude for himself" must also be a "consul," leading others from charity (cf. Jb 3).[2] Granted, such life is tempting and dangerous, but to the elect, the "very poison of the serpent" is a "remedy," and "evils are of service to them"; while for the wicked, "even good things are injurious."[3]

Whatever trials and temptations assault the soul, the good Christian preserves a balanced soul. He has the strength and courage of Ezechiel, whose name means *fortitudo dei*,[4] and he shares the equanimity of Job,

---

1. *Mor.* 7.15.18 (CCL 143, 345–46). For other such conversions see *Mor.* 8.10.20 (CCL 143, 396–97); *Mor.* 31.43.84 (CCL 143B, 1608); *Mor.* 6.16.23 (CCL 143, 299–300); *Mor.* 30.10.38 (CCL 143B, 1518); and *Mor.* 30.10.37 (CCL 143B, 1517–18).

2. *Mor.* 4.30.59 (CCL 143, 203–4).

3. *Mor.* 34.22.45 (CCL 143B, 1765).

4. *HEz.* 1.2.6 (CCL 142, 20). For writers associated with Stoicism, such as Cicero and Seneca, courage is the ability to endure trials: cf. Cic. *Tusc.* 3.17.36, where *fortitudo* is defined as what "te animo tanto esse coget, ut omnia, quae possint homini evenire, contemnas et pro nihilo putes"; also *fin.* 1.15.49; Sen. *epist.* 64.4. Joseph Pieper, *Fortitude and Temperance*, trans. D. F. Coogan (New York, 1954) treats the interconnection of these virtues in the Christian tradition, especially with St. Thomas. See also Michel Spanneut, "Le Stoïcisme dans l'histoire de la patience chrétienne," *MSR* 39 (1982): 102–3.

the stability Gregory calls *constantia mentis*.[5] Whether battered by suffering or buoyed by wealth and good fortune, Job maintains the proper balance of spiritual health. His dynamic constancy is the temporal analogue of Adam's prelapsarian stability, now adjusted to the realities of daily life. While certain saintly contemplatives may strive to attain Adam's changelessness, even they must on occasion serve others and bear the burdens of the flesh. The prelate and the average Christian have an even greater need to preserve spiritual balance. Ideally, the mind can be like a tree, "deeply rooted." Though buffeted by contending winds, the Christian can remain firm and stable.[6] "Fixed by the weight of constancy," such a mind can withstand the "wandering" and "flux" of the world.[7]

The soul's constancy in adversity and prosperity is found in writers associated with the Stoic traditions, such as Cicero and Seneca, and the theme proved especially attractive to early Christian writers.[8] Gregory embroiders the theme by stressing the interconnection of body and soul, and the paradoxical nature of God's blessings and punishments. For

---

5. *Mor.* 7.32–33.47–49 (CCL 143, 370–71). See also *HEz.* 2.7.11–20 (CCL 142, 324–34); *In lib. I Reg.* 1.106 (CCL 144, 117f.); *HEv.* 1.6.2 (PL 76, 1096–97); *Reg. Past.* 2.3 (PL 77, 28–30). For other passages on the general structure of adversity and prosperity, see: *HEz.* 1.6.8 (CCL 142, 72); *Mor.* 10.21.39 (CCL 143, 564–65); *Mor.* 15.50.62 (CCL 143A, 789); *Mor.* 20.33.65 (CCL 143A, 1051); *Mor. praef.* 8 (CCL 143, 13–15). Some of the material in this chapter is from my paper *"Adversitas et Prosperitas*: une illustration du motif structurel de la complémentarité," in Fontaine et al., eds., *Grégoire le Grand* (Paris, 1986), 277–88.

6. *Mor.* 22.7.17 (CCL 143A, 1105). Sinners are rootless trees; cf. *HEz.* 1.2.3 (CCL 142, 18); *Mor.* 12.53.60 (CCL 143A, 665).

7. *Mor.* 19.5.8 (CCL 143A, 961). In this passage, *stabilitas consilii* is a synonym for the *gravitas constantiae*, itself a *pondus*.

8. Frequent terms are *aequibilitas, constantia, stabilis anima, tranquillitas*; cf. Hor. *Carm.* 2.3, 2.11, 11.12; Cic. *off.* 1.20.69, 1.26.90; *Tusc.* 4.6ff., 4.13; Metellus in *Tusc.* 1.35.85 and Rupilius in 4.17.40 are similar to Job; Sen. *dial.* 2, an entire essay on *constantia*; also *dial.* 1, on *providentia* 1.2, 2.6, 3.1, 4.1, 8.10; *epist.* 36.5, 39.3–4, 45.9, 67.4, 67.14–15, 75.17–18, 91.18; *dial.* 9, on *tranquillitas* 2.3; 2.11; 11.12; Boeth. *cons.* 2.4.2; 2.8.3f. In *dial.* 9.2.3, Seneca defines *tranquillitas* as a translation of εὐθυμία in Democritus: *placido maneat nec adtollens se nec de primens*. For Seneca, virtue alone can preserve us in changes of fortune, *vit. beat.* 15.5; evil is in one's perception of fortune, *epist.* 91.21–33. Gregory's most immediate inspiration is probably Cassian *conl.* 6.8–10 on Job and adversity and prosperity. Gregory echoes *conl.* 6.8–12—an explanation of being ambidextrous from Judges 3:15—in *HEz.* 2.7.15–20 (CCL 142, 329–34) and *Reg. Past.* 2.3 (PL 77, 28–30) and elsewhere. See also *conl.* 4.12; *inst.* 5.41.10; 9.13.1–10; 11.11.13–17. Aug. *civ.* 14.8–9 treats *constantia* and the difference between the Christian's range of feelings: fear and desire, grief and joy, strength and weakness, and the presumably Stoic's *apatheia*, or *insensibilitas*, cf. Sen. *vit. beat.*15.4–6. See also *civ.* 14.8–9, a second major influence, where Augustine speaks of Cicero's *constantia mentis*, likening it to the εὐπάθεια of the Greeks. He says Christians both rejoice and grieve in temptations and desire to be examined and tried by the Lord (Ps 26:2); this differs from the "insensibility" of the Stoics. Gregory echoes this passage in *Mor.* 2.16.28–29 (CCL 143, 77). Cf. Aug. *Enn. in Pss.* 64.13; 36.9–10; 50.4; 54.2; 70, s.1.10; 137.12; *catech. rud.* 17.27; *civ.* 17.23; Ambr. *off.* 1–2; and *Iac.* 7.28–32. Cyprian and other Fathers do mention the idea, however, as it is something of a commonplace.

Gregory, the equilibrium of the soul allows the Christian to remain stable despite all the physical and spiritual changes of life, which Gregory divides into "prosperity" and "adversity." Prosperity, the good fortune man enjoys, is God's smile, his grace, blessings, and gifts.[9] Prosperity includes all the good fortune Job enjoys and more: flocks, friendship, household, sons, possessions, riches, and health.[10] The worldly delights of prosperity are alluring and almost irresistible; sweet pleasures caress and soften the body. Prosperity also comprises temporal power and command over others.[11] Honor, glory, and success invariably elicit the praise of others. Riches, food, and comforts are luxurious "fats" feeding one's humors, while beauty delights the eyes.[12] Like the day, the morning, and sunlight, prosperity is warm and nourishing, and makes things flourish.[13] The happiness, joy, tranquillity, and hope of such good fortune can all serve to soothe and refresh the pilgrim on his way.[14] It is the meat that sustains, and an ointment that heals.[15] Finally, even man's spiritual success and achievement, his virtues and good works, are prosperities: a wholesome fruitfulness, God's gifts of grace and man's good fortune.[16] All prosperity tends to elevate the soul (*extollere, elevare, erigere*), and prosperity is an ascendant state (*celsitudo, culmen, sublimitas*).

In direct contrast, man also faces the adversity of the world. The misfortune and bad luck man suffers evidence God's wrath, his discipline, and his vengeance.[17] As prosperity is God's gift, adversity is the loss of his gift. Job endured a series of losses: a house overturned, death, poverty, illness, opprobrium.[18] Adversity is every kind of suffering: grief,

9. *Mor.* 20.3.8 (CCL 143A, 1007–8); *Mor.* 30.10.38 (CCL 143B, 1519–20); *Mor.* 9.13.20 (CCL 143, 470–71); *Mor.* 5.2.2 (CCL 143, 219–20); *Mor.* 23.26.52ff. (CCL 143B, 1185ff.); *Mor.* 10.10.16–19 (CCL 143, 549–51).

10. *HEz.* 2.7.20 (CCL 142, 332–34); *Mor.* 14.13.15 (CCL 143A, 706–7); *Mor.* 8.54.91–92 (CCL 143, 453–55); *Mor.* 30.10.38 (CCL 143B, 1518).

11. *Mor.* 5.11.17 (CCL 143, 229–30).

12. *Mor.* 5.2.2 (CCL 143, 219–20); *Mor.* 12.44.50–51 (CCL 143A, 659–60); *Mor.* 4.21.40 (CCL 143, 188); *Mor.* 6.6.8 (CCL 143, 288–89).

13. *Mor.* 5.2.2 (CCL 143, 219–20); *Mor.* 2.9.15 (CCL 143, 69–70); *Mor.* 10.18.35 (CCL 143, 562–63).

14. *Mor.* 8.54.92 (CCL 143, 454).

15. *Mor.* 14.13.15 (CCL 143A, 706–7); *Mor.* 5.40.71 (CCL 143, 271); *Mor.* 8.54.92 (CCL 143, 454–55).

16. Cf. *Mor.* 23.25–27.51–54 (CCL 143B, 1184–87); *Mor.* 10.10.16–19 (CCL 143, 549–51); *Mor.* 2.52.83 (CCL 143, 109–10); *Mor.* 2.49.78–79 (CCL 143, 106–8).

17. *Mor.* 20.19.45f. (CCL 143A, 1036f.); *Mor.* 9.27.42 (CCL 143, 485); *Mor.* 9.21.33 (CCL 143, 480); *Mor.* 20.3.8 (CCL 143A, 1007–8); *Mor.* 5.10.16 (CCL 143, 228); *Mor.* 7.25–26.31–32 (CCL 143, 355–56); *Mor.* 2.14.23 (CCL 143, 74).

18. *Mor.* 2.13.22ff. (CCL 143, 73ff.); *Mor.* 8.2.2 (CCL 143, 382–83); *Mor.* 8.8.15 (CCL 143, 392–93); *Mor.* 14.7.8 (CCL 143A, 702); *Mor.* 20.22.48–49 (CCL 143A, 1038–39); *Mor.* 6.12.14 (CCL 143, 293–94); *Mor.* 26.46–47.84–85 (CCL 143B, 1328–29).

tears, pain, affliction, physical and mental anguish. Spiritually, adversity is vice and the loss of one's virtue or contemplation through temptation and sin.[19] A battle against the devil and against God,[20] adversity is most frequently a scourge or whip (*flagellum*). It is also the surgeon's knife lancing the tumor of pride, cutting and draining evil humors as it wounds the soul.[21] Like the night, adversity is dark; it is also sad and bitter.[22] Like the winter, its frost and storms oppress man.[23] Adversity straightens, narrows, hardens, and dries the body; it deflates and depresses the soul with fear (*deprimere, gravare*). Misfortune can even break the soul, or make it become hard and numb.[24]

Using the concepts of prosperity and adversity, of good and bad fortune, Gregory explains how man should respond to the blessings and the suffering God sends. Adversity and prosperity so alternate continually that they "become confused with each other,"[25] and man can scarcely distinguish between them. The alternating states of contemplation and temptation, virtue and sin, are God's comings and goings, his grace and his wrath.[26] But because of sin man cannot discern the meaning of God's visitations:

> Therefore, the coming and going of God from our mind cannot at all be known, and we are ignorant of the final end of these alternating stages, since it is uncertain whether temptation proves us or kills us in our trial, and we can never discern whether gifts remunerate those abandoned, or whether they nourish along the way those who are returning to the fatherland.[27]

Both gifts and temptations can precede election or damnation.[28] Adversity is not necessarily a deserved punishment for sin, nor prosperity

---

19. *Mor.* 9.13.20 (CCL 143, 470–71); *Mor.* 20.3.8 (CCL 143A, 1007–8); *Mor.* 23.26.52ff. (CCL 143B, 1185ff.); *Mor.* 10.10.16–19 (CCL 143, 549–51); *Mor.* 6.22.39 (CCL 143, 312–13); *Mor.* 2.49.78–79 (CCL 143, 106–8).

20. *Mor.* 8.2.2 (CCL 143, 382–83); *Mor.* 14.37.45 (CCL 143A, 725–26); cf. also *Mor.* 3.21.29 (CCL 143, 140): "tribulationum bellum."

21. *Mor.* 5.40.71 (CCL 143, 271); cf. *Mor.* 3.21.39–40 (CCL 143, 140–41), where adversities are darts lacerating wounds.

22. *Mor.* 4.1.6–7 (CCL 143, 167–68); *Mor.* 16.61–63.75–77 (CCL 143A, 842–43); *Mor.* 26.46.84 (CCL 143B, 1329); *Mor.* 2.9.15 (CCL 143, 69); *Mor.* 5.2.2 (CCL 143, 219–20); *Mor.* 14.15.17 (CCL 143A, 707–8).

23. *Mor.* 29.30.65 (CCL 143B, 1480).

24. See above n. 9 and *Mor.* 5.45.71 (CCL 143, 271); *Mor.* 8.10.20 (CCL 143, 396); *Mor.* 9.46.71 (CCL 143, 506–7).

25. *Ep.* 3.51 (CCL 140, 196).

26. *Mor.* 9.13.20 (CCL 143, 470–71).

27. *Mor.* 9.13.20 (CCL 143, 471).

28. *Mor.* 5.1.1 (CCL 143, 218–19); *Mor.* 14.6.7 (CCL 143A, 701–2); *Mor.* 24.18.44 (CCL 143B, 1221–22); cf. *Mor.* 12.25–26.30–31 (CCL 143A, 647–48).

a reward for virtue. Prosperity can reward virtue and foreshadow the joys to come, or it can be the temptation sent to undermine the soul with the only sweet rewards the damned are ever to receive. Adversity can purge the soul of sin and return it to health, or it can break the soul if it evokes blasphemous anger and impatience. Thus both prosperity and adversity are ambiguous:[29] both can be dangerous as well as good. To maintain the security of his soul, the Christian should treat both as trials, for to assume the worst prevents unpleasant surprises.

Unfortunately, few have the discipline to respond properly to the alternations of adversity and prosperity. Rather, many Christians fall into error by adopting one of two extremes of behavior, either a spiritual or a carnal extreme. Gregory chastises the hyperspirituality of the philosophers (presumably the Stoics) who aim to be insensitive to God's scourges,[30] for being numb to pleasure and pain, they will also be hardened to God. Such *apatheia*, based on a denial of God's involvement in his creation, fails to recognize the pedagogic uses God can make of the world to bring about man's return. Hypocrites pose other problems. Self-righteous and flamboyantly ascetic, they criticize the powerful position the Church holds in the world and condemn those who serve in the world, bearing the burdens of others.[31]

As the spiritual extreme separates spirit and flesh too completely, so that the mind becomes numb with *apatheia*, the carnal extreme connects flesh and spirit too directly, so that the soul becomes overly sensitive to changes in the body and the world. The carnal, such as Job's wife and friends, wrongly assume that they deserve to prosper in the world and are not to suffer unless they have sinned. They believe their status in the world should reflect their spiritual state with God. Consequently, they launch "impatient insults" against God when they suffer unwarranted adversities, blaming God for the evils they endure and wrongly impeaching his justice.[32] Should the carnal enjoy prosperity, they believe they possess the world's good fortune as a result of their own worthiness, and so forget to thank the Creator for his gifts.[33] Being tied to the world instead of to God, the carnal puff up proudly in prosperity. But in adversity they are utterly crushed by despair, because they love the world and its delights too fervently.[34]

29. Pierre Boglioni calls this a "double ambivalence"; "Miracle et nature chez Grégoire le Grand," in *Cahiers d'études médiévales*, I: *Epopées, légendes et miracles* (Montreal and Paris, 1974), 52.

30. *Mor.* 2.16.28 (CCL 143, 77).

31. *Mor.* 26.40.73 (CCL 143B, 1320–21); *Mor.* 26.41.76 (CCL 143B, 1322–23).

32. *Mor.* 2.16.28 (CCL 143, 77); also *Mor.* 11.34.47 (CCL 143A, 612–13).

33. *Mor.* 8.36.59 (CCL 143, 428–29).

34. *Mor.* 4.1.3 (CCL 143, 165–66); also *Mor.* 8.21.37 (CCL 143, 408); *HEv.* 1.1.6 (PL 76,

Job mediates these extremes. He perceives the relation God has with the world and preserves the proper dialectic obtaining between flesh and spirit. One should learn to suffer adversity and prosperity as Job did, both loving and fearing God equally in prosperity and adversity.[35] Where the hypocrite would fear God only when disciplined for his sins in adversity, would love God only when blessed with rewards in prosperity, Job undergoes a deep conversion of heart, recognizing that both discipline and rewards can precede either election or damnation. In facing adversity, Job is patient; he is chastened and fears, yet he still loves God and thanks him for the scourges.[36] In prosperity, he loves God and thanks him for his blessings, but he never ceases to fear the Giver of his gifts. Job's "constancy of mind" allows his soul to "stand" in adversity and prosperity.[37]

Here again Gregory depicts a pattern of polarity in which the members of an opposing pair of qualities or states take on one another's characteristics. Prosperity is good in moderation, for it soothes and refreshes the soul and encourages the pilgrim on his travels to the homeland. But prosperity turns to adversity when the discipline of the soul relaxes, and excessive humors soften the flesh and push the soul to pride, lechery, and any number of despicable vices.[38] Even spiritual prosperity is dangerous.

Spiritual prosperity turns into adversity when the success of virtue turns to pride. The good works and virtue give the soul hope for salvation, but this hope can easily swell to an excess of security and confidence.[39] The soul foolishly begins to blur the distinction between divine gifts and human weakness and imagines virtue comes from itself, rather than from God.[40] Pride arises so easily in prosperity because discerning where human strengths end and God's gifts begin is very difficult. Prosperity may be like a day, but it is a day of such confusions.[41] Hypocrites

---

1096). Cf. Cassian *inst.* 9.13.11–13 where they should be "immobiles perdurantes nec casibus deiecti praesentibus nec prosperis . . . elati," and *inst.* 11.10.1–11.18.

35. *Mor.* praef. 3.7 (CCL 143, 12–13). God allowed Job to be tried because his patience was as yet unproved, *Mor.* 2.9.15 (CCL 143, 69–70); *Mor.* 7.32–33.48–49 (CCL 143, 370–71); *Mor.* 11.34.47 (CCL 143A, 612).

36. See preceding note and *Ep.* 10.12 (CCL 140A, 838–39).

37. *Mor.* 7.32.48 (CCL 143, 370–71). Job was attacked by his friends. "Videntes corporis uulnera, sed mentis constantiam nescientes, dum me de iniustitia increpare ausi sunt, usque ad me necdum uenerunt; sed dura me inuectione pulsantes, dum stare animum inter aduersa deprehendunt, quasi ad me uenientes erubescunt."

38. *Mor.* 3.7.10 (CCL 143, 119–20); *Mor.* 16.69.83 (CCL 143A, 848); *Mor.* 5.11.17 (CCL 143, 229–30); *Mor.* 8.10.22 (CCL 143, 397–98); *Mor.* 6.6.8 (CCL 143, 288–89).

39. *Mor.* 7.18.21 (CCL 143, 347–48); *Mor.* 8.10.20 (CCL 143, 396–97); *Mor.* 2.49.78 (CCL 143, 103–4); *Mor.* 16.59.72 (CCL 143, 841); *Mor.* 9.53.80 (CCL 143, 511–12).

40. *Mor.* 2.49.78 (CCL 143, 106–7); cf. *Mor.* 5.10.16 (CCL 143, 228–29).

41. *Mor.* 4.2.7 (CCL 143, 168).

flourish in prosperity and the devil disguises himself as an angel of light. The devil brings gifts of prosperity, but they are false ones, vices under the cloak of virtue: anger disguised as justice, excess as mercy, fear as humility, pride as authority.[42] All are excesses on either side of the line of discretion. In prosperity it is difficult to discern whether man loves God for his own sake or for the gifts he gives; thus confession in prosperity means nothing.[43] For all these reasons, the promises of prosperity are actually adversities.[44] Its gifts can be fraudulent, and prosperity becomes a kind of persecution.[45] Prosperity can be a greater burden than adversity; holy men fear it more; they trample it down and despise it.[46]

Gregory's pessimism about the nature of good fortune stems from his vision of life as a trial, a continual challenge to test man's loyalty and strength. God's athlete is assaulted on all sides by temptation and suffering, and, like Job, he never knows what will happen next. All too easily the day of prosperity turns into the night of adversity, all the smiles vanish, and the light becomes loathesome.[47] The sweetness of prosperity is actually bitterness and worms.[48] God may have given man prosperity not as a blessing, not as a reward for his virtue nor a comfort along the way. Prosperity may have been sent as a temptation, a provocative trap luring man to damnation. From this perspective, adversity is easily the true prosperity. Adversity is bitter and hard, it pierces the soul with salutary fear.[49] The external loss of worldly goods and status, or the internal loss of virtue from sin, adversity reveals man's weakness to himself. God's favor is withdrawn; on his own, man confesses his nothingness. Eternal damnation may actually be his fate.

But just as prosperity turns into adversity, so too adversity becomes prosperity. Used rightly, adversity chastens the soul and humbles it, restoring the soul to health through repentance.[50] The wrath of God is part of his mercy, and adversity is the discipline of a loving father preparing his son for inheritance.[51] Adversity collects and purifies the carnal nature

42. *Mor.* 3.33.65f. (CCL 143, 155f.).

43. *Mor.* 8.36.59 (CCL 143, 428–29).

44. *Mor.* 4.2.7 (CCL 143, 168).

45. *Mor.* 4.21.40 (CCL 143, 188).

46. *Mor.* 5.1–2.1–2 (CCL 143, 218–20); *Mor.* 7.18.21 (CCL 143, 347–48); *Mor.* 14.8.10 (CCL 143A, 703).

47. *Mor.* 23.24.48 (CCL 143B, 1181); *Mor.* 4.2.7 (CCL 143, 168).

48. *Mor.* 23.25.49 (CCL 143B, 1181); *Mor.* 16.49.83 (CCL 143A, 848).

49. *Mor.* 2.49.76 (CCL 143, 105–6); *Mor.* 9.56.85 (CCL 143, 516–17); *Mor.* 26.46.84 (CCL 143B, 1329).

50. *Mor.* 2.52.83 (CCL 143, 110); *Mor.* 9.53.80 (CCL 143, 511–12); *Mor.* 9.56.85 (CCL 143, 516–17); *Mor.* 20.32.64 (CCL 143A, 1050). Also, *Mor.* 5.40.71 (CCL 143, 271).

51. *Mor.* 21.4.8 (CCL 143A, 1069–70); *Mor.* 9.56.85 (CCL 143, 516–17); *Mor.* 7.18.21 (CCL 143, 347–48); *Mor.* 5.9.15–16 (CCL 143, 227–29).

loosened and scattered in prosperity. The scourge of adversity disciplines the wild ass (Jb 11:22), yokes him to the commandments, and checks his freedom to run in the woods of his desire.[52] The disciplined flesh is hardened by adversity, as if congealed by frost and winter winds.[53] Adversity awakens the mind and clarifies confusion. The grief of penitence stabilizes the soul, reason returns, and discretion is sharpened so man can separate the divine gifts from human weakness.[54] The Lord may give gifts in prosperity, but he reveals them truly in adversity.[55] The scourge of temptation cuts through the flesh and reveals the bone of man's hidden strength. But though adversity makes known man's patience and love of God, still man's relative weakness is revealed.[56]

In *Moralia* 26, Gregory explains succinctly how the spiritual adversity of temptation and even sin becomes prosperity:

> By a marvelous dispensation our Creator permits the soul elevated by prosperity to be stricken suddenly with temptation, so that it may see itself more truly in weakness, and now improved may descend from the pinnacle of pride which it claimed by its virtues. . . . [F]rom that very adversity of temptation you will know how vainly you formerly prided yourself in your greatness. . . . [S]ince humility advances through temptation, that very adversity which keeps the mind from pride is prosperous.[57]

When temptation deflates the prosperity of virtue, it is as if the hand of sin has entered the heart, or the house of one's virtue has been overturned. Almost every virtue and good work can be lost, even prayer and contemplation.[58] The mind is pierced with fear of judgment and becomes penitent. But with a confession of humility, which is a sacrifice in imitation of Job and Christ, spiritual health returns. Because Christ has reor-

---

52. *Mor.* 10.13.23–24 (CCL 143, 554).

53. *Mor.* 29.30.65 (CCL 143B, 1480).

54. *Mor.* 2.46–50.73–80 (CCL 143, 101–8); *Mor.* 8.10.20 (CCL 143, 396–97).

55. *Mor.* 23.26.52 (CCL 143B, 1185–86).

56. *Mor.* 23.25.51 (CCL 143B, 1184–85); *Mor.* 23.1.1 (CCL 143B, 1143–44); *Mor.* 5.16.33 (CCL 143, 240–41); *Mor.*23.24.48 (CCL 143B, 1180–81); *Mor.* 2.43.68 (CCL 143, 100); *Mor.* 9.53.80 (CCL 143, 511–12).

57. *Mor.* 26.44–45.81–82 (CCL 143B, 1327): "Mira autem dispensatione agitur, ut conditor noster subleuatum prosperis animum subita concuti temptatione permittat, quatenus semetipsum in infirmitate uerius uideat; et ab eo quem de uirtutibus sumpserat, iam seipso melior elationis fastu descendat . . . in ipsa aduersitatis temptatione consideras quam frustra prius de te magna elatus aestimabas . . . cum per temptationem humilitas proficit, prospera est ipsa aduersitas quae mentem ab elatione custodit." Cf. Cassian *inst.* 12.8.12–15, where God heals by opposites, that those who are ruined in pride may be restored in humility; also *inst.* 11.6.19–20; *inst.* 11.10.26–27; *conl.* 4.3–4.

58. *Mor.* 26.45.82 (CCL 143B, 1327–28); *Mor.* 11.50.68 (CCL 143A, 624–25); *Mor.* 24.11.29 (CCL 143B, 1208–9); *Mor.* 2.49.79 (CCL 143, 107–8); *HEz.* 1.5.11–12 (CCL 142, 62–64); *HEz.* 1.1.15 (CCL 142, 12–13); *HEz.* 2.2.3 (CCL 142, 226–27); cf. Cassian *conl.* 4.3; 4.12; 4.16.

dered the world in redeeming man, virtue and vice can be complementary remedies.[59]

> What is virtue unless a medicine? and what is vice unless a wound? Therefore, since we make a wound of our medicine he makes a medicine from our wound, and we who are wounded by virtue are healed by vice. For we pervert the gift of virtue to the practice of vice, and he applies the delights of vice to promote virtue. He wounds our health to heal it, so that we who flee from humility when we run, may cling to humility as we fall.[60]

Virtue is a medicine when it supplies spiritual merits, but it can turn into a vice when it inflates self-importance and induces pride. Vice usually wounds the soul with sin, but it can turn into the medicine of humility. Both are positive and negative, spiritual and carnal; when joined, the negative potential of virtue and vice is checked. All of this is possible through Christ. The Mediator joins spiritual and carnal paradoxically in himself and extends this paradoxical order to govern all human experience, mysteriously reuniting body and soul, carnal and spiritual sides of life.

Gregory sees the equilibrium of the Christian as a mean between extremes, a point of balance between the spirit and flesh of which man is a composite. Vices and virtues, good works and temptations keep the natural propensities of spirit and flesh in the right equilibrium: for this reason we endure the Pauline warfare of spirit and flesh. Gregory explains:

> For the flesh drags us to the depths lest the spirit puff us up, and the spirit draws us to the heights lest the flesh fall down. For if the spirit did not raise us, we would be in the depths, and if the flesh did not weigh us down, we would exalt ourselves because of the heights.[61]

It is the balance of body and soul that enables one to avoid dangerous extremes of pride and despair. In an exegesis of Job 28:25 ("And he apportioned with waters"), Gregory depicts the hearts of the elect as regulated like water weighed out in proportion, presumably on a scale, an image found in Cassian.[62]

> By a certain control when each of the saints is caught up to the heights inwardly, he is still tempted outwardly that he may neither fall into de-

---

59. Cf. Cassian *inst*. 12.8.1 ff.
60. *Mor*. 33.12.25 (CCL 143B, 1695).
61. *Mor*. 19.6.12 (CCL 143A, 964): "Ad ima quippe trahit caro ne extollat spiritus; et ad summa trahit spiritus ne prosternat caro. Spiritus leuat ne iaceamus in infimis; caro aggrauat ne extollamur ex summis." See the balance of flesh and spirit described in Cassian *conl*. 4.12.
62. Cassian *conl*. 4.12; *conl*. 1.20–21.

spair nor rush into pride. Neither does external temptation accomplish sin, because interior intention draws him up, nor again does interior intention elevate him in pride, because exterior temptation humbles him, and weighs him down. Thus very appropriately, we recognize what we receive for interior perfection and what we are by external defects. And it happens in a marvelous way that one should neither be exalted because of virtue, nor hopeless because of temptation, for when the spirit draws us, the flesh drags us back again, and by the most subtle moderation of internal judgment the soul is balanced in a certain mean between the highest and lowest things. So it is well said, "And he apportioned the waters."[63]

Like waters apportioned in a balance, the heart of the saint is in equilibrium. By setting off virtue against temptation, the wondrous dispensation of God allows inward and outward, high and low, spirit and flesh, pride and despair to be balanced. Spiritual virtue checks the carnal excess of sin and despair caused by sin. Temptation checks spiritual excess and pride by making the soul humble; indeed "weakness" is the very "guardian of virtue."[64] The midpoint or mean between spiritual and carnal elements is a balance point of health that gives man both humility and hope. When the enemy attacks, it is precisely this balance of soul and solid intention of thought that he disrupts.[65] In the *Homilies on Ezechiel*, Gregory returns to the imagery of apportioned waters and expands the reconciliations. Explaining how temptation and contemplation are mutual remedies, he continues:

> By a marvelous dispensation, the soul is balanced in a certain mean, so that it neither vaunts itself in good things nor falls down in evils. Whence through blessed Job it is said of the Lord, "And he apportioned the waters" [Jb 28:25]. Indeed for God to apportion the waters is to keep the sensibility of the soul in humility between prosperity and adversity, gifts and temptations, high and low things.[66]

63. *Mor.* 19.6.12 (CCL 143A, 964): "Sed fit certo moderamine ut dum unusquisque sanctorum iam quidem interius ad summa rapitur, sed adhuc temptatur exterius, nec desperationis lapsum, nec elationis incurrat; quoniam nec temptatio exterior culpam perficit, quia interior intentio sursum trahit; nec rursum intentio interior in superbiam eleuat, quia temptatio exterior humiliat dum grauat. Sicque magno ordine cognoscimus in interiori profectu quid accipimus, in exteriori defectu quid sumus. Et miro modo agitur, ut nec de uirtute quisquam extolli debeat, nec de temptatione desperet, quia dum spiritus trahit et caro retrahit, subtilissimo iudicii interni moderamine, infra summa et supra infima in quodam medio anima libratur. Bene ergo dicitur: 'Et aquas appendit mensura.'"

64. *Mor.* 19.6.12 (CCL 143A, 964): "infirmitas custos uirtutis."

65. *Mor.* 8.24.43 (CCL 143, 414).

66. *HEz.* 2.2.3 (CCL 142, 226–27): "Sed mira dispensatione in quodam medio anima libratur, ut neque in bonis superbiat neque in malis cadat. Vnde et per beatum Iob de Domino dicitur: 'Et aquas appendit mensura.' Aquas quippe Deo mensura appendere est inter

The saint and the good Christian keep their hearts in a mean, balanced between the trials of adversity and prosperity, sin and virtue, the high things of heaven and the low things of the earth.

The soul's constancy, its equilibrium and balance, is effected by *discretio*. The interior "scale" of discretion weighs and balances all decisions.[67] Discretion entails not only the ability to discern virtue and rectitude but also the ability to control one's behavior, to temper one's actions so that pernicious excesses are avoided. The line of discretion is extended as a mean between the extremes of authority and humility, and the discretion of the good Christian avoids extreme behavior by exercising and relaxing virtues as the situation demands. Discretion is especially important for the proper ascetic practices. The monk should travel the road to Bethsamis, turning neither to the right nor to the left (cf. 1 Sm 6:12); that is, he should not afflict the flesh beyond measure, for spiritual works consist in more than just defeating the flesh. But if the flesh is not afflicted sufficiently, it becomes proud and refuses to submit in servitude to the mind.[68] Gregory's ideal of moderation secures this proper balance: just as the strings of the lute are tightened or loosened to achieve the proper tension, so virtues must be moderated to attain a suitable harmony.[69]

With the most careful discernment and discrimination, holy men are able to distinguish necessity from pleasure, so the needs of the flesh do not turn into occasions of vice.[70] And the prelate possessing discretion knows the proper remedy for each spiritual illness and each particular patient, as Gregory explains in *Pastoral Rule*.[71] Ultimately, discretion keeps the soul balanced, both by illuminating the narrow path between moderate virtue and vicious excess, and by balancing all experience, the external changes of adversity and prosperity. Gregory quotes Ecclesiastes 11:27, "In the day of good things, do not forget evils, and in the day of evils, do not forget the good,"[72] and comments:

> For whoever accepts gifts, but does not also fear the scourges in the time of gifts, falls into pride through joy. Moreover, whoever is stricken by scourges, but never consoles himself with the gifts allotted him, is

---

prospera et aduersa, inter dona et tentationes, inter summa et infima animarum sensum in humilitate custodire."

67. Cf. *Mor.* 33.35.60 (CCL 143B, 1725); *Mor.* 8.4.5 (CCL 143, 384); *Mor.* 3.13.24 (CCL 143, 130).

68. *In lib. I Reg.* 3.112 (CCL 144, 261–62).

69. *Mor.* 20.51.78 (CCL 143A, 1061).

70. *Mor.* 20.14.28 (CCL 143A, 1024–25).

71. See Dagens's discussion, *Saint Grégoire*, 123ff.

72. *Mor.* 3.9.16 (CCL 143, 124–25).

pulled down from his stability of mind by every kind of despair. Thus each should be joined to the other so that one is always supported by the other. Just as memory of gifts should temper the punishment of scourges, so fear and expectation of scourging should pierce the joy of gifts. Accordingly the holy man, to soothe his depressed mind amidst his wounds, considers the sweetness of his gifts during the pain of his scourges, saying, "If we have received good things from the hand of the Lord, why should we not endure the evils?" [Jb 2:10].[73]

To recognize that both prosperities and adversities are sent by God is to understand that God has designed both to be used as medicinal remedies for spiritual health. Thus prosperity becomes a healing ointment, and adversity an excision of the wound.[74] Memory of sweet gifts heals the pain of the scourge, while recollection of the scourge cleanses the mind of excessive joy and pride. In *Homilies on Ezechiel* 2.7.15, Gregory expresses a similar idea of attaining balance through memory. The Christian holds a palm in the right and left hands, being neither elevated to the right by pride in prosperity, nor deflected and broken at the left by despair in adversity. A palm encircles his forehead, for the Christian remembers adversity in prosperity to check pride, and prosperity in adversity to preserve hope. In a related image, the soul is held in balance between an upper and lower millstone of hope and fear. Hope of salvation lifts the soul, while fear of damnation depresses it. The good Christian holds these two millstones balanced in his breast, for he hopes in vain for mercy if he does not fear justice, and he fears justice in vain if he does not hope for mercy.[75] Having such a memory and balance, Job's soul is "moderated marvelously between high and low things."[76]

From Gregory's descriptions of the soul's equilibrium one can deduce a spiritual topography of the *anima in medio libratur* (Figure 2). The series of complementarities can also be depicted as a Pythagorean square (Figure 3).

Carnal can become spiritual, and spiritual carnal. The "contradictory" of spirit and flesh are each ambivalent, being both positive and neg-

73. *Mor.* 3.9.16 (CCL 143, 125): "Quisquis enim dona percipit sed donorum tempore nequaquam etiam flagella pertimescit in elatione per laetitiam corruit. Quisquis autem flagellis atteritur, sed flagellorum tempore nequaquam se ex donis quae eum contigit accepisse, consolatur ab statu mentis omnimoda desperatione destruitur. Sic ergo utraque iungenda sunt ut unum semper ex altero fulciatur; quatenus et flagelli poenam memoria temperet doni et doni laetitiam mordeat suspicio ac formido flagelli. Sanctus igitur uir ut oppressam mentem inter uulnera mulceat in flagellorum doloribus blandimenta donorum pensat dicens: 'Si bona accepimus de manu Domini mala quare non sustineamus?'"

74. *Mor.* 5.36.71 (CCL 143, 271).

75. *Mor.* 33.12.24 (CCL 143B, 1694); cf. *Mor.* 7.32.48–49 (CCL 143, 370–71).

76. *Mor.* 26.17.30 (CCL 143B, 1287): "inter alta et infima mirabiliter temperatur."

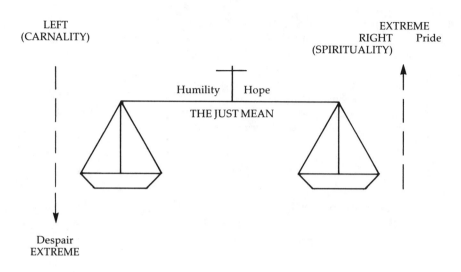

2. The Balanced Soul

ative, but also complementary, for the negative extreme of each checks the other. The healthful balance of humility and hope is produced from reciprocal remedies.

This pattern of the complementarity of spiritual and carnal governs the Christian's life, not only inwardly in his own virtue and sin but also outwardly in the life he pursues and in the Church he loves and serves. To achieve the requisite sacrifice of will, man cannot be allowed to pursue either a contemplative or an active life exclusively. Both lives must be held, for activity balances the pride of spirit, where man forgets his virtues are the gifts of God, and contemplation balances the pride of flesh, where man forgets God by scattering his soul in God's external gifts. The horizontal width (*latitudo*) of action is countered by the vertical height (*altitudo*) of contemplation.[77] He who extends himself in the breadth of practice must also raise himself to the heights of contemplation.[78] Since the width of charity and the height of contemplation are proportional,[79] the two lives reinforce one another. The heart first poured upward in contemplation is poured back down with knowledge and charity to execute

77. *HEz.* 2.2.15 (CCL 142, 235–36).
78. *Mor.* 6.37.56 (CCL 143, 325–26). See Patrick Catry, "L'Amour du prochain chez saint Grégoire le Grand," *StMon* 20 (1978): 287–344.
79. *HEz.* 1.12.10 (CCL 142, 188).

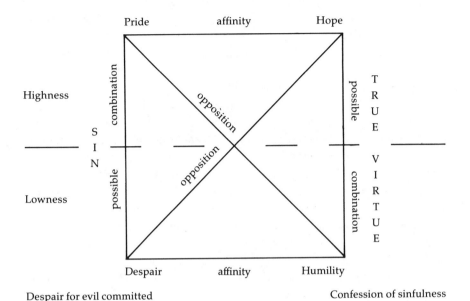

LEFT (CARNALITY)
Pride in good works
Sin of Spirit

RIGHT (SPIRITUALITY)
Goodness
Virtue of Spirit

Pride   affinity   Hope

Highness

combination

opposition

S
I
N

possible

opposition

Lowness

possible

T
R
U
E

possible

V
I
R
T
U
E

combination

Despair   affinity   Humility

Despair for evil committed
Sin of Flesh

Confession of sinfulness
Virtue of Flesh

3. A Pythagorean Square of the Soul's Balance

external works.[80] Conversely, like prophets returning home from the fields (Ez 3:24), by going outside, one is led to highest vision;[81] by bending, one is made erect.[82] As the height of contemplation pulls man upward and counters the outward dispersion of the active life, the "dust" of temptation and minor sins contracted in the active life checks the possible pride that might arise from satisfaction in the purity of the contemplative life.[83] A man is perfect only insofar as he bears the sorrows of others,[84] and the light of secret vision is given only as a reward for good works.[85]

The imagery Gregory uses to express the complementarity of active

80. *Mor.* 6.37.56 (CCL 143, 325–26); *HEz.* 1.12.10 (CCL 142, 188); *Mor.* 12.52.59 (CCL 143A, 664).

81. *HEz.* 1.12.10 (CCL 142, 188).

82. *Mor.* 7.15.18 (CCL 143, 345).

83. *Mor.* 1.13.31 (CCL 143, 42).

84. *Mor.* 19.11.18 (CCL 143A, 969): "Tanto enim quisque perfectus est, quanto perfecte sentit dolores alienos."

85. *In lib. I Reg.* 3.116 (CCL 144, 263).

and contemplative lives is rich and varied.[86] In addition to Rachel and Leah, Mary and Martha, there are also the two wives of Helcana from 1 Kings,[87] Isaiah and Jeremiah,[88] the angels of Ezechiel's vision who hold the hand of good works under the wing of contemplation (Ez 1:8),[89] and the twice-dyed garments of the priest in Mosaic Law.[90] Paul descends from the third heaven to serve his neighbor;[91] Jacob returns home from his fields;[92] and Christ himself is a cornerstone who perfectly unites activity and contemplation, love of God and love of neighbor (cf. Jb 38:6).[93] In all cases, the active life of loving and serving one's neighbor complements the contemplative life of loving and serving God. Love and service of neighbor and of God successively increase one another.[94] One moves first from love and service of neighbor to love of God; and the love of God returns man to earth with greater love with which to serve his neighbor.[95]

As the individual reconciles the more carnal and the more spiritual vocations, so the corporate identity of the Christian in the Church is based on the reconciliation of spiritual and carnal elements. Gregory's notion of concord in diversity in the Church embodies the complementarity of spiritual and carnal.[96] The more spiritual members of the Church are the eyes who adorn the body with sight and beauty, the more carnal are the feet who serve and protect the eyes, suffering to labor in the dust of Babylon. Each member needs the other to supply what it lacks, and each remedies the other in a concord that checks carnal extremes. That the eyes humble themselves to serve the feet checks the possible pride of the contemplative's retreat and isolation. Indeed the contemplatives grow more perfect recognizing their own imperfection and need of others: "[And the eyes] penetrate the highest things more subtly, the more

86. *Ep.* 1.5 (CCL 140, 5–7); *HEz.* 2.2.15 (CCL 142, 235–36); and *HEz.* 1.3.9 (CCL 142, 37).

87. *In lib. I Reg.* 1.64 (CCL 144, 89–90).

88. *Reg. Past.* 1.7 (PL 77, 20); *Ep.* 7.5 (CCL 140, 448ff.).

89. *HEz.* 1.3.9 (CCL 142, 37).

90. *HEz.* 2.4.3 (CCL 142, 259). See also *Reg. Past.* 2.3 (PL 77, 29), and *Mor.* 6.37.56 (CCL 143, 325–26). See Catry's further discussion of images in "L'Amour du prochain," 287–94.

91. *Reg. Past.* 2.5 (PL 77, 32); Cf. *Mor.* 6.35.54 (CCL 143, 322–24).

92. *Mor.* 5.11.20 (CCL 143, 231–32); cf. *HEz.* 1.12.10 (CCL 142, 188).

93. *Mor.* 28.13.33 (CCL 143B, 1420).

94. *HEz.* 2.3.11 (CCL 142, 243); *HEz.* 2.2.15 (CCL 142, 235–36); cf. *Mor.* 7.24.28 (CCL 143, 352–53).

95. *Mor.* 10.15.31 (CCL 143, 559–60); see also *HEz.* 1.5.12–13 (CCL 142, 63–64).

96. Paul Meyvaert, "Diversity Within Unity, a Gregorian Theme," in *Benedict, Gregory, Bede, and Others,* Variorum Reprints CS 61 (London, 1977), VI:141–61. Meyvaert deals with the direct political applications of this theme—i.e., Gregory's acceptance of different liturgical practices—which is an excellent example of the connection between thought and action.

humbly for love of the Creator they do not scorn the lower ones."[97] That the feet submit themselves for spiritual guidance remedies their sinfulness and pride in the world; otherwise they would not be saved at all. Too, each member serves as a visual reminder to the other of humility. The weaknesses of the active man are public, his strengths hidden. The strengths of the contemplative are public, his weaknesses hidden. Therefore the contemplative should grow humble by considering the hidden strengths of the active man, the active man by considering the open strengths of the contemplative.[98]

A complementary relationship even exists between the Church and the secular powers. The emperor is within the Church, and, as Gregory admonishes Emperor Maurice, he has been given power to do good, to open the way to heaven more widely, so that the earthly kingdom may wait upon the heavenly kingdom.[99] Christ has committed his priests to the emperor's care, and he may be called upon as a "warrior of the Lord" to fight "enemies of the Church."[100] While the Church depends upon secular powers to wield the sword on her behalf, secular powers must look to the Church for moral guidance. The princely rhinoceros in Job 39:9–10 must feed humbly at the crib of spiritual wisdom supplied by the Church.[101] Again, the knowledge that each needs the other for reciprocal tasks should ensure humility and concord.

Members of the Church are also like the creatures in Ezechiel's vision who stretch their wings under the firmament to one another (cf. Ez 1:23).[102] Each has virtues to impart to the others. By extending their wings to touch the tip of another's, they communicate their gifts in a loving caress. One enlightens the darkness of another's ignorance, the second (with whom Gregory identifies himself) uses his temporal power to comfort and defend the first. Similarly, the Church is the temple of Jerusalem rebuilt in marvelous order (Ez 40). As stone is placed upon stone, so in the holy Church each one carries another and in turn is borne by another.[103] If a stone in the wall is thrown too far outward, in secular cares and desires of worldly honor, it is recalled inward. Conversely, if a stone

---

97. *Mor.* 31.13.25 (CCL 143B, 1568).

98. *Mor.* 31.13.25 (CCL 143B, 1568).

99. *Ep.* 3.61 (CCL 140, 210).

100. Ibid.; *Ep.* 1.72 (CCL 140, 80–81).

101. *Mor.* 31.3.3–4 (CCL 143B, 1551–2). The exegesis of the rhinoceros as a type of the secular powers is in *Mor.* 31.2.2–6.8 (CCL 143B, 1549–55). For a discussion of this passage and its implications for political theology, see Marc Reydellet, *La royauté dans la littérature latine de Sidoine Apollinaire à Isidore de Seville* (Rome, 1981), 441–503.

102. *HEz.* 1.7.21 (CCL 142, 96).

103. *HEz.* 2.1.5 (CCL 142, 211).

is too inward, seeking to be hidden and bearing only its own cares, it is led outward, so that it can be useful to many.[104] Each soul is humbled, recognizing its dependence on others for what it lacks; each soul is charitable in serving the needs of the other.[105] So also, rich and poor perform services to one another, cementing the Church together: the rich give alms to the poor, and the poor pray for the rich. Being especially near God, their intercession is very powerful.[106]

This reconciliation of the more spiritual and the more carnal members of the Church is also expressed hierarchically. Abraham, Isaac, and Jacob represent three levels of Christian progress: the moral, the natural, and the contemplative lives—equivalents of the ethical, physical, and theoretical lives in ancient Greek tradition.[107] Proverbs, Ecclesiastes, and Song of Songs form a "ladder" leading the Christian to higher and higher degrees of understanding.[108] Gregory's church encompasses varying levels of the faithful: the preachers, the continent, and the good married couples, symbolized by Noah, Daniel, and Job.[109] Their merits are unequal, yet each has a place in the Church. They are made of the same "earth," though distinguished diversely; they have one faith and one charity, even if unequal.[110]

This pattern of complementarity arises from the basic paradoxes of Christ's Incarnation and the exchange of spiritual and carnal that takes place through Christ. Classical ideas of virtue as a mean between extremes, of health as a balance of opposites become part of this paradoxical order. To what extent Gregory draws on Christian sources long steeped in classical tradition or returns anew to classical sources is impossible to say; in general Gregory certainly prefers Cassian, Ambrose, and Augustine to Cicero or Seneca, and hellenistic ideas of medicine and geography are simply his cultural heritage. Whatever the source, Gregory uses ideas of balance and opposition to shape Christianity in a new way. The mu-

---

104. *HEz.* 2.1.10 (CCL 142, 216).

105. *Mor.* 28.10.22 (CCL 143B, 1413).

106. *HEv.* 2.40.10 (PL 76, 1309–10); a traditional Christian theme, cf. William Countryman, *The Rich Christian in the Church of the Early Empire: Contradictions and Accommodations* (New York and Toronto, 1980), esp. 118ff.

107. *Cant.* 9 (CCL 144, 12), cf. Rufin. *Orig. in cant.* 1.1. For a full discussion of the sources Gregory used comparing the commentary, see Rodrigue Bélanger, *Grégoire le Grand, Commentaire sur le Cantique des Cantiques*, SC 314 (Paris, 1984), 29–49.

108. Ibid.

109. *Mor.* 1.14.20 (CCL 143, 34); *Mor.* 30.6.23 (CCL 143B, 1506); *HEz.* 1.8.10 (CCL 142, 107); *HEz.* 2.1.7 (CCL 142, 213–14); *HEz.* 2.4.5 (CCL 142, 261); *HEz.* 2.7.3 (CCL 142, 317).

110. *Mor.* 30.6.23 (CCL 143B, 1506). See Aelred K. Squire, "The *ordo amantium* in Gregory the Great," *Studia Patristica* (to appear), who argues that the *ordo amantium* in *In lib. I Reg* refers not exclusively to monks, but to all the faithful.

sical harmony and complementarity of the universe is deeply reassuring, not because it necessarily adumbrates God's mercy, for this is not implicit, but rather because it provides the Christian with a chance to help himself. Through the exercise of *discretio* the Christian learns to anticipate changes and conquer them through self-control. At least the Christian knows the terms of God's trial, and he is challenged to struggle and fight with all the weapons available to him.

In this struggle the Christian's great defense lies in the *arx mentis*, that unassailable citadel of self-control which allows one to remain safely disengaged from worldly affairs, though deeply involved in them. Prosperity is undertaken reluctantly, with detachment and disinterest, even as adversity is sought willingly.[111] Admittedly, engagement in worldly activities is an ambivalent enterprise, lawful in intention and yet unlawful in practice, like the ways of the camel: "Thus earthly dispensations, like the ways of the camel, agree with the Law in the head, and disagree in the foot, since the things that they desire by living justly are of heaven, and the things in which they are busied in work are of this world."[112]

But as long as the heart clings to God internally, one can brave the temptations of external affairs. Being both *in mundo* and *extra mundum*,[113] one is also like Adam sleeping, unconscious of the world, yet awake to dreams of God.[114] The bride of Song of Songs expresses this same division, "I sleep, and my heart is awake" (5:2). Man's mind should be always fixed upon God;[115] his worldly position borne externally, as a carnal shell. Just as he governs his body with temperance and restraint, so should he exercise his office with moderation and discernment.[116] Despising power, he should keep it "secret" and "hidden" from himself, only making such power "public" and "knowing" it so that he might perform good deeds.[117] With such internal dissociation from power, "citizens of Jerusalem [can] serve in the work of Babylon," for the elect of God have "moral excel-

---

111. *Mor.* 35.14.30 (CCL 143B, 1794): "Debet ergo oboedientia et in aduersis ex suo aliquid habere, et rursum in prosperis ex suo aliquid omnimodo non habere, quatenus et in aduersis tanto sit gloriosior quanto diuino ordini etiam ex desiderio iungitur, et in prosperis tanto sit uerior quanto a praesenti ipsa quam diuinitus percipit gloria funditus ex mente separatur."

112. *Mor.* 1.28.40 (CCL 143, 46): "Terrenae igitur dispensationes, quasi camelorum more, capite legi concordant, pede discrepant; quia et caeli sunt quae iuste uiuentes appetunt et huius mundi sunt ea in quibus opere uersantur."

113. *Mor.* 22.16.35 (CCL 143A, 1117).

114. *Mor.* 30.16.54 (CCL 143B, 1528).

115. *Mor.* 23.20.38 (CCL 143B, 1173).

116. Cf. *Mor.* 18.43.68 (CCL 143A, 933–35).

117. *Mor.* 26.40.73 (CCL 143B, 1320–21); *Dial.* 1.9.7 (SC 260, 80–82); *Mor.* 9.25.37 (CCL 143, 481–82).

lence" and "moderation," and they "do not seek their own gain."[118] The elect can sit on the sidelines (*ex latere respicere*), "using" the things of this world to comfort them on their pilgrimage, rather than being "possessed" by them.[119]

Outwardly there is highest honor, but inwardly the grief of afflictions engenders humility; outwardly the glory of power, but inwardly the secret sacrifice of a contrite heart.[120] One should be like David, who conquered the pride of his power through the inward sacrifice of humility.[121] Those exalted by God to perform worldly offices must always remember they are sinful and thus equal to the rest of the human race.[122] Yet more than this, those who serve should be humbled by their involvement in the world. Prelates are oxen, who chew the "cud" of contemplation. Nevertheless, they are "yoked" with the burden of office and become defiled with the "dust" of the world.[123]

To engage in worldly life is to sacrifice the chance for attaining purity and innocence, since sin is inextricably mixed in worldly affairs.[124] The active life is a "descent to torture."[125] One can be subjected to the torture of praise, though it will purify the just even as it damns the wicked.[126] Service is to be a sacrifice of charity in imitation of Christ.[127] "Following the Lord, they bear the cross the more truly, the more sharply they conquer themselves and are tortured by compassion and love for their neighbors."[128] Christ's law of charity commands that we bear one another's burdens (Gal 6:2). All Christians have a duty to take care of their family in the Church and to use the gifts God has given to benefit others.[129] For Gregory, this charity is not simply a concern for souls; bodily needs must

118. *Ep.* 8.33 (CCL 143A, 557–59).

119. *HEv.* 2.36.11 (PL 76, 1272).

120. *Mor.* 20.38.73 (CCL 143A, 1056–57); see also *Mor.* 26.26.46 (CCL 143B, 1301–2).

121. *Mor.* 26.26.47 (CCL 143B, 1302): "Ecce humilitatis hostiam ab intimo cordis oblatam crebro replicat, et iterum atque iterum confitendo offerre non cessat; eamque multipliciter loquens iudicis sui oculis ostentat. . . . Et quomodo istud sacrificium Deo, placere cognouerat . . . nisi quod uicina esse superbia potentibus solet, et paene semper rebus affluentibus elatio sociatur, quia et saepe humoris abundantia duritiam dat tumoris?"

122. Cf. *Mor.* 21.15.22 (CCL 143A, 1082); *Mor.* 26.26.46 (CCL 143B, 1301–2).

123. *Mor.* 7.12.14 (CCL 143, 343–44).

124. *Mor.* 17.22.32 (CCL 143A, 869).

125. *Mor.* 13.41.46 (CCL 143A, 693); this is said of the Church as well as of the minds of the good.

126. *Mor.* 26.34.62 (CCL 143B, 1314).

127. E.g., *HEv.* 2.34.2 (PL 76, 1247).

128. *Mor.* 30.25.74 (CCL 143B, 1542): "Qui sequentes Dominum tanto uerius crucem tollunt, quanto acrius et se edomant, et erga promixos suos caritatis compassione cruciantur."

129. *Reg. Past.* 2.5 (PL 77, 32–33).

be succored as well.[130] Ultimately, to prefer solitude and privacy to the service of others is wrong. Our compassion for others easily "washes away" the temptation aroused by helping them.[131]

Despite Gregory's condemnations of the active life and temporal prosperity, in the end he affirms them in a regenerated form. Temporal power, like marriage,[132] is good, though attendant circumstances may push the Christian to extremes of carnality if discretion is wanting. But if internal humility can be preserved, all is well: "That temporal power is great which in being well administered has a special reward from God; and yet sometimes it swells in pride from being set over others."[133] Wealth and property are not faults, but the reaction toward such fortune may be.[134] Some are lifted by good fortune to pride, others to do great works of mercy. All things of God's creation are good, the abuse of them is the cause of sin. Even the rich are not endangered if they are humble; Abraham was prosperous and elect.[135] Certainly both rich and poor can lead carnal lives.[136]

Precisely because Gregory believes so strongly in internal humility and in the power of repentance to restore humility continually before God, he is blessed with a generosity of vision rare among the early Fathers of the Church. What counts is the internal disposition of humility, not external circumstances, whether they be considered prosperous or adverse in the eyes of those proud of their seeming virtue or those benumbed by carnal comforts.[137] The purity of the truly righteous man is a "lamp despised by the rich" (Jb 12:5), by those "swollen" with either spiritual pride or carnal goods.[138] As long as the Christian inwardly shines with virtue in God's sight, he will sit among the predestined at Judgment Day, even if he is despised in this life by the sanctimonious, or by the

130. *Ep.* 1.44 (CCL 140, 58).

131. *Reg. Past.* 2.5 (PL 77, 32–34).

132. Sexuality and power are connected, both being dangerous "elations," assertions of self that tend to puff one up. On the need for clergy to refrain from marriage, thus keeping their power pure, see Samuel Laeuchli, *Power and Sexuality: The Emergence of Canon Law at the Synod of Elivra* (Philadelphia, 1972).

133. *Mor.* 26.26.44 (CCL 143B, 1299).

134. *Mor.* 10.30.49 (CCL 143, 571–72): "Nam sunt nonnulli quos census per tumorem non eleuat, sed per misericordiae opera exaltat. Et sunt nonnulli qui, dum se terrenis opibus abundare conspiciunt, ueras Dei diuitias non requirunt atque aeternam patriam non amant, quia hoc sibi sufficere, quod rebus temporalibus fulciuntur, putant. Non est ergo census in crimine sed affectus. Cuncta enim quae Deus condidit bona sunt; sed qui bonis male utitur profecto agit ut, quasi per edacitatis ingluuiem, eo per quem uiuere debuit pane moriatur."

135. Ibid.

136. *Mor.* 15.56.65 (CCL 143A, 790–91).

137. *Mor.* 10.30.49–51 (CCL 143, 571–75).

138. *Mor.* 10.30.49–50 (CCL 143, 571–72).

wealthy. And, to Gregory, this means that not merely "a few will reach the summit of perfection," for God has said, "I will number them and multiply them above the sands."[139]

The soul's perfection lies in recognizing imperfection, in remembering how short one has fallen of Christ's rule, in recalling to mind the faults and wickedness that leave their ugly, indelible traces on the soul. Imperfection ensures humility, and for this reason Providence leaves at least one vice, so man will not be carried off in pride: for the mind shines all the more truly for contrast with smaller faults.[140] The Christian can advance in virtue through temptation,[141] and the recollection of sin only makes him cling to God with greater gratitude and longing.[142] This perfection in imperfection not only defines the Christian's relation to God but also supports his ties with his neighbors. Recognizing his own imperfection increases the Christian's tolerance and sympathy for others. To be perfect is to tolerate a neighbor's imperfection with patience.[143] The Christian becomes willing to help others, and his own imperfection is no bar in helping them advance. At the very moment holy men think themselves ruined, they are actually most successful in reaching others.[144] The righteous are wounded physicians who nevertheless heal others.[145]

Humility refines compassion, and compassion in turn strengthens the soul. Man finds true stability giving himself to others, true perfection recognizing he is but human and fallible. The omnipotent God even permitted Peter, the shepherd of the Church, to be frightened by a handmaiden and to sin in denying Christ in a moment of panic.[146] We must ask ourselves why God did this, Gregory says, and he offers an answer relevant to all who bear power:

> This we recognize certainly as an act performed by [God's] dispensation of great mercy, so that he who was to be shepherd of the Church might discern in his own sin how he should have compassion for others. And so first [the Lord] shows [Peter] to himself and then sets him over others, so that from his own weakness he might recognize how to bear mercifully with the weaknesses of others.[147]

139. *Mor.* 10.31.52 (CCL 143, 575–76), cf. Ps 139:18.
140. *Mor.* 4.23.43 (CCL 143, 189).
141. *Mor.* 34.22.45 (CCL 143B, 1765).
142. *Mor.* 4.36.72 (CCL 143, 216–17).
143. *Mor.* 5.16.33 (CCL 143B, 241): "Ille enim uere perfectus est qui erga imperfectionem proximi impatiens non est. Nam qui alienam imperfectionem ferre non ualens deserit, ipse sibi testis est quod perfecte necdum proficit."
144. *Mor.* 5.3–4.4–5 (CCL 143, 220–22).
145. *Mor.* 3.16.30 (CCL 143, 134–35).
146. *HEv.* 2.21.4 (PL 76, 1171–72).
147. *HEv.* 2.21.4 (PL 76, 1172).

CONCLUSION

The continuity Gregory perceives between spiritual and carnal realms yields different degrees and intensities of complementarity. We can diagram the continuities and polarities of spiritual and carnal by imagining a line of creation unfolding from God downward and then bending this line at midpoint (Figure 4). The original polarity of spirit and flesh is thereby displaced and duplicated, so that the carnal and spiritual axes are mirror images of each other, and each axis has a harsh and soft aspect. The intensities of the complementary oppositions vary, from radical opposition at the bottom of the diagram to identity and unity at the top. But in the series all the oppositions are analogous. Sacrifice effects the balance that unites spiritual and carnal; at the point of equilibrium, members of an antithetical pair exchange polarities.

God and the devil are certainly opposed, as goodness is to evil, yet the two have a complementary relationship. The devil is God's *exactor*, and the devil can even fulfill God's kindness as he vents his own anger. The devil and God each have two sides. God is the merciful and benevolent Creator as well as the just Judge, who will avenge sin and melt man in his wrath. The devil is both the fearsome enemy bent on destroying man and the comic trickster who teases St. Benedict. The Church and the state have a similar complementary relationship. The secular prince is the cruel rhinoceros who tramples others, yet he becomes the tame rhinoceros bound to serve the Church. The Church first suffers persecution and endures pitiful adversities, quite at odds with the world, yet becomes triumphant and prosperous, even exercising temporal power and enjoying great honor. The Church and state are interdependent: the Church needs the secular powers for protection and advancement of her interests, while the state needs the Church for moral instruction and redemption.

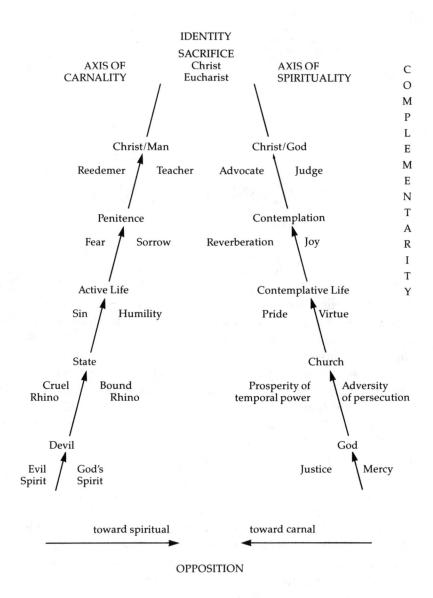

IDENTITY
SACRIFICE
Christ
Eucharist

AXIS OF
CARNALITY

AXIS OF
SPIRITUALITY

C
O
M
P
L
E
M
E
N
T
A
R
I
T
Y

Christ/Man

Christ/God

Reedemer   Teacher

Advocate   Judge

Penitence

Contemplation

Fear   Sorrow

Reverberation   Joy

Active Life

Contemplative Life

Sin   Humility

Pride   Virtue

State

Church

Cruel
Rhino

Bound
Rhino

Prosperity of
temporal power

Adversity
of persecution

Devil

God

Evil
Spirit

God's
Spirit

Justice   Mercy

toward spiritual

toward carnal

OPPOSITION

4. A Scale of Complementarity

An analogous complementarity exists between active and contemplative lives. Both have negative extremes. The active life can so entrap the soul in the world that the soul becomes numb and sinful. But the contemplative life is also dangerous, for the monk can be tempted by pride or may retire so completely from the world that he becomes forgetful of others. Too, the virtue and sin of these lives are reversible: virtue can wound in causing pride, and sin can become a cure when it restores humility. When joined, active and contemplative lives balance and even promote each other. From the active life the Christian gathers strength for contemplation, and from contemplation he brings insights to the active life. Contemplation and temptation alternate in much the same cyclical pattern. One's joy in contemplation is invariably struck down by temptation or worldly memories, yet this very failure humbles the soul and reconstitutes penitence, the first step of a reunion with God. Thus the compunctions of fear and love are related dialectically: love comes through fear, and one is lifted through penitential tears to joy. Yet joy often returns to sorrow, and fear replaces love, when the Christian returns to recognition of himself and regret for his carnal life.

At the center is Christ, joining flesh and spirit, God and man. Christ's sacrifice changes man's vision of God. If God is the terrifying judge, Christ's sacrifice reveals God to be merciful and gentle, for his Incarnation displays God's humility in becoming man and dying for man's sake. As man, he is the Redeemer who suffers in the flesh as only a human being can. Yet his life on earth also teaches perfect righteousness, for Christ is guided entirely by the divine Logos. As God, Christ will visit man with fierce vengeance on Judgment Day, yet he will also serve as the Advocate for the sinners he redeemed, continually interceding for mercy on their behalf. Christ is both Priest and Sacrifice, reconciler and reconciled. Through sacrifice, directions change and a cosmic equilibrium is attained. Christ's sacrifice is a lesson for man. If man rebels against God and is an enemy in sin, he becomes a son when he immolates his rebellion in sacrifice. Paul is the archetype of this conversion, for he changes from a cruel persecutor to a gentle victim, willing to fill up the suffering of Christ in his own body.

Sacrifice purifies and transforms the flesh of sinful humanity, restoring man to God, even as Christ's sacrifice makes this restoration possible. A marvelous cosmic equilibrium exists, for man's willingness to be a living sacrifice to God becomes his repayment of Christ's sacrifice. Finally, the sacrifice of the Eucharist symbolizes this cosmic reunion and balance, for at the moment of consecration, the heavens open, and visible and invisible, high and low, angels and man are joined and reconciled.

The balance of this system recalls Athenagoras's remark: "There is nothing disordered nor negligent in the constitution of the Universe; each thing happens rationally."[1] The intricate complementarity between carnal and spiritual shows that God's order is comprehensible or, as Gregory would say, it encourages hope. Yet the very dynamism of this reversible world shows that man must also preserve a salutary fear. Sacred and profane, carnal and spiritual, human and divine are interwoven and blended in a mysterious complementarity. Yet discretion must always be preserved to discern the individual lines of God's pattern for each human life.

1. *Leg.* 25, quoted by Spanneut, *Le Stoïcisme des Pères de l'Eglise de Clément de Rome à Clément d'Alexandrie* (Paris, 1969), 401.

BIBLIOGRAPHICAL ESSAY

The past ten years have brought such renewed interest in Gregory that extensive bibliographies are available. This essay is then extremely selective, and for further information the reader should consult the bibliographies provided by: Robert Markus, "Gregor I, der Grosse," *Theologische Realenzyklopädie* (Berlin and New York, 1985); 14: 135–45; Luigi Serenthà, "Introduzione Bibliografica allo Studio di S. Gregorio Magno," *Scuola Cattolica* 102 (1974): 283–301; Vera Paronetto, "Note Gregoriane: A Proposito di Alcune Recenti Pubblicazioni su Gregorio Magno," *RSCI* 34 (1980): 174–87; and *Obras de San Gregorio Magno*, B.A.C. 170 (Madrid, 1958), with an extensive bibliography by Melquiades Andrés. Recently published works can be located in the *Bulletin de théologie ancienne et médiévale*, *Bulletin d'histoire Bénédictine*, *L'Année Philologique*, and the Elenchus Bibliographicus published annually in *Ephemerides Theologicae Lovanienses*. An important aid for research has just been published in the Corpus Christianorum Series Latina, a dual volume *Thesaurus Sancti Gregorii Magni*, edited by CETEDOC (Brepols-Turnhout, 1986). The Thesaurus will at last help settle the redaction of the *Dialogues* and *In librum 1 Regum*.

A general overview of Gregory's era is provided by A. H. M. Jones, *The Later Roman Empire*, 2 vols. (Norman, Okla., 1964). A more detailed treatment is given in the excellent work by T. S. Brown, *Gentlemen and Officers: Imperial Administration and Aristocratic Power in Byzantine Italy, A.D. 554–800* (Rome, 1984), which makes extensive use of Gregory's letters. Brown offers major revisions to the older work on the exarchate of Ravenna by Charles Diehl, *Etudes sur l'administration byzantine de l'exarchat de Ravenne* (Paris, 1888), and he also modifies many conclusions drawn by André Guillou, *Régionalisme et indépendance dans l'empire byzantin au VIIe siècle: L'Exemple de l'exarchat et de la Pentapole d'Italie* (Rome, 1969). Several papers from Jacques Fontaine, Robert Gillet, and Stan Pellestrandi, eds., *Grégoire le Grand*, Colloques internationaux du Centre National de la Recherche Scientifique, Chantilly, 15–19 September 1982 (Paris, 1986) supply the latest research on Gregory's historical situation: Michel Rouche, "Grégoire le Grand face à la situation économique de son temps," 41–57; Charles Pietri, "Clercs et serviteurs laïcs de l'Eglise romaine au temps de Grégoire le Grand," 107–22; Lellia Cracco Ruggini, "Grégoire le Grand et le monde byzantin," 83–94.

The culture of Rome as a city is treated well by Peter Llewellyn, *Rome in the Dark Ages* (London, 1970); Bryan Ward-Perkins, *From Classical Antiquity to the Middle Ages: Urban Public Building in Northern and Central Italy, A.D. 300–850* (Oxford, 1984); and Carol Heitz, "Les Monuments de Rome à l'époque de Grégoire le Grand," Fontaine et al., eds., *Grégoire le Grand*, 31–39. Broader sketches of Gregory's society are provided by André Guillou, *Culture et société en Italie byzantine* (London, 1978); O. Bertolini, *Roma di fronte a Bisanzio e ai Longobardi* (Bologna, 1941), esp. 189–282; Robert E. McNally, "Gregory the Great (590–604) and His Declining World," *Archivum Historiae Pontificiae* 16 (1978): 7–26; Vincenzo Recchia, *Gregorio Magno e la società agricola*, Verba Seniorum, n.s. 8 (Rome, 1978).

Several volumes from the series *Settimane di Studio del Centro italiano di Studi sull'alto Medioevo* are pertinent in reconstructing Gregory's society and culture: vol. 9: *Il passaggio dell'Antichità al Medioevo in Occidente* (Spoleto, 1962); vol. 14: *La conversione al Cristianesimo nell'Europa dell'Alto Medioevo* (Spoleto, 1967); vol. 17: *La storiografia altomedievale* (Spoleto, 1970); vol. 19: *La scuola nell'Occidente latino dell'Alto Medioevo* (Spoleto, 1972); vol. 22: *La cultura antica nell'Occidente latino dal VII all'XI secolo* (Spoleto, 1975); vol. 23: *Simboli e simbologia nell'Alto Medioevo* (Spoleto, 1976). Useful too for the general climate of the times are Jacques Le Goff, *La Civilisation de l'occident médiéval* (Paris, 1964); Walter Emil Kaegi, Jr., *Byzantium and the Decline of Rome* (Princeton, 1968); and Averil Cameron, *Procopius and the Sixth Century* (Berkeley and Los Angeles, 1985).

For general biographies of Gregory, see Jeffrey Richards, *Consul of God: The Life and Times of Gregory the Great* (London, 1980); Emilio Gandolfo, *Gregorio Magno, Servo Dei Servi di Dio* (Milan, 1980); Raoul Manselli, *Gregorio Magno* (Turin, 1967); V. Battistelli, *Consul Dei: San Gregorio Magno*, La Via 5 (Alba-Rome, 1942). Such older works as F. Homes Dudden, *Gregory the Great: His Place in History and Thought*, 2 vols. (London, New York and Bombay, 1905), and Pierre Battifol, *Saint Gregory the Great*, trans. John L. Stoddard (New York, 1929) can be useful if read with caution. Gregory is generally credited with founding the medieval papacy; see the standard works of Erich Caspar, *Geschichte des Papsttums von den Anfängen bis zur Höhe der Weltherrschaft*, 2 vols. (Tübingen, 1933); Horace K. Mann, *The Lives of the Popes in the Early Middle Ages*, vol. 1, pt. 1 (London, 1925), esp. 1–250. More specific are works by Max Walther, *Pondus, Dispensatio, Dispositio* (Kriens, 1941); articles from Robert Markus's collection *From Augustine to Gregory the Great: History and Christianity in Late Antiquity*, Variorum Reprints (London, 1983); Neil Sharkey, *St. Gregory the Great's Concept of Papal Primacy* (Washington, D.C., 1950); and G. Kopka, "The Pope as Diplomat: A Study of Selected Correspondence of Gregory the Great with the Secular Authorities of His Day" (Diss., University of Texas, Austin, 1967). Three works on the general state of the Church and her bishops are essential to understanding Gregory's historical situation as pope: Peter Llewellyn, "The Roman Church in the Seventh Century: The Legacy of Gregory the Great," *JEH* 25 (1974): 363–80; A. H. M. Jones, "Church Finance in the Fifth and Sixth Centuries," *JThS* 11 (1960): 84–94; André Guillou, "L'Évêque dans la société méditerranéenne des VIe–VIIe siècles. Un Modèle," in *BECh* 131 (1973): 5–20.

Further research on Gregory as pope has been conducted by Paul Meyvaert, "Gregory the Great and the Theme of Authority," in *Benedict, Gregory, Bede, and Others*, Variorum Reprints, CS 61 (London, 1977), no. V: 3–12; Claude Dagens, "L'Eglise universelle et le monde oriental chez saint Grégoire le Grand," *Istina* 20 (1975): 457–75; E. H. Fischer, "Gregor der Grosse und Byzanz: ein Beitrag zur Geschichte der päpstlicher Politik," *Zeitschrift der Savigny Stiftung für Rechtsgeschichte. Kanonistische Abteilung* 36 (1950): 15–44; and Karl Morrison, *Tradition and Authority in the Western Church, 300–1140* (Princeton, 1969), 117–40. A number of papers dealing with Gregory's activities as pope and related topics appear in Fontaine et al., eds., *Grégoire le Grand*: Jean Batany, "Le Vocabulaire des fonctions sociales et ecclésiastiques chez Grégoire le Grand," 171–80; Dag Norberg, "Style personnel et style administratif dans le *Registrum epistularum* de saint Grégoire le Grand," 489–97; Charles Pietri, "Clercs et serviteurs laïcs de l'Eglise romaine au temps de Grégoire le Grand," 107–22; Vincenzo Recchia, "I protagonisti dell'offensiva romana antimonofisita tra la fine del quinto e i primi decenni del sesto secolo dai *Dialoghi* di Gregorio Magno," 159–67; André Tuilier, "Grégoire le Grand et le titre de patriarche oecuménique," 69–82.

On Gregory's education and intellectual background, see Pierre Riché, *Education and Culture in the Barbarian West, Sixth through Eighth Centuries*, trans. John J. Contreni (Columbia, S.C., 1976), 145–57. The works of Pierre Courcelle are extremely important for linking Gregory with the classical past; see his *Late Latin Writers and Their Greek Sources*, trans. Harry E. Wedeck (Cambridge, Mass., 1969), esp. 361–421; *Recherches sur* des *"Confessions" de saint Augustin* (Paris, 1968); *"Connais-toi toi-même,"* vol. 1, *De Socrate à saint Bernard* (Paris, 1974); "S. Grégoire à l'école de Juvénal," *Studi in onore di Alberto Pincherle* (Rome, 1967), 170–74; "*Habitare secum* selon Perse et selon s. Grégoire le Grand," *REAug* 12 (1967): 97–117. Jacques Fontaine's *Isidore de Seville et la culture classique dans l'Espagne wisigothique*, 2d ed., 3 vols. (Paris, 1983) gives an excellent picture of the basic intellectual climate Gregory shared with Isidore, a younger contemporary. Claude Dagens treats Gregory's attitude toward secular learning in "Grégoire le Grand et la culture: de la *sapientia hujus mundi* à la *docta ignorantia*," *REAug* 14 (1968): 17–26; as do A. Sepulcri, "Gregorio Magno e la scienza profana," *Atti della reale Accademia delle scienze di Torino* 39 (1903–4): 962–76; Vera Paronetto, "Gregorio Magno e la cultura classica," *Studium* 74 (1978): 665–80; F. Buddenseig, "Gregory the Great, the Destroyer of Pagan Idols. The History of a Medieval Legend Concerning the Decline of Ancient Art and Literature," *JWI* 28 (1965): 44–65. For a discussion of the diverse versions of the Bible Gregory used, see Jean Gribomont, "Le texte biblique de Grégoire," Fontaine et al., eds. *Grégoire le Grand*, 467–75.

Gregory has been considered the first exponent of a truly medieval spirituality. The classic treatment is the rather jaded work of Adolf Harnack, *History of Dogma*, trans. Neil Buchanan, 3d ed. (New York, 1961), 5: 262–73. More sympathetic surveys appear in Robert Gillet, "Grégoire le Grand," *DS* 6: 872–910 and his introduction to Grégoire le Grand, *Morales sur Job I–II*, trans. André de Gaudemaris (Paris, 1975), SC, 32 bis, 7–113; Ariside Bocognano's introduction to his translation of Grégoire le Grand, *Morales sur Job XI–XIV*, SC 212 (Paris, 1974), 7–32; Karl Baus et al., *The Imperial Church from Constantine to the Early Middle Ages*, trans. Anselm Biggs, vol. 2 of *History of the Church* (New York, 1969), 602–756; Jean Leclercq, *The Spirituality of the Middle Ages*, trans. The Benedictines of Holme Eden Abbey, Carlisle, vol. 2 of Louis Bouyer et al., *A History of Christian Spirituality* (New York, 1961), 3–30; J. Leclercq, *The Love of Learning and the Desire for God: A Study of Monastic Culture*, trans. Catharine Misrahi (New York, 1962), esp. 19–43; Gustavo Vinay, *Alto Medioevo Latino: Conversazioni e no* (Naples, 1978), 11–82. A survey of Gregory's writing, with an emphasis on style and grammar, is given by Ferruccio Gastaldelli, "Osservazioni per un profilo letterario di San Gregorio Magno," *Salesianum* 26 (1964): 441–61. Several works by Adalbert de Vogüé elucidate connections between Gregory and earlier sources, among them: "La Règle du Maître et les Dialogues de s. Grégoire," *RHE* 61 (1966): 44–76; "Grégoire le Grand, lecteur de Grégoire de Tours?" *AB* 94 (1976): 225–33.

Scores of articles have been devoted to aspects of Gregory's theology. The biographies cited above offer extensive lists of such articles; those I have found useful are cited in the text. Surprisingly few books have appeared dealing with Gregory's spirituality. The most important is Claude Dagens, *Saint Grégoire le Grand. Culture et expérience chrétiennes* (Paris, 1977), a very thorough and impressive work. The recent book by G. R. Evans, *The Thought of Gregory the Great* (Cambridge, 1986), should be read with caution: see the review by Paul Meyvaert in *JEH* (to appear). Although many earlier works raise certain questions because of their neo-scholastic approach, certain are still important; see, for example, Franz Lieblang, *Grundfragen der mystischen Theologie nach Gregors des Grossen Moralia und Ezechielhomilien* (Freiburg im Breisgau, 1934); Leonhard Weber, *Hauptfragen der Moraltheologie Gregors des Grossen* (Freiburg in der Schweiz, 1947); Michael Frickel, *Deus totus ubique simul: Untersuchungen zur allgemeinen Gottgegenwart im Rahmen der Gotteslehre Gregors des Grossen* (Freiburg im Breisgau, 1956).

Of Gregory's works, the *Dialogues* have attracted most attention. The reader should begin by reading the excellent introduction to Grégoire le Grand, *Dialogues* (SC 251) by Adalbert de Vogüé. For the *Dialogues* as historical sources, see especially Georg Dufner, *Die Dialoge Gregors des Grossen im Wandel der Zeiten und Sprachen* (Padua, 1968), who shows that the *Dialogues* were taken up by the laity. See also Roger Sorrell, "Dreams and Divination in Certain Writings of Gregory the Great" (B. Litt. Thesis, Oxford, 1978); and several works by Sofia Boesch Gajano: "Demoni e miracoli nei *Dialogi* di Gregorio Magno," in *Hagiographie, cultures et sociétés iv–xii siècles*, Actes du Colloque organisé à Nanterre et à Paris (2–5 May 1979) (Paris, 1981), 263–81; "Dislivelli culturali e mediazioni ecclesiastiche nei *Dialogi* di Gregorio Magno," *Quaderni storici* 14 (1979): 398–415; "La proposta agiografica dei *Dialogi* di Gregorio Magno," *StudMed* 21 (1980): 623–64; "Narratio e expositio nei *Dialogi* di Gregorio Magno: tipologia dei miracoli e struttura dell'opera," *Bulletino dell'Istituto Storico Italiano per il Medioevo e Archivio Muratoriano* 88 (1979): 1–33. See also Giorgio Cracco, "Ascesa e ruolo dei *Viri Dei* nell'Italia di Gregorio Magno," *Hagiographie, cultures et sociétés iv–xii siècles* (Paris, 1981), 283–97; Jacques Le Goff, "*Vita et Preexemplum* dans le 2 livre des *Dialogues* de Grégoire le Grand," in *Hagiographie*, 105–20; W. F. Bolton, "The Supra-historical Sense in the *Dialogues* of Gregory I," *Aevum* 33 (1959): 206–13; F. Tateo, "Struttura dei *Dialoghi* di Gregorio Magno," *VetChr* 2 (1965): 101–27; A. Vitale Brovarone, "La forma narrativa dei *Dialogi* di Gregorio Magno. Problemi storico-litterari," *Atti dell'Accademia delle Scienze di Torino* 108 (1974): 95–173; Adalbert de Vogüé, "La Règle du Maître et les Dialogues de s. Grégoire," *RHE* 61 (1966): 44–76; idem, introduction to Grégoire le Grand, *Dialogues* (SC 251).

On Gregory's influence in the Middle Ages, see: R. Wasselynck, "L'Influence de l'exégèse de s. Grégoire le Grand"; and his "Présence de s. Grégoire le Grand dans les recueils canoniques (X–XII)," *MSR* 22 (1965): 205–19, and "Les Compilations des Moralia in Job du VIIe au XIIe siècle," *RecTh* 29 (1962): 5–32; Georg Dufner, *Die Dialoge Gregors des Grossen*, and his "Zwei Werke Gregors des Grossen in ihrer italienischen Überlieferung," *IMU* 6 (1963): 235–52; Jean Leclercq, "The Exposition and Exegesis of Scripture: From Gregory to Saint Bernard," in *The Cambridge History of the Bible. The West from the Fathers to the Reformation*, 3 vols., ed. G. W. H. Lampe (Cambridge, 1976), 1:183–97; and Beryl Smalley, *The Study of the Bible in the Middle Ages* (Notre Dame, Ind., 1970), esp. 32–36.

INDEX

Abandonment, by God, 1, 10, 63, 138
Abbots, 73; authority over monks, 71–
    72; obedience and humility to,
    179n3; as physicians, 204n61
Abel, 85, 183
Abnegation: of carnal life, 188, 190–92,
    213; of self, 84, 188, 190, 197
Abraham, 252, 255; sacrifice of, 180n5
Abstinence, 68, 83n120, 196, 197; of
    Christ, 170
Accidents, transcendent truths in, 48–
    49
Achsah (daughter of Caleb), 224
Active life, 234; vs. contemplative life,
    19, 20, 21, 91, 189–93, 215n13, 234–
    35, 236, 248–51, 259; dangers of,
    259; and temporal power, 255; tor-
    ture of, 254
Adam, 19, 34, 61, 98, 111n22, 113, 115,
    118n67, 119, 122–23, 126, 145, 173,
    253; proud mistakes of, 151; soul of,
    165; stability of, 78–79, 96, 106, 109,
    112, 237
Adeodatus, bishop of Numidia, 90
Adriatic Sea, 52
Adversity, 23, 48, 59, 145; of Christ,
    169; conquest of, 214; of Gregory,
    88, 184, 185; inflicted by devil, 14;
    inflicted by God, 10, 11, 26, 42, 52,
    212, 238; of Job, 11, 60, 63, 64, 184,
    238, 241; and prosperity as ambigu-
    ous, 10, 23, 26, 108, 195, 229, 237–
    46, 253, 257; resentment of, 217;
    and resurrection, 179; salutary ef-
    fects of, 208–15 passim, 220–21;

submission to, 149; unwarranted,
    240. See also Afflictions; Misfortune;
    Scourges; Suffering; Trials;
    Tribulations
Advocate, Christ as, 150, 176, 259
Affections: complementary, 87; and
    afflictions as complementary,
    225n101
Afflictions, 10, 208, 239; of Gregory
    and Job, 184; grief of, 254; as heal-
    ing, 218; merciful, 63–64, 219; from
    penitence, 219; as purge, 142–43.
    See also Adversity; Scourges;
    Suffering
Afterlife, 58–60
Agapitus I, Pope, 5; vs. Equitius, 72,
    74; and healing, 104
Agatho, Bishop, 105
Agilulf, 88
Almsgiving, 59, 182, 252
Altars, for relics, 57, 67
Ambivalences, 12, 22–27 passim, 52–
    53, 59, 108, 146, 147–48, 185, 186–
    87; of body and earthly life, 128; of
    Christ's role, 177; of fear and love,
    225–26; inner, of Gregory, 185, 186;
    of power, 81; of prosperity and ad-
    versity, 10, 23, 26, 108, 195, 229,
    237–46, 253, 257; of sexual pleasure,
    134–35; of spiritual and carnal
    realms, 46, 64–65, 176, 247–48. See
    also Balance; Complementarities;
    Paradoxes
Ambrose, 9, 13, 14, 15, 16, 103, 111,
    172n60, 180, 185, 186n37, 195n8, 252

Designer:	Mark Ong
Compositor:	Wilsted and Taylor
Text:	10/13 Palatino
Display:	Palatino
Printer:	Braun-Brumfield
Binder:	Braun-Brumfield